JOHN W. LANNAMANN

SMALL GROUP
DECISION MAKING
Communication and
the Group Process

SMALL GROUP DECISION MAKING

Communication and the Group Process

THIRD EDITION

B. Aubrey Fisher

Late Professor of Communication
University of Utah

Donald G. Ellis

University of Hartford

McGraw Hill Publishing Company
New York St. Louis San Francisco Auckland
Bogotá Caracas Hamburg Lisbon London Madrid
Mexico Milan Montreal New Delhi Oklahoma City Paris
San Juan São Paulo Singapore Sydney Tokyo Toronto

SMALL GROUP DECISION MAKING
Communication and the Group Process

3 4 5 6 7 8 9 0   DOC DOC   9 4 3 2 1

ISBN 0-07-021099-3

This book was set in Plantin by the College Composition Unit
in cooperation withWaldman Graphics, Inc.
The editors were Hilary Jackson, Judith R. Cornwell, and Bernadette Boylan;
the production supervisor was Denise L. Puryear.
The cover was designed by Carla Bauer.
R. R. Donnelley & Sons Company was printer and binder.

Library of Congress Cataloging-in-Publication Data

Fisher, B. Aubrey, (date).
    Small group decision making: communication and the group process.
    — 3rd ed./B. Aubrey Fisher, Donald G. Ellis.
        p.   cm.
    Bibliography: p.
    Includes index.
    ISBN 0-07-021099-3
    1. Small groups.   2. Decision-making, Group.   3. Communication.
I. Ellis, Donald G.   II. Title.
HM133.F55   1990
302.3'4—dc20   89-8297

About
the Authors

B. Aubrey Fisher completed his Ph.D. at the University of Minnesota in 1968. From 1971 until his death in 1986 he was Professor of Communication at the University of Utah. Aubrey Fisher was a very respected and accomplished communication scholar and teacher. He wrote many articles and chapters on communication theory and group processes and was the author of *Small Group Decision Making, Perspectives on Human Communication,* and *Interpersonal Communication: Pragmatics of Human Relationships.* He was the editor of *Western Journal of Speech Communication* from 1982 to 1984 and was the President of the Western Speech Communication Association in 1985, in addition to holding offices in national organizations.

Donald G. Ellis holds a Ph.D. from the University of Utah. He has been on the faculty of Purdue University and Michigan State University and is currently an Associate Professor and Chairman of the Department of Communication at the University of Hartford. He has authored numerous articles on communication theory with particular emphasis on language and interaction processes in interpersonal and group contexts. He and William Donohue edited *Contemporary Issues in Language and Discourse Processes* for Lawrence Erlbaum Associates, and Ellis currently serves as the advisory editor for Erlbaum's communication series in language and discourse processes. He participates in various national organizations and lectures and writes in the fields of language behavior, group decision making, interpersonal communication, and related topics.

This book is dedicated to the memory of Aub Fisher,
his family, his work, and his friends.

Contents

CHAPTER 1

The Group Process   10

CHAPTER 2

Dimensions of the Group Process   32

CHAPTER 6

The Process of Group Decision Making   140

CHAPTER 7

Anatomy of Communication in Decision-Making Groups: Improving Effectiveness   170

CHAPTER 8

Behavioral Standards: Roles and Norms   202

CHAPTER 9

Leadership and Power   222

CHAPTER 10

Social Conflict and Deviance   256

Preface

This is the third edition of *Small Group Decision Making: Communication and the Group Process*. It is a testimony to the strength and pervasive importance of Aubrey Fisher's work with groups and their communicative processes. After Aubrey's untimely death, I was asked if I would take on a revision of his text. I agreed, but with some trepidation, because my goal, which was to revise, sharpen, and update the text in the tradition of Fisher's perspective on small group behavior, was probably unattainable. Even though I could feel Aubrey's presence in every sentence, I am sure that I have done him some injustices somewhere. Nevertheless, I assume full responsibility for my own biases and idiosyncrasies. Aub would understand.

Groups serve many purposes, but their most typical purpose is some form of decision making. This book emphasizes decision making and communication. It draws from all facets of group life—including training groups, family groups, and therapy groups—but its principal interest is the group that makes decisions in face-to-face interaction.

This book is also about communication. Communication is often defined as merely transmitting and receiving messages. While there is some truth to this definition, this book emphasizes the *process* of communication. Communication is considered *the* organizing element of the group. Through communication, human beings process information, test ideas, exchange opinions, and achieve consensus on decisions. Through communication, they develop interpersonal relationships and form "groups" from aggregates of individuals. Thus, communication is the crux of the task and social dimensions of all groups.

This book is intended for university students studying group discussion. The students' primary interest may lie in group formation, in task performance, in social systems, in decision making, in social conflict, or in a variety of other areas. The common point of departure, however, is communication that organizes people into an active social system for the purpose of performing some task—notably decision making. Therefore, this book may be used in a variety of courses in a variety of university departments at different levels in the curriculum.

You will find an overview of the book detailing each chapter's contents on page 7 in the Introduction. The instructor's manual for this edition features an outline of the course, key terms, discussion questions and test items, activities and/or projects, group-process observation forms, and, for the first time, an entire transcript of group interaction providing actual beginning-to-end samples.

Although I assume full responsibility for this revision, I have benefited from many influences direct and indirect. The work of a number of reviewers was invaluable. They provided me with resources and insights that have found their way into many of the chapters that follow. I may not have lived up to all of their expectations, but I am grateful for their help. In particular I would like to thank Katherine Adams, California State University at Fresno, who also prepared the instructor's manual; Don Boileau, George Mason University; Rolayne DeStephen, Sinclair College; Bill Donohue, Michigan State University; G. Lloyd Drecksel, University of Utah; Randy Hirokawa, University of Iowa; John Hocking, University of Georgia; Scott Poole, University of Minnesota; and Cynthia Stohl, Purdue University. Judith Cornwell of McGraw-Hill was also an excellent associate editor. She was friendly, helpful, and a pleasure to work with.

I am also fortunate to be associated with many friends and colleagues in the Department of Communication at the University of Hartford. I have learned much about group cohesiveness from them. I am especially indebted to Lynne Kelly and Bob Duran and hereby publicly promise to return their books and material.

My wife, Karen Beyard, deserves a very special thank-you. She proofread the entire manuscript and assisted with many of the pesky details of writing a book. Her work and commitment to this project were invaluable.

And to David and Alex who are warm, wise, and wonderful and just a joy to be part of.

Donald G. Ellis

SMALL GROUP
DECISION MAKING
Communication and
the Group Process

Introduction

We must inform you at the outset that we're well aware of many of the jokes concerning decisions made by groups and the process of group decision making generally. We know that the camel is a horse designed by a committee and that a committee is a group of people that keeps minutes and wastes hours. We have also heard that a committee is a group of people who can do nothing individually but, as a group, can meet and decide that nothing can be done. Group decision making has been defined as the confusion of the loudest-talking member multiplied by the number of members present. In regard to the propensity of organizations to appoint committees at every opportunity, it has been said that if several average Americans found themselves on an airplane about to crash, at least one of them would take time to appoint a landing committee.

Occasionally one of the jokes will contain a germ of truth. One of our favorite stories about group decision making involves the *blinder system*. As the story goes, a farmer always plowed his field with a single horse hitched to the plow. Nevertheless, the farmer yelled, "Giddyup, Jack! Giddyup, Casey! Giddyup, Jerry! Giddyup, Tom!" Day after day, his neighbor heard the farmer shouting all those names at the lone horse. One day his curiosity and bewilderment proved too much. He went to the farmer and asked why he called his horse by all the different names. "Oh," replied the farmer, "the horse's name is Jack. But, you see, he doesn't know his own strength. So I put blinders on him, and I yell all those other names. Then he works hard, and he pulls the plow mighty fine. All the time, you see, he thinks he's got all those other horses helping him."

The blinder system may indeed be less of a joke than it appears. Perhaps it is simply another name for the *assembly effect* discussed in Chapter 2. Despite all the witticisms and the alleged limitations of the group process of making decisions, it remains one of the most potent and valuable tools of our society.

The process of decision making in a social setting is vitally important in a democratic society. Nearly every facet of our society—political, legislative, judicial, economic—functions through decisions made by groups. Laws are formulated by large groups of legislators and small groups of legislative committees. National executive decisions come from meetings of the President and the Cabinet or small groups of advisors. The decisions of juries determine the fates of civil and criminal defendants in our courts. Negotiating teams decide the wages and benefits of millions of labor-union members. The functioning of every business, educational, and political organization relies on decisions made by management teams. Group decisions ultimately determine what television programs we are able to view, what products are available to purchase, what new automobiles will look like, what taxes we will pay, and so forth. Although we are often unaware of the pervasive influence of group decisions, the effects of those decisions on our lives are inescapable.

The small group has been a very common phenomenon in every society from the beginning of civilization. In our society, probably the most common small group is the family. In many respects, the family is a decision-making group that has as its principal task the rearing of children. On the other hand, the family group is little more than a biological accident. Group members do not choose to belong to the family group, nor are they typically free to remove themselves from its confines; runaway children and deserting mothers and fathers are not condoned by our society. Nevertheless, since families do engage in many decision-making activities, they may be considered examples of decision-making groups and included in our study.

Certainly many other types of groups exist in our society, but they are not included in the following discussions of group decision making. The encounter group, the laboratory training group, the consciousness-raising group, the creativity workshop, the awareness group, the assertiveness training group, etc., exist for purposes other than the performance of a group task. Moreover, such groups do not function as bona fide "groups." Rather, they remain collections of individuals, each of whom is pursuing a basically individual goal. The purpose of such groups is to provide individual members with some outcome—perhaps increased sensitivity, increased awareness, increased assertiveness, self-identity, or ventilation of aggressions and feelings. In some respects, these groups are oriented to therapeutic goals; that is, they provide a group context for the behavioral change of individual members.

This book discusses the type of group with a specific identity of the group in which each individual member experiences a sense of membership or loyalty. The group is not merely a convenient context in which individuals make decisions; rather, it is a specific process of making decisions socially. Group decision making, as a process, is quite different from the decision making performed by individuals.

Task-oriented group is a generic term that identifies any one of an enormous variety of groups whose very existence depends on its performing some task. An outside authority often assigns the task to the group, although individuals may, of their own volition, form a group by themselves. They may decide to form a group in order to perform some task that either cannot be accomplished by a single person or cannot be accomplished as effectively by persons acting alone. The nature of what constitutes tasks performed by groups varies widely, ranging from an assembly-line work group whose assigned task is to put bolts A, B, and C through holes 1, 2, and 3 to a group of jury members who ponder the evidence presented at a trial and decide on the guilt or innocence of a defendant. Some tasks, such as that of the jury, obviously require verbal and oral interaction. Others, such as the assembly-line group, require no oral interaction at all.

The task-oriented group is by far the most prevalent group in our society. Every human organization—business, educational, service, and political—includes numerous task-oriented groups to carry out the various functions of that organization and other task-oriented groups to coordinate the efforts of all other groups. Perhaps the most interesting of these organizational subgroups are the management groups—those groups charged with the task of organizing various organizational groups and subgroups into a unitary, efficiently functioning organization. Management groups may be the most interesting because they deal directly with issues confronting every social system. And much of being a group member is knowing how to work productively with others in a social situation.

Our focus in this book is narrower than the broad variety of purposes implied by the term *task-oriented group*. Specifically, our concern is with one of those purposes, probably the most common group purpose of all—decision making. Decision-making groups make up the bulk of all groups in most human organizations. Groups decide what new products will be manufactured, for example, and how they are to be designed, advertised, and sold. Groups decide which laws will govern a society, how those laws will be enforced, how they are to be interpreted, and even how those who violate the laws will be dealt with. Our entire society functions through the organizations that it comprises. And each organization functions through decisions made by groups within that organization. This type of group—the decision-making group—is the primary concern of this book. As later discussions will demonstrate, group decision making differs inherently from individual decision making, both in the process of making decisions and in the nature of the decision-making task. Thus, the *group* is considered a decision-making *system*.

Effective decision making is regarded as a natural consequence of the members' abilities to analyze and understand the process of group decision making. But no one can acquire such an ability without active participation in group decision making. Although some people may argue that one cannot effectively experience any phenomenon without thoroughly studying it from the impartial and objective perspective of the observer, others argue just as vehemently that there is no substitute for experience. Both sides of this hackneyed controversy between the values of education and experience are probably at once both right and wrong. Knowledge of anything without experiencing it is as sterile as experiencing it without any knowledge. Students of group decision making are strongly urged to incorporate their understanding of group decision making, gained from reading this book and others, with actual participation in groups engaged in decision-making tasks. Combining understanding with experience leads to the most fruitful results and maximizes the effectiveness of group decision making.

Too often overlooked in the study of group decision making is the process of communication—the vitally essential ingredient of any social system. Communication is *the* organizing element of a social system. To highlight the study of group communication, the group is defined in a face-to-face setting that absolutely requires verbal and oral communication as the principal mode of interaction.

WHAT TO EXPECT

Some expectations have probably been established at this point. The first is that the group will be treated as a *whole*. That is, the group is a phenomenon quite distinct from its individual members. In this sense, we are employing the concept of holism, or nonsummativity—a tenet of general systems theory. We shall think of a group as a social system characterized by wholeness and inseparability. In this respect, we can say that the group is different from (and sometimes more than) the sum of its members. The many references to the "group" in the following chapters assume a single entity that, in the context of task performance, is more significant than the specific characteristics (such as the personalities, intelligence, and abilities) of the individual persons who constitute the membership.

A second expectation should also be clear. Our focus will be on decision making, a specific task orientation of the group. The title of this book should make this emphasis clear. Every chapter is oriented to this emphasis. Certainly, aspects of groups other than the specific task are also important in understanding how groups develop and how they make decisions, and the following chapters will include discussions of such aspects. Although these aspects are not unique to decision making, they contribute to understanding the group process; for example, norms and roles exist in all groups, whether they make decisions or not. The book includes discussion of these group concepts because they are characteristics of decision-making groups.

This book is not a how-to-do-it manual for being successful in decision-making groups. You will find few lists of things to do and things not to do. You will find some suggestions for improving the effectiveness of communication and the group process, but you will probably be disappointed that these suggestions are rarely specific enough to qualify as surefire principles for ensuring success in group decision making. Some textbooks may make promises to the readers and suggest that if they follow the guidelines in the book, they will know how to "control" or "win" the conference or the group. But this book's perspective on group decision making, viewing the group as a whole and communication as an interactive process, deemphasizes the possibility of an individual member controlling other members. Such control is simply not available in most groups. And when it is available (such as to the "boss" in a group of subordinates), group decision making does not exist. Rather, the boss makes the decision and informs the others, in which case the assumption that a group exists is superficial and misleading.

The primary purpose of this book is to generate in students an understanding of communication and the group process, and hence of group decision making. We shall consistently emphasize understanding rather than mere knowledge. Under-standing involves experience—not merely *knowing* what to do, but *understanding* what is going on and then adapting to that experience.

We advocate in this book that each group member should develop the feeling of being both a participant and an observer of group decision making. In other words, the quality of group decision making improves when members are sensitive to the process of communication and group development and thus experience this process while it is occurring. As a result of observing the group during this process, you will be able to participate in the process more effectively. Being a participant-observer—that is, both a participant and an observer—requires you to understand group decision making as well as to be knowledgeable about it. Knowing group decision making is one thing; understanding it is much more significant. We hope that the distinction between understanding and knowledge will become apparent as you continue your reading.

CONVENTIONAL WISDOM: A BARRIER TO UNDERSTANDING

There was once an instructor of instrumental music who contended that we in-structors of communication "have it easy" teaching high school students the prin-ciples of communication because the students are able to benefit from experience. After all, they have spent 10 to 15 years actually communicating every day. But teaching a beginning student how to play the trombone is much more difficult, he maintained, because the student has no benefit of past experience in trombone play-ing. We maintained that it is precisely for this reason that learning the trombone is probably less difficult. Because the students in our communication classes have vast communicative experience, they possess a large repertoire of alleged "knowledge" gained from this experience—beliefs widely held and tenaciously main-tained, whether or not they reflect reality. And this knowledge serves to inhibit, rather than assist, the students' understanding of communication principles.

Nonspecialists' beliefs that are widely (if carelessly) held fall into the genre of "conventional wisdom." Principles from conventional wisdom are considered cred-ible and true, not because they are actually true, but because they are conventional—because many people believe them to be true. The advertising slogan "Fifty million Frenchmen can't be wrong" reflects the simplistic wisdom based on convention-ality. If so many people believe it to be true, then it must be true. But if fifty million Frenchmen believed the earth were flat, they would be wrong nevertheless. Con-ventionality may lead to increased credibility, but it has no direct bearing on reality.

Belief based on conventionality often takes the form of a cliché or an adage believed to possess truth because it is so familiar. We sometimes call such beliefs folk wisdom and fall prey to their influence. How and why conventional wisdom gains credibility through familiarity is a matter of some conjecture. The axiom "Early to bed, early to rise" can be traced to Benjamin Franklin's mother trying to urge her recalcitrant son into bed at the appointed hour. Conventional wisdom is also not necessarily easily identified as conventional wisdom. It is difficult to resist the influence of the familiar antecedent that often precedes a principle from conventional wisdom—"Everyone knows that . . . ." Who wants to be out of step with the rest of the world?

Dangers of Conventional Wisdom

Because conventional wisdom is conventional, it is not necessarily false. On the contrary, many clichés have some basis in fact. But accepting such "wisdom" at face value is nevertheless dangerous. At its worst, conventional wisdom is blatantly false and leads to greater problems than originally existed. At its best, conventional wisdom oversimplifies the situation and desensitizes us to reality. In the case of group decision making, members either create more social problems for themselves because of false "wisdom" or are led to inefficient and unproductive effort by the demands of irrelevant "wisdom."

Most important, axioms based purely on conventionality masquerade as real knowledge and thwart genuine understanding. In the case of group communication, which abounds with folk wisdom, conventional wisdom severely inhibits the improvement of decisional quality and of group communication. In almost no other area of human endeavor do we rely so heavily and so trustingly on conventional wisdom. Although some persons suffering from arthritis continue to wear copper bracelets on their wrists, we generally seek the expert assistance of a physician when illness strikes. Although we may "starve a cold and stuff a fever" (or is it the other way around?), we don't seriously believe that eating an apple every day will protect us from illness. We generally don't rely on a pain in the foot to predict bad weather or take delight from a red sky in the evening. When we really want to know what weather is in store, we seek out the forecasts made by expert meteorologists. But when it comes to communication and the group process, everyone seems to be an expert, reverting to the oversimplifications of conventional wisdom.

Conventional Wisdom about Group Decision Making

Representative examples of conventional wisdom about group decision making are listed below. Many of these examples may seem sensible and eminently reasonable, and you will probably discover that you have believed more than a few of them. The examples come from various areas of communication and the group process, represent only a tiny portion of the clichés about group decision making, and have only one trait in common: They are all false.

1. Discussion differs from debate in that members of a group discussion do not advocate argumentative positions but maintain an open mind and a spirit of free inquiry. *Corollary:* The effective decision-making group exhibits a minimum of argument and interpersonal conflict.
2. To be effective, the group should strive for nearly equal participation among group members.
3. Each member of the group should perform certain duties required of group

membership. *Corollary:* The duties of the leader differ from the duties of the other group members.

4. In the group context, getting the job done—that is, making the decisions—is more important than getting along with other group members. *Correlative opposite:* In the group context, developing close interpersonal relationships is more important than the actual performance of the decision-making task.
5. Some people are natural-born leaders. *Corollary:* Some people possess the characteristics (or quality) of leadership.
6. The personalities of the members exert the most significant effect on the process of group decision making.
7. In the long run, a group will achieve better results through using democratic methods than through achieving specific results by other means.
8. Almost any job that can be done by a committee can be done better by having one person responsible for it.
9. We talk with one another, but we just don't communicate.
10. Two-way communication is preferable to one-way communication.
11. Compromise is the most effective strategy for resolving social conflicts.

Relying on conventional wisdom is a formidable barrier to the understanding and knowledge of group decision making. By the time you have read the following chapters, you should understand why and how these examples of conventional wisdom are not true. At that time you should also be able to add many other examples to the list. When you are able to do that, you will have taken one giant step forward toward a robust understanding of group decision making.

AN OVERVIEW OF THE BOOK

The preceding pages have established the primary focus of this book—group decision making. There are dozens of methods one can use to approach the study of group decision making. The subtitle of this book provides an insight into the perspective employed in the chapters following; although "communication and the group process" may imply two perspectives, the chapters will illustrate that communication and the group process comprise a single, unified perspective.

Chapters 1 and 2 lay out the framework of the group process, and Chapters 3 and 4 describe the nature of the communicative process. While reading these chapters, you will probably note that both "communication" and "group" are defined as a process—in fact, a single process. As a process, communication and the group are composed of patterned behaviors (or actions) that are constantly in a state of change. Neither communication nor a group should be considered a "thing." Rather, each is a process that is constantly *in process* of continually developing. Both are continually evolving and changing over time. Some theorists have described this concept as "Being is becoming."

Chapter 1, The Group Process, describes the leaderless group discussion (LGD) as essential for understanding the complete and natural group process. Of course, a "pure" LGD (a group with 100 percent capacity for and freedom of self-regulation) probably doesn't exist, but every group is to some degree free to control its own functioning and its own destiny; that is, every group is to some extent an LGD. This initial chapter emphasizes how individuals organize themselves into a single entity, a group, and thereby develop the social system that is essential to effective group decision making.

Chapter 2, Dimensions of the Group Process, illustrates the interdependence of the social and task dimensions of group decision making. For group members to be effective as a decision-making system, their interpersonal relationships must also be effective. In fact, effectiveness in one dimension is usually tantamount to effectiveness in the other. But groups can be effective only to the extent that they perform tasks that are appropriate to a group. In this way, they take advantage of the uniquely social elements of group decision making.

An analysis of the communicative process reveals both structural (space-oriented) and functional (time-oriented) elements. Chapter 3 (Group Communication: Structural Elements) and Chapter 4 (Group Communication: Functional Elements) discuss these characteristics of the communicative process as they are specifically adapted to the group setting. The structural elements of group communication (e.g., feedback responses, networks, gatekeeping, breakdowns, and barriers) are the most commonly known, but the functional elements may be more significant to understanding the process of group decision making. Chapter 4 illustrates how the communicative process can be viewed from a pragmatic perspective. These functional elements (e.g., feedback sequences, analysis and punctuation of interaction sequences, and the content and relationship dimensions) are vital to our understanding of group decision making.

Chapter 5, Observing and Analyzing Small Group Communication, focuses on how information about the communicative process in small groups is collected. The chapter describes common observational methods and emphasizes techniques for observing group interaction. Any student of group decision making should have some "feel" for observing and analyzing the interaction of group members in the process of actual group decision making. This chapter will not make you an expert researcher, but it does give you a sense of observing and analyzing real groups.

Chapter 6, The Process of Group Decision Making, traces various approaches and models that have been used to understand group task performance. This discussion emphasizes a four-phase spiral model of decision emergence, a process defined in terms of punctuated interaction sequences. This descriptive model indicates not so much that groups *make* decisions as that decisions *emerge* from the ongoing group interaction.

Chapter 7 is titled Anatomy of Communication in Decision-Making Groups: Improving Effectiveness. The chapter begins with an illustration of the "flavor" of group interaction during the four phases of decision emergence described in Chapter 6. The Chapter gives samples of the interactions in real decision-making groups; these samples provide a verbal picture of what decision making looks like. The chapter then provides guidelines for group members; these guidelines center around attitudinal factors, interpersonal factors, and group-identity factors that can improve effectiveness in groups.

Developing standards for members' behavior unifies the participating persons within a functioning social system. Chapter 8 emphasizes the two most common group standards—roles and norms—and discusses them in terms of communicative behaviors. In the same sense that decisions "emerge" from group interaction, so, too, do group norms and each member's role.

Chapter 9, Leadership and Power, focuses on the most common of all group roles—that of leader. The discussion utilizes the functional perspective on leadership, a perspective that is consistent with the view of communication and the group process. Furthermore, the process of leader emergence is described as a counterpart of decision emergence, discussed in Chapter 6. In fact, this description suggests that as group members succeed in achieving consensus on group decisions, they develop a status hierarchy and leadership at the same time and as a part of the same process.

Chapter 10, Social Conflict and Deviance, adopts a functional approach in explaining group phenomena that are typically regarded as socially disruptive and are therefore to be avoided or resolved. The process view of group decision making employed throughout this book suggests that conflict and deviance are really quite typical components of the group process. Therefore, they should be expected and should even be considered normal aspects of the entire group process. This chapter emphasizes *managing* (rather than resolving) conflict and deviance in order to take advantage of their positive functions and to avoid excessive fear of them (which fear is inherently destructive of the group process).

Definitions of important concepts and terms in this book are given as they are introduced, and the glossary in Appendix 1 briefly defines most of the book's specialized terms. But keep in mind that while *defining* a concept is easy, *understanding* it is more difficult and infinitely more valuable.

In your classroom study of group decision making, you may well decide to emphasize some chapters more than others, to omit one or more, to rearrange the chapters, and to provide supplemental information. No book's content and organization are sacred; rather, you should adapt them to suit your specific classroom purposes. Each and every chapter of this book emphasizes an understanding of how a group is structured, how it functions, and how it evolves through the process of human communication.

Understanding is the key to effective participation in group decision making. Central to this understanding and to effective participation is human communication in the group. One must always keep in mind that, however members of a small group may differ from one another as human beings with a unique combination of personality and abilities, they all have one thing in common—they are communicating individuals.

But no one can really *teach* effective communication and group process; it can only be *learned*. We hope the truth of this seemingly paradoxical statement will become apparent during your reading of *Small Group Decision Making: Communication and the Group Process*.

CHAPTER 1

The Group Process

Robert Stroud, better known as "the birdman of Alcatraz," was truly an amazing person. Without previous background or professional training in ornithology, he became an expert on birds and bird diseases while a prisoner in solitary confinement. For most of us, the most astonishing part of Stroud's story is not his self-developed expertise in ornithology, but the fact that he could endure so many years of solitude. We cannot even imagine the interminable tedium of loneliness—no one to talk with day after day, no one to laugh with or argue with or just sit in silence with year after year. Most of us would probably prefer death to an indefinite sentence of absolutely solitary confinement.

One of the techniques associated with brainwashing involves social isolation. The prisoner is separated from all other prisoners and cut off from all communication with family, friends, or even the author of a book. It is not surprising that the prisoner often develops an interpersonal bond akin to friendship with the jailer. Satisfying the compelling need for companionship is preferable to insanity. The feeling of being absolutely and totally alone is simply intolerable for a normal human being.

The human is indeed a social animal. Few of us could exist as a social hermit, and we generally consider those few hermits who do exist to be crazy. This is not to say, however, that humans crave to live in huge metropolitan communities, although a glance at any of our overcrowded and smog-ridden megalopolises would seem to indicate that many do. But a person can feel just as alone in a large city as in solitary confinement. Humans have developed a need for intimate social relationships. In other words, we have developed a need to belong—typically to a small group.

The small group is the oldest and most common of all social organizations. Nations and entire civilizations have come and gone, but the small group has continued throughout all recorded history. We belong to family groups, groups of close friends, groups of associates at work, recreational groups, ad infinitum. While our membership in some small groups may involve only interpersonal friendship and serve no purpose other than the gratification of social needs, our membership in many small groups serves a much broader purpose. Work groups in an office or a factory exist in order to perform some task within the larger social organization. Almost everyone works in an organization of some type. These organizations must meet goals by coordinating the activities of employees and making decisions about productivity and quality. Organizations expect individuals to be competent group members. As a member of a group, you will be expected to (1) participate, (2) work well with others, (3) assume leadership responsibilities, (4) present ideas clearly, (5) disseminate information both internally and externally, (6) be sensitive to the decision-making process, and (7) possess good oral and written communication skills (Hunt, 1980).

We are concerned with small groups that exist for a definite purpose. For the moment, we won't quibble about how small a small group must be; certainly the group must be small enough that every member is able to know and communicate with every other member. We are also concerned with communication. A group, however large or small, cannot and does not exist without communication among its members. Communication and only communication binds individual human beings together into group membership. Communication and only communication allows group members to fulfill the group's purposes.

Communication, for our purposes, inherently includes speech, or oral communication. Of course, people communicate nonverbally as well, through gestures, movement, and space. But speech is the basic mode of communication in every small group. Furthermore, for our purposes, the communicating members of a small group are in a face-to-face situation. While it is theoretically possible for a group to exist by communicating only through letters or telephone, the face-to-face situation is far more typical in this society.

But our primary concern involves a more specific purpose—the purpose of making decisions. While many aspects of a small group are common to numerous types of groups with a greater variety of purposes, group decision making is not only more common but also allows for greater sophistication in developing the group process. We shall, of course, be interested in other group purposes from time to time as they contribute to our understanding of group decision making, but the emphasis of this book remains on decision making.

"Group" and "process" are two words common to nearly everyone's daily vocabulary. We use these words flippantly as though we understood them thoroughly. And, for the most part, this understanding is sufficient for everyday conversation. But writers of textbooks use these words and others as though they and their readers understood the words in the same way. We want to take no chances in this book.

This chapter is devoted to providing a working definition of *group process*. Essential to this definition is an understanding of each of the two words individually. To provide these working definitions requires a certain amount of courageous self-assurance. Although the words are common, definitions for them abound. The reader will discover in this chapter (and in others to follow) that the viewpoint expressed in this book is in substantial agreement with some other authors and in substantial disagreement with perhaps even more.

PROCESS DEFINED

A single sentence is not sufficient for an adequate definition of *process*. As with most terms, *process* cannot be *defined* nearly so easily as it can be *understood*. A dictionary provides several elements of the term that offer a starting point for such an understanding. According to any good dictionary, four elements are inherent in a process—action, or acts, a continuous *change in time*; advancement, or *progress;* over time, and a *goal,* or result. Thus, a process clearly implies a time dimension, as well as a space dimension, in which action occurs in a continuously changing progression toward some goal.

David Berlo (1960, p. 24), an early communication theorist, offered an excellent and often-quoted definition of *process:*

> If we accept the concept of process, we view events and relationships as
> dynamic, on-going, ever-changing, continuous. When we label something as
> a process, we also mean that it does not have *a* beginning, *an* end, a fixed
> sequence of events. It is not static, at rest. It is moving. The ingredients
> within a process interact; each affects all of the others.

Berlo's definition is richer than the dictionary's and emphasizes the time dimension as a fluid, ever-changing evolution of ingredients. Because it is so deeply imbedded in the time dimension, any beginning or end of a process is an arbitrary point in time since the "something" is different from one instant to the next. Berlo also provides a clue to why every process is continually changing: interaction among the ingredients. Each ingredient affects and is affected by every other ingredient. The ingredients, then, are interdependent; that is, any change in one of the ingredients affects all the other ingredients.

Clearly implied in the nature of a process is a marriage of the space and time dimensions—structure and action. For example, "wooden table" is a statement about the *structure* of various pieces of wood. But the *process* of "wooden table" requires an explanation of how wood was sawed from a felled tree (an arbitrary starting point in time), the sequence of steps involved in cutting and assembling those pieces of wood, applying the finish, etc., until the finished table appears (an arbitrary stopping point in time). Thus, a process involves not only structure but also how and why structural changes come about during the passage of time.

The term *process* means that individuals and their groups are continually changing and modifying themselves. Group members respond to internal and external stimuli and alter their ideas and behaviors in accordance with the group's needs and goals. Because a group changes from moment to moment, it is misleading to attempt a complete understanding of a group at any particular point in time. Rather, the group must be examined as an entity that has developed over time—where change, not constancy, is the group's key characteristic.

GROUP DEFINED

A Smorgasbord of Definitions

Marvin E. Shaw (1976, pp. 6–12), in his integration of the research knowledge of small group phenomena, summarizes the various approaches to defining *group*. Most of the definitions cited by him indicate that members of a group *share* something in common. And it is this common something that defines the existence of a group. One definition considers a group to be any collection of individuals with shared perceptions; that is, a group is composed of individuals who perceive the existence of a group and their membership in it.

Perhaps more familiar is the definition that stipulates the sharing of a common motivation or goal. Thus, workers unite to form a labor union since they have a common need to satisfy, such as higher wages and better working conditions. The collective strength of the union, then, has the common purpose of securing those goals.

Still another definition based on commonality specifies the sharing of a common fate. For instance, a basketball team or a debate team wins or loses as a group and not as individuals. The outcome affects all members of the group as a whole and not each member individually.

Other definitions imply that commonality is insufficient for an adequate understanding of *group*. This class of definitions looks to the structure of the group—the relationships and ties among group members that bond them together into a group. Such an organizational definition perceives the social organization as the "glue" of group structure. Thus, roles, norms, values, status hierarchies, power relationships, etc., are laws that govern the behavior of group members and tie them to the group. The presence of these ties defines the nature of the group.

A final category of definitions perceives the central element of a group to be interaction among its members so that the members are interdependent among themselves. It is this type of definition that Shaw (1976) and Gouran and Fisher (1984) find most acceptable; Shaw (1976, p. 11) defines a group as "two or more persons who are interacting with one another in such a manner that each person influences and is influenced by each other person." In this book we use *interaction* and *communication* interchangeably, considering the two terms to be synonymous. The term *interaction* implies the coordination of behavior between two people; *communication*, moreover, implies that symbols are exchanged and shared between two or more people. As you will see later, coordinated behavior has some message (or meaning) value and is therefore communicative. Shaw's definition is not very complete, but it forms the basis of our definition of *group*.

] *def*

Interaction ≠ comm unless observer perspective is brought into the sequence.

The Principle of Groupness

Common sense should tell us that not every collection of individuals who talk with one another and who even exert minimal influence on one another is a "group" in the strictest sense of the term. Consider several individuals who congregate in an elevator or at a bus stop. They may carry on a conversation, but they do not constitute a real group.

Arguing whether a particular collection of persons makes up a group is about as worthwhile as arguing about the number of angels who can dance on the head of a pin. But identifying those characteristics which differentiate a group from a collection of individuals does provide insight into a more complete understanding of the nature of a group. John K. Brilhart (1978, pp. 20–21), for example, specifies five characteristics of a group:

1. A number of people sufficiently small for each to be aware of and have some reaction to each other....
2. A mutually interdependent purpose in which the success of each is contingent upon the success of the others in achieving this goal.
3. Each person has a sense of belonging or membership, identifying himself with the other members of the group.
4. Oral interaction (not all of the interaction will be oral, but a significant characteristic of a discussion group is reciprocal influence exercised by talking).
5. Behavior based on norms and procedures accepted by all members.

You will note that Brilhart employs the smorgasbord of definitions within his five characteristics—common perceptions (1 and 3), common fate and common goal (2), interdependence and interaction (4), and organizational structure (5). Brilhart adds to the interactional characteristics the stipulation that a significant proportion of communication will be through speech, thereby virtually requiring that the group be in face-to-face confrontation. He also places a general limitation on size, assuming that the people interact within the framework of a *small* group.

But Brilhart is more concerned with illustrating the principle of groupness, which he considers a property that groups possess and collections of individuals do not. According to Brilhart (1978, p. 21):

> "Groupness" emerges from the relationships among the people involved, just as "cubeness" emerges from the image of a set of planes, intersects and angles in specific relationships to each other. One can draw a cube with twelve lines (try it), but only if they are assembled in a definite way. Any other arrangement of the lines gives something other than a cube. Likewise, one can have a collection or set of people without having a group....

Brilhart emphasizes that a group exists as something apart from the persons who constitute the membership. Just as the twelve lines form cubeness when placed in the proper relationships to one another, groupness forms from the relationships among the members. As the individual lines lose their individual identity when cubeness is perceived, so do members lose their identity as individuals when groupness is perceived. Shaw (1976, p. 14) appears to be making a similar observation when he states that "a group is real to the extent that it is perceived as an entity."

For several scores of years a controversy existed among sociologists regarding the existence of a "group mind." In oversimplified terms, a group was thought to have a "mind" of its own—a way of thinking and a pattern of emotions quite separate from those of the individual members. The "group mind" idea was rejected several decades ago on the basis that the group can not be substantially different from the individuals who make up its membership. A group simply cannot have a mental life external to the mental lives of its members. In analogical terms, a finished product is limited by the raw materials of its composition; without sulfur, oxygen, and hydrogen, for instance, sulfuric acid cannot exist.

Although a group mind is not implied, a group does possess an identity of its own apart from the identities of its individual members. In fact, individual members often take on the identity of the groups to which they belong as part of their identity as individuals. For example, John Doe is identified as a Democrat, a student, a communication major, a suburbanite, a Kiwanian—all groups with corresponding identities and with alleged characteristics of their own. We shall return to this point later, when we discuss the law of partial inclusion.

The Group as a System of Communicative Behaviors

The identity of a group apart from the identities of its individual members—groupness—has been established. A more common method of expressing this same principle is literally a cliché—that is, a group is "more than the sum of its parts." This principle of nonsummativity assumes that individual components constitute a single entity and, moreover, is characteristic of a group system.

An entire body of theoretical knowledge, commonly known as general systems theory, may be beneficial to furthering our understanding of the group process. A *system* may be defined simply as an entity that behaves as an entity because of the interdependence of its component parts. A group system, then, is a group that behaves collectively as a group because of the interdependence of its members. Every system has three elements that describe its existence—structure, function, and evolution.

The *structure* of a system may be regarded as the physical arrangement of its components in space at any given point in time.

The *function* of a system may be defined as the relationships between its components in time. It is the day-to-day operation of the system. The function of the system gives it order and regulation, and our society provides laws that allow the system to function in a desired (i.e., normal) manner. Of course, a system's operational process must necessarily be described in terms of the *combined* complex of structure and function—as *structure* refers to the relationship between a system's components in space, *function* refers to the relationships between these components in time.

The *evolution* of a system creates the history of the system—its progressive and possibly regressive changes through time. Every system needs a history—time to develop into an orderly structured and functioning system. The behavior of the system contains that history. Open systems, of which a group is one, possess the capacity of self-determination. Hence, the system itself may accelerate the process of systemic development.

The principles of groupness and process are consistent with the evolution of a system. It takes time for a collection of individuals to form groupness. And the process of forming a group from a collection of individuals is embodied in the evolution of the group system. Those evolutionary changes as the group changes its character are also included in the evolution of the system.

If the point is not yet clear after the discussion of the many definitions of a group, we shall be explicit now. None of the definitions of a group is false or incorrect; that is, each definition is true and correct. As Shaw (1976, p. 6) says, "It is evident that different authors are simply looking at different aspects of the same phenomenon." It is a fact that the observation of reality must always proceed from the perspective of the observer. And perception is always fragmentary. Remember the story about the blind men who encountered their first elephant. The point is that none of the blind men was incorrect. Each perceived the same phenomenon from a different perspective and generalized about the whole phenomenon on the basis of his perceived information.

The truth is that reality is quite elusive. It is not so much *discovered* as it is *constructed* and manipulated. When considering human behavior from a process perspective, we confound even further the problems involved in constructing reality. Again, Berlo (1960, p. 25) explains:

> The basis for the concept of process is the belief that the structure of physical reality cannot be *discovered* by man; it must be *created* by man. In "constructing" reality, the theorist chooses to organize his perceptions in one way or another. He may choose to say that we can call certain things "elements" or "ingredients." In doing this, he realizes that he has not discovered anything, he has created a set of tools which may or may not be useful in analyzing or describing the world.... The dynamic of process has limitations; nevertheless, there is more than one dynamic that can be developed for nearly any combination of events.

In constructing a definition of the "reality" of a group, each author attempts to organize perceptions by emphasizing those elements he or she considers most significant. By creating a "set of tools," the author has used only one dynamic for describing a group and has based the definition of *group* on that perspective.

The perspective of this book is communication. It should not be puzzling, then, that our definition of *group* will utilize this perspective. The common way of defining a group has viewed individual human beings as the components of the group system. The definition that we shall derive by the end of this subsection does not deny that human beings constitute the group, but the individual person is not the primary unit of analysis. Rather, what the individual does—how he or she behaves—constitutes the set of tools used to describe, analyze, and define the group.

If components of a system are interdependent, they influence and are influenced by one another. Unless we consider some form of supernatural power, then the only means by which one person can influence another is by behaviors—that is, the communicative exchanges among people provide the sole method by which influence, or effects, can be achieved. Our emphasis, then, is on what group members do and less on what they think and feel. Thus, the components of our group system are the communicative behaviors produced by individual members.

Karl Weick (1979, p. 90), in discussing "collective structure," stresses the point that as people organize into a group system, they organize their behaviors: "Having *first* converged on shared ideas of how a structure can form (i.e., on means), the persons *then* activate a repetitive series of interlocked behaviors—that is, they form a collective structure." One group member's behavior is dependent on another's and collective structure emerges when patterns of behavior emerge that characterize the group. A collection of individuals, then, develops into a group as each member interlocks his or her behaviors with those of the other members. Consider the analogy of a basketball team. All the previous definitions of *group* are applicable to the team. But for our purposes, the team possesses groupness to the extent that the behaviors of the players are interdependent, interstructured, and predictable. Sportscasters are fond of saying that a team has played together so long that the players "know each other's moves." To rephrase this cliché, players can, on the basis of their own acts, predict what other players will do next and what they themselves will do subsequently. A "fast break" or "out-of-bounds play" is based on structuring the players' behaviors interdependently so that the result of the cluster of interdependent behaviors is a player "free" to take a shot. On the other hand, some basketball teams are characterized by "free-lancing," which may be another way of saying that the players' behaviors are not interdependent but are based on each player's behaving as an individual. Hence, a free-lance team is more a collection of individuals than a group.

Weak reasoning

Weick expresses more concern, however, with the interact or double interact than with the single act. In fact, interacts and double interacts are simply groupings of acts. An *interact* is composed of two contiguous acts, while a *double interact* is a combination of three contiguous acts. A emits an act (a single act), which is followed by an act from B (an interact), which is followed by a third act from A (a double interact). If the emphasis is on interdependent acts, the more important unit of analysis is the interact or double interact. In this way, acts are seen within the context of preceding and succeeding acts. The structure of the group, then, is defined by those sequences of acts which recur so often that one can predict what kinds of acts tend to follow or precede other kinds of acts.

Communication is the medium of group decision making, and the sense of groupness emerges from the communication. Consider the following example of group communication. The group members are discussing integration in public schools.

BOB: My research shows that 79 percent of the minority students in the community are concentrated in 15 percent of the school districts.
ANN: Yeah, but if you believe in the concept of the neighborhood school, then those students are attending school with their friends and community members.
JIM: But it also means that students are not exposed to kids with other backgrounds and cultures, and that is not good for a child's education.

Each subsequent person's contribution to the group is a communicative *act,* but these acts are responses to the messages of others. You cannot really understand Ann's or Jim's statements without knowing what they are responding to. As the group develops longer sequences of *interaction,* it begins to form recognizable patterns, and this is what Weick means by "collective structure." In order to understand the group you must understand the systemic patterns of interaction. What we have in the above example is "disagreement," because Jim and Bob are arguing in favor of the forced integration of schools, whereas Ann is opposed. What is im-

should be interaction

portant is that the group members are interdependent through communication, and the best way to understand the group is through the analysis of interaction—not the analysis of individuals.

Viewing a group as a system of behaviors may be disconcerting to some. A system of behaviors is not tangible. You can't touch or hold a behavior. It doesn't exist in space. Hence, a group seems somewhat mystical as a result. In a way, this is very true. Groups are less tangible than we often believe. But communicative behaviors can be observed—unlike such internal phenomena as interpersonal liking, beliefs, and feelings. And communicative behaviors are apparently the only method by which interdependence or mutual influence can be achieved or observed.

As the discussion of communication in Chapter 4 will illustrate, the processes of communication and of group merge into virtually a single process. In this sense, the subtitle of this book, *Communication and the Group Process*, refers not to two different elements, but to a single process. The process of communication is virtually indistinguishable from the process of group. The element that unifies the communicative process and the group process is, theoretically, the broad framework of general systems theory—a popular theoretical view within the study of groups and social organizations.

Therefore, a group will be defined as a collection of individuals whose communicative behaviors—specifically, acts, interacts, and double interacts—become interstructured and repetitive in the form of predictable patterns. To the extent that the communicative behaviors of group members are interstructured, the attributes used to characterize a group may be assumed to exist.

The Leaderless Group Discussion (LGD)

For the purpose of understanding fully the "natural" process of a group, this book will utilize what has been called the leaderless group discussion (LGD). Contrary to the implication of its name, the LGD is not a group of talkative people who do not have a leader. The characteristic that distinguishes an LGD from other groups is the group's capacity for self-determination. That is, an LGD is affected or influenced by a minimum of authority or forces external to the group. For example, a committee formed within a larger organization is subject to the demands and pressures of the larger organization. The organization imposes on the committee certain assigned duties, deadlines for task completion, etc., and the activities of the committee are restricted by the need to meet the needs and goals of the organization. The LGD, on the contrary, has a broader capacity to decide for itself its own goals, its own norms, its own roles, and its own status hierarchy. Rather than having its leadership assigned by some external authority, the LGD determines its own leader. Hence, "leaderless group discussion" implies not the absence of leadership altogether, but the absence of a single, externally assigned leader.

A second characteristic of an LGD concerns the external pressure on all status levels. We shall assume the membership of the LGD to be mostly peers at the time the group is formed. A large organization endows its members with status, and it structures the status levels into a hierarchy. A corporation, for example, has directors, managers, assistant managers, supervisors, and assembly-line workers. A committee formed within this corporation would reflect the status hierarchy of the larger corporation. Consider the military—perhaps the most status-conscious of all human organizations. Members of the military visibly display their status on their sleeves or shoulders. Understandably, a group composed of military personnel would be highly susceptible to the status demands of the larger organization. But to avoid the external pressures of a larger organization's status hierarchy, the LGD is generally thought to consist of members with similar initial status. *a historical*

For our purposes, we shall also consider an LGD to be a *zero-history group*. That is, our LGD is observed from its first formation—the point of zero history. It is not a group that has existed for a long time. It has already been established that the process of developing groupness takes time. So that the complete process of group formation can be observed, observation of the group must begin at the point of its inception as a collection of individuals. The zero-history group, then, embodies the total history of the group.

To the extent that external forces impinge upon the self-determination of the group members, the "natural" group process is incomplete. This is not to say that a group that is subject to external pressures is not natural. Indeed, most groups are not "pure" LGDs. But an LGD embodies the entire group process—the development of its entire group culture. Our purpose is to look at the entire group process, and the LGD allows us to do this. A non-LGD reflects something less than the whole process, with a portion of the group process predetermined by external authorities or by its history. Thus, the LGD reflects the group process in its more natural state.

Realistically, of course, no group is either totally free from external authority or totally controlled by external forces. In fact, forming a true LGD in a classroom is practically impossible. Every classroom group is subject to external restrictions— the presence of the instructor, the "captivity" of the classroom, the status distinctions from the student culture, the environmental pressure of classroom assignments at the end of the quarter or semester, or the due date for a group project. Even if the instructor does not assign a specific task, but allows the classroom group to select its own, the group is "forced" to choose its own task rather than voluntarily forming around a common need "felt" by the group members. But to the extent that a classroom group is not purely an LGD, it reflects most group experiences.

One might ask at this point why we are employing the LGD as the model for a group. Such a question, however, misses the point. Every group is, to some extent, an LGD. In other words, being an LGD (that is, having the capacity to regulate itself) is not a characteristic that a group possesses or lacks. It is a continuum— a characteristic that every group possesses to some degree. In a pure LGD the capacity for self-regulation is highly prominent. The members are keenly aware of their own self-regulatory powers. In groups that are not LGDs to any significant extent (i.e., groups whose regulation by external authority structures is strong, such as groups within a larger organization and families), *some* self-regulating capacity is still present. On the other hand, members of such groups are less keenly aware of their power to govern themselves. Their informal structure may not be recognized or approved by the external authority, but it is often much more powerful than the official (or formal) structures of authority.

Later chapters will briefly discuss specific types of groups that are not LGDs to the same extent as others are. But the self-regulating capacity of all groups is still present in these groups when the group is viewed as a process. Often the group process is delayed, and occasionally it is thwarted, by overly powerful external authorities. However, with some exceptions (e.g., the military, prisons, and some bureaucracies), the decision-making group is an LGD to a considerable extent and is thus capable of a good deal of self-regulation. To the degree that external authorities usurp the group's capacity, the entire group process is not allowed to develop.

Therefore, to utilize the LGD in its fullest possible sense is to provide a benchmark against which other groups can be compared. At that point, it becomes possible to evaluate whether any group (depending on the nature of the task and on whether the group can function effectively to perform that task) should have more or less self-regulating capacity.

The Size of the "Small" Group

Our definition of *group* as a process and as a system of behaviors does not include the characteristic of size that seems to be implied by the word "small." You will recall, however, that Brilhart's (1978) five characteristics of groupness include the characteristic that the group be small enough that each member knows, and is able to react to, every other member. Beyond this very general limitation, however, the criterion of size is rather trivial in defining a group as a process.

Sociologists have long defined various levels of human society—individual, dyad, group, organization, and society (or culture). Communication specialists have also found these distinctions popular in separating the field of communication into various sociological settings—that is, interpersonal communication, group communication, organizational communication, and mass communication. Within the study of communication, at least, these distinctions are decreasing in importance, so that the process of communication is typically viewed as the same, regardless of the sociological setting in which it occurs. Under any circumstances, the distinction between one sociological level and another, on the basis of size alone, is difficult to determine. For our purposes, we intend to draw no distinction between group communication and what is typically called interpersonal communication. It is the process of communication that is most important.

Given the nature of a group as a process, then, we cannot provide any upper limits of size. That is, we will not provide any size limitation at which a group, after having increased to that size, becomes an organization. We shall adhere to Brilhart's very general characteristic that a group is sufficiently small for each member to be able to know and react to every other member. At the lower limit of the size criterion, however, we will stipulate that a group includes at least three people.

Although a dyad (that is, two persons) is similar in many respects to a group, it is a much simpler—that is, a less complex—social system. The difference created

? Selvini ?

See the Bavelas article re N way interaction

by adding even one person to a dyad (thus involving three members instead of two) provides a much more complex social system. Even a three-person group embodies many characteristics not present in a dyad. For example, in a dyad only one channel exists to "connect" the communicators. In other words, a dyad cannot have a communication network in the sense that some channels are used more often than others. A network in a dyad is impossible. In a three-person group, however, three channels are possible (A-B, A-C, and B-C). Thus, a network involving channel selectivity is possible.

It is also impossible for a deviant to exist in a dyad. Any norm that exists between two persons must have the recognition and consent of both members; otherwise, it ceases to exist as a norm. On the other hand, a norm in a three-member group may result from the imposition of the norm by a majority (or coalition) of two members on the third member. In a three-person group you have the possibility of majority rule (two against one), which is not possible in a dyad.

Mortensen (1972, pp. 267–268) also indicates several characteristics of dyadic interaction that are quite different from the interaction in a group. For one thing, he says that the dyad is "a highly unstable, tension-producing form of interchange. It is unstable because everything depends on the continuous reactions of only one person—either A or B." In other words, either member of a dyad can stop all the interaction by simply withdrawing. In a three-member group, however, interaction does not cease because of the whims or the actions of only a single person. That is, no one person has the power to destroy or disrupt completely the entire social system.

Mortensen goes on to indicate that dyads are also susceptible to a highly complementary interactive relationship. That is, the dyad tends typically to gravitate, for example, toward a dominant-submissive relationship between the two participants. A dyad in the form of an interview exemplifies such a relationship. One of the members is quite active, and the other member is quite passive. In other words, one person asks the questions, and the other person answers the questions. But because the dyad is so vulnerable to the activities of either person, the passive member also has ultimate veto power over the relationship. The passive member can, at any time, void the relationship by refusing to respond. As a result, the dyad is much more unstable than a group of three or more members.

Yet complementary can form overly stable ruts as well

Mortensen summarizes the distinctions between dyadic and group interaction. He suggests that, particularly in a task-oriented situation, a dyad exhibits more tension and is more unstable than a three-member group. Furthermore, the proportion of verbal activity and the nature of the verbal activity are quite different from the interaction that occurs when three or more members are present.

Perhaps the most significant difference between the dyad and the group is the feeling of identification with the larger system—a feeling that is seldom present in a dyad. One member of a classroom group verbalized this feeling of interdependence most vividly in responding to the group's interaction during a specific group meeting. She described her personal reactions in her diary: "A group project, such as this, creates a great amount of tension in those involved, because how you do certain things may be quite different from someone else. And yet, you're dependent on each other for the overall success or failure. And you feel a responsibility for success of the others as well as yourself."

This feeling of mutual interdependence, the feeling of interpersonal responsibility for the success and failure of other members as well as for yourself, is similar to what we have called groupness. Groupness implies a mutually interdependent purpose so that individual success is contingent upon the success (or failure) of the entire group. The responsibility for success is, furthermore, a two-way responsibility. Members of a group tend to feel responsible for the success of the entire group as well as to develop even greater resentment toward any other group members who do not share their portion of the responsibility.

In a group, then, individual members tend to be highly aware of their responsibility, whether it stems from social pressure or the fulfillment of a personal need. Nevertheless, that feeling of interdependence in a group is much stronger and more vital than it is in a dyad. In the two-member social system, any responsibility is toward only one other person and not toward an entity apart from the individual members—that is, the group.

Our definition of *group* is now rather complete—*three or more individuals whose communicative behaviors become interstructured and repetitive in the form of predictable patterns.* We hasten to reiterate that although the group process includes a minimum of three people, the process of communication in a group is not unlike the process of communication in a dyad. The reverse, however, is not so evident. Some characteristics of a group are not present in a dyad. Nevertheless, discussions of the social and task dimensions of a group (in Chapter 2) will also reflect what is known about dyadic interaction. We shall continue to assume that what is true of dyadic interaction is also true of group interaction.

WHY WORK IN GROUPS?

There is little doubt that working in a group can be an irritating and frustrating experience. The act of communicating with other people requires patience and tolerance as the people work to understand one another and accomplish goals. One researcher (Sorensen, 1981) even developed the concept of "grouphate" and found that many people dislike working in groups; but more importantly, Sorensen also discovered that people were more satisfied with groups as they improved their training and skills associated with effective group operation. Even when groups are maddeningly slow and clumsy, they are important because of the participation and recognition they offer individuals. Our democracy is founded on the principle of the informed citizen who is capable of taking part in decision making. None of us wants others to make our decisions for us. And for that reason alone, it behooves us to understand the subtle workings of communication in groups. In any case, groups are capable of performing functions and achieving some goals more efficiently and accurately than individuals can. Although there is evidence that individuals sometimes perform better than groups (Shaw, 1981), the quality of decision making is enhanced in groups working under certain conditions.

(groups superior for complex dec)

Groups tend to perform best as the complexity of a task increases. The most plausible justification for this is that individuals are limited to their intellectual and information-processing capabilities (Abelson and Levi, 1985). Regardless of how hard a person works to solve a problem, he will not succeed if he simply lacks the required knowledge or ability to solve the problem. Individuals tend to simplify problems that are too complex. Groups, on the other hand, can draw on the available pool of information and talent. If you were a member of a student-government committee charged with deciding how much money to allot to the student paper and you were not very knowledgeable about how much money it took to run the newspaper, your decision would benefit from the expertise of others. Working with others would allow you to determine more accurately the needs of the student paper.

Even experts, who have the sophisticated knowledge necessary for some complex tasks, have something to gain from working in groups. A number of researchers have found that experts are not immune to problems in decision making (Alpert and Raiffa, 1982; Tversky and Kahneman, 1983). They found that even experts can (1) become overconfident, (2) misinterpret inconsistent evidence, and (3) engage in reasoning fallacies.

Judgment.

Groups are better at judgment decisions than individuals are. Some decisions require judgment rather than expert knowledge because the nature of the task is more ambiguous or because there is no clear-cut solution to the task. This generalization is related to the one above but is more concerned with uncertain tasks, including those which are diffuse and ill-defined. If you were a member of a student group that was asked to develop a student-oriented campaign to attract new students to campus, you would be dealing with a task that had a variety of alternatives, no one of which is necessarily correct. Groups are superior at tasks that require the consideration of a number of judgmental alternatives.

Many of the problems that groups try to solve require the group members to be creative in deciding on possible decisions, to be sensitive to a range of new information, to change beliefs in the face of new information, and to make decisions with incomplete information (Zeev, 1981). The limits to creativity and valuable interpretation of information are extended when individuals have others to stimulate them, and groups have a greater capacity to store and process information. This does not mean that the larger the group, the better the group will perform. On the contrary, there is a point of diminishing returns. But some optimal number of group members will produce more information and decision possibilities, and these factors are characteristic of high-quality decisions (Janis and Mann, 1977).

THE INDIVIDUAL AND THE GROUP

Each human being is, to some extent, unique. Each of us is composed of attitudes, beliefs, and values that define who we are. Some people may believe that engaging in group decision making will have little impact on oneself. Others might conclude that the individual's self-concept is overpowered by the group; therefore, the self is subjected to the social pressures of conformity and is influenced by the group process rather than influencing it.

In actuality, both of these explanations are flawed. There is no simple one-way influence between a group and the individual. The situation is far more complex than this. In all likelihood, and individual's nature and self-concept develop simultaneously with the group process, each influencing the other and being influenced by the other. Individual members will certainly affect the performance of any group. Moreover, the nature of the group will affect all members within it. Hocking, Margreiter, Hylton (1977) demonstrated the "intra-audience" effect, or the fact that the opinions of group members have a strong influence on individuals. But rather than providing a simple choice between which influence is stronger (the group or the individual selves), the relationship between the two is more accurately understood as a *mutual* development. The selves of the individual members nurture and grow with the group just as the entire group process nurtures and grows with each individual self.

Social Comparison

Leon Festinger (1950, 1954), a social psychologist, argues that every human being has a need to evaluate self. That is, each person's self-concept includes some quest or desire for evaluation. For example, a person with a certain opinion is generally dissatisfied unless or until that opinion can be judged to be correct. A person feels that he or she has certain abilities and needs to know how good these abilities are. Often the need to evaluate one's own self-perceived abilities and qualities leads to comparing these abilities and qualities with those of other people. Simple nonsocial and objective means for comparison are often unavailable or do not exist at all. Festinger therefore developed his theory of "social comparison."

Festinger suggests that people are most likely to compare themselves with other people who are quite similar and with whom they are in close interpersonal contact. It would be foolish, for example, for junior high school students to compare their intellectual achievements with those of college graduates; the comparison with another person would most likely involve another junior high school student, probably a friend or classmate. In other words, the evaluation of the self will be more accurate when the differences between oneself and others are relatively small.

In the case of extreme dissimilarity between the persons being compared, Festinger suggests that the man or woman engaging in social comparison can still cope merely by avoiding situations that are very dissimilar. In other words, social comparison also includes the notion of selectivity. That is, a person chooses to engage in social comparison with similar persons and tends to avoid comparison with those who are extremely dissimilar.

This selective phenomenon of social comparison thus leads to the formation of groups that are quite homogeneous—that is, whose members have similar opinions, abilities, and qualities. In this way, liberals tend to associate with other liberals and consequently compare their own liberal qualities with those of their fellow members. Conservatives associate and compare themselves with other conservatives and succeed in maintaining their own conservatism.

Festinger's theory of social comparison, then, may explain why and how self-concepts remain relatively stable over long periods despite the vast amounts of social interaction. These interactions involve comparisons with people who have similar selves, so that the person's self-concept is maintained and even reinforced through social comparison.

Of course, any change in a person's life (such as a move to a new town, a transfer to a new job, or a change in schools) will bring that person into contact with a different—and unfamiliar—social situation. The new situation will thus lead to new social comparison processes because of the reduced capacity to exercise choice or selectivity in objects for social comparison.

The point is this: When social-comparison processes are functioning and a person is attempting to evaluate his or her own abilities, opinions, and qualities, the self-concept remains quite stable and unchanging, owing to the selection of appropriate objects (persons) and social situations used for comparison. These persons and situations are considered to be "appropriate" to the extent that they are quite similar to one's present self-concept. Nevertheless, changes in social situations, perhaps due to normal life changes during the process of living in our mobile society, often bring the person into contact with new social situations and thus with other persons to be used as objects for social comparison. In this case the self-concepts change, sometimes quite drastically.

Self-Disclosure

Each person has many different selves rather than a single, uncomplicated self-concept. One differentiation between these selves is that between "public self" and "private self." That is, each person has a self that is visible to, and known by, friends and acquaintances. At the same time, parts of the self remain private in the sense that they are qualities of which others have little or no knowledge. Of course, the closer a friendship, and thus the greater the communication between two persons, the greater the proportion of each individual self that will be public to the other.

A person who is providing information to someone else about the private self may be said to be engaging in self-disclosure, or self-disclosing communication. It is important to note, however, that self-disclosures do not necessarily include anything and everything that one may relate to another about oneself. Self-disclosing communication is said to occur when the information about self that is given to another person includes some information that the other would not know or be able to discover through other means (Jourard, 1964; Bochner, 1984). Most groups have members who self-disclose, and for this reason it is important to understand the concept.

One significant characteristic of self-disclosure is the phenomenon of reciprocity; that is, as one person makes self-disclosures to another, the other typically responds with self-disclosures. In reviewing the research on self-disclosure, Pearce and Sharp (1973, p. 418) call reciprocity the "best documented characteristic of self-disclosing communication." In other words, as A self-discloses to B, B tends to self-disclose to A. This reciprocal self-disclosing communication, then, results in something of a snowball effect. As communication contains a certain amount of self-disclosure, more self-disclosure will be contained in further communication in ever-increasing amounts. Thus, if B reciprocates A's self-disclosure with further self-disclosing communication of his or her own, A will typically reciprocate and engage in even more self-disclosing communication, thereby influencing B to engage in additional self-disclosure, and so on.

Consider a hypothetical example of unreciprocated self-disclosure. You tell an acquaintance something about yourself that you consider quite private. Your acquaintance appears to be interested in this information but doesn't give you any intimate information in return. You are unlikely to continue exposing your private self to the other person unless you get something in return. This communicative procedure is analogous to an economic transaction in which you have invested something of yourself but feel that the other person has invested nothing. Self-disclosure, then, is similar to a financial transaction in which information about the self is the commodity being transacted.

Although self-disclosing communication tends to escalate over time—that is, to increase steadily during the formation of a social relationship—there is reason to believe that this escalation does not continue indefinitely. The self-disclosure is rather slight at the beginning of social relationships, soon increases as a result of the reciprocated self-disclosing messages of the participants, and then reaches a point at which it decreases in terms of both its amount and its degree of reciprocity; therefore, mature groups contain less self-disclosure than less mature groups do. This decrease in self-disclosing communication appears to be intuitively sensible: After so much self-disclosure during the development of relationships, each person's private self contains less information of which the other person is unaware. And because this information has become part of the public self during past self-disclosures, there is less information about each person's self to be disclosed to the other. Furthermore, there is now less need for self-disclosing communication, because in the closeness of their relationships the participants have already made large investments, or commitments. Having made these commitments, the participants need progressively less self-disclosure in order to maintain their relationships.

A further characteristic of self-disclosing communication is appropriateness. A self-disclosure may be appropriate or inappropriate in *timing:* that is, *when* the act of self-disclosure takes place. Indeed, the timing of certain communicative behaviors is a highly important factor in communication and the group process and will be discussed again and again throughout this book. There may also be appropriateness or inappropriateness of *content*. Before discussing appropriateness of self-disclosing communication, it is necessary to note differences in content between various kinds of self-disclosure. One self-disclosing comment is not necessarily the same as another self-disclosing comment. For example, certain topics are much more easily disclosed than are others. If a friend informs you that she once attended the University of Hartford, she is engaging in self-disclosure; this is information about herself that you would probably not know (or care about, for that matter) unless she told you. This topic is "safe" and is quite appropriate as self-disclosing communication to an early acquaintance; on the other hand, some topics (such as her sex life or love life) would be highly inappropriate. Furthermore, within any given topic area the depth of self-disclosure can vary considerably; that is, one could make self-disclosures about one's sex life or love life in a very intimate or a non-intimate manner. A simple statement, "I dated my wife for three years before we were married," is a self-disclosure about one's love life, but it is not a very intimate statement. (We are not willing to provide an example of a statement with high intimacy on this particular topic.) Altman and Taylor (1973) list thirteen topics that differ (for most people) in their level of intimacy. These topics include religion; marriage and children; dating, sex, and love; parental family; physical condition and appearance; money and property; politics; emotions; interests and hobbies; interpersonal relationships; personal attitudes and values; school and work; and demographical or biographical characteristics. Keep in mind, also, that specific self-disclosing communication within any of these thirteen topics ranges from a very intimate statement to a not-so-intimate remark.

It is now possible to discuss the appropriateness of self-disclosing communication itself. We often tend to believe, quite erroneously, that self-disclosure (or "openness" of communication with others) leads to a close interpersonal relationship and generally to more effective communication. Although self-disclosure is quite common and typical of (perhaps even essential to) friendship and close interpersonal relationships, the timing of self-disclosing communication is nevertheless highly significant. Horenstein and Gilbert (1976) conducted some research which discovered, for example, that when strangers engage in communication for the first time, self-disclosure leads to a dislike of the self-disclosing person and a desire to avoid further interaction with that person. While more intimate self-disclosures would probably lead to greater anxiety and increased discomfort in that person, the researchers suggest that any self-disclosure between strangers (i.e., first acquaintances), tends to make the other person feel uncomfortable, experience anxiety, and therefore avoid further interaction. This reaction may be similar to embarrassment and a feeling that "I don't know you that well."

Altman and Taylor (1973) also assert that reciprocity of self-disclosure is more important in forming interpersonal relationship than is the actual amount of self-disclosure. That is, the interpersonal relationship is never one-way. It is the result of the group's investment in member relationships, so that one person's self-disclosing communication leads to self-disclosure by the other person and back again. Thus, when someone tells you something about himself or herself, this disclosure is your cue to reciprocate, to engage in your own self-disclosure, if you want the relationship to continue to grow (Johnson and Johnson, 1987).

As a part of human communication, the self-disclosure phenomenon is important to the group process. It bridges the gap between the self and the group by providing one significant interpersonal aspect of the individual self. Central to the notion of self-disclosure is the realization that, as noted earlier, each person has a part of self that is public as well as another part that is private. The person, then, is able to choose whether to reveal a part of his or her private self to the other person and how much to reveal. In making the revelation, the person is committing a part of self to the relationship, and this commitment is likely to result in further commitment to the relationship. Moreover, as the relationship becomes a significant part of the act of communication, it thus becomes greater than the self of each individual communicator. This phenomenon of the social relationship embodied in every act of human communication is implicit in the groupness characteristic.

Interpersonal Trust

There is trust in a relationship when the individuals believe that each person will behave in a mutually beneficial manner (Johnson, 1986). Interpersonal trust is a characteristic of every successful decision-making group. Without trust between their members, groups are destined to substandard performance.

Keep in mind that trust characterizes the *relationship* rather than an *attitude* held by any of the persons. Trust is not one-way, but involves all members in the situation engaging in the same relationship called trust. If *A* trusts *B* but *B* does not trust *A*, then trust cannot be said to characterize the relationship. Rather, it would refer to a person's attitude.

Developing interpersonal trust is, like a group, a process. It takes time. In order for each person to develop some expectations of the other person and to be able to predict that person's behavior, trust must include some past history of interaction between the members of the relationship. A trusting relationship cannot develop overnight. It is not an immediate occurrence; rather, it emerges from the relationship after it has endured for some time.

Furthermore, the mutuality of interpersonal trust involves the achievement of goals and objectives. No one engages in a trusting relationship with another for purposes of self-satisfaction or self-aggrandizement. Rather, interpersonal trust involves objectives that are shared by, or common to, all participants in the situation. Typically, such a goal is one that either cannot be accomplished or can be accomplished only with the utmost difficulty by one person functioning alone. A team, or group, is thus essential to accomplishing the goal.

Pearce (1974) suggests a further characteristic of interpersonal trust that will become even more important when the social and task dimensions of the group process are discussed in Chapter 2. According to Pearce (p. 242), "even if the trusted person is well-intentioned and knowledgeable..., he must be perceived as capable of performing the appropriate behavior to be trusted." If you go swimming on the "buddy system" with a fellow swimmer, the expectation is that you will help if your buddy gets into trouble and that your buddy will save you if you get into danger in the water. Nevertheless, if either of you is a poor swimmer, interpersonal trust cannot exist to a significant degree. Despite your respective good intentions and helpful attitudes, the capability of performing the necessary lifesaving behaviors essential to the trusting situation of the buddy system may be highly questionable. Consequently, the expectations and predictions of the other person's behaviors must include some expectation and predictability of that person's capability of performing the trusting behavior appropriate to that situation. All the good intentions in the world are not likely to increase your trust in your swimming buddy unless you also believe in his or her capability to save you should the need arise.

Interpersonal trust, then, is a characteristic of the entire social situation. It involves not just the attitudes of one or more individuals but also the mutually other-directed definitions of the relationship. And these definitions are reciprocated by all participants in the situation. Furthermore, the situation must involve some history of past interaction—the development of a set of expectations and predictions of one another's behaviors. Of course, this predictability of one another's actions is based on what occurred during the past interaction. The situation of interpersonal trust also allows for the possibility of alternative options as responses to each person's invitations to engage in trust.

In this respect, as Pearce (1974) points out, to talk about interpersonal trust with any understanding is to consider the interdependence involved in the situation, the attitudes and expectations of all participants, and the mutuality and reciprocity of these attitudes and expectations as well as the behaviors and reciprocated behaviors during human communication.

Risk

Scholars who write about self-disclosing communication often discuss the "stranger on the plane" phenomenon: the tendency of human beings to reveal more of their selves to strangers with whom they never expect to engage in further interaction (such as a fellow plane-rider) than to an acquaintance whom they do expect to see again. The plane-rider phenomenon emphasizes the fact that interaction with strangers whom one will probably not meet again involves very little risk to the person. There is simply no commitment to the relationship or to developing the relationship. Therefore, nothing you say in the relationship will come back later to haunt you. Consequently, such communication involves little commitment to any social relationship and is thus of little importance to the social self.

The concept of commitment will arise again in future chapters dealing more specifically with communication and the group process. Fundamental to any commitment, to any development of a group, is the element of risk that is present in the situation. Commitment to any group, loyalty, or person inherently and inevitably involves the risk of being wrong, of appearing foolish in the presence of others. When you are alone, it is easy to do things that would be extraordinarily difficult or embarrassing if done when you are with others. Engaging in group decision making requires the ability to risk (and if necessary, to endure) frustration, disappointment, and ridicule or shame. Without this commitment by all or nearly all members of a decision-making group, little will be accomplished; and decisions, if made, will be of predictably poor quality.

We are all probably familiar with the saying "It is better to keep your mouth shut and be thought a fool than to open it and remove all doubt." This cliché contains the questionable advice to avoid risk, to avoid commitment, to be safe when interacting with others. Such advice not only reveals a naive view of social interaction but—more important—is incredibly bad counsel for prospective members of decision-making groups. Nevertheless, many people implicitly adhere to this axiom in social relationships and avoid the risk inherent in committing themselves to a group or a social environment.

When we engage in social risk, we are essentially gambling on a successful outcome. One who "hides" self and avoids risk is refusing to gamble. But whereas one only risks the possibility of failure by committing oneself to a social situation, one positively ensures a lack of success by avoiding the commitment. Social commitment and risk taking allow us the possibility of success, which includes increased self-esteem and successful decision making in a group—but when we avoid commitment and refuse to gamble, there is no possibility of success for either the self or the group process.

The element of risk cannot be overemphasized in the group process. Anyone who engages in communication with another person, if that communication is to be effective and meaningful, must inevitably assume some risk of self. Communicators, to be right, must risk being wrong. Of course, everyone who takes a risk must be aware that the consequences may be negative. But avoiding negative consequences will accomplish little. Moreover, achieving positive results more than compensates for any earlier feelings of risk. There is a biblical parable concerning the servant who buried the talents he was given. He thus avoided losing his money, but he did not profit either. Stated another way, to avoid any situation that includes an element of risk is ultimately to lose.

Engaging in risk, increasing vulnerability to fellow members of a group, is prerequisite to an effective group process. To avoid risk, for whatever reason and with whatever strategy one wishes to employ, is to deny the group its ability to function with maximum effectiveness. Furthermore, it is to deny your own self the opportunity to grow and to develop your own abilities and qualities. It may well be a form of social paranoia, although probably not in any psychopathological sense that would require therapy. Rather, such paranoia is a common neurosis that discourages the development of the human potential and fosters ineffective communication and inadequate group functioning.

SUMMARY

Understanding the nature of the group process requires an understanding of the nature of *group* and *process*. A process involves the dynamic relationships of events in an ongoing, continuous sequence of time. Each ingredient of the process affects, and is affected by, every other ingredient as changes in the process evolve through time. Although many perspectives have been used to define *group*, this book utilizes the perspective of interdependence and interaction. A collection of individuals develops groupness over time, so that the identity of a group exists apart from the separate identities of its individual members.

A group is conceived to be a system characterized by its structure (the pattern of relationships between its components at any given point in time), its function (the regulatory, recurring day-to-day relationships between its components through time), and its evolution (the continuous changes of structure and function over a long period). Rather than perceiving individual persons to be the components of the group system, this book considers communicative behaviors to be the units for defining, observing, and analyzing the group system. Thus, a group is a collection of individual persons whose communicative behaviors—specifically acts, interacts, and double interacts—become interstructured and repetitive in the form of predictable patterns. The prototypical group that embodies all the elements of group process and is minimally inhibited by external, or environmental, constraints is the leaderless group discussion (LGD).

Individuals work in groups because groups are better at some types of tasks. And after joining groups, individuals go through a social-comparison process. Successful group decision making is thus a direct result of each person's integration into group membership. Central to this integrative process are the mutual and reciprocal functionings of self-disclosure, interpersonal trust, and risk.

CHAPTER 2

Dimensions of the Group Process

Our society has long tended to draw rather clear distinctions between allegedly opposing phenomena. For example, we classify a person as a liberal or a conservative, a Democrat or a Republican, a blue-collar worker or a white-collar worker. It is no wonder, then, that we differentiate between two dimensions of group decision making—task and social. Because people are involved in a group, the social dimension is evident. And because the group is expected to come to agreement on a decision, the task dimension is also evident.

It is unfortunate, but true, that the task and social dimensions of group decision making are often viewed in conflict with each other. This view seems to reflect the hackneyed conflict between reason and faith, science and the humanities, classicism and romanticism, logic and emotions. There have been numerous attempts to provide detailed plans and instructions for making a group decision that avoids social or emotional influence. The assumption underlying these proposals is apparently that a decision is better when based on an impersonal and critical evaluation of the facts. We are cautioned against emotional reactions in the apparent belief that such reactions lower the quality of the group decision.

The purpose of this chapter is to provide an insight into the social and task dimensions of the group process. Consistent with the perspective of interdependence involved in group process, these two dimensions will be viewed as inseparable. This chapter illustrates how the social dimension affects group decision making and how group decision-making tasks are different from decision-making tasks performed by individuals.

INTERDEPENDENCE OF THE SOCIAL AND TASK DIMENSIONS

Both task and social dimensions are inherent in the process of group decision making. No decision-making group exists without both dimensions. It is important to understand each of them in order to understand effective group decision making and to participate effectively in a decision-making group. *Task dimension* refers to the relationship between group members and the work they are to perform—the job

32

they have to do and how they go about doing it. *Social dimension* refers to the relationships of group members with one another—how they feel toward one another and about their membership in the group.

For some reason, the task and social areas of the group process have typically been viewed separately. Some theorists separate the task and social dimensions and indicate that two problems continuously confront a group during its period of development—group structure (social) and task activity. Thus, group members deal with each type of problem separately throughout their existence as a group. According to one early theorist (Tuckman, 1965), certain comments aid in developing the group's structure, and other comments are directed toward accomplishing the group's task. Robert F. Bales's (1950) first system of classifying the behaviors or acts of group members—interaction process analysis (IPA)—specifically labeled every comment as oriented toward either the social area or the task area. Such a total separation is probably unwise. Common sense should tell us that a comment such as "Aw, you don't know what you're talking about!" implies not only an outright rejection of a contributed idea (a task comment) but also an impact on the social relationship of at least two members. Bales's revision of his IPA categories of acts (Bales and Cohen, 1979) seems to reveal second thoughts about drawing such a clear distinction between social and task comments. The task and social dimensions of group process are highly interdependent—in fact, virtually indistinguishable from each other. That is, one may separate the two from a theoretical perspective, but the interaction between the two makes them virtually inseparable in practice.

There is a reason for using the term *dimension* to refer to the task and social areas of group process. Figure 2-1 illustrates the two-dimensional existence of a plane geometrical figure. A rectangle exists in two dimensions—height and width. Height cannot be separated from width without altering the rectangle itself. Although the height or width may be observed and measured separately, the two dimensions are inseparable within the definition of the rectangle. The same inherent and inseparable relationship is true of the task and social dimensions of a group process. Without either dimension, the group process does not exist.

Cohesiveness and Productivity

You can probably remember being a member of a group you thoroughly enjoyed. There was an esprit de corps among the members, a spirit of camaraderie, a feeling of close personal ties. You undoubtedly felt that the group was worthwhile and rewarding to you, and you felt a sense of loyalty to the group—a personal commitment. In a group such as this, members are proud to be members. Occasionally such groups evolve from classroom groups. The following comments, for example, are selected from the final entries in diaries kept by members of a group formed within a class studying group communication. Their feelings were unanimous:

"I feel a close bond with the other members of our group and would like to continue working with each one."

Figure 2-1 "Dimensions" of the group process.

"I am very grateful for this group experience and feel a very close bond of friendship and understanding with each member."

"What I really want to emphasize is the way that we learned to function as free-
thinking people unacquainted, really, with the others (at the beginning of the
term) and evolve into an extremely cohesive group."

"I developed a great amount of respect for and a relationship of oneness or unity
with each member individually and the group as a whole."

"It may sound a little corny, but I feel [list of the other members' names] are good
friends and, when this class is over, I will feel, if nothing else, that I have
made some friends for life."

On the other side of the coin, you have perhaps been involved with groups
that were less than appealing. There may have been bickering among some members, but probably you were more bored than hurt by the group experience. Rather
than feeling a sense of commitment or pride in the group, you probably searched
for excuses to avoid group meetings. If you had any choice in the matter, you probably dropped out of the group; otherwise, you endured it only as long as you had
to. One comment from a final diary of another classroom group illustrates this type
of group: "One thing that really affected the development and behavior of our
group was not being able to get together for a meeting. It seemed that the five of
us could never find one time that was good for everyone. But as they say, you can
always find time for the things that are important."

The two types of groups just described illustrate a difference in *cohesiveness*—
the ability of group members to get along, the feeling of loyalty, pride, and commitment of members toward the group. It would not be inaccurate to say that cohesiveness is, more than anything else, the degree of liking that members have for
one another. To the extent that members like one another, they are committed to
the group and feel loyal and proud of their membership status. Cohesiveness may
also be viewed as the output of a group's social dimension. That is, cohesiveness is
not a process so much as a state of being. As groupness emerges from group interaction, the group may be characterized at some level of cohesiveness. Such a
characteristic describes the outcome of the process in the group's social dimension.

In a similar fashion, the output from a group's task dimension may be described as *productivity*. To the extent that a group accomplishes its task, it is productive. As with cohesiveness, the amount of productivity is not always easily de-

termined. Of course, the productivity of a group on a manufacturing assembly line may be measured by counting the number of products its members complete in a given time period. Or the productivity of a basketball team may be determined by the number of games it wins. But what of a decision-making group? The number of decisions is seldom a good indication of productivity. A jury, for example, may have only one decision to make—the guilt or innocence of the defendant. As in most decisions, quality rather than quantity is the best determinant of a decision-making group's productivity. And the quality of decisions is exceedingly difficult to measure.

Despite the difficulties of observing and measuring productivity and cohesiveness, they serve as useful concepts to describe the general success of a group along its task and social dimensions. Caution must be exercised, however, in utilizing these descriptive terms. Cohesiveness and productivity are not qualities that a group does or does not have. Each is a characteristic that describes to some degree the success of the group process in every group.

In every group, both cohesiveness and productivity exist in some amount. That is, a group's productivity or cohesiveness should each be visualized as some point along a continuum. For example, in terms of cohesiveness a group may be low, moderately low, moderately high, high, and so forth. Another analogy may illustrate this point. Height is a characteristic of every person. We measure height conveniently in feet and inches, and everyone has height to some degree. We may describe someone as tall or short, but we would never say that a person has no height. In the same way, we may describe a group as "low" with respect to cohesiveness or productivity, but it is foolish to say that the group is "not productive" or "not cohesive." Even though we commonly use such expressions to characterize a group, we must keep in mind that we actually mean that the group is rated at the lower end of the continuum of either productivity or cohesiveness.

Since the interdependence of the task and social dimensions has been established, it seems reasonable that the outputs of these dimensions—cohesiveness and productivity—should also have an interdependent relationship. Although we can visualize a group whose members hate one another but are able to be quite productive, this type of group is unusually rare. Common sense would dictate a direct relationship between productivity and cohesiveness—that is, the more cohesive a group is, the more productive it is likely to be. And this dictum is true—up to a point. As a group raises its level of cohesiveness, the more likely it is to raise its level of productivity. Conversely, the more productive the group, the greater the likelihood that it will be more cohesive. However, the relationship breaks down toward the upper end of the two continuums. Figure 2-2 illustrates this relationship between cohesiveness and productivity. According to this diagram, extremely cohesive groups are more likely to have moderate to low productivity. Although the productivity of highly cohesive groups probably doesn't sink to the level of groups that are extremely low in cohesiveness, such groups are not nearly as likely to be as productive as groups with moderately high cohesiveness.

Several explanations account for this phenomenon. First, the group may have been together so long that its original purpose—its task—has suffered simply be-

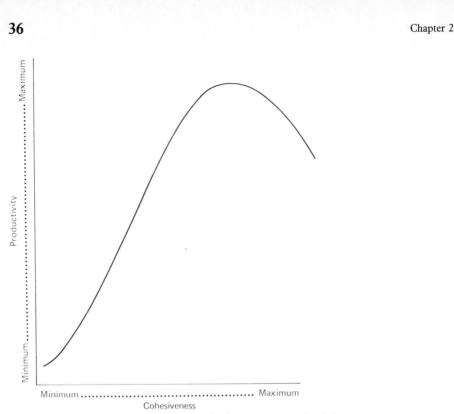

Figure 2-2 The relationship between cohesiveness and productivity.

cause the members enjoy one another's company too much. Many local community service organizations find that over the years the primary purpose of their organization has changed from assisting their community to having a good time. The greater proportion of their activity, then, is socializing rather than working on community service. We are familiar with one group whose purpose, at the time the group was formed, was to raise money for an annual charity drive. The group still raises money annually, but it continues to meet regularly during the year to play cards, eat dinner, and generally entertain itself. The greater proportion of its effort is social enjoyment, not raising funds.

Another explanation is that a group which is highly cohesive but has low productivity has a great deal of "reserve productivity." That is, the group is capable of much more productivity but simply does not expend the effort to be productive. Hence, its productivity lies dormant, or in reserve. The classic example is the extremely bright student who does just enough work to earn a passing grade but doesn't earn an A; teachers, parents, and friends would say that this student isn't working to capacity. Another example is the athletic coach of a losing team who bemoans the fact that the players are capable of winning every game but just aren't playing to the level of their abilities. In either case, the assumption is that the group or the person is capable of superior productivity but actually achieves only average or below-average productivity—hence the term *reserve productivity*. If actual productivity and reserve productivity were added together, the total would be a superior level of productivity.

Whatever the explanation for the relationship between cohesiveness and productivity, the point to remember is that the outputs of the two dimensions of group process affect each other reciprocally. For example, an increase in productivity tends to increase the cohesiveness of a group. The legendary football coach, Vince Lombardi, had all the characteristics that would normally lead to low cohesiveness. He was aloof from his players—highly dictatorial and a slave-driver. The players were forced to perform behaviors they would normally find abhorrent. They were subject to stringent training rules more appropriate for Little League juveniles than mature adults. They endured torturous practices above and beyond the normal practice routines. But they won games. They ruled the National Football League during the decade of the 1960s and became famous for their "Packer pride." Apparently the team was a tightly knit, highly cohesive group. We can only wonder how cohesive it would have been had it been a losing football team.

Conversely, an increase in cohesiveness generally precipitates a corresponding increase in productivity. The classic example of this phenomenon is commonly known as the Hawthorne effect. Deriving its name from a series of investigations performed in the Hawthorne plant of the Western Electric Company, the Hawthorne effect generally refers to the increase in productivity that results from an environmental change in the social dimension. Organizational managers may single out a work group within the organization and give that group special attention or special favors, such as enlisting its aid in a research situation. That group is likely to increase its productivity as a result. Athletic coaches talk about getting their teams "psyched up" for the big game with a great deal of group activity: rallies, team dinners, yelling, and so forth. Corporations spend an increasing amount of time and money on facilitating pleasant and positive social relationships. The company picnic, softball game, noon exercise hour, and a host of social activities are all designed to increase the sense of cohesiveness and satisfaction with the organization so that the workers become more productive.

Occasionally, however, the increase in productivity precipitated by an increase in cohesiveness may be more a rationalization by the group members to account for their otherwise low level of productivity. That is, the group members probably realize that their group has accomplished little in its task dimension, and so they rationalize that the group actually accomplished more than it did. One method of rationalization is to change the nature of the task. Members of a classroom group often feel that their decision-making task was not very worthwhile, anyway, and so they arbitrarily change their perceptions of what the task really was. The following excerpt from a classroom group's final self-analysis illustrates this rationalization:

> Because our information would not be used for anything of real importance,
> we felt we were wasting our time to meet.... The only real purpose in our
> group was to get in the assignments.... As it turned out, our group was
> more a social group than anything else. We never really got into any real
> conflicts. But we felt some very important things came out of the experience
> of being in a group. We learned better how a group functions and

> why.... All the different topics that we had discussed in class about what
> happens in a group became clearer to us as we related to each other about
> what had happened in our group. This gave all of us a better understanding
> of group methods.

In reality, little groupness ever emerged for these group members. They experienced a spurt of social success toward the end of the term and began the process of rationalizing their previously low productivity. Although they did perceive the "real task" of the classroom group, these members were probably attempting to impress the instructor rather than actually describing their group's level of productivity. It is, unfortunately, probably true that comments like these are more typical of the classroom group than the comments of the extremely cohesive group cited earlier.

How to Promote Cohesiveness in Groups

In order to function well, a group must cohere; it must work together and promote a "we" feeling among its members. As their cohesiveness increases, the members become even more committed to the group's goals, accept the group's tasks and roles more readily, and conform to the group's norms more frequently. Cohesiveness is that powerful appeal which attracts group members to one another and creates a collective identity, so that the success of the group means the success of the individuals.

As you will see throughout this book, we offer no magic formulas for the simple and surefire creation of effective groups. The same is true of cohesiveness. You cannot do a few simple things to ensure that a group will be cohesive and therefore productive. Nevertheless, you can apply some intelligence to the problem. Cohesiveness develops when certain conditions exist in the group—and if you can understand and control these conditions, you will have a better chance of producing a cohesive group. Below are six strategies for increasing cohesiveness in groups.

Encourage External Threats This may sound a little harsh, but group members become much more unified when they perceive a threat to their existence or dignity. A threat is indeed one of the most effective cohesiveness devices. Many groups are characterized by argument and dispute, but this all stops when an outsider criticizes the group. Countries have been known to pull together and become much more patriotic and chauvinistic when they are threatened by other countries. Managers use this technique all the time when they set up competitive situations between groups. Forcing groups to compete with one another and then rewarding the winner is one example. Even friendly competition helps. If, for example, a sales group from a company challenges a group from another company to a baseball game, the group members are likely to strengthen their bonds as they work to meet the challenge.

Create History As time passes and the members of a group share some experiences, they usually draw closer together. This is especially true when the experiences are difficult or trying. Soldiers in combat, work groups that accomplish difficult tasks, and juries that struggle with a decision are examples of groups whose members work hard together and become closer as a result. Often members of an organization will retell stories and humorous incidents pertaining to the company. These stories become part of the historical mythology of the organization and help create a sense of organizational history, and this history contributes to cohesiveness. Some managers arrange special events, such as retreats, parties, or workshops, to discuss the work and problems of group members. These occasions are often used to build cohesiveness because they give group members a common historical experience to refer to.

Establish Interdependent Goals The goals of a group must be in the interest of all members and, more important, should be goals that require coordination and contribution from everyone in the group. As group members increase their reliance on one another, they increase their need and desire for cohesiveness. There is no need for unity when a job can be done by one person. A factory worker has no incentive to be a positive and productive member of a group when his pay is based on individual work or accomplishment. But if he is a member of a work team that is responsible for an entire project, and if the pay or compensation is based on the quality of the project, then he is much more likely to become a productive member of a group.

Accomplish Something When members see that they are making progress toward a goal, they feel much better about the group; conversely, there is a decline in cohesiveness when the group stops making progress. The factory worker mentioned above will feel very good about himself and the group if the group makes progress toward its goals. A good strategy for a manager is to set short-term, easily attainable goals for a group so that its members can experience a sense of accomplishment and establish enough cohesiveness to continue their work. Fund-raising committees and capital campaigns often set easily attainable goals in order not only to present an image of success but also to give their committee members a sense of accomplishment in their work.

Develop Relationships and Shared Norms Obviously, groups are more cohesive when the members like one another; and obviously, group members will like one another when they are cohesive. It is a "chicken or an egg" issue, because it is impossible to say which comes first. Do people like each other because they are cohesive, or are they cohesive because they like each other? In either case, when group members are friendly and show intimacy and understanding, they are more likely to be cohesive.

The group should also develop common norms and standards of behavior. If group members develop the norms for which they feel a sense of committment, they will support and accept these norms. Mutually accepted and understood norms of behavior introduce regularity, making cooperation and coordination easier to achieve. It is true that cohesive groups are able to tolerate some differences in people, even appreciating and taking pride in these differences, but it is also true that too much variation in the norms and values of the group reduces cohesiveness.

Promote Acceptance for Group Members   Secure group members are cohesive group members. When anxiety is reduced and self-esteem is heightened, the members are more likely to perform with energy and enthusiasm. When a person is not threatened by a group, and is accepted by its members, the person is much more likely to participate in the group. Group members need to be told that their contributions and behaviors are valued by the group, for group acceptance is of the utmost importance. If a supervisor is more interested in assigning blame to an individual than solving a problem, the threat of blame will seriously hinder cohesiveness.

All in all, cohesiveness results in a better group, but it has one negative consequence. Janis (1983), a social psychologist, discusses a phenomenon called *groupthink*. We will encounter groupthink elsewhere in this book: namely, its influence on decision making (Chapter 6), conformity (Chapter 8), and conflict (Chapter 10). But for now, groupthink is a negative consequence of highly cohesive groups. It is also an interesting example of the interdependence between the task and social dimensions of the group process. Groupthink is related to the quality of output from the group rather than to the amount of effort that cohesive group members exert.

One consistent research finding about groups is that group consensus changes individuals' opinions and preferences (Moscovici, 1985). In other words, when a group is cohesive and in strong agreement about a decision, the opinions and preferences of the individuals in the group change to conform more to the preferences of the group as a whole. The members are so committed to the group that they use it as a basis for their own opinions, suspending their own critical thinking in favor of the group's opinions. The group exerts both conscious and unconscious pressures on individuals to conform to the group's decisions. And because individuals value their membership in the group and feel a strong sense of commitment, they conform quite easily. Often their conformity is not a matter of willingly giving in to the group; when people are very reliant on groups for acceptance and security and have a strong in-group loyalty, they literally conform their opinions and judgments without knowing it. In fact, they will defend what they do.

Groupthink occurs when a group makes an extreme or poor decision because members suspend their critical faculties in favor of consensus. You will see in Chapters 6 and 10 that conflict over ideas is an important part of the group process. Groupthink results when the group short-circuits this process because cohesion and consensus are more important than honest disagreement. The group members usually convince themselves that the judgments and decisions of the group are correct and superior to the opinions of any one member. One person in a classroom group, suffering from what she thought was groupthink, wrote, "Everyone in the group gets along almost *too* well. Ideas that come about, therefore, are shallow and unclear. Members of my group are afraid to challenge or question ideas." Groupthink is a defective and low-quality decision that results when the group is too cohesive and more concerned with agreement and consensus than with quality.

THE SOCIAL DIMENSION

Our society has long recognized the worth and dignity of the individual. The individual's right to life, liberty, and the pursuit of happiness is inviolate. Advertisements sell products by appealing to the wish to "get away from the crowd" and assert individuality. Laws protect each person's rights to privacy, to earn a living, to gain an education—in short, the right to be an individual. But we also recognize that the human being is a social being. Although a few people choose to be hermits, most human animals seek the company of other humans and apparently need membership in a variety of social systems.

To understand a group is to understand the relationship between the individual and the group. Moreover, to understand this relationship is to understand the individual. This section deals with the reciprocal relationship between the individual and the group. Specifically, the development of the miniculture that constitutes a group entails the development of a climate that socializes the uniqueness of the individual into the social system of the group. The term *socioemotional climate* refers to this merger of the individual into the social system.

Perspectives on the Socioemotional Climate

The most common perspective used to discuss the socioemotional climate of a group is cohesiveness. But cohesiveness, a very general and abstract concept, is synonymous with the concept of socioemotional climate. Understanding how cohesiveness develops is indeed equivalent to understanding the development of a group's socioemotional climate.

Interpersonal Attraction   One common approach to discussing cohesiveness is to discuss how and why people are attracted to one another: that is, how and why people like one another. The assumption is that people who like each other develop a cohesive group. So a cohesive group is cohesive because members develop interpersonal liking.

Attitudinal similarity is the most frequent reason why people are attracted to other people. As Berger (1973, p. 181) wrote, "one of the most robust relationships in all of the behavioral sciences is that which exists between perceived attitudinal similarity and interpersonal attraction. We like persons whom we perceive to hold attitudes which are similar to ours, especially when these attitudes are concerned with issues which are important to us." Members of a group will like one another if they perceive that the group is composed of people with similar attitudes and preferences. Even if group members disagree about something, there will be an accompanying pressure to communicate about it, and the increase in communication will usually (but not always) lead to more agreement and therefore to greater interpersonal attraction. Thus, whenever possible, it is best to compose groups of similar types of people.

But there are other factors that relate communication to attraction in the group. Below are four strategies for increasing the attractiveness that group members have for one another. While there are no guarantees that members of a group will like one another and then become cohesive, it is possible to increase the probability of interpersonal attraction.

1. *Increase the Frequency of Interaction* How often people communicate is associated with interpersonal attraction. As people communicate with one another more often, they increase their mutual attraction. One consistent finding in communication (Bochner, 1984) is that there are pressures toward agreement and liking. People basically want to like other people. If members of a group spend time together and talk about anything—task or nonrelated social matters—they will increase their attraction for each other. It is possible, of course, to find that you dislike someone after talking to the person for a while, but the odds are that this will not happen. As the frequency of interaction increases, however, it is difficult to know whether this frequency is the cause of the attraction or its effect; that is, are people attracted to each other because they communicate more frequently, or do they communicate more frequently because they like each other? Another "chicken or an egg" question. Nevertheless, increasing the contact time among group members is always a good idea.

2. *Reciprocate Liking and Interaction* A second factor associated with interpersonal attraction is the perception of reciprocated attraction and interaction. Interpersonal liking is a two-way street. We like people who like us. Moreover, we tend to be attracted to people we think we are going to be working with; even though we have never met them, the natural pressure toward liking and attraction "kicks in" when we think we are going to be communicating with them. Sometimes a few group members are not very interested in other members of the group and can seriously impair the group's progress. If you can communicate to these few members that they will be interacting with others who are interested in them, you can improve the chances of attraction. We begin building perceptions of others even before we communicate with them, and we will be attracted to those who are attracted to us.

3. *Self-disclose* Self-disclosure may be defined generally as statements made to another about oneself—what one thinks, feels, believes, wants, needs. It is verbally communicated personal information to another person (see Chapter 1). Rosenfeld (1988) explains the complexities and conditions that make self-disclosure successful, and his fundamental conclusion is that self-disclosure is potentially very beneficial to interpersonal relationships in groups. Self-disclosure does have its risks; group members who choose to self-disclose can meet with rejection or a negative image from other people. But if disclosive communication is handled properly, group members will experience closer relationships and increased understanding. And the best way to get others to self-disclose is to do it yourself.

If your group is experiencing interpersonal tensions, it might behoove you to attempt a disclosure.

It is true that self-disclosure is risky, but so are all strategies for improving relationships. Research indicates that positive disclosures are associated with highly cohesive and successful groups. In task-oriented groups, that exist in classrooms or organizations, disclosure can help maintain relationships. Disclosure in task-oriented groups requires some skill. People sitting around in business clothes making decisions do not reveal personal information about themselves very readily. But the presentation of at least slightly disclosive information about yourself presents you as agreeable and nonthreatening. It "humanizes" you to the extent that disclosure makes you appear open, warm, and friendly. Other people will usually respond in kind. Self-disclosure is a very useful way to improve the interpersonal attractiveness among group members.

4. *Develop Bonding Competence* An important aspect of being a capable, competent communicator is developing relationship skills, or what Bochner (1984, p. 588) calls *bonding competence*. There are a number of dimensions to becoming a competent member of a group (see Andersen, 1988), but skill at promoting interpersonal relationships is one of the most important. Skilled group members usually achieve their communication goals by using appropriate social skills and by remaining sensitive to the needs of others. People are attracted to socially competent individuals, ones who not only achieve their own goals but also satisfy the goals of others. Competent relationship bonders show solidarity with others. They communicate in such a way as to indicate to the group that everyone is important and has status. They offer to help, and they make personal sacrifices for the group. Their communication behaviors evidence flexibility and adaptability.

Member Satisfaction Cohesiveness may also be viewed as the extent to which members enjoy, or are satisfied with, their group experiences. Rather than viewing an individual's relationship with another individual, this perspective on cohesiveness attempts to view one element of an individual member's perception of the group as a whole. The term *satisfaction* is used here to refer to morale, loyalty, or any way in which individual members are pleased with their group experience. Marston and Hecht (1988) have written an interesting essay in which they report the results of an intensive study of a small group where the observers noted the variables that influence group members' satisfaction. How satisfied the group members are with the group is clearly correlated with group consensus, productivity, and general performance and effectiveness (Hecht and Riley, 1985).

Marston and Hecht (1988) report six qualities of groups that are associated with satisfied group members.

The first is the importance of *participation*. Group members get generally grumpy and disaffected when they feel as if they are not allowed to participate or that the participation is unequal. Group members are most satisfied when they feel included in the discussion, and they are least satisfied when they feel as though others are dominating the discussion. Both the frequency and the duration of the participation are important. Another important factor in participation is bidirectional communication. People are satisfied not only when they are allowed to communicate often but also when others direct messages to them; it is naturally reinforcing to have someone direct questions or information to you. Also, group members must perceive that they have a free, unfettered opportunity to participate. An early study by Heslin and Dunphy (1964) found that actual participation rates were less important than the perception of freedom to interact. You can improve participation rates by controlling group size and making sure that leaders are skilled at including everyone in the discussion.

The *types of messages* are a second important contributor to the group member's satisfaction. There are, of course, many types of messages that influence the group, but the most important are (1) negative communication, (2) ambiguous communication, and (3) orienting communication. Negative communication, which includes personal criticism, decreases the member's satisfaction; group members must be able to express disagreements, but they must learn to do it in a manner that is not offensive to individuals. Vague and ambiguous messages also decrease satisfaction; they make for confused meaning, and they generate confusion and equally ambiguous responses from other group members. Orienting communication directs the group discussion by means of clarification, questions, answers, and relevant information; helping the group to keeps things organized and focused, orienting communication promotes satisfaction with the group.

Feedback is a third component of satisfaction. Group leaders and other members of the group must do everything they can to provide feedback to other members. Feedback is a statement that is responsive to the behaviors of other group members and group members should receive both positive and negative feedback. Positive feedback (being told that what you have done is good or helpful to the group) is desirable, but negative feedback is also important. If you can change a group member's behavior so that it becomes more aligned with the group's goals, then you have significantly contributed to satisfaction in the group. The best way to communicate negative feedback is to be performance-descriptive; that is, focus on describing the performance of the group member, not the person's emotions or attitudes.

Interaction management is a fourth element of establishing successful group satisfaction. Interaction management refers to one's skill in regulating and coordinating the flow and direction of interaction. The interaction is being poorly managed when people interrupt one another and speak in a confused and uncoordinated manner. One very important factor in interaction management is *turn taking*, which refers to the smoothness of the back-and-forth exchanges among speakers. If the group is composed of people who are poor speakers and awkward about who speaks when, there is likely to be confusion and frustration among the group members. The leader should ensure that turn-taking expectations are not violated.

Fifth, satisfaction is highest when group members are comfortable with the *status* hierarchy in the group (discussed in detail in Chapter 9). Status is the prestige or position that a person holds in the group. High-status group members are able to influence other group members because they have some skill or resource that the group values. Group members are very dissatisfied when there is confusion and disagreement over status. If one member acts more important then he or she is given credit for, then other members of the group will become irritated. Groups like to think of their members as having equal status, but this is probably impossible to achieve. All groups have some status differential. But agreement on the nature of that differential is important. An individual, say a leader, may have status and power in the group, but there will be no problem if the other group members understand and support the person.

The final source of group members' satisfaction is *motivation*. When everyone in the group has a desire to remain in the group and wants to contribute and devote time to the group, then the members are motivated to perform. There is no substitute for people who really want to be involved in a project. A person will be more motivated when a group is able to reward the person and to be a significant part of the person's identity. Also important is conversational motivation (the motivation to engage in interaction), for satisfaction increases when the members are enthusiastic about taking part in the discussion. Motivated communicators ask questions, seek information, do research, request clarification, and are generally highly involved in and focused on the interaction.

Group Identification Another perspective from which to view individuals and their relationship with the group is the extent to which they identify themselves with that group. Many scholars discuss group identification as the member's internalization of group goals—the extent to which the group's goals become the goals of the individual members. Group identification here implies a broader meaning. To the extent that each group member feels a part of the group or recognizes membership in the group, group identification may be said to exist.

There are some observable manifestations of a growing group identification even in the classroom group. Student members will change their classroom seating patterns and begin to sit beside or near their fellow group members. The member will begin to refer to the group in the first person as "my" group or "our" group. When members keep diaries of their reactions after each group meeting, the diaries themselves reflect a developing group identification. A diary in the early stages of the group meetings will include a reference to another member in the third person: for example, "I am having trouble with one of the people in this group. He seems to criticize everything I say." Later, that same member will use first names exclusively in referring to fellow group members—"Steve is still the critic of our group. But I am beginning to realize that he just wants us to think about what we are saying."

Occasionally group members have difficulty establishing group identification, so an impetus is needed to stir their feelings of unity. An example from one such group indicates a possible impetus for increasing group identification. One group member, frustrated by the obvious apathy of his fellow group members, sought help from his instructor. This group, as might be expected, was not very productive and had received a rather low evaluation on a preliminary group project, and the members were naturally disappointed over their low grade. The instructor and the student arranged a group conference. During this conference the entire group, acting as a unified group, complained to the instructor about the low grade, and throughout the conference the instructor remained firm and proceeded to justify the low mark, often using rather shaky grounds for his justification. The conference proved to be successful in that the group developed much closer ties of group identification. They became united against a common "enemy"—the instructor. At the end of the term, when they were informed of the contrived incident, the group members had almost forgotten it. Group identification, in this instance, was spurred by conflict with some external foe. But more important, the feelings of increased group solidarity were maintained in the absence of the foe.

Symbolic Convergence

"Symbolic convergence" sounds a little daunting, but it is really a pretty clear and interesting concept. Whereas the preceding section discussed some well-established perspectives on the social dimension of the group, symbolic convergence is a special theory of communication that has been evolving in recent years (see Bormann, 1986). It is a realistic picture of the communication in groups and helps explain the social dimension of groups, especially how they come to form a group identity; moreover, it is significantly correlated with cohesiveness. Groups establish their own culture with information and stories that are unique to the group, and these cultural stories are evidence that the group is forming a special identity that is of value to the group's members.

Symbolic convergence theory is concerned with the evolution of certain patterns of communication in the group. More specifically, it deals with attempts to find recurring communication patterns in the group that are indications of group consciousness. The term *symbolic convergence* refers to the coming together (or unifying) of certain symbols in the group that are important to group members. When group members share and understand symbols in a particular way, they form a common understanding and consciousness with which they can identify; this identification is *symbolic* because it deals with the human tendency to interpret signs and signals and infuse them with meaning. When people participate in a group, they share stories and fantasies and make sense out of human action by attributing meaning to human events. When symbolic worlds overlap or come more closely together, they are said to *converge*. And people are sharing a common consciousness when they understand one another's symbolic worlds.

Bormann (1986) cites *dramatizing messages* as an example of how symbolic themes develop in a group and then the members converge. In 1950, Robert Bales devised categories to code the communication in small groups (see Chapter 6). One of his original categories was "shows tension release," but it was later changed to "dramatizes." A group member dramatizes a message when he or she portrays something in dramatic terms. Bormann (1986, p. 224) wrote that "A dramatizing message is one that contains one or more of the following: a pun or other word play, a double entendre, a figure of speech, analogy, anecdote, allegory, fable, or narrative."

Over the years, small group researchers noticed that some of the dramatizing in groups would cause an explosion of symbolic material that the group became very enamored with. This led to the concept of group fantasy and fantasy-chain analysis. The researchers noted that dramatic messages were not important any time one member made a pun or a joke; rather, they became important when group members became excited, interrupted one another, and showed a lot of emotion.

Sharing Group Fantasies Researchers observed that a group might be working along in a normal manner and then come to a point where the members would get off track and depart from the group's main direction. This might begin with a simple dramatic message. Often the people would lean back in their chairs and get quiet for a while, and then all of a sudden someone would say something completely off the subject and unrelated to the task at hand. She would tell a story about a strange incident or about something that had happened to her. Then other group members would join in and add to the story, and the group would get lively and emotional as everyone contributed to the narrative. It was not uncommon to observe group members taking part in these stories and expressing fear, sadness, and joy. Then, just as abruptly as it began, the episode would end, often with one member directing the group back to the task.

These were moments of dramatization. The group had participated in a fantasy. The term *fantasy* does not refer to something unreal or bizarre, but to the act of sharing interpretations of events to satisfy the group's need to organize experience and form communal bonds. Group fantasies often deal with news, television, organizational stories, desires, or things that have actually happened to group members. They serve to achieve an empathic symbolic convergence. The group members take pleasure in their joint experience of emotions. Group fantasies are also thematic; they have a story with characters and patterns of action. Group fantasies are not chaotic and confused, but organized. They are composed of characters (sometimes heroes and villains) that are engaged in human activities that represent themes of power, control, failure, success, the future, and other common lifescripts.

The example below is from a classroom group. It is a fantasy chain with a power theme; that is, it illustrates how a group shares fantasies related to power. The group members are experiencing frustration at their inability to accomplish the task. After a few moments of silence, Rick begins:

RICK: You know, I'd like to bag this whole project.
PETE: Yeah, screw this guy. Let's just tell 'em we're not going to do this group assignment.
SUE: Be serious, we'll all get F's.
RICK: No we won't. We'll get in touch with all the other groups and none of us will turn in the assignment. He can't fail the whole class.
BOB: Let's just take over the class, like the students did in the sixties. I mean really,

what could he or the university do? We'll just insist on not having to do this assignment.

RUTH: I read about these kids once who took over a class. They determined themselves what they were going to do, what books they would read, and who was going to get what grade.

BOB: Sure, I've often thought we should have more say so in what goes on in class.

RUTH: There was a movie about it or something.

RICK: It could be done.

SUE: Come on, you guys, we gotta get this done.

This interaction is a power fantasy. It offers the group an exciting way to discover emotional common ground related to frustrations, attitudes, lines of action, and opinions. This power fantasy has heroes (the class), villains (the professor), and scenarios where people carry out behaviors. The pattern of communication allows the group to dramatize its attitudes, and this dramatization becomes an important part of the group's culture. The communication of an individual or group always reveals attitudes and values. Imagine a bunch of fraternity boys sitting around talking about getting drunk, big parties, and scoring with women. The attitudes and values inherent in their culture are apparent. The same is true of a collection of women who talk about shopping, getting married, and having their nails done.

Fantasy chains are very important to establishing a common group identity. All new groups and LGD groups must spend time communicating in such a way that they develop a sense of common identity. Group members succeed at such an identity creation by recognizing that they are in a group and that this group has an existence and purpose of its own. They become aware that they are different in some ways from people who are not members of the group. You can always tell groups that have a strong identity and are probably very cohesive because they have fantasies about "outsiders" and "insiders." They develop a sense of "our group." They use phrases to refer to themselves, such as "our group," "we," or "us." Groups that have pet names for themselves are especially symbolically converged. We have known groups that called themselves the *Testmasters*, the *Bluebirds*, or the *Hawks* (after their school mascot). These names are symbolic of the strong sense of common identity the group has created, and they serve to mark the boundaries for membership in the group.

Social Tension

The feeling of tension is familiar to all of us. A person who feels tense is nervous and irritable. Television commercials have endowed tension with a certain fame, along with its accompanying headache. But tension does indeed have its physiological signs—contracted muscles, the familiar sweaty palms, the averted eye gaze. This is the tension experienced by an individual person. Social tension is not unlike the tension experienced by an individual. Persons in a group suffering from extreme social tension may exhibit many of the signs of individual tension. Extreme social tension is characterized by an electric atmosphere. The very air seems charged. The individual members are uncomfortable. All in all, extreme social tension is not a pleasant experience.

Primary and Secondary Tension There are two types of social tension—primary and secondary. The difference is one of kind rather than degree. During the initial period of a group's formation, primary tension is inevitable and to be expected as a normal occurrence. One might compare primary social tension to stage fright. Social inhibitions create a lack of assurance about how to behave. Comments are quietly spoken and very tentative. Long pauses occur between comments. Members rarely interrupt one another; and if two members should speak at once, profuse apologies reveal the extent of primary tension present.

Secondary tension is potentially much more serious. Unlike primary tension, it is not always predictable or easily overcome merely through the passage of time. The hallmark of secondary tension is typically an abrupt departure from group routine. Sometimes a sharp increase in tension begins with an outburst from one of the members. There may be a heated exchange between two or more members. A flurry of verbal activity will be followed by an unbearably long pause. During the heated exchange, members may attempt to shout over one another's comments for extended periods. Usually two or three members will do most of the talking while other members remain rigidly silent, staring at the floor. Extreme secondary tension is definitely an unpleasant sensation and, if uncontrolled, threatens the social health of the group.

The causes of secondary tension are many and varied. Overt interpersonal conflict, occasionally even a personality conflict, may precipitate severe secondary tension. Environmental pressures, such as a shortage of time to accomplish the task, will cause it to rise sharply. Quite often, a feeling of frustration among the members foments tension. Such frustration may stem from an acknowledged lack of success in task accomplishment or the feeling that the group performance was far short of expectations. A nonconforming member might cause frustration—particularly one who is habitually tardy or absent from group meetings or who consistently fails to fulfill promises made to the group. Whatever the cause, extreme secondary tension, once experienced, must be brought under control if the group is to survive.

Managing Social Tension Up to this point we have discussed tension as harmful and destructive to a group's socioemotional climate. Certainly excessive tension is harmful to the group, but some tension is both normal and essential. In fact, some tension is always present in a functioning group. Tension implies activity. An actor, for instance, is not relaxed when performing, but is tense, concentrating on the performance. The successful athletic team is "up for the game." After a group overcomes the natural social inertia in the early stages of group development, the members experience tension. They are alert, on their toes—tense. The functioning group is not at rest, but active, and hence is experiencing some degree of tension.

The problem of social tension, then, is not that it exists, but that it may exceed an optimal level. Every group has a "tolerance threshold" of social tension above which it cannot function effectively. If the tension level is below that threshold, the group is able to function well. But when the tension level rises above the group's tolerance threshold, it becomes the overpowering priority in the group's socioemotional climate. The group must reduce that tension level before it can do anything else.

Of course, the tolerance threshold varies from group to group. Some groups can tolerate a rather high level of tension. That is, some groups are able to function effectively although a rather high level of tension is present. Another group whose tolerance threshold is lower will find that level of tension intolerable. Just as some individuals can endure more pain than others, some groups can endure more tension that others. The problem for the group, then, is to develop successful mechanisms for reducing tension when it rises above the tolerance threshold.

Some groups overcome the initial primary tension but fail to control the secondary tension. Thus, the secondary tension level remains above the tolerance threshold, and the group is unable to function effectively throughout. For the members of this group, the socioemotional climate is extremely unpleasant. No group can withstand indefinitely the pressures of secondary tension above the tolerance threshold. One can predict that the life expectancy of this group will be short. The members will probably disband their group rather than suffer such social agony much longer.

In another type of group the members are never able to overcome their initial primary tension. They remain a collection of individuals. Members do not identify with the group; they exhibit extraordinary apathy and have virtually no commitment either to the group or to the task at hand. One is reminded of the joke about the community meeting called to protest apathy, but no one showed up at the meeting. This group—or, more accurately, this collection of individuals—will not exist long either. If the members do continue to meet (in the event that they are a "captive" aggregation compelled to meet), they will accomplish little.

A third type of group seems ideal. The members overcome primary tension and never suffer from secondary tension above their tolerance threshold. They seem to be a happy, healthy group of contented people. And that may be true. More likely, however, members of this group either are bored stiff or are suffering from an abnormal fear of social tension. It is simply not healthy, perhaps not normal, for group members never to experience secondary tension above their tolerance threshold. One explanation for never doing so would assume that they just don't care enough to get excited about anything. As a result, members do what they are told but have little commitment to the group's activities. Another plausible explanation would assume the members to be hypochondriacs about social tension. They fear tension so much that they conscientiously avoid any stimulus that would raise the tension level above the tolerance threshold. Hence, members retreat or take flight from any potential source for a social problem. Rather than solving their social problems, they ignore them and hope they will go away.

A fourth type of group is most likely to enjoy the ideal socioemotional climate. This group has frequent moments of secondary tension above its tolerance threshold, and it consistently dispels the excess of tension. This group successfully manages its social tension and obviously has no fear of secondary tension. Its past behavior is a series of instances of successful management of tension. The members have obviously developed mechanisms for successfully coping with secondary tension and have incorporated them into their system's functional patterns. The social fabric of this group is strengthened with each success in managing social tension. The socioemotional climate is vibrantly healthy, and the members undoubtedly find the group exciting and stimulating.

The mechanisms developed by successful groups for reducing excessive tension are also many and varied. Moreover, what works in one group may be totally unsuccessful in others. Often one or two persons assume the role of tension relievers, and the group looks to them for help when the time arises. Sometimes a tension reliever is a jokester—a person who is carefree, happy-go-lucky, and makes people laugh. But laughter is not always a clear sign of tension release; it may even signify excessive tension. When members laugh at comments that are really not funny, they are probably exhibiting, rather than releasing, tension. Quick, abrupt, high-pitched laughter is generally a sign of tension rather than of tension release. One group successfully relieved primary tension through a member who constantly told jokes, often at her own expense. But when secondary tension arose, her self-deprecating jokes were unsuccessful. In fact, the other members resented her carefree attitude and finally demanded that she take a more serious attitude toward their task. Thus, the behavior that dispelled primary tension was unsuccessful in coping with secondary tension, even in the same group.

Another tension-relieving role may be that of a mediator between two conflicting members. When secondary tension erupts from such an interpersonal conflict, the conciliator who is respected by both the conflicting members is a tension reliever. Sometimes excessive tension is reduced by finding a scapegoat as a mediating agency. When tension arises from frustration over environmental or task pressures, that frustration must be vented at someone or something. In a classroom group, the instructor serves as a convenient scapegoat (as in the power fantasy in the previous section). In a business organization, the "boss" becomes the outside "enemy." The successful scapegoat is generally outside the immediate group membership. Most important to the group, though, is not *how* it manages tension, but *whether* it does.

One strategy for successful tension management is to *confront social problems head on.* More problems are created by avoiding or ignoring potential problems than by facing them squarely. Such overt action is rarely easy, however, and generally requires old-fashioned guts! But the social benefits are worth the momentary and perfectly normal reluctance. One member's diary, written immediately after a particularly productive group meeting, emphasizes the wisdom of confrontation:

> But almost everyone got the preppie stereotype impression of me. It goes to show, first impressions are really terrible, because everyone is so different from what I thought. I told them all exactly what I thought of them and they told me. I thought this would be a total disaster, and everyone would end up hating each other. But it brought us very close together, I think.

This meeting was a great accomplishment for our group. Now I think we can start moving.

Whatever the social problem, the importance of confronting it head on cannot be overestimated. Occasionally the group is in for a painful period of agonizing tension during this confrontation. But in the long run the group not only survives, but becomes stronger. One classroom group provides an excellent example of extreme measures used to confront a social problem centered in a single person. This example also demonstrates the constructive effects of confrontation on the group's socioemotional climate. This five-member group was composed of four women and one man. For a variety of reasons, the man was considered a male chauvinist by the women members, a thorn in their side. They deeply resented what they considered to be his domineering behavior, although they had not directly verbalized their resentment. At one climactic meeting they finally decided to let him know—clearly and forcefully. The following excerpts from the male member's paper analyzing his group most clearly illustrate what happened during the confrontation and its aftermath:

> Then there was the meeting when one of the members hit me with the comment, "Go to hell, you egotistical creep!" It was then that I began to realize the value of this class and how our group reacted. There was, of course, a great deal of tension that day. I was very nervous and uncomfortable....In being blasted I, more than anyone else, I think, felt what a brutal force and what brutal pressure can fall on someone in the social dimension of a group when people begin to attack you.

> ...It was exciting to have each member of the group become confident enough to bare his or her soul to the rest of the group.

A comment from another member of the group corroborates the positive effects of this extreme confrontation:

> My first reaction to Marilyn's "Tom, go to hell" was that it was uncalled for. I thought that that type or degree of honesty was not needed. However, it was exactly what was needed because it opened the door to real communication. We all became very sober and honest with each other....By the end of the meeting my mind was so elated that I felt completely free of anxiety or pressure, and I felt very much at peace with myself and with the world.

Granted, not every confrontation will have such immediate and such positive effects. Nor will every confrontation be centered on a single member or even on a person at all. But avoiding potential social problems will have even fewer immediate effects and many less positive ones. The important point is that the group overtly and conscientiously confronted its problem.

But what of compromise as a solution? Surely problems are not always win-or-lose propositions. A group should be able to effect some sort of "golden mean." The spirit of compromise is healthy. No one should belittle the wisdom of the spirit of compromise. Nor should one assume that compromise is the cure for all social problems. Often compromise is a tactic used by a group to avoid facing its problems. The following excerpt from a classroom group's final self-analysis reflects this point:

> It was surprising that our first task was completed because we had competition within the group that became disruptive. In order to achieve the task we had to compromise and stop competing.... However, compromise never was the ultimate solution, as we were to learn. Our group suffered from tension because we did compromise. The only thing our first compromise did was to produce a paper but leave the members with a subconscious feeling of "something is wrong." We concluded that compromise is an easy way of dismissing tensions that could go beyond the threshold—an escape from facing the ultimate questions that have to be answered for group survival.

In this group, compromise was a substitute for the solution of social problems. The members compromised as the easy way out. Rather than facing up to their problems, they escaped from them through compromise. We must conclude, then, that compromise is a useful mechanism for tension management. But compromise should come *after* the group confronts its social problems and should not be used as a substitute for facing up to its problems.

In summary, there is one vitally important point to remember. The successful and socially healthy group is not characterized by an absence of social tension, but by successful management of social tension. No group should expect, or even hope for, an absence of problems caused by social tension. Instead, a group should expect social problems to occur, should confront those problems, and should develop mechanisms for their control. This means that the members must learn to overcome their personal inhibitions, be honest, and require or demand the same behavior from other members. Such "good advice" is, of course, deceptively simple. It is more easily said than followed. But a successful group requires not only time for development but also the overt effort of its members to make it a success. One student group encapsulated this good advice in a pithy slogan that may be worth repeating: "The group that fights together stays together." A later version of this slogan may be even better: "The group that fights, unites."

THE TASK DIMENSION: DEFINITION

The nature of the task dimension of the group process has long been a topic of considerable concern among scholars of small group phenomena. In most cases, group tasks are imposed on the group by some external authority—that is, some authority outside the group. For example, the legal system assigns its decision-making task to a jury after a courtroom trial. A group in a business organization that must decide, for example, how to market a specific product is assigned this task by some organizational superior for the purpose of furthering the goals of the larger organization.

Occasionally, however, individuals form into a group for the purpose of performing some task that can be accomplished more productively with group effort.

For example, political-action groups are often formed by persons who wish to respond as a group to some perceived problem, such as improving environmental quality, lobbying for specific legislation, or electing a candidate to political office.

Certain types of tasks will place different "critical demands" on group members in terms of specifying what behaviors or procedures they need to perform in order to accomplish those tasks adequately. Some scholars have attempted to specify those critical demands by listing the various types of tasks actually performed by groups. Hackman (1968), for example, has identified three types—production tasks, discussion tasks, and problem-solving tasks. A production task calls for the presentation of ideas concerning some stimulus, such as "Write a critical analysis of *Othello*." A problem-solving task requires the group members to specify an action to be taken regarding some pressing need, such as "What should be done to resolve the problem of insufficient housing on campus?" Hackman's discussion task, the most general of his three types, deals with an evaluation of issues that typically have no right or wrong answer. For example, "Is the American economy truly free enterprise?"

The task dimension of the group process central to our interests involves the more comprehensive task of decision making. In virtually any group's decision-making effort, all three of Hackman's tasks (production, discussion, and problem solving) will be involved. Although the discussions in Chapter 6 will indicate some minimal differences between problem solving and decision making, the task efforts of decision-making groups resist any clearly specifiable restrictions as to the nature of the group task.

Much more significant, however, is the tendency to view any task as one that can or even should be performed by a group. We shall take the position that in order to maximize the quality of task performance, certain tasks should be performed by groups, and other tasks would be best performed by expert individuals. Our distinction, then, is based less on what types of tasks are given to groups and more on the particular type of task most appropriate to the group process.

THE TASK DIMENSION: INDIVIDUAL VERSUS GROUP DECISION MAKING

Surely the process of making decisions in a group differs from that of one person working alone. This statement should not be too startling. After all, a group is different from a single individual. For one thing, there are more people in a group. This bit of wisdom contains several important implications. A group has a greater variety of resources. There are more minds to contribute to the decision-making effort, more sources of information. Unlike the lone individual, a group is able to divide labor among its members so that, for example, members can work on their own specialties.

On the other hand, a group has potential problems not inherent in individual decision making. The problem of achieving consensus is present in a group. The many examples of hung juries are ample evidence of the existence of this problem.

And, with the addition of more people, there is greater opportunity for conflict. At the same time, there are many more sources to generate new ideas. Also, there are more viewpoints from which to evaluate those ideas critically. In other words, a critical exchange of ideas is much more easily accomplished by a group.

Group Polarization

Among the differences discovered when individual and group decision making have been compared is the phenomenon known as group polarization (Moscovici, 1985, pp. 396–399). Simply stated, *group polarization* refers to the tendency of groups to make decisions that are more extreme than the initial opinions of its members. Some early group researchers found that the decisions made by groups rather than individuals tended to be extreme. This was termed the *risky shift*. They found that groups would select an alternative that had a bigger payoff but a lower probability of attainment. If a group and its individual members were to place bets on a horse race, for example, the group would more likely bet on a 100-to-1 shot than would any of the individuals deciding alone. Apparently the group interaction stimulated individuals to take greater risks and be less conservative.

One reason the risky-shift phenomenon generated so much research interest was that it contradicted some prevailing theories of the time. Theories of conformity would predict that groups would avoid deviant opinions because there are interpersonal pressures in groups to accommodate your opinions to those of others. The risky-shift phenomenon also contradicted what was called normalization theory. This theory held that group decisions would reflect an average of opinions and norms. One member of a group might be a risk taker, but another would be more conservative; the result would be an average of the two members and not an extreme decision. There were various explanations of the risky shift, but the most popular explanation attributed group risk to the diffusion among group members of the responsibility for the group decision. Individuals were more willing to take chances because they could not be blamed. It is the same explanation that accounts for lynch-mob behavior in the old west. No good citizen would think of lynching the man in jail, but in the anonymity of the group, "mob fever" was the result.

Later research concluded that the risky-shift phenomenon should be considered a matter of attitude change. Group polarization means that individuals change attitudes according to the communication and information in the group. Initial involvement in and commitment to the group and its decisions are an important part of any attitude change. When group members hold more extreme opinions, they also tend to be highly committed and to exert more pressure on moderate group members, who find it easier to shift. Communication in a group structures information around group norms, and the norms that a group develops are more polarized (or extreme) than are the norms and opinions of individuals. Myers and Bishop (1971) found that groups composed of racists became more racist after discussion. Polarization effects were found in groups discussing attitudes about women, abortion, and a number of other social issues.

It is also true that group consensus changes individual attitudes and opinions.

The groupthink hypothesis discussed earlier is about groups that make faulty (and sometimes extreme) decisions because there are pressures toward uniformity. Our tendency is to be influenced by members of groups who are like us. Groups in organizations are typically composed of people who value their membership in the group and realize that the group has tremendous reward potential. Whenever people are interdependent, as they are in group discussions, there is an attraction toward the majority and there are pressures to conform to the majority. The fact that groups polarize their opinions is the result of highly susceptible group members who establish new norms and then pressure others, often subtly, to be consistent with the prevailing norm, thereby continuing to validate the norm. This spiral leads to riskier decisions. These are the behaviors that lead to polarized opinions, and group members would do well to be aware of them.

Efficiency and Speed

Few people have accused a group of being efficient. Referring a proposal to a committee in order to kill it is a well-known parliamentary tactic. Simple arithmetic should illustrate that, in terms of hours expended, groups are destined to be less efficient than individuals. Say that one person can complete a decision-making task in 1 hour. A three-person group would have to complete this task in 20 minutes in order to equal the 1 hour spent by the individual—but the group would probably spend more than 1 hour, thus taking more than 3 times as long *per person* to complete the task.

Compared with individuals, groups are abominably slow. You will recall that it takes time for groupness to evolve. The group must establish a history before it can function effectively as a decision-making system. For a group member, patience is an important virtue. Inevitably, group members become highly frustrated, particularly in the early stages of group development, over the group's apparent lack of progress. Members are anxious to "get the show on the road," to quit wasting so much time and attend to the task at hand. Although these feelings of frustration and discouragement are typical, they should not be considered serious. Progress is not very visible in the early stages of group development, but the seemingly rapid progress later is a direct and cumulative result of the activities that have come before.

There is one possible explanation for the apparent inefficiency and slowness of group decision making. Researchers have discovered that a group's effective attention span is quite small. In fact, the average length of time a group discusses a single theme is only *58 seconds*. In other words, groups tend to jump from topic to topic very quickly without dwelling on any one topic for very long. Groups tend to make decisions in spurts of activity, whereas an individual may be more capable of lengthy periods of sustained effort.

At this point one may be tempted to ask, "If groups are so slow and inefficient as a decision-making system, why bother with them at all? Let individuals make all the decisions." If efficiency and speed were the sole criteria by which decision makcussed in Chapter 4), one cannot avoid making a feedback response (Haslett and Ogilvie, 1988). For example, if you are waiting in line at a supermarket checkout counter, you are often surrounded by strangers; nevertheless, you and all the other shoppers are involved in a common situation—waiting in line.

Assume that a stranger in front of you turns to you and remarks, "They sure are slow at this time of day, aren't they?" Your response to this statement is inevitably a feedback response. You have numerous responses available to you, such as the following: (1) You could agree and respond by saying, "They sure are." (2) You could disagree, offering a statement such as "Oh, I don't know. The line seems to be moving rather quickly, even though they are quite busy." (3) You could be noncommittal or perhaps even change the subject—"I hate standing in line" or "I'm in a hurry" or "That other checkout counter seems to be moving faster." (4) You could ignore the original statement by turning or looking away from your new acquaintance. Whatever you choose to do in responding to the stranger's initial statement, you are engaged in providing a feedback response. Even your attempt to ignore the other person and not engage in communication is a feedback response.

The fact is that you are involved in that communicative event, that common situation, whether you want to be involved or not. Even response 4 (ignoring the other person) is a feedback response. You have, in essence, said to the stranger, "I'm not interested in continuing this communication. I don't wish to speak with you." Your behavior, both verbal and nonverbal, is a feedback response that conveys information to the other person about yourself, about that other person, and about your relationship to each other. Even your attempt to ignore the other person leads to some interpretation. The stranger may consider you something of a snob, an unfriendly person. The relationship is not likely to be interpreted as a desirable one or to be continued. Furthermore, the other person's self-concept may be damaged to some small extent. He or she may wonder whether body odor or bad breath has provoked your antisocial reaction.

Since a feedback response is absolutely inevitable within a communicative event, the common notion of one-way or two-way communication would appear to be of limited usefulness or importance—at least when one is talking about communication in a face-to-face setting. Once two or more people are involved in a common social situation, even strangers who are standing in line together at a supermarket checkout counter, any behavior performed by any of these strangers is potentially communicative. Furthermore, any behavior performed by a person after receiving a source's message is naturally interpreted as a feedback response. How, then, can one-way communication occur in a face-to-face communication setting? The answer is that it cannot. For purposes of communication and the group process, there is no such thing as one-way communication. All communication is inevitably and inherently two-way. All behavior following another person's behavior is inevitably and inherently a feedback response. Thus, feedback responses are constantly occurring throughout the interaction among group members.

One's self-concept, or one's beliefs and attitudes about self, also develop through communicating with others. Every person is constantly receiving new information, which then serves to validate or invalidate one's own beliefs and self-concepts. Every feedback response provides some information to the source about his or her self-concept. Such responses provide information about how others view us.

We do not mean to imply that every statement or feedback response that is received always contains specific information about self. Rather, information that is conveyed to the source must be interpreted. If you disagreed with the person in the checkout line at the supermarket, that may have had an effect on the person's self-concept. For example, that person may have had a friendly, outgoing self-image and taken pride in having the ability to relate to other people very well. Your disagreement (or, even worse, your failure to answer) may have damaged this self-concept or cast it into doubt.

One of the problems in interpreting feedback responses is to determine how honest or authentic those feedback responses are. How sincere is the person who is providing the feedback response? Is the other person merely trying to "make us feel good" while actually masking or hiding true feelings? Some people may believe that all feedback responses should always be honest, genuine, and reflect "true" feelings if the communication is to be effective. If we reflect upon such a belief for a moment, however, we will probably not accept it as a universal principle. In a situation in which a genuine feedback response might be harmful to another person, we often provide a response that is less than authentic— in reality, a lie. Often those dishonest feedback responses occur because we do not wish to hurt anyone's feelings unnecessarily. In other words, we often interpret our friendly relationship with the other person to be more important than the honesty of our feedback responses.

What if a play directed by a friend of yours was terrible? The actors were awful, as was the stage movement, and the pace was agonizingly slow. In short, the play failed miserably. Nevertheless, talking with your friend after the performance, you told him what a fine play it was and how much you enjoyed seeing his production of a well-written drama. If in reply to his "How did you like the performance?" you had given him a truly honest feedback response, his feelings may have been hurt. More important for you, he may have wondered about the future of what was then a friendly relationship. Your dishonest response may thus have been a compliment, not so much to his directorial abilities as to his status as a friend. You valued the relationship more than you valued the principle of honest and authentic feedback response.

The stronger the relationship, the more valuable the feedback responses. The closer the ties of interpersonal liking (cohesiveness) among members of a group, the more honest and authentic these responses will be. Typically, feedback responses among close friends will include more negative evaluations than will the responses among acquaintances, although many positive responses will also occur during the interaction among friends. One might summarize this discussion by suggesting that the most effective feedback responses occur in groups or social relationships which are strong and in which the interactants like one another. On the other hand, honest and authentic feedback responses do not necessarily cause or lead to interpersonal liking. Rather, because persons like each other, they are more likely to be more authentic. That is, interpersonal liking allows for the probability of more authentic and genuinely honest feedback responses.

Nearly everyone is familiar with the process of response reinforcement in the familiar sense of psychological "conditioning." We are all aware of Pavlov's classical experiments in which the dogs were conditioned to salivate at the ringing of a bell, even without the presence of food. In a very simple sense, all of us are "conditioned" throughout our lives in the sense that we have been trained to perform behaviors that are appropriate to our culture. We have been taught to say "Please" and "Thank you," to eat with a fork, etc. This acculturation into our society in which we learn manners and other appropriate behavior is, in a way, a certain kind of conditioning. After all, we were rewarded when we remembered the appropriate action and were punished when we failed to behave in the socially approved manner.

Conditioning, however, is not the major thrust of this discussion. Rather, we are more concerned with feedback responses. But feedback responses may reinforce the behaviors that precede them. That is, our reactions or responses may or may not be favorable to the preceding comment. We may nod, smile, say "Uh-huh," "I agree," or "Yes," or express approval in some other way. On the other hand, our feedback response may be negative and may express disapproval. We may shake our heads, scowl, or say "No," "I disagree," and so forth. When we express disapproval through our feedback responses, these responses tend to inhibit or extinguish that behavior. In this way, we have negatively reinforced the other person's behavior. When our feedback responses express approval, they tend to enhance or encourage continuation of that behavior—positive or a negative reinforcement. Therefore, a feedback response may serve as a positive or a negative reinforcement of the preceding behavior.

Many people fear the potential effects of such reinforcement patterns when the power to condition members of a society is in the hands of an unscrupulous leader or tyrant. We fear being manipulated or controlled or even "brainwashed" by a government, an advertising agency, or a group leader. We are all too aware of the fictional accounts of some futuristic society of conformists who are conditioned to accept the will of some "big brother." Books and movies such as *1984* and *Road Warrior* depict the future in depressing and apocalyptic terms. We worry about being "conditioned" by violence on television or by manipulative advertising that will control our buying and even our voting habits. In short, our society suffers from a rather irrational fear of the alleged power of psychological conditioning.

Of course, the human being is not a machine and is not so easily manipulated or so easily conditioned as the writers of fiction would have us believe. Basically, the human being is highly obstinate. The human is able to decide what messages to receive, what messages to believe or disbelieve, what messages to remember and what portions of messages to receive, remember, distort, and revise. In short, the control over the message (and over feedback responses too) lies in the hands of the receiver. In fact, some scholarly research (Nokes, 1961) has discovered that feedback responses which seemed obviously positive in their reinforcement (and were intended as such) were interpreted by some receivers as being negative. Furthermore, some receivers interpreted negative feedback reinforcement as being rather positive. We should not underestimate the awesome power of each human being as a processor of information.

The discussion of group norms in Chapter 8 will emphasize the tremendous power that the social unit of the group has over its individual members. At the same time, however, the discussion will illustrate the capacity of the individual members to shape the formation and the function of the group. Feedback responses (as positive or negative reinforcement) certainly do affect our behavior, and through feedback responses we also affect other people's behavior—but we must keep in mind that feedback responses (as attempts to influence) can be, and often are, successfully resisted by the receivers of these responses.

The psychological function of feedback responses (or communicative reactions) as reinforcement emphasizes feedback as a means of controlling human behavior. In Chapter 4, the discussion of feedback as a more functional (rather than purely structural) aspect of communication will also emphasize feedback as a means of "control," although in a much different sense. In both cases, however, we need to keep in mind that feedback as reinforcement is only an *attempt* to control and cannot be an omnipotent influence on defenseless and unsuspecting human beings.

CHARACTERISTICS OF MESSAGES

Mechanistically speaking, when people communicate, they exchange messages with one another. One person encodes a message and directs it to another person, who decodes the message, provides some understanding or interpretation of it, and then encodes a message in response. In this way, communication occurs as the messages flow back and forth between the sources and the receivers (i.e., between the members of the group). In this mechanistic framework of communication, a message is a structural phenomenon; that is, it is conceptualized as some *thing* that is transmitted across space on a channel and received at another point in space. This mechanistic framework emphasizes the structural elements of communication, in which the message and the channel are indeed the central elements.

From such a mechanistic view of communication, it seems reasonable to think of effective, or "good," communication as the exchange of "good" messages. If a lady tells a new acquaintance that she is a faculty member in a university department of communication, the acquaintance is likely to respond with something like "I'd better watch what I say." Conventional wisdom dictates that the messages we transmit and receive carry certain characteristics that render them desirable, effective, or otherwise "good." A structural approach to group communication therefore includes those attributes (or characteristics or qualities) which a "good" message has.

Haslett and Ogilvie (1988, p. 397) offer a list of eight suggestions for giving feedback in group discussions. They offer these eight as desirable characteristics of messages—characteristics that can be used to improve contributions to group interaction. These characteristics are: (1) be specific and clear, (2) support comments with evidence, (3) separate the issues from the people, (4) soften negative messages, (5) sandwich negative messages between positive ones, (6) pose the situation as a mutual problem, (7) use good timing, and (8) use a proper manner of delivery.

You will probably note that not all these characteristics refer to the structural elements of messages themselves. For example, a message is "specific" only if it can be compared with the earlier messages during the group discussion and thus be seen to be more specific. Also, "pose the situation as a mutual problem" is more an attitude of the people than something contained in a message. Further, a message is "softened" only to the extent that the receiver interprets the message that way; if subsequent discussions continue the train of thought contained in the softened message, one could assume that the message may have provoked it. It is difficult, however, to determine structurally if any message is softened at the time it is first uttered.

The most important of these eight characteristics may be "use good timing." As later chapters on the group process consistently illustrate, what is said, how it is said, and even who says it may not be nearly as significant to the group process and to effective decision making as *when* it is said. Therefore, it is difficult to determine whether any single message, in isolation, is structurally desirable or undesirable in terms of its characteristics alone. Only when the message is placed within its context of the ongoing group interaction can it be assessed as to its specificity, evidence, softness, and good or bad timing.

There is also the matter of the "codability" of messages during group communication. The codability of messages is very similar to Haslett and Ogilvie's "clarity" characteristic. The important characteristic of the message is how easily it can be interpreted by the receiver. On the other hand, it is difficult to think of the meaning of a message being contained *in* the message. Rather, we typically tend to think of the meaning of messages as being within people—a property of the process of interpretation. We have even coined clichés which say that meaning is located within the person and not in the message—"Meaning is perception" and "Words don't mean; people do." Phrased another way, the meaning of the message is *assigned* by the human interpreter and does not exist in the coded message itself. Nevertheless, a message may be encoded in such a manner as to increase the likelihood that it will be interpreted quickly, easily, and in a manner similar to the meaning intended by the source.

Messages during group communication are often highly ambiguous or unclear; that is, they have low codability. Members of groups frequently appear to be very tolerant of these ambiguous messages and do not often seek clarification of them. Naturally, ambiguous messages have communicative advantages as well as obvious disadvantages. In terms of the disadvantages, an ambiguous message may drastically affect the efficiency of group conversation in the sense that members may argue at length before discovering that they have been in agreement all along but have been unaware of that fact because they were using messages of low clarity or low codability. The same can be true of a group in apparent agreement on an ambiguous issue, although there may be much disagreement that remains unexposed because of a lack of sufficient clarity.

On the other hand, ambiguous messages often occur early in a group's interaction history and are used by the group members as a means of coping with the group's decision-making task—that is, with the problem to be solved. As Chapter 6 will show, highly ambiguous messages (i.e., messages whose codability or clarity is low) are neither "good" nor "bad" in and of themselves. There are times when such messages are quite typical of, and beneficial to, the making of decisions by a group. At other times during the group process, however, they may be quite inappropriate and detrimental to the group's decision-making efforts.

Eisenberg (1984) makes the very interesting argument that ambiguity can be used strategically and to the benefit of the communicator. In short, it is simply naive to assume that clarity is the norm and the responsibility of the speaker. Some particularly skilled group members are not only unclear, but purposefully so. Sometimes vagueness or lack of clarity can head off conflict; groups often have to juggle many purposes, and there are fewer chances for conflict and tension when some things are vague. Groups can also benefit from general rather than specific goals because they allow for flexibility and change. Pacanowsky and O'Donnel-Trujillo (1983) show that interpersonal relationships in groups and organizations are close, but not too close. Many people in groups form valuable and positive relationships with other groups members that facilitate the work they must do, but these same people also keep some distance. Ambiguous messages permit the expression of thoughts and feelings but also allow for deniability. In a very interesting way, ambiguity allows a person both general and specific interpretation. Someone can say, "I don't feel very good about this group," and then deny a specific interpretation of this utterance, such as "You mean you don't like the other group members?" Ambiguity in this case makes for the expression of feelings while at the same time saving face.

Under any circumstances, it is difficult to make once-and-for-all statements concerning what specific characteristics should be reflected in messages exchanged during the entire process of group decision making. Generally speaking, in terms of the eight characteristics listed earlier, we suggest that messages exchanged by members of decision-making groups should probably be informative, sufficiently long (actually, quite brief, as in normal conversations), and relevant to the task and to prior interaction. We shall not, however, advance any hard-and-fast rules concerning the characteristics that *all* messages should contain throughout the group's interaction. The discussion of group decision making in Chapter 6 should make abundantly clear the overriding significance of the timing of messages (when they occur) rather than the characteristics they may contain.

NETWORKS

Examining communication networks is the most common structural approach to understanding communication among individuals in the group. Most people are familiar with networks in terms of highways, telephone lines, and water pipes, but interpersonal communication networks in groups are composed of more abstract communicative behavior and are sometimes more difficult to understand. *Communication networks are regular patterns of person-to-person contact that are typically char-*

acterized by the exchange of information between humans (Monge, 1987, p.243). By observing who talks to whom and what information is connected to which people, we can infer a communication network. Alba (1982) notes that group networks are composed of patterns of contact and communication among people who interact more with each other than with members of larger networks. Groups are very often defined according to what networks emerge.

Monge and Eisenberg (1987) have described three major approaches to networks: the relational, positional, and cultural approaches. Our primary concern, however, is with the *relational* approach. Group networks are relational in that they focus on the direct communicative connections between members of a network; the emphasis is on describing the network and identifying who is in what role. The positional school is concerned more with the hierarchical structure of organizations and society, while the cultural school focuses on the more abstract meanings that are transmitted throughout society and cultural communities. The hierarchical network of an organization (president, vice president, managers, directors, etc.) exists before the formation of particular groups; this formal network is typically established by an outside authority, and although informal networks may arise during the process of interaction among organizational members, the organization recognizes the formal network as the optimum one for the group's task performances. When a member of an organization utilizes formal channel linkages, it is often called going through channels.

But discussion groups (especially LGDs) have a limited established network. There may be some members who are designated leaders, for example, but over time the process of communicating significantly alters networks and allows the group's members to perform a variety of functions and occupy many roles. So even though networks are usually thought of as stable relationships, they change over time because relationships and people change. Nevertheless, as the process of group interaction continues, members use some linkages very frequently and others quite sparingly; thus, a network emerges during group interaction, and this network reflects the developing social structure of the group. Figure 3-1 illustrates four common networks that may emerge in a five-member group. The all-channel network is a theoretical possibility, but it rarely describes actual groups because it implies that every possible interpersonal channel linkage is used and that there is equal channel usage. It is not uncommon for group members to have access to others (links), but it is rare that all links receive equal usage.

There are some interesting concepts that apply to group networks. They are relatively easy to understand and to measure, so they can be very useful for beginning group analyses. The most common network measurements are size, reachability, density, and centrality (Tichy, 1981).

Network *size* simply refers to the number of people to which a person is linked. It is possible to establish the size of an individual's network and the size of the network as a whole. In the wheel configuration in Figure 3-1, member C is linked directly to four people, so his network size would be 4. Member B is linked only to one, so his individual network size is smaller, 1. In terms of the entire network, the wheel is "smaller" than the all-channel network because it has fewer linkages.

Circle

Wheel

Chain

"Y"

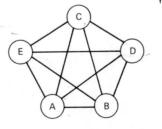

All-channel

Figure 3-1 Common networks in five-member groups.

Reachability is the number of links it takes to connect one individual to another. In the wheel network, *C* is very "reachable" by *B* because they are directly linked, but *D* is less reachable by *B* because *B* must go through two links. On the network level, reachability is the average number of links separating people. Persons *A* and *E* in the chain network have low reachability because they must go through so many others. The numbers in parentheses in Figure 3-1 refer to the total number of links that a person must go through to reach everyone in the network. The number 10 above person *A* in the chain network means that the sum of all the links to everyone in the network is 10. This may sound momentarily confusing, but if you count up the links you can see where the numbers come from: *A* must go through one link to reach *B*, two links to reach *C*, three links to reach *D*, and four links to reach E, and $1 + 2 + 3 + 4 = 10$. Compare that to the reachability of C in the wheel; person C can reach everyone quite easily. The average reachability in the chain is higher than that in any of the other networks.

Density is related to reachability. It indicates the number of linkages that exist in proportion to the number that would exist if everyone were linked directly. In the all-channel network, everyone has reachability; this network is also dense because of the possible 10 linkages. Your personal network is dense if you are directly connected to a lot of people.

Centrality is a frequently studied concept. Every member of the network is assigned a centrality figure on the basis of how close he or she is to all other members of the network. The most central person is the one with the *fewest* links between everyone else. Thus, the parenthetical numbers in Figure 3-1 indicate centrality; they show which person has the most "betweenness," or lies on the shortest path between others. Person C in the wheel network is the most central because everyone else must go through C to reach any other member of the network.

Using various points of comparison, studies comparing communication networks have revealed many differences between the types of networks. In terms of speed and efficiency, for example, centralized networks (such as the wheel and the chain) are found to be superior to decentralized networks (such as the circle, the least centralized). But this finding is tempered by a further comparison in terms of problem-solving accuracy: Centralized networks solve simple problems most accurately, but decentralized networks are more accurate in solving complex problems. In terms of group morale, the members of decentralized networks experience greater satisfaction with their group experiences than do members of groups employing a centralized network. In short, whereas centralized networks are considered superior in terms of accomplishing tasks (at least simple ones), decentralized networks foster more cohesive groups and appear to have an advantage in performing more complex tasks.

Results from past comparisons of communication networks, however, may not be particularly significant to LGD decision making. In the first place, nearly all such comparisons have been performed in research laboratories under rigidly controlled conditions. The laboratory context itself is no reason to dismiss comparison results as insignificant, but one of the typical laboratory controls has unfortunately been the severe restriction of time allowed for group interaction. A few studies that allowed more time for group interaction revealed that the differences between groups using different network patterns diminished significantly over time. (Network research has also typically restricted other aspects of communication, such as sending only written messages without face-to-face confrontation, but the restriction of time may be a more significant restriction of the group process.)

A group needs time to develop any satisfactory organization. As soon as the group members accustom themselves to the network they are using, the particular pattern or network they employ should be of little consequence. The success of centralized networks in the task dimension of the group process should increase the cohesiveness of group members over time. Time is absolutely essential for the natural interdependence of the two dimensions of the group process to asset itself.

And, too, the social success of decentralized networks should also allow members to strive harder in the task dimension and thereby increase their speed and efficiency of task performance. Whatever the causes, the differences between networks in terms of speed, efficiency, accuracy, organizational stability, and group morale appear to diminish over time.

When a group does not have sufficient time to establish its social organization, the members begin to compensate. Functioning under sever time pressure, they simply don't have sufficient time to proceed through all the steps of decision modification in order to achieve consensus on their decisions; therefore, they compensate by short-circuiting the group process. One shortcut method used by groups in the absence of a clear social organization is to substitute the simple majority vote for the process of validating decisions by consensus. The inevitable result of such shortcuts, of course, is false or superficial consensus. The members allegedly perform their tasks and make their decisions, but since no real consensus has been achieved, they do not commit themselves to carrying out these decisions.

The structural view of communication networks does contribute to the understanding of the group process in many respects. For instance, the concept of centrality has consistently been related to leadership and status. The most central position in an emergent network is most apt to be the position occupied by the emergent leader, and the various levels of centrality generally reflect the status levels of the group's hierarchy. Figure 3-1 illustrates two status levels (level of centrality) in the wheel network; the relative centrality of C is 4, and the relative centrality of all other positions is 7. Three status levels are reflected in the chain network; C is the apparent leader with a relative centrality of 6, B and D occupy the second status level with relative centralities of 7, and A and E occupy the third status level with centrality figures of 10. The Y network illustrates four status levels, a rather uncommon status hierarchy to emerge in a five-member group. Only the circle network has a single status level, and this is an extremely improbable network to emerge in a decision-making group.

The network that finally emerges from extensive group interaction is not the only network employed by the group during the process of decision making. A group may employ one network at one stage of the process and shift to a different network later on as the group enters a new phase of the process. In this respect, centrality does not necessarily reflect leadership or even high status during the intermediate stages of the group process.

For example, the verbally active "problem member" may at some point during interaction be the recipient of influence from every other member verbally attempting to modify the problem behavior. During this period of group interaction, the network would probably show the deviate in position C in the wheel network—a highly central position. This network, showing a problem member in a central position, would undoubtedly be temporary, for a problem member or extreme deviate who does not modify his or her behavior will eventually be ignored by the others and excluded from their interactions. Such action virtually expels the extreme deviate from the network and from effective group membership. Therefore, while centrality is often linked to that leadership and status in the network which finally emerges from group interaction, during intermediate stages in the process of group decision making it may also indicate an extreme deviate under group pressure to conform.

Another stage of network development involves the coalitions or subgroups formed during various phases in the group decision-making process. The network used at that time generally reflects the existence of coalitions. To illustrate, the Y network might reflect the presence of two coalitions, one composed of three members (C, D, and E) and the other composed of two members (A and B). We might hypothesize further that each coalition has formed around its own contender for leadership; the two most central positions, B and C, would then represent these two contenders.

No discussion of the network structures of group communication would be complete without a comment about the limited number of networks described above. There are obviously more possible network combinations than the four (omitting the all-channel network) shown in Figure 3-1, but the other combinations are simply variations of these basic models. For example, the wheel and chain networks can be combined by adding to the wheel network two additional channel linkages between A and B and between D and E. The same network can be formed from the chain network by adding channel links between A and C and between A and E. This wheel-chain network is thus a network formed by combining channel linkages included in two of the basic network models.

Further variations should be obvious. The important points are that emergent network structures can be observed in a small group and that these structures provide insight into various aspects of the group's decision-making process.

A final point to remember about network structures concerns the nature of processes. Interactional patterns change through time as the group moves from one phase to another in the decisional process. Network structures also change. Because changes in structure reflect changes in process, the developing structure of the network can be viewed as an emergent process that changes over time and culminates in the final, emergent network characterizing the group's status hierarchy. Thus, a network's attributes are not purely structural (spatial), but include attributes of action (time).

GATEKEEPING

Viewing communication structurally (as the transmission and reception of messages on a channel) reveals a further structural characteristic of communication. The networks illustrated in Figure 3-1 provide a graphic depiction of the concept of *gatekeeping*. You will note, for example, that some group members in each of those networks (except for the all-channel network) do not communicate directly with every other member of the group. In the wheel network the person occupying position B does not communicate directly with the member occupying position D. Rather, B exchanges messages with the member in position C, who, in turn, exchanges messages with D. Member C, in all networks except the all-channel network, is the intermediary (or link) in a chain of communication channels between members B and D. That is, B communicates with D only through C's intermediation in the circle, wheel, chain, and Y networks.

The member who occupies that middle link in the network is in a position of greater relative centrality. In the Y and chain networks, for example, member B is the gatekeeper between A and C. In the chain network, member D is a gatekeeper between C and E. In the wheel network, member C is the gatekeeper between every possible pair of members--A and B, A and D, A and E, B and D, B and E, and D and E. In other words, all messages sent and received in the wheel network are transmitted either to or by the group member who occupies position C. For this reason, the wheel network is the most centralized network of all.

It seems reasonable, then, that a gatekeeper is a person who occupies a position of considerable potential influence. This member receives more messages from more different sources than members who are in less central positions in the network. Given this informational advantage over other group members, a gatekeeper (in the sense of a centralized position in a small group network) often becomes a group leader or, at least, a member with above-average influence. The concept of leadership will be discussed in more detail in Chapter 9.

When persons sit around a table in a face-to-face situation—for example, a group in a classroom setting—the notion of networks seems somewhat artificial. After all, there appears to be nothing that would prohibit any group member from exchanging messages with every other member in the group. Thus, the all-channel network should be the network used by most "real" groups. Nevertheless, networks typically emerge in face-to-face groups after a period of time. They are characterized by a predominant usage or neglect of certain channels. That is, some members tend to communicate more with some members and less with others.

The gatekeeping role in classroom groups may also be a factor in activities that occur outside the face-to-face situation. Therefore, gatekeeping is not readily apparent in the actual group meetings during the performance of its decision-making task. One classroom group, in particular, contained one member—Marilyn—who performed an important gatekeeping role, but this role was apparent only in situations outside the face-to-face meetings of the group. Marilyn was neither a leader nor a particularly high contributor during the group's discussions at its meetings. Nevertheless, she, probably more than any other single member, was responsible for the group's successful decision-making performance.

Marilyn's group had a problem. The problem was Carol. Carol proved to be quite irresponsible in her interactions with the group. She was often absent from the meetings, usually with a legitimate excuse (employment and other classroom pressures). But reasons for absences from group meetings are of little concern to a functioning group. Quite reasonably, the other group members resented Carol's absences because she was not doing her part to help the group do its work—a task that placed it under considerable time pressure. Regardless of the legitimacy of Carol's absences, the other group members found themselves having to assume a heavier burden in the group's task efforts. Carol just didn't accept her share of the group's responsibility. Moreover, she also had what appeared to be a personality conflict with a few of the group members, a conflict that probably stemmed from a disagreement over proper social behavior.

During the meetings that Carol did attend, her contributions were not frequent and were not directed to any one member of the group more than others. When she was unable to attend the meetings, she consistently contacted Marilyn outside class meetings, often giving her material to bring to the meetings. Soon Marilyn was the person who spoke for Carol during group meetings and who explained Carol's absences or reported on her progress. In other words, Marilyn became the gatekeeper between Carol and the other group members. While the others resented Carol's lack of commitment to the group, they considered Marilyn to be a valuable member. Through Marilyn, they came to accept Carol as a member of what developed into a rather cohesive group.

The gatekeeping role does not necessarily imply influence in a group, although it often does. Nevertheless, this role serves a valuable structural position in the processing and dissemination of information among all members of the group. Moreover, the position carries with it enormous responsibilities for the exercise of judgment of what information should be relayed from one person to another, what information should not be retransmitted, and what information should be augmented or emphasized.

When gatekeeping occurs in the exchange of messages in a group, communication is mediated in the sense that communication between a source and a receiver "goes through" a mediator. On the level of an entire society, we often refer to this phenomenon of mediated communication when thinking of the mass media— radio, television, newspapers. Our mass media serve as the go-between for informational sources and the larger society—us, the consumers of information. Mediated communication is thus rather efficient in terms of mass information processing. Too many data are available in our informational environment for us to process or consume them all—that is, to interpret all the data as meaningful information. The gatekeeper plays a structural role that reduces considerably the quantity of data available. By relaying information to the receiver, the gatekeeper converts much data into a manageable amount of information and typically conveys this information in a more understandable form.

Gatekeepers have an awesome responsibility. They must make many crucial decisions before relaying or retransmitting the messages. For example, should information be transmitted in the same manner and the same form in which it is received? Often, relaying identical information is quite impossible. There is simply too much of it to be relayed. The gatekeeper must then reclassify the information into larger "chunks." At this point, the selectivity of the gatekeeper becomes highly significant. The mass media, and particularly newspaper and television news reporters, have often been accused of allowing their biases to dictate what information they select and retransmit to the public.

Gatekeepers have no choice but to exercise their selective processes. They must recognize, interpret, and then retransmit information. The gatekeeper who uses the selective processes adequately is called objective—as in the "objective news reporter." More often, however, the objectivity of a news reporter is determined by the extent to which the information received is consistent with the biases of the reporter in the gatekeeping position. But before we hasten to condemn, keep in mind that this use of the selectivity processes in information processing is quite normal.

A gatekeeper not only retransmits information but also withholds information, thereby not allowing it to pass through to the next receiver in the chain. In the same sense that a dam holds back some amount of water in a reservoir and allows only a portion of the water over the spillway, a gatekeeper also holds back some information from the receiver and allows only certain other information to "spill over." Withholding certain information and retransmitting certain other information must also be a part of the gatekeeper's process of selectivity. Although information may not necessarily be distorted, the omission of some information may lead to a different interpretation of the information that *is* received. In this sense, a gatekeeper who does not perform the role adequately may be guilty of both an error of commission (distorting information in the retransmitting) and an error of omission (withholding pertinent information).

When the person in a gatekeeping position must deal with information that exceeds his or her capacity to store and retrieve information, the result is called *information overload*. Information overload is more of a problem in a large-scale organization (which would involve many more people and much more information in various forms—for example, written memoranda, oral conversations, formal letters, market reports, sales reports) than it is in a small group. The face-to-face interaction of a decision-making group would normally use information in the same limited forms—verbal and nonverbal speech.

Furthermore, as Chapter 6 will discuss, groups soon develop methods of coping with too much information. They handle many different pieces of information for very brief periods of time rather than simultaneously discussing the same items over a long period. Information overload, then, is rarely a problem during small-group decision making, although it may be a significant problem within a large organization. Most important, overload occurs not throughout the entire group or organization, but at a specific point or position in the network, and this position must be relatively central—that is, a gatekeeping position.

An interesting concept related to the gatekeeping process is *boundary spanning*. A boundary spanner is a person who communicates and processes information *between* networks. In organizations, it is the person within the organization who communicates with the environment and influences the flow of information from the organization to the environment and back again (Adams, 1980). The chief executive officer of a company is often a boundary spanner, and his or her skill in representing the company to the community, and the community to the company, is an important part of the job. Marilyn in the above example was a boundary spanner; she could move between the network boundaries of the group and the environment. Boundary spanners act like gatekeepers because they have access to information that is usually unavailable to other members of their group. Similar to a media gatekeeper, they select and transmit information that less well informed people should have.

There are three types of highly connected individuals, but only one of the three is a boundary spanner (Tuchman and Scanlan, 1981). The first is called an *internal star*. This person is well-connected within an organization or group. This might be a person in your group who knows everyone well and can reach the right person at the right time; he or she is well-connected, but not a boundary spanner. The second type of well-connected person is an *external star*. This person has primary contact with people who are external to a group. The third type, a boundary spanner, is well-connected both internally and externally and translates knowledge from one network to the other. If you are a member of a group that must deal with other groups, and if one person in your group communicates with the other group and then carries that information back to your group, this person is spanning the boundaries of the two networks.

Boundary spanners are very important people in corporations. Because they work in a multitude of information environments, they have access to many ideas and types of data. Moreover, they are the people an organization turns to when it needs influence with some component of the environment.

SOCIAL STRUCTURE

The social structure of roles and status levels in a group also affects the communication among the group members. The members communicate with one another in different patterns and networks, dependent to some extent on the status levels (such as leader and followers) in their group's social structure.

It is clear that the social structure in a group affects the structural aspects of its communication. Leaders and other high-status persons, for example, are major participators during group interaction, both as initiators and respondents of messages. Low-status members communicate for a disproportionately large amount of their time with high-status members, thus affirming that network centrality is linked with leadership and status. The typical explanation for this structural phenomenon in the group's use of networks involves the individual member's desire to aspire to higher status. An individual who finds it impossible to rise to high status through his or her own achievements will substitute for actual status a vicarious membership in a higher status by communicating upward in the status hierarchy.

During the process of leader and status emergence, however, the structural patterns of communication change over time. During early stages of the emergent process, contenders appear to communicate most often with their lieutenants and not with one another. Such a communicative structure is consistent with the assumption that coalitions form around leader contenders. The communication network also reflects these coalitions. After a group completes its process of leader emergence, however, the leader tends to initiate and receive messages to and from all group members and to assume a central position in the network.

Certainly the status of the group member affects the messages that he or she initiates and receives. *Who* says it is as important to perceiving the relative importance of the message as *what* is said. Status endows a message with value. In the study of persuasion and attitude change, the credibility (or "ethos") of the communicator appears to be a significant factor in how people attend and react to persuasive messages. Thus, the communicative structure in a small group affects, and is affected by, the social structure of the group members. Communicative structure and social structure exert a mutual and reciprocal influence on each other and may therefore be considered interdependent.

BARRIERS AND BREAKDOWNS—A FALLACY

Too often, instances of ineffective communication are dismissed as the result of communication barriers or breakdowns. This mechanistic rationalization of communicative failures has enjoyed widespread popularity in everyday usage and even in group communication research. It is not necessary to dwell on this common misconception of the communicative process. Fisher (1978), among others, has already illustrated the fallacy in the reasoning allegedly justifying the existence of barriers and breakdowns in communication.

Briefly, a communication barrier or breakdown is a purely structural attribute of communication, on the assumption that messages travel through space from one person (a source) to another person (a receiver). Thus, communication is not so much a process as a linear flow of messages across space. A *barrier* is a "dam" that blocks the flow of messages so that the receiver cannot receive an initiated message. A *breakdown* assumes that the connecting link between communicating individuals ceases to exist—in the same sense as a broken telephone line. In any case, the concept of barriers and breakdowns depends on the idea that a linear flow of messages across space is the central feature of communication.

The basic analogy of communication barriers and breakdowns is the machine in which a barrier (e.g., a clogged fuel line) or a breakdown (e.g., a broken fuel line) could certainly be said to exist. If human communication were so mechanistic, it would certainly be much less complex than it is. Fortunately, human beings and their social systems do not correspond accurately to the mechanistic analogy.

The assumption of linearity is contrary to the principle of interdependence. Communicators don't send and receive isolated messages; they engage in a process—the development and maintenance of an interpersonal relationship. And this relationship is defined by the recurrent, sequential patterns of messages in the context of the entire interaction. Communication as an interaction process denies the possibility of its being partially blocked or breaking down. Can an interpersonal relationship be blocked or break down? In group communication the interpersonal relationship is groupness, inextricably interdependent with the process of group communication. As long as any vestige of groupness exists, communication continues to exist. A barrier or breakdown assumes an absence of communication, but it ignores the more important problem of ineffective communication.

Furthermore, Chapter 10 will demonstrate the normality of social conflict and deviance. If the linear flow of messages is central to group communication, social conflict and deviance must by definition be inherently disruptive. That is, conflict will lead to closed channels and communication barriers or breakdowns. That social conflict disrupts the free flow of messages is blatantly false for much, if not most, social conflict and deviance.

Occasionally, members of an unsuccessful group believe that social conflict is harmful and disruptive. Because of their belief, the members overtly avoid conflict until their tension level and suppressed hostility become so extreme that communication barriers and breakdowns do seem to exist. Such a group illustrates a classic example of the self-fulfilling prophecy in action. If group members believe that conflict is disruptive and harmful, they tend to behave as if it were and eventually succeed in disrupting effective group communication and harming the group process.

To take seriously the notion of communication barriers and breakdowns is to regard communication mechanistically, to be sure. More important, however, too much emphasis on barriers and breakdowns subverts even a mechanistic conception of human communication—at least when it occurs in a face-to-face situation, such as in group decision making. Thinking of effective and ineffective communication is much more valuable and beneficial than believing in the myth of noncommunication.

Subsequent discussions in this book will ignore the possibility of barriers and breakdowns in human communication. We shall emphasize, instead, the improvement of communicative effectiveness and the effectiveness of the group process. What you might otherwise have considered to be a communication breakdown, at least in terms of the conventional wisdom you continue to possess, shall be treated as communication, but ineffective communication. Try to reconceptualize barriers and breakdowns and interpret them in the sense of a communicative process that is not operating adequately or effectively, but is working nevertheless.

Too many common misconceptions about communication and the group process prevail in our society. One step in improving the effectiveness of communication is for all members to discard their misconceptions about groups and about communication. Truly, understanding communication and the group process includes not *mis*understanding it.

NONVERBAL COMMUNICATION AND GROUP STRUCTURE

Members of groups usually attend to the words and intentional meanings of other group members. But the meanings of words and messages are also influenced by *nonverbal* communication—eye contact, pauses, gestures, intonation, spatial relationships, and the like. In this section we will consider the structural and functional aspects of nonverbal behavior. The next chapter will consider those aspects of nonverbal behavior which are part of the functional nature of communication. A functional approach to communication emphasizes what communication does, how it affects other people, and how messages function in groups, whereas a structural approach examines the physical and spatial forms that influence meanings and perceptions.

One way to describe the variety of possible nonverbal behaviors is to categorize them into three types:

1. *Proxemic behavior* This is how people are affected by spatial and distance orientations.
2. *Kinesic behavior (body motion)* This includes gestures, body shifts, eye movements, facial expressions, and posture. These physical movements can be described structurally, but they are more usefully discussed as motions that accompany spoken words and modify verbal meanings.
3. *Paralinguistic qualities* These include loudness, pitch, tone, and rate of speech. They are vocal qualities which have no dictionary meaning but which add to the interpretation of words.

We will now examine the fundamental structural issue in nonverbal communication in groups—proxemic behavior. Then in Chapter 4 we will examine how the other two types of nonverbal communication work to clarify messages, orient speakers, and signal power and emotional states.

Proxemic Behavior

Proxemics is the study of the communicative use of space—the ways in which we use, arrange, and perceive physical space.

Have you ever had somebody stand too close to you and make you feel uncomfortable?

Have you ever been even slightly intimidated by someone who was taller than you, or have you intimidated someone who was smaller?

Have you ever noticed the difference between the arrangement of objects in your living room and the organization of a classroom?

Have you ever placed your books or coat on a table to "save" a seat for yourself in the cafeteria or library?

If you have experienced any of these things, you have experienced the influence of proxemic patterns on your behavior. The spatial and distance orientations that group members maintain exert considerable influence on the flow and patterns of communication in the group. Communication is facilitated when the distances between people are comfortable, and it is hindered when we deviate from these comfortable distances, because the organization of space relates to some of our most fundamental human needs.

Territoriality and Personal Space The possession of one's own territory is an example of a fundamental human need with respect to proxemics. *Territory* is space that you feel ownership toward; it is an area or object that you have rights to and defend accordingly. If you place your books and coat on a cafeteria table and then go off to get lunch, you will be surprised—and feel that your territory has been violated—if someone moves your books and sits down. Group members often claim territory for themselves. A chair or position at a table might be the territory of a particular group member, and tension can result if someone else invades this territory. Such tension is usually subtle and may appear as aggression later in the group discussion. But the very subtlety of such influences makes them more insidious, because they are less apparent and it is more difficult to identify the source of the problem.

In an interesting study, Taylor and Lanni (1981) wrote about what they called the "resident advantage." This is the advantage that accrues to the group or group member who is using space that he or she owns. You have undoubtedly heard of the "home-court advantage" in basketball and other sports. Individuals and teams simply perform better in space that they "own." The same is true for groups and their members. If a group has a favorite place to meet, such as a dorm room or library study room, then it will perform better if it continues to meet in its own "territory." Taylor and Lanni also found that individuals who host the group in their home or some other private location are more likely to communicate in a dominant manner; this is even true for group members who are not predisposed toward dominance. So the nature of physical space influences how group members feel about the group and themselves.

An idea related to territory is personal space. *Personal space* is that psychological outline of space around your body which you define as your own. If people or objects get too close and "violate" your personal space, you feel strange or uncomfortable. For instance, if a group member moves his or her chair too close to you and you feel awkward, then that group member has violated your personal space; as a result, you might feel anxious and withdraw from the discussion. The area around our bodies that constitutes personal space expands and contracts to meet the social needs of a situation; we keep this area wide in the presence of strangers, for example, but narrow it for intimate relationships. The anthropologist Edward T. Hall (1959) identified four categories of personal space and their corresponding social functions, and all four categories have implications for group behavior:

1. *Intimate distance* (0 to 8 inches) is for body contact and intimate relationships. Your group will probably not use this distance unless the group is composed of people who have very well developed, perhaps intimate, relationships. Children, who have yet to become socialized about personal distance, will often penetrate your intimate space. If some group members interact at such personal distances, they will probably make the other members nervous.
2. *Personal distance* (1½ to 4 feet) is the most typical interactional distance for friends and acquaintances. Touch is a little more difficult and less expected at this distance. Most groups interact within this zone.
3. *Social distance* (4 to 12 feet) is clearly out of the range of touch but allows us to recognize the other person. This distance is used for casual contact with strangers and for some business functions.
4. *Public distance* (12 feet and beyond) is for formal encounters, speeches, platform presentations, and encounters with public officials. This is the distance at which groups can break up into smaller groups if they are not careful; people feel as

if they cannot make contact with others at the outer edge of this zone, so they turn their attention to those around them.

These distance zones are useful and generally accurate, but other factors also influence how group members use personal space. Women, for example, sit closer to one another than men do because women are typically more involved in personal relationships and more receptive to symbolizing closeness. Groups consisting mostly of women interact differently than groups consisting mostly of men. The topic of conversation also influences the use of personal space; group members who are in a serious conversation about an important, impersonal topic related to the group's task tend to sit far apart, whereas they tend to sit close together for intimate discussions.

Group Spatial Ecology The area of proxemics that relates to the influences of physical space (such as furniture arrangements, architecture, doors, and walls) is called *group spatial ecology*. We seldom think about the influence of the physical environment, but it can dictate patterns of communication; it has a strong impact on which people we communicate with and on how we communicate. For instance, the living room in your family home is probably arranged for conversation and relaxation; there are comfortable chairs facing one another so that people can talk. A classroom, on the other hand, where the seats are arranged in rows, is designed so that everyone focuses attention on one place (the teacher) and conversation between students is more difficult (although they manage it). For the most part, groups should be concerned about arrangements that bring people together and facilitate face-to-face communication.

Environmental psychologists and communication theorists have been studying how various arrangements of space influence communication. Two basic types of arrangements are shown in Figure 3-2. Environmental arrangements that encourage contact and communication are called *sociopetal* arrangements. Living rooms and restaurants, for example, are designed to bring people together and to foster interaction; you can see in Figure 3-2 that the furniture forces people to face one another and limits the physical barriers between people. The tables in a restaurant or bar are the only space for food and drinks; the customers are therefore environmentally "pressured" to make contact with one another. Arrangements that keep people away from one another, discouraging communication, are called *sociofugal* arrangements. They separate people by turning them away from one another (e.g., back-to-back seating), placing greater distances between them, and using physical barriers to make contact difficult.

The effects of proxemics on small-group behavior have been examined in a number of studies, which find that it is possible to discourage or facilitate good group communication by manipulating proxemic variables. The physical environment either limits or extends the options and types of communication available to people. For instance, it is easier to interact with people who are opposite you than with those on either side; also, individuals at the corners of a table will contribute the least to discussions, while those at the head or in central positions will con-

Figure 3-2 Some environmental arrangements. (*Source:* Burgoon, 1988.)

tribute the most. Knapp (1978) concluded that people would prefer to sit in adjacent seats around a table or face-to-face and that these arrangements are the most conducive to cooperation. Groups should choose seating arrangements that encourage eye contact and face-to-face interaction.

People in high-status and leadership positions are granted special places. In groups, they will occupy *high-interaction* positions; these are locations that offer the most contact with people. Leaders and dominant people gravitate toward the end of rectangular tables and choose to sit opposite other people. Holding a dominant seating position in a group enables the person to monitor and influence other persons in the group. It is pretty obvious what you have to do if you want to be a leader or to exert influence in the group: Sit in a place that makes you the symbolic leader of the group. Likewise, if you want to increase the participation of a particular group member, you might succeed by placing the person in a centralized seating position, for a central position in a seating arrangement confers status and authority on an individual.

Spatial arrangements are also related to interpersonal relationships in the group. The members use each other's distance orientations as signals of how involved each person is in what the other has to say and of what each thinks of the other. When people like each other and are involved in their relationship, they lessen the distance between themselves. When people are angry or displeased with each other, they choose an extreme proximity. They might withdraw and move away, or if they are especially aroused, they might move very close in order to shout. Group members can use their knowledge of proxemic choices to their advantage. If you want to communicate exclusion to certain group members, you can physically distance them from other group members, whereas moving closer to them will indicate your interest and interpersonal acceptance.

SUMMARY

Viewed as a process, communication has both structural and functional dimensions. The structural elements are consistent with the view that communication involves the transmission and reception of messages on channels. One structural element of communication is feedback; feedback responses are unavoidable and occur continuously during the give-and-take of group interaction. Effective feedback responses during group interaction depend on the cohesiveness of the group members and on the interpretations of the feedback responses by the persons who receive them.

Certain characteristics of the messages that constitute the group interaction are important to decision making. For effective group decision making, the timing of the messages may be more significant than their content.

Viewed structurally, group communication can be seen as a network—a pattern of channels that link members of the group. Networks are distinguished from one another by size, reachability, density, and centrality. The most central position in a network is apt to be occupied by a leader or by a deviant who is under extreme social pressure to conform. During the process of group decision making, several networks generally emerge from the group's interactive patterns; these networks reflect the coalition formation and leadership at various stages in the group process.

The gatekeeper in a network is someone who is responsible for receiving, transforming, and retransmitting information to other members of the group. Because gatekeepers are usually in central and pivotal positions, they possess much authority and responsibility. A boundary spanner is someone who acts like a gatekeeper but transmits information between networks. Who says what to whom is also influenced by the social structure of the group; high-status members and leaders of a group initiate more communication than low-status members do, and this fact confirms that status is linked to network centrality. The concept of communication barriers and breakdowns is untenable, for it is inconsistent with the view that communication is a process.

Proxemic behavior is also part of the structure of communication in groups. Proxemics is the study of the communicative use of space. All of us have personal space and territoriality needs; that is, we have a sense of ownership about the objects and space around us. Group members often claim territory (such as chairs and tables) for themselves. Spatial distance can be either intimate, personal, social, or public. The physical environment can be arranged to encourage communication (in sociopetal arrangements) or to keep people away (in sociofugal arrangements). The use of personal space is related to a number of other variables, such as sex, leadership, and interpersonal relationships.

CHAPTER 4

Group Communication: Functional Elements

You have undoubtedly been trained in various aspects of communication through-out your experience in elementary and secondary schools and in college. You have probably mastered, to some extent, the syntactic dimension of communication, its grammar. For example, you know about placement of nouns and verbs, agreement between subject and predicate, etc. The semantic dimension is also emphasized in our schools, generally in the sense of finding a referent for a word in order to de-cipher its meaning. That is, a word stands for something. Early in your educational career, you learned to use the dictionary and provide definitions for words—se-mantics. The dimension of communication that rarely appears in our schools' cur-ricula, however, is the pragmatic dimension. *PRAG*

The pragmatic dimension of communication deals with the relationship be-tween words and people. Another way of understanding the pragmatic dimension of communication is to think of the functions performed by a message or a unit of communication. That is, what does the action *do* in the communicative process? Beyond the grammar of the sentences and the meanings of the words is the prag-matic notion of how the action functions in the communicative situation as, for example, a bluff, a threat, a plea, or an expression of intimacy. Anytime someone in the group utters a sentence or phrase, he or she performs a type of action that has some meaning for and influence on the hearer of the action. In the following example, Jim is talking to another group member (Ben):

JIM: You know, Ben, if you don't have that information from the Department of Transportation by Monday, I'm going to ask someone else to get it and give you a poor evaluation.

Whenever you speak, you perform actions with your words. The words in Jim's sentence perform some *communicative* function. If you were asked what Jim was doing in that utterance, you might say he was *threatening* Ben, telling Ben that there would be negative consequences if he did not get the necessary information. You could say that Jim was "performing" a threat. *Perform Prag if*

Now in Jim's utterance we took the words at their face value. Jim threatened

Ben with a loss of status and a poor evaluation if he did not get the information that the group needed. It was a genuine and serious threat. But what if Jim had said in a rather playful manner, "Ben, old boy, you'd best get that information we need or I'm gonna kill you." Obviously, these words are not to be taken literally. This would not be genuine threat. It is still a statement indicating what Jim wants Ben to do, but its *effect* is different; its pragmatic function is different. An emphasis on the pragmatic functioning of human communication is an emphasis on the functions of communication. Later in this chapter it will become apparent that the same comment (even using the same words) may perform different functions, depending on the intent of the speaker and on when it occurs in a sequence of interaction. The function of any particular communicative act often depends on what precedes or follows it during the normal course of human communication.

The ideas in this chapter are not particularly complex. However, they may appear to be more difficult than they are, probably because understanding the functional elements of communication requires revising the way we normally think of communication. In the following pages, for example, the concept of transmitting and receiving messages on a channel is of little relevance. The emphasis is now on the entire group or social system, taken as a whole—a single whole, composed of all the members of the group. The focus is on the group as a system—a single information-processing entity of which each individual person is a part. In other words, the whole (the group) is different from the sum of its parts (the individual members). Rather than focus on the individual human being (for example, on self-concept, attitudes, values, or beliefs), we will concern ourselves with the social relationship, the organization of individuals into a single unit called a group.

PRAGMATICS AND COMMUNICATION

A pragmatic approach to the study of communication in groups is only one approach among many (see Shaw, 1981, and Hirokawa and Poole, 1986), but it leads us to consider a number of important issues. For example, we must take into account the context in which communication takes place; we must know who the speaker and the hearer are, at least, and we should know when and where the communication takes place.

Many people think of communication as synonymous with the ways people make contact; thus, communication is easily equated with telephones, computers, radio, and television, and these perspectives emphasize the channels for transmitting and receiving messages. However, as explained in Chapter 1, we are using the terms *communication* and *interaction* interchangeably in this book. When a speaker utters words that have some message value and does so in a particular social situation and at a point in the unfolding stream of talk, the speaker is both communicating and interacting: *communicating* because the language carries meaning and content, and *interacting* because the language functions to express social relationships. It is impossible to do one without the other.

Communication Defined

Our definition of *group* in Chapter 1 emphasized that a group is a system of communicative behaviors composed of identifiable patterns of interaction. Our definition of *communication* closely parallels this definition of *group* because we consider the group process and the communicative process to be precisely the same process (whereby this book's subtitle, *Communication and the Group Process*, indeed refers to a single process). At the same time, because small group decision making is our focus of attention in this book, we are viewing the communicative process in terms of the group—and particularly in terms of the group as a holistic decision-making system.

The analysis of communication in groups is the analysis of language in use. We will define *communication* simply as *the process of people exchanging messages, which are formulated according to the principles of a code, in a context*. The important words in this definition are "process," "messages," "code," and "context." The definition simply says that people use language to create messages and that these messages acquire their meaning both in a situation and in relation to previous and subsequent messages.

Your language is a code (or set of principles) for organizing symbols. Readers of this book are competent users of the English-language code, but there are other ways to organize symbols. There are other languages (e.g., French and Swahili) and others ways to express the code (e.g., sign language and mathematics). All of the above are linguistic codes; that is, they are governed by formal rules about how sounds and words can be organized. Linguistic codes have a grammar. There is a grammar of French, of Swahili, and of sign language. Sign language is not non-verbal communication just because the symbols are not spoken; even though it expresses linguistic meaning through the use of hand and body movements, it still functions according to linguistic principles. Nonlinguistic codes are what we often call nonverbal communication, which includes body movements, facial expressions, physical features, and much of what passes for "animal communication."

We are concerned with the social-interaction aspect of language, not with the formal grammatical and linguistic properties of language. We want to know how an utterance in the group (such as a threat, promise, or piece of information) counts as social action. The meaning and significance of what people say in groups is not based on the grammar or strict content of a statement by a group member; rather, it is based on the coherence of conversational sequences and on the actions performed by those sequences. A pragmatic approach to communication locates the action and meaning of utterances *in the interaction*. That is, meaning results from applying one's knowledge of the contexts and the people in them to the words that group members utter. In the following example, Sue and Howard use their shared knowledge to accomplish communication:

SUE: What time is it?.
HOWARD: Kelly's class just ended.

Howard's response is not a literal answer to the question because he never states what time it is. But the relationship between Sue and Howard is such that they share knowledge of a Professor Kelly and when her class ends. Howard's utterance is perfectly sensible and responsive to the question, but only in relationship to what preceded it and the context of his relationship with Sue as a member of his group.

Communication is the major vehicle for accomplishing tasks, and it soon becomes clear that many concepts in groups are apparent in the communication. The following example is of a group argument. The group has been discussing case studies of a business that behaved unlawfully in order to reap a small profit. The group's goal is to analyze the cases and decide what it would do, given the conditions of the case. Only a portion of the entire argument appears here:

JOY: Well, I finished the case. It was interesting but disgusting.

ANN: Uh hum.

JOY: It was so dumb. I'm a business major, and real businesses don't do those things. I mean, you know, it was so dumb to cheat.

PETE: Just cuz you're honest doesn't mean these things don't happen.

JOY: I know, but...

PETE: I think it's very common. That's exactly how lots of millionaires got started. I've even known companies like that.

JOY: That was some time ago. I don't think it relates any more.

PETE: Sure it does. My friend had trouble with a company like that.

JOY: Yes, but...(The argument continues.)

The group members are providing valuable information that will be important when they make their final decision. Pete and Joy are interrelating their personal experiences with the subject matter the group is discussing. Their differing opinions are being worked out in the interaction that characterizes the group's decision-making processes. All communicative utterances are interpreted by the participants in the communication, and each participant assumes that a message "counts as" a type of social action. Pete's statement, for example, that just because Joy is honest does not mean that others are might be counted as a put-down. Joy can choose to treat it as nonthreatening and unimportant—or she might take offense at the statement, and at some point her argument with Pete could get emotional and begin to have negative consequences for the group. It is important to underscore that actual communication consists of the data that people use to conduct the business of the group.

When the focus of communication shifts from the individual human being to the social system (the group), the most significant elements of communication become the *relationships* between group members rather than the internalized feelings, attitudes, emotions, or beliefs of individual members. The only way two persons can establish a relationship with one another is to act toward one another, to engage in communicative actions. How *A* "feels" about *B* cannot affect their social relationship unless and until this feeling becomes observable to *B* and to other group members—that is, until this feeling is expressed in the form of action, a communicative behavior. Although the internalized feeling may be highly important to *A*, it is significant to *B* and to other group members only to the extent that they are able to become aware of it. In other words, private elements of a person's self can be important to the group system (and to group decision making) only if they become public and knowable or if they affect behaviors that are then public and observable. In either case, the focus is on the communicative actions, the behaviors.

Any behavior that a person can perform is based on a choice from among alternative behaviors available to each communicator. Every person is capable of performing any of a vast array of possible actions. The action that is performed at any given instant is inevitably a product of some process of choice, a process of choosing to perform one or more behaviors from among the enormous repertoire of available behaviors. In this sense, everyone possesses a repertoire of behaviors capable of being performed at any given time. The performance of a behavior is thus a result of each person's choice.

Why do we choose to perform some behaviors and not others in any given situation? Although we are capable of free choice and free will, this fact does not imply that our choice is random, that we choose to behave in a purely happenstance or capricious manner. Rather, we choose to behave on the basis of what we consider to be appropriate to a given situation. Stated another way, our repertoire of choices is *constrained* in the sense that many alternatives are eliminated and are thus not available to be chosen in any given situation. As paradoxical as it may seem, we have the capacity of choice among behaviors at the same time that our behavioral choices are subject to numerous constraints that limit the range of alternatives available to us. In many instances, we are only vaguely aware, or even unaware, of any of these constraints, but we submit to them nevertheless. For example, we wear clothing in public rather than appear nude. We speak in a language that contains specific rules of syntax and semantics and conform to those rules (although often rather loosely), even though we may not be aware of the rules that operate to constrain our choices.

Often constraints occur as a result of a particular social situation in which we find ourselves. For example, in your family group the constraints that fellow family members place on your behaviors are quite different from the constraints present when you are in a group of close personal friends. Furthermore, either of these situations will place constraints on your actions that will be different from those constraints evident in a group of strangers or new acquaintances. We will communicate in one way with a boss or an employer and in a different way with a close friend or fellow family member. The social environment places many constraints on our behavioral repertoire and significantly influences the communicative process.

The principal origin of the constraints on our behaviors is the previous interaction itself. That is, constraints result from our past behavioral choices during interaction as well as from the past behaviors of others. When communicating with someone, you *must choose* to perform some behavior; that is, you have no alternative but to choose and thereby perform some behavior. Regardless of what your initial behavioral choice is, your subsequent behavior in the situation is thus constrained as a result of what you and the other communicators have elected to perform in past communicative behavior. Watzlawick, Beavin, and Jackson (1967, pp. 131–134) refer to this phenomenon as the "limiting effect of communication" and describe it as follows: "In a communicational sequence, every exchange of messages narrows down the number of possible next moves" (emphasis deleted).

An example may illustrate this limitation principle of communication more clearly. A man was riding to campus on a city transit bus when an elderly woman boarded the bus and sat beside him. After a few minutes, she remarked that it was shameful that the city had cut down so many of the big trees along the street on which they were riding. Without really thinking, he responded, "Yes, it sure is." This single exchange of messages functioned to place both of them in a communicative situation that limited the man's subsequent behavioral choices. At the very least, he experienced some degree of involvement in this casual relationship. This involvement, virtually involuntary on his part, proceeded directly from his agreeable response to the woman's initial attempt to make conversation. They continued the conversation and became more involved.

Each time a person enters into a communicative situation, he or she brings to that situation some preliminary definition of the relationship and of the situation. The exchange of messages (i.e., the interactional behavior) that occurs during the communicative event defines the communicative situation more clearly until a single definition of the situation exists. The definition is characterized by a particular variety of message exchanges. In other words, our definitions of the situation that we bring to the relationship are redefined in conjunction with those of the other communicator.

A communicative relationship thus evolves during the process of interacting with others. Each communicator soon learns which behaviors are appropriate to the situation and which behaviors are inappropriate. The interaction soon stabilizes, if the communication continues for a sufficient time. Stated another way, each person in every communicative situation learns how "to play the game": learns what the rules are that govern the communication. As a result, the individual communicators constrain their behavioral choices until an identifiable pattern of message exchanges evolves to characterize or define that relationship.

Communication is thus a series of actions. That is, communication becomes a sequence of events that occur in time. An action is not a "thing." It has no material existence; it is not extended; it does not take up any space. A behavior is fleeting. It exists only in time and is thus related to other behaviors or other events in time. Viewed in this manner, communication becomes somehow less "real" than the structural elements of communication discussed in Chapter 3. We can easily visualize, in a physical sense, messages being transported on a channel from one place in space to another place in space, from source to receiver on a channel path. These elements are all conceptually "thinglike" in the sense of a material existence of the elements of communication. However, communication as a sequence of behavioral events reflects no comparable physical quality.

Despite the absence of physical communicative elements, a pragmatic perspective of communication is understandable as certain sequences of acts become familiar. That is, certain acts tend to follow other acts so frequently and are repeated so often that we come to expect the next act in the sequence even before it occurs. The interaction becomes familiar because it has been repeated so often in the past. In this way, past sequences of interaction constrain future interaction even though the communicators themselves may be unaware that their actions are being constrained. Communicative relationships are thus characterized by what sorts of actions are performed by communicators who are familiar with the appropriate sequence.

Some people have certain friends with whom they engage in mutually insulting behaviors. Either one will insult the other, and this insult is a clear sign that the next act in the sequence will be another insult in response. And some interpersonal relationship are characterized by argumentative interaction; that is, virtually anything that one person says will be followed by the other's disagreement. Both of these sequences of interaction are symptoms of very close interpersonal friendships. These particular people would never have dreamed of insulting or disagreeing with the woman on the bus, however; that sequence was characteristic of a casual first acquaintance. Insults and disagreement would have been quite inappropriate in such an early stage of interaction. The close relationships characterized by mutual insults and argument have developed over a long period and are based on frequent exchanges of similar behaviors in the past. Those past sequences are now familiar and constrain the present interaction.

This view of communicative functions does not ignore a person's self. Rather, such a perspective considers the behaviors performed by a person (particularly those behaviors performed in sequence with the behaviors of other persons) as a very adequate representation of the self. In other words, every person's self grows, develops, and possesses an identity in relationship with other people. It does not exist in isolation. Furthermore, relationships with other people are defined and characterized as sequences (interacts and double interacts) of communicative behaviors or actions. As behavioral sequences (determined by past interactions) become familiar to the communicators, the social relationship becomes identifiable and "comfortable" to the communicators.

Communication, then, is a series of events, each one following the other in a stream of ongoing actions, or behaviors. These actions performed by the communicators are "connected" with one another within this ongoing stream. Therefore, we think of the "connectedness" among the various actions rather than of each individual action in isolation. We talk about *inter*action or communication to signify the entire conversation, the entire process of communication.

The process of communication involves considering the entire conversation of the communicators (for our purposes, members of a decision-making group) as a single process. It is in this sense of a single "system" of communication that Birdwhistell (1959, p. 104) characterizes communication as an entire process (or system) in which an individual participates. An individual "does not originate communication," but rather "engages in or becomes part of communication." Viewed pragmatically, the communicative process emphasizes the interconnections between the actions performed by the individual communicators. Together with their connections, all the actions by the individual communicators from the entire system (or process) of communication. For our purposes, the communicative system is the group and the group process.

Group communication, then, involves a sequence of the actions that are contributed by individual members. As a sequence, each action follows after or precedes another action. The person, when engaging in, or becoming part of, communication, contributes actions (or behaviors) to the overall process of communication. In a sense, each person takes turns in contributing actions, particularly in the form of verbal utterances in a face-to-face conversation or discussion. For some period of time, any individual group member gets the floor and later relinquishes his or her turn to another member, who then has the floor for some additional period of time.

Communication or interaction is the sequence of the actions contributed by the communicators in the sense that they take turns in contributing to the sequence. Each person's action is connected in some manner to the action that precedes it and to the action that follows it. An example of such connectedness occurs when we say that a comment following a question may be regarded as an answer. Rather than think of each individual action separately, we think of the *connections* between actions and thus view the communicative process as a *system* of communication rather than as actions and reactions by individual persons.

One Cannot *Not* Communicate

When communication is viewed as a sequence of behaviors, one factor becomes immediately apparent—one cannot *not* communicate. It is literally impossible not to behave. For example, try this exercise: For the next 10 seconds, *do not behave.* Your first reaction should be the realization that such an instruction just doesn't make any sense. The idea of *not* behaving is nonsensical. Even silence or remaining motionless is behavior. Sleeping is behavior of a sort. Lying or standing still is behavior. Thus, if behavior has no opposite, and if communication is defined as behavior, then communication also has no opposite. Hence, one cannot *not* communicate.

Watzlawick, Beavin, and Jackson (1967, pp. 48–51) were probably the first to coin the now familiar phrase "One cannot not communicate." This catch phrase has often been the object of considerable misinterpretation. For example, is all communication to be considered behavior? The answer to this question is affirmative. (No problem so far.) On the other hand, is all behavior communication? The answer here is less clear.

Certainly not all behavior can be communication. On the other hand, any behavior performed during communication potentially has some message value. That is, any behavior is potentially communicative in the sense that it can affect subsequent interaction. But any behavior that is not public or observed (such as random foot-tapping or fidgeting under a table, out of view) is not a significant part of the communicative situation. Moreover, such behavior *cannot* be significant precisely because it is not public or capable of being observed.

Any behavior, though potentially communicative, may eventually prove to be insignificant. To understand communication, then, is to discover those parts of the interaction, the particular kinds of actions, which are the most significant elements of the interaction. Other behaviors would be considered rather unimportant, but not necessarily noncommunicative. Is all behavior communication? Not necessarily. But any behavior that is public and thus observable within the ongoing inter-action is potentially communicative.

The impossibility of not communicating also suggests that communication need not be intentional or successful to be definable as communication. We some-times believe that communication takes place only when it is effective—that is, when the source and the receiver have interpreted the message similarly, or are "one the same wavelength." But in the event that interpretations are not similar, we tend to believe that communication has not even occurred. For example, we often say, "We talked to each other, but we didn't communicate." Such an ob-servation apparently suggests that communication has not been totally successful or has not fully resolved disagreements. Obviously, such a communicative situation may not be particularly effective or successful. But to suggest that no communi-cation has taken place is absurd.

When people are talking (that is, behaving verbally and nonverbally) with one another, they have no choice but to become involved in a series of behavioral ex-changes. These interactions are, by definition, communication. It is not, however, necessarily effective communication. Indeed, misunderstanding may characterize many communicative situations. But its presence does not mean that no commu-nication has taken place, although it may imply that the communication was not particularly effective in establishing a mutually satisfactory relationship.

The Content and Relationship Dimensions

To this point, our discussion has focused on actions performed by individual com-municators. We have said little or nothing concerning the interpretation of these actions or what they might contain. Assume that any action (or behavior) performed by any person during a communicative event can be called a message. As such, it contains information. Pragmatically, this information involves two dimensions—a content dimension and a relationship dimension. As dimensions, the content and relationship aspects of communication are inseparable and are always present in every communicative behavior.

Gregory Bateson (1935), a social anthropologist, first discussed the concept of two aspects of language that he termed the *report* and *command* characteristics. His original analysis of language has since been extended to communication, generally, as content and relationship dimensions. The content dimension of communication refers to the aspect of behavior that deals with specific data. The content is the topic of conversation, the subject matter. The relationship dimension refers to that prop-erty of communicative behavior that provides direction as to how the message's content is to be interpreted. It enables the members of the communicative situation to develop some definition of their social relationship.

The content and relationship dimensions of communication may be compared, respectively, with the *information* contained in a message and the *style* in which the information is expressed. To express a message that contains some information is to express that message *in some way*. Stylizing a message is absolutely unavoidable. In other words, a message will contain some content, and it will also be stylized.

We teach children early in their formative years to stylize messages in order to develop satisfactory relationships. We call such training in stylizing messages "being polite" or "having good manners." The child soon learns not to say, "Gimme the potatoes." Instead, we teach children to ask, "Please pass the potatoes," along with other stylizations, including "Thank you," "You're welcome," and "Excuse me." The *content* of the two messages requesting potatoes is precisely the same, but the relationship dimension within the two messages differs significantly.

In every exchange of messages in a sequence of interaction, the content and relationship dimensions of communication are present. Within group decision making, the two dimensions are even more apparent and probably more meaningful than in normal everyday conversation. We hasten to add that these dimensions are no more important in group decision making than in other communicative situations; but because of the task and social nature of decision-making groups, these dimensions seem more obvious and are directly involved in the effective functioning of the group process. Ultimately, these dimensions are related to effective decision making. Members of decision making groups are quite likely to be aware of the content and relationship dimensions of communication.

It is important to remember that whenever communication occurs, the communicators are dealing with information at the same time that they are developing a social relationship. This relationship dimension of the communication may develop into one of friendship, enmity, cooperation, equality, superior-subordinate, or any of many possible social relationships. Moreover, these relationships develop during the sequence of interactive behaviors and may or may not be consistent with the expectations arising from the situation. For example, you have probably had communicative relationships with some "bosses" who interacted with you as though they were indeed superior to you; another boss, however, may have been more of a colleague or an equal in your interactions. Many husband-wife pairs interact in the form of a superior-subordinate relationship, while others have developed a more equal relationship. Inevitably, the relationship (together with the content) is an inherent part of, and is reflected in, the communicative behaviors exchanged by the participants during group communication.

Group decision making is clearly a social enterprise. While members are communicating with one another, they are simultaneously attempting to achieve consensus on decisions and establishing a social relationship that unites individuals into a functioning group. Thus, group members perform their decision-making task at the same time that they are developing their group relationship. Every act of communication performs a content (informational) function as well as a relational function.

Consider the following excerpt abridged from the interaction of a classroom decision-making group. The students are discussing the pros and cons of establishing a coal-burning plant to generate electricity in southwestern Utah.

TIM: Well, the environmental groups are certainly opposed to a power plant so close to the national park.

JACK: Frankly, I think that the environmentalists are all a bunch of nuts.

MIKE: I don't think I understand. What do you mean?

JACK: They just don't seem to care about the people who live in that area. The residents want the plant.

MIKE: Don't care? You've got to be kidding. They care more about the future of those people than lining the pockets of a few utility companies.

JACK: But look at all the jobs that will be created.

MIKE: And look at all the pollution that will float into the park.

JACK: What *are* you? Some kind of Sierra Club freak?

MIKE: What are *you?* A Bircher?

TIM: Does anybody know what time it is?

This brief excerpt illustrates the interplay of the content and relationship functions within the interaction. Jack and Mike are engaged in an argument over specific information related to the topic at hand. Apparently their argument includes relational overtones as well. Their conflict over the content issues leads to a rather competitive relational conflict. Their final comments are as much a personal attack on the relationship level as they are inquiries into the ideational basis of each other's opinion.

Tim's last comment illustrates clearly that the content and relationship dimensions are simultaneously functioning during the interaction. In terms of the content of his final comment, Tim is asking a question that seeks information concerning the time of day. The question changes the subject matter of the discussion on the content level. In fact, one of the other group members responds and tells him the time according to her watch. More important to the relationship dimension of the interaction, however, Tim's request breaks the tension that has been developing in the group as a result of the informational and interpersonal conflict between Jack and Mike. Tim's abrupt change of topic leads to the release of relational tension created by Jack and Mike's interpersonal rivalry.

Similar to the social and task dimensions of group process, in every act the content and the relationship functions of communication always operate simultaneously during the process. Every act of communication contains information in the content dimension as well as some additional indicators as to how that information should be interpreted (that is, the relationship dimension). Sometimes the relationship dimension is reflected in the manner in which the words are said (in the inflection, vocal emphasis, etc.), or perhaps in the choice of words used to express the information, or even in the movements, gestures, or facial expressions during the utterance of the words. Under all circumstances, then, the content and relationship functions of communication occur simultaneously in every act.

These two dimensions of communication should not be construed as a difference between kinds of acts or types of behavior. In other words, one act of communication is no more content-oriented or relationship-oriented than another. The content and relationship functions of communication are inseparable and inherent within each and every act of human communication.

Interaction Analysis

One method that attempts to understand the ongoing stream of interaction during group decision making involves categorizing each participant's contribution to the communicative process. In this way, any action contributed by an individual member is perceived to be of a certain type. Chapter 6 includes this method of understanding group communication in order to facilitate a fuller understanding of how group members make decisions (task dimension) and relate to one another (social dimension). The practice of interaction analysis, in which categories (or classes) of actions are used to analyze the ongoing process of group communication, is also the subject of a more detailed discussion in Chapter 5.

Of course, any action performed by an individual group member fulfills different functions. For example, the above conversation between Tim, Jack, and Mike about the power plant provides several examples of multifunctional comments. Tim's final remark, for instance, serves several functions. He is not only requesting information, but he is also releasing the social tension that has developed because of the increasingly personalized conflict between Jack and Mike. Also, Tim's comment serves to change the topic of conversation.

Keep in mind that it is always difficult to interpret the communicative behavior of others and feel confident about the interpretation. Some communication scholars have spent considerable time studying how it is that we can know what others mean by their communication (Folger and Poole, 1982). But there is always the question of whose interpretation is more useful. If you ask any participants in communication what they meant by a particular utterance, they are certainly biased according to their perceptions of the situation and of other people. In the example above it may appear as though Mike is attacking Jack, yet Mike might not see it that way at all. But on the other hand, an outsider may not know as much about a speaker's intentions. Participants in interaction are usually preoccupied with their own intentions, as are observers of interaction. Communication in the group not only performs many functions but also serves the interests of many people.

The point of understanding group communication, then, is not to identify which function is the most important one served by any given action. We should recognize that each individual action performs several functions in the communicative and group process. The categories used to analyze interaction focus on specific classes of functions in order to let us understand the interaction from a restricted viewpoint. Another list of categories, however, may focus on other functions and lead to an understanding of the interaction from the perspective of a different set of functions. Therefore, one can regard the interaction of the same decision-making group from the viewpoints of several different category systems. Combining the results from such analyses will provide a more complete description, explanation, and understanding of the process of group decision making.

Using different category systems to understand the ongoing interaction appears to be quite sensible. We wouldn't think of looking at a painting in only one way in order to understand it completely. A study of the colors and the artist's combinations of them in the painting would provide only one way of understanding the work of art. Concentrating on the composition of figures and objects in the frame would be another way of looking at the painting. We might also consider such factors as the mood or impression created in the painting, the artist's purpose and style, the school of art the painting represents, the reactions of critics and the public, and so forth. Communication is understandably a complex phenomenon. It is multifaceted and involves many different functions. Thus, different categories of human actions are necessary in order to achieve the fullest possible understanding of communication and the group process.

Later in this chapter we shall discuss specific lists of categories (or functions) of communication that have been used to analyze ongoing interaction in group decision making. Keep in mind that any list of categories of interaction must inevitably reflect some way of understanding that which is considered most important in the communicative process. If we look for certain functions in group communication, we will find those functions. But in doing so, we must also ignore other functions. In a sense, the categories that are used to analyze interaction are eyeglasses through which we look in order to view the communicative process. Using a different set of categories to analyze interaction, then, is similar to looking at communication through a different set of glasses and thus seeing something different.

Punctuation of Interaction

We suggested earlier that the functional view of communication seems less "real" or less "actual" than a view of communication as messages traveling along a channel. The ongoing sequences of communication, because they are events, are certainly less real in the sense that they are not tangible. They are not objects, but occurrences—events in time. Moreover, as a series of events, interaction continues indefinitely in an ongoing stream of continuous occurrences. After all, time doesn't stand still; it moves forward in only one direction—toward the future. Some events may be of longer duration than others, but duration does not necessarily make an event more or less important. Furthermore, how does one interpret an event, a behavior, or a message within an ongoing stream (or sequence) of communication? Recall that, as a process, a stream of communicative behaviors has no beginning and no end other than one that is arbitrarily selected.

An analogy may best illustrate how one can organize, and thus derive meaning from, a sequence of communicative acts. Consider a stream of letters of the English alphabet strung together, unorganized and ongoing, such as the following: *aneatdeskisasignofasickmind*. These letters come from a wall sign found in many an office, but the sign presents the letters in organized groups of words. That is, the letters are *punctuated* (organized) into words by placing spaces between the letters. The groups of letters are more understandable, more meaningful, than the letters by themselves. Properly punctuated, the sign reads, "A neat desk is a sign of a sick mind."

Punctuating is nothing more than organizing or grouping elements in order to enable one to interpret their meaning more easily and more meaningfully. Unpunctuated letters themselves have no intrinsic meaning or significance. But words (punctuated groups of letters) do endow the letters, in combination with other elements, with an interpretable meaning and hence with significance. Furthermore, if you change the punctuation rules, you tend to change the possible interpretations of the sequence of elements. Several years ago, after discussing the punctuation of interaction sequences, a student attended the next class meeting with a hand-lettered sign on his shirt. The sign consisted of the "words" *toti emul esto*. He asked us to interpret the phrase. Not one of us was sure, but we all felt that the phrase was vaguely Latin. Since none of us knew Latin, we were unable to decipher the three words. His response was to punctuate the apparently Latin phrase into four English words. He did not change the sequence of the letters. He merely revised the punctuation rules of the sequence and got "to tie mules to." The punctuation, then, allows for a meaningful interpretation of the meaning (or significance) of communication. We are all familiar with the famous experiments of Pavlov, who conditioned dogs to salivate at the ringing of a bell even without the presence of food. On the other hand, *that* punctuation of the sequence of events was the scientist's interpretation. If one of Pavlov's dogs had been able to speak, it might have said, "See how I have this dumb human trained! Every time I feel hungry, I just salivate. Then he rings the bell and gives me food." Pavlov himself, the dumb human, punctuated the sequence of events quite differently. He thought Fido was the one who was conditioned.

If a single behavior of an individual group member is an act, then groupings of acts result from punctuating the interaction sequence. At this point it is necessary to introduce *interact* and *double interact,* two terms used to denote specific groups of acts. We already have terms to designate the grouping of letters of the alphabet in the written mode of communication. We call these groupings *words*. Groupings of words are called *sentences,* and groupings of sentences are called *paragraphs.* Our present purpose requires similar terms to designate groupings of actions (or behaviors) within an ongoing sequence of interaction during group decision making.

The *act,* then, is the contribution to the discussion of a single individual. One act following another act (that is, a pair of acts) is called an *interact.* Thus, an interact is composed of two contiguous acts. A *double interact* is a combination of three contiguous acts in the interaction sequence. Member *A* emits an act (a single act), which is followed by an act from member *B* (thus forming an interact), which is followed by a third act from member *A* (a double interact). Because our emphasis is on communication, or *inter*action, the most important units of analysis are the interact and the double interact—that is, the connectedness of acts to form interaction. In this way, the individual acts are always within the context of the communicative process—the preceding and succeeding acts.

The earlier excerpt of interaction from the group composed of Tim, Jack, and Mike comprises a total of ten acts (count them). Those ten acts also contain nine interacts (or possible combinations of two contiguous acts); Tim's first remark followed by Jack's comment is one interact, Jack's comment followed by Mike's subsequent comment forms another interact, and so on. If one numbers those ten acts from 1 through 10, then the nine interacts are 1-2, 2-3, 3-4, 4-5, 5-6, 6-7, 7-8, 8-9, and 9-10. Each individual act, then, is the second act of one interact (in combination with the preceding comment) and the first act of another interact (in combination with the following comment); note that because the first act has no antecedent and the last act has no subsequent act, there are always fewer interacts than there are acts. The same is true in forming eight double interacts from the same list of ten acts. The eight double interacts are 1-2-3, 2-3-4, 3-4-5, 4-5-6, 5-6-7, 6-7-8, 7-8-9, and 8-9-10.

The question remains as to which groupings of acts (interacts and double interacts) are to be regarded as the appropriate ones. The rules for punctuating acts within the interaction sequences are less explicit and less readily identifiable than the punctuation rules for grouping letters into words, phrases, and sentences. The punctuation of the sequence of letters, discussed earlier, into *toti emul esto* does not conform to those familiar punctuation rules. The alternative punctuation (*to tie mules to*), however, does conform to those rules. The latter punctuation reveals four recognizable English words. The former punctuation produces no recognizable English words among the three. And why are the words recognizable? One reason is that they are familiar in common usage. That is, we have used these words so often in the past that they become recognizable when we use them again.

Although the rules are not quite so specific in punctuating acts into interacts and double interacts, some sequences of interaction are recognizable as sequences. Consider the following list of three acts that are scrambled (that is, out of sequence) in terms of a recognizable double-interact pattern:

"Fine."
"Fine, thank you. How are you?"
"Hi. How are you?"

Clearly this double interact is in reverse order. The sequence is recognizable as the greeting ritual of our American culture. The sequence is so familiar, so patterned, and has appeared so often in the past (and is thus familiar) that we respond to the question as a ritualistic greeting and not as a realistic inquiry into the state of our health.

How, then, are interaction sequences punctuated into interacts and double interacts? The most common method of punctuating them is to organize the sequences into interacts and double interacts that are familiar—and they become familiar, of course, to the extent that they have been repeated often in the past. The punctuation of interaction sequences is therefore typically a matter of sheer redundancy. The more often the interacts and double interacts have occurred in sequence in the past, the more we are able to expect them to occur again in the future, and the more we will tend to punctuate them as recognizable sequences in the present. In Chapters 5 and 6, you will find that the discussions of the decision-making process and of the development of social relationships are based on the punctuation of interaction sequences in terms of their past frequency of occurrence: that is, in terms of how their repetitiveness (or redundancy) makes them recognizable as sequences of interacts and double interacts.

Occasionally, breaking the familiar sequence and substituting a novel or unexpected action has greater impact than would normally be expected. The information value of such an action is enhanced precisely because the action is out of the ordinary, unexpected, and/or novel. These are characteristics of human communication that will become increasingly important as we delve more deeply into the analysis of communication and the group process.

THE THEORETICAL PERSPECTIVE

We continue to emphasize throughout this book that understanding communication and the group process depends on the perspective from which we choose to view it. A perspective on communication in groups precedes a definition. Given our way of looking at communication and the group process, a definition will follow from a specific viewpoint and will reflect it. We want to emphasize understanding rather than solely definition or solely knowledge. To understand is to know not only *what* you know but also *how* you know and *why* you know. Without understanding, knowledge includes only *what* you know.

There is no unified theory of small groups, and there is no unified theory of communication. Anyone who purports to describe and analyze small group communication must necessarily select that perspective which seems most useful and advantageous. Not all perspectives lead to the same conclusions, and no single perspective has achieved anything approaching universal popularity. Therefore, choosing one theoretical perspective means omitting others. And there are many theories, models, and descriptions of small groups and communication. We will not, for example, devote time to Lewin's (1951) field theory, Bales's (1953) equilibrium model, Homans's (1950, 1961) external and internal "systems," Blau's (1960) social integration model, or Thibaut and Kelley's (1959) exchange model. We will allude to these perspectives at various points in this book, but we will essentially ignore their basic theoretical precepts.

The theoretical perspective employed throughout this book is taken from general systems theory (more specifically, modern systems theory). While many fields of endeavor, ranging from biology to computer science, have employed versions of systems theory, the particular systems approach used has been specifically adapted to communication and group decision making. More specific discussions of the theoretical underpinnings of systems theory applied to communication appear in Fisher (1978), but the following few basic principles will help clarify the relationships between groups, communication, and systems theory.

Wholeness

The first principle of systems is *wholeness*—that every component of the system affects and is affected by every other component and that a change in one component necessarily effects changes in all other components. A system is composed of interdependent parts that function as a whole unit. Because all the parts are related, focusing on one part to the exclusion of another distorts the functioning of the system. For instance, analyzing the personality traits of each group member is not consistent with the wholeness principle, which would neglect a comprehensive analysis of individual members in favor of a comprehensive analysis of the group as a single entity.

A term related to wholeness and often applied to systems is *nonsummativity*. This means that the whole is different from the sum of the parts. In other words, when parts of a system are related, the result is a collectivity that has an identity separate from the identities of its individual components. In Chapter 2 we discussed how groups have an identity and sometimes behave in a way that no individual would; this is an example of the nonsummativity effect. A group's behavior cannot be accounted for by analyzing the individual components of the group. Two adults and three children could be a simple collection of individuals, but if they live and interact together, they constitute a system called a family, and that family is identifiable as a single unit.

Nonsystems do not interact in any meaningful way. What if we took everyone in school who was over 6 feet tall and put them in a room. They would not be a system, because they do not relate to each other in any meaningfully interdependent way. A single individual feature (height) explains their collectivity but they do not affect one another because of their height. On the other hand, a decision-making group, a labor union, a political party, a family, or a church does function as a whole system in meaningful ways. All of us are part of many systems, and each system is operating meaningfully when we are behaving in the system.

Structure, Function, and Evolution

All systems have a structure, a function, and an evolution. These are quite simple concepts. *Structure* refers to spatial relationships. We talk about things being above, below, beside, face-to-face, and so forth. The organization chart in a company represents structural relationships; it is possible to study the chart and see who is *above* whom and who is *below*. Likewise, the words "superiors" and "subordinates" represent structural relationships between people. Physical objects also have structural relationships. A table can be composed of four legs and a top, but if these component parts are not arranged correctly, the four legs and a top cannot be called a table. Chapter 3 was devoted to the structural elements of communication in groups; in discussing networks and proxemics, it discussed such structural (or spatial) concepts as the *centrality* and communicative *distance* within a network.

Functional relationships focus on actions rather than on spatial relationships. They pertain to what group members do. They are usually repeatable actions that define how one group member is relating to another; for example, a person may be acting as an information giver, questioner, energizer, or respondent. In a functional relationship, the person is not as important a component as are the actions the person performs in relationship to other group members. For example, if we say that a group member functions as an information giver, we mean that the person performs actions defined as information-giver behaviors and that these actions serve some purpose in the group.

Evolutionary relationships trace the group's history. In studying the evolution of a group, we are concerned with the changes in structure and function that occur over time. As the term *evolution* implies, change is usually slow and gradual rather than sudden and immediate. And, of course, the evolution includes periods of no change—periods when the structural and functional relationships in the group are constant.

As an example of the structural, functional, and evolutionary relationships in a social system, consider any rather typical company:

- Structurally, the company might be divided into four components: executive, management, production, and sales.
- The functional relationships of the four might be defined as a process of product manufacturing in which the executive component handles the broad policy and decision-making tasks, management deals with the day-to-day operations, production performs the manufacturing duties, and the sales force markets and sells the product to the public. These functions are interdependent (i.e., each is affected by the other). Thus, the salespeople cannot guarantee delivery if the production people cannot meet their quotas, and poor executive decisions will influence all parts of the company's structure.
- The evolutionary relationships trace the history of the company, the changing products, markets, management decisions, people, and economic considerations. The company might be highly structured, with very strictly defined relationships between people and with clear-cut status relationships and role specializations, or it might be loosely structured, with informal and relaxed relationships between people.

Openness

Group systems are open systems. An *open* system takes in and processes new information; it has a free exchange of information with the environment. A *closed* system, on the other hand, is isolated from the environment and does not accept information from the outside world. Imagine a group that could not gather information from various sources and talk to people outside the group, but was limited to the information and resources of the group members. Such a group would be a closed system, and it would be characterized by retarded development

The openness of a system is actually a variable property, ranging between 0 percent (totally closed) and 100 percent (totally open). A totally open or totally closed physical or biological system is very unlikely except under severely controlled laboratory conditions. Social systems are never closed; they must always be viewed as open to some degree.

Groups are open systems because they have free interchange with the environment; they have inputs and outputs. If a group is trying to decide on a policy toward integrated schools, for example, it will need input from sources other than the group. It will consult specialists, research studies, programs in other communities, and so on. The group's output might be in the form of a report and a series of suggestions; this report would be discussed and analyzed and then used as input.

Open systems are also characterized by self-regulation and growth. A group can grow and change itself because it controls how it adapts to the environment; it uses information from the environment to alter its course of action. A classroom group, for instance, takes instructions from the professor and then alters the way it behaves. The following section discusses a very important aspect of the group's adaptability and self-regulation—feedback.

FEEDBACK SEQUENCES

Usually, feedback is thought of as a response (or reaction) to a previous action. In a functional, pragmatic view of communication, feedback is not merely a response— it is an entire sequence of actions. This concept of feedback stems directly from the field of cybernetics, which has been credited with coining the term *feedback*. Cybernetics involves the study of control—how machines (and humans) develop normal functioning by controlling any deviations or departures from what is considered "normal."

An analogy may explain this notion of control and the way in which feedback functions to maintain the steady or normal operation of the system. Figure 4-1 depicts a feedback sequence that is often used to illustrate the notion of cybernetic feedback. You will note that feedback, as a sequence, involves a cycle of events, each one of which affects the next event in the sequence. In this way, any change in any one event will precipitate a change in every succeeding event, including itself.

For example, assume that the thermostat of Figure 4-1 is preset at 68°F. Beginning at any arbitrary point on the cycle, we should be able to visualize a change (or deviation) in the normal operation of the thermostatic mechanism. Perhaps the temperature of air in the room falls to 65°F. This change is a deviation from the "normal" functioning of the system, with the "normal" temperature defined by the preset temperature of 68°F. The deviation from the preset temperature causes the thermocouple to close, thus completing the electric circuit and opening the gas jets in the forced-air furnace. The pilot light ignites the gas flame, thereby superheating the air in the furnace chamber, which in turn causes the fan to turn on, which in turn increases the flow of air through the furnace ducts to the room, which in turn raises the air temperature in the room. The feedback cycle is then complete.

Figure 4-1 The feedback cycle of a thermostat.

Note that the "cause" of the rise in room temperature is the original decrease in room temperature. The effect of feedback is to reflect back on itself by setting in motion a sequence of events. Each of these events affects the next event in the sequence until the cycle is completed by returning to the original event. At this point, the feedback cycle begins again in a never-ending cyclic pattern of self-reflexive regulation of the temperature in the room.

Feedback as a sequence is not simply a knee-jerk reflex to some antecedent stimulus. In fact, feedback is not a single action at all. Rather, it is a process initiated by some action. The action (that is, some change in a preset "normal" standard of actions) sets in motion a sequence of actions, each of which stimulates the next action in the sequence until the sequence closes the cycle by exerting influence on the original source of the action. Feedback is a cycle, or loop, because the action exerts influence on itself through direct influence on each link in the chain of events contained in the cycle.

The urbanization process clearly illustrates feedback loops. In brief, farmers occupy a rural area and create a demand for goods and services, such as groceries, machinery repair, the distribution and sale of agricultural products, a post office, and medical care. Soon a small village blooms in the middle of the rural area. Soon a company builds a small factory near the town because of the available supply of labor. More people move to the town in order to secure jobs at the factory. With more people available for work, the market for more services is larger, so more stores selling consumer goods are necessary. Shopping centers and more factories are built as more people move to the city. The small town booms to form a megalopolis. Each deviation from the originally rural area stimulates more and more deviation in a classic illustration of feedback.

The international arms race is another classic example of feedback loops. The spiraling arms race has brought an extraordinary amplification of innovations in weapons development, leading from the invention of gunpowder to dynamite and to the atomic bomb, the hydrogen bomb, the cobalt bomb, the ICBM and MIRV, ad infinitum.

Progress, growth, and change in a social system can occur only through feedback cycles. Naturally the social system must devise methods to manage feedback, along with progress, growth, and change, or the deviation gets out of hand. Urbanization may symbolize much progress in our nation, but unmanaged urbanization has created the serious problems we have only recently faced. The severity of these problems, such as air and water pollution, urban decay and blight, urban crime, inadequate civic services, and overpopulation, has prompted the observation that a megalopolis, such as New York City, may be ungovernable. Nations, too, have recently attempted to set limits on the current arms race through treaties and multilateral agreements. And arms-limitation talks among the powerful nations of the world will probably continue for some time.

Compared to the notion of feedback as response, the functional view of feedback (that is, as feedback cycles or sequences) is probably more valuable as a means of understanding feedback in communication and the group process. The notion of feedback as response is not so much unimportant as it is only a partial view of feedback in the context of group decision making. Feedback as simply response seems more important to the individual member and less significant to the group as an entire social system. Because this book stresses group decision making (specifically, communication and the group process), the greatest emphasis in Chapter 6 will be on feedback cycles during the process of group interaction during the making of decisions. Chapter 6 will therefore illustrate more specifically those feedback cycles which function during group interaction as groups go about their task of making decisions.

DIMENSIONS OF COMMUNICATIVE BEHAVIOR

Earlier in this chapter we discussed the two dimensions of communication—content and relationship. As you will recall, content refers to the specific subject matter or information of communication, and the relationship dimension indicates how the information is to be interpreted. That is, every communication serves to establish some identifiable social relationship between the communicators regardless of the content or the subject matter of the communication. From the previous discussion of interaction analysis in this chapter, you will recall that any category system used to analyze communication focuses on specific functions performed by communicative actions. Thus, it is possible to focus on the content or the relationship aspect of communication with a given category system while still recognizing the fact that the content and relationship dimensions are both present in each communicative act. In this section we will examine how the ongoing interaction of decision-making groups can be viewed in terms of either the content dimension or the relationship dimension, or both. Such analyses, of course, involve using different category systems to analyze communicative behavior.

In referring to content and relationship as "dimensions" of communication, we have adopted the view that *every* act contains both a content aspect and a relationship aspect, although we may focus on only one of the dimensions in a given category system to analyze interaction. Therefore, any attempt to separate acts into those which are primarily oriented to either content or relationship is quite impossible.

Earlier discussion has also indicated that this viewpoint is in substantial agreement with those of some scholars and in substantial disagreement with those of some others. This observation is still another way of saying that one's understanding of communication and the group process depends on the viewpoint, or perspective, used to understand it. One can safely assume, then, that the perspective adopted in this book is quite different from that of others.

Viewing the content and relationship dimensions of communication pragmatically, we are able to examine different lists of interaction categories that emphasize one or the other dimension. Some of these lists of categories will be discussed in this chapter, with the purpose of providing an explanation of the specific category systems—specific lists of functions performed by communication during the process of group decision making. The methods of interaction analysis will be discussed in

Chapter 5. The results obtained from actually observing the interaction of decision-making groups will be discussed in Chapter 6.

The Content Dimension

One way to view the interaction of decision-making groups is to consider each act in terms of how it functions to influence the opinions of other group members toward a specific issue being discussed. Central to such a category system is the concept of *decision proposal*. Each issue or topic of discussion during group decision making is potentially a decision that the group can make. In other words, each topic of conversation is a proposed decision which may be incorporated in the final consensus or which must be resolved as a preliminary step to achieving consensus on a final decision.

For example, a jury whose decision-making task is to determine the guilt or innocence of a defendant undoubtedly discusses many issues preliminary to that final verdict. That is, the jury members may need to determine whether a specific eyewitness is credible, whether the prosecution proved beyond a reasonable doubt the existence of motive, whether extenuating circumstances were sufficient to excuse the defendant from a crime, and so forth. In this way, each individual act during the jury's deliberations functions on a given proposal in such a way that it attempts to influence the perceptions of other members toward that proposal.

Once a decision proposal is identified, the categories of interaction provide a list of functions performed on that potential decision. This analytical system, based on decision proposals, includes the following categories:

1. Interpretation
   - **f.** Favorable toward the decision proposal
   - **u.** Unfavorable toward the decision proposal
   - **ab.** Ambiguous toward the decision proposal, containing a bivalued (both favorable and unfavorable) evaluation
   - **an.** Ambiguous toward the decision proposal, containing a neutral evaluation
2. Substantiation
   - **f.** Favorable toward the decision proposal
   - **u.** Unfavorable toward the decision proposal
   - **ab.** Ambiguous toward the decision proposal, containing a bivalued (both favorable and unfavorable) evaluation
   - **an.** Ambiguous toward the decision proposal, containing a neutral evaluation
3. Clarification
4. Modification
5. Agreement
6. Disagreement

Even the act that initiates the decision or introduces a topic for discussion functions on the proposal in some way. It may *interpret* favorably, unfavorably, or ambiguously, with or without substantiation. But under any circumstances, every act functions on a decision proposal in terms of how that idea should be viewed by the group members. This category system, based on the concept of decision proposals and used to observe the interaction of actual decision-making groups in real life, provides the categories for the model of decision emergence that will be discussed extensively in Chapters 6 and 7.

Significant to this category system are the favorable, unfavorable, and ambiguous categories of interpretation and substantiation. A comment that is classified as favorable is a comment that functions on the decision proposal by expressing a favorable attitude toward it, thereby implicitly attempting to influence the perceptions or opinions of other members toward a favorable position regarding the proposal. Similarly, a comment that is unfavorable toward the proposal attempts to influence other members to reject the proposed idea.

It is possible, however, to interpret or substantiate (that is, to interpret with evidence) a decision proposal ambiguously. An ambiguous comment is one in which the speaker's attitude or opinion is not explicit in the act itself, either because it is neutral (for example, "That's interesting") or because it contains both a favorable and an unfavorable evaluation (for example, "That's a good idea, but it needs a lot of work before it is acceptable").

Using this category system to observe the earlier excerpt showing the interaction of Tim, Jack, and Mike provides some indication of what that interaction is like. Even without being thoroughly familiar with these interaction categories, one can clearly see that the interaction between Jack and Mike reflects a sequence of favorable and unfavorable interpretations or substantiations of the decision proposal regarding the establishment of the power plant so near a national park. Their resulting interaction is a sequence of favorable-unfavorable-favorable (f-u-f) interaction—a clear indication of conflict over ideas or over the subject matter of the discussion. This conflict arises over a decision proposal—a conflict in the content dimension of communication. Whereas Tim's comments may reflect a neutral or ambiguous attitude toward the proposal, the comments of Jack and Mike are definitely not ambiguous.

Mike's first comment, in which he asks for clarification of Jack's preceding act, is the only act of either member that reflects neither a favorable nor an unfavorable interpretation or substantiation of the decision proposal. Mike is merely asking for more information in order to determine "where Jack is coming from." When Mike gets this information from Jack's subsequent comment, he solidifies his position and takes a clear ideational stance on the decision proposal.

This category system for analyzing decision-making interaction is specifically related to the content dimension of decision-making tasks. Although the system may not be entirely appropriate for examining the interaction in other types of tasks, it is altogether appropriate for examining group decision making, our focus in this book.

Later chapters will be discussing the categories of decision-making interaction listed above. Chapter 5 will show how they are applied, and Chapters 6 and 7 will refer to them explicitly.

The Relationship Dimension

There are certainly many ways to view the possible relationships that can unite the individual members within a group. Such relationships may be defined in terms of one or more previously discussed interpersonal factors. For example, we can define a relationship in terms of its level of intimacy, how much interpersonal trust is present, or how much self-disclosure occurs and is reciprocated among members. The category system of social relationship to be discussed in this section, however, defines the relationship in yet another manner.

We must recognize that the nature of a relationship is also definable within a variety of different perspectives, and hence within different systems of interaction categories. The present category system has been used more extensively than any other to show the nature of social relationships in groups. It is presented here not necessarily because it is the best way to view a social relationship, but because it has been used often.

Gregory Bateson, a social anthropologist, is an important scholar in the content and relationship dimensions of communication. He has defined *relationship* (1972) in terms of what he calls *control modes* of communicative actions. We often use this same concept of control-mode relationships in everyday conversation when we describe the game of one-upsmanship. We often characterize a conversation, for example, by suggesting that someone is trying to one-up the other. *One-upsmanship* means an attempt by one person to control the other, to achieve a higher social status than the other, and in some respects to be dominant over the other.

Viewing communication in terms of control modes involves three basic categories:

↑ One up: An attempt to restrict the behavioral options of the other person
→ One across: An attempt at mutual identification
↓ One down: An attempt to relinquish one's own behavioral options to the other person

At the risk of oversimplifying these categories, we can look at certain examples of how an individual may contribute a one-up, a one-down, or a one-across act. Actually, however, the only way to define a comment as either one up, one down, or one across is to consider that comment in relation to the interaction sequence, particularly the comment preceding it. For example, returning to the Tim-Jack-Mike interaction, Mike's comment "You've got to be kidding!" is probably a one-up act. Mike is relationally saying to Jack, "I am not going to allow you any behavioral options other than the one of agreeing with me." His statement is highly imperative; it is didactic. Mike commands Jack to change his mind and conform to Mike's own opinion.

Jack might have responded by saying to Mike, "Yes, I guess you're right. You've convinced me." If he had done so, he would have clearly relinquished his behavioral options to Mike in making this one-down comment. In reality, however, Jack responded by arguing with Mike. That is, he refused to relinquish his behavioral options to Mike and responded with another one-up comment.

A one-across comment does not attempt to control the other person. Nor does such a comment acquiesce to the other person's control. Such an act serves to define the relationship as one of equal status. It may function to restate, repeat, or clarify the previous act. Some group interactions, particularly in encounter or training groups, encourage one-across actions. Often such a comment is preceded by the ritualistic and explicit declaration that the comment is restating a previous act for the sake of clarification: "What I hear you saying is..."

Obviously a single utterance by one person cannot hope to establish a social relationship. The relationship is definable only by a sequence of individual acts. A one-up comment does not establish a social relationship, but in the context of other acts it can be part of a relationship. In this sense of a social relationship, it becomes apparent that a person "engages in," or "becomes part of," the communication (that is, the relationship). No one individual can unilaterally define a communicative relationship. Rather, it is defined by individual actions in concert with the actions of other persons.

There are two identifiable social relationships under the general headings of "symmetry" and "complementarity." The minimal instance of one of these relationships is, of course, an interact. A *symmetrical* relationship is an interact in which the antecedent and subsequent (first and second) acts in the sequence are the same function—either ↑ ↑ , ↓ ↓ , or → → .

A *complementary* relationship is an interact in which the antecedent and subsequent acts "fit together" to form a complete relationship. In the same sense that two angles that together form a right angle (90°) are called complementary angles in geometry, two acts that fit together to form a complete social relationship are called a complementary social relationship. Thus, a complementary relationship involves one person's attempt to assert control over the other and the other person's acceptance of that control: ↑ ↓ and ↓ ↑ . A complementary relationship may take the form of any of the following common social relationships: dominant-submissive, question-answer, buying-selling, giving-receiving, employee-employer, parent-son or parent-daughter, superior-subordinate, husband-wife, teacher-learner, source-receiver, etc. We do not mean to imply, however, that these social relationships are complementary in their use of control modes; rather, they are complementary in the sense that they fit together.

The two forms of complementary relationships (↑ ↓ and ↓ ↑) are essentially the same. One is a mirror image of the other—that is, the reverse of the other. Member A is dominant and member B is submissive, or member A is submissive and member B is dominant. The three forms of symmetry (↑ ↑ , ↓ ↓ , and → →), however, are quite different from one another. The ↑ ↑ symmetrical relationship is one of competition—competitive symmetry. Each person is trying to one-up the other. They are competing with each other, as shown in Mike and Jack's interaction.

Submissive symmetry (↓ ↓) is not so overtly competitive, but it may reflect an underlying competition, nevertheless, in the sense that each person is attempting to force the other person to take the initiative. If you have ever played chess, you will know that it is sometimes to your advantage to force your opponent to attack or to make the initiating moves. A boxer who is a strong counterpuncher may want the opponent to lead with the punches. Submissive symmetry is also apparent in an interaction familiar to all of us. It is the conversation that occurs in situations that involve such decisions as how to spend the evening. The conversation may go something like this:

"What do you want to do tonight?"
"I don't know. What do *you* want to do?"
"I don't care. It's up to you."
"No. Really, you decide."
"But I really don't care."
"Neither do I."

Relationships characterized by submissive symmetry are often the most difficult and frustrating of all.

Equivalent symmetry ($\rightarrow$ $\rightarrow$) is characterized by the establishment of a peer relationship—equal partners. Equivalent symmetry, according to a commonsense interpretation, would probably characterize a democratic relationship, such as a decision-making group composed of equals and led by a democratic leader. We must be careful, however, to avoid thinking of any relationship, including equivalent symmetry, as the most desirable type of social relationship. In certain contexts, one kind may be more valuable than another. We doubt, for example, that a relationship of equivalent symmetry would be highly desirable in a group of soldiers in combat or in an orchestra or a flight crew. Such situations probably call for a highly complementary relationship between officer and enlisted personnel, between conductor and players, and between captain and crew.

It should be obvious that not all these relationships can be sustained for an indefinite period. For example, competitive symmetry ($\uparrow$ $\uparrow$) must be resolved in some manner, or the relationship will be highly uncomfortable. Mike and Jack's competition was apparently so unpleasant that Tim found it necessary to relieve the social tension with his innocuous comment asking for the time. Submissive symmetry ($\downarrow$ $\downarrow$) is also not likely to be sustained for any long period. The participants simply won't get anywhere. No progress will be made. It is a relationship that is temporary at best.

The complementary relationships ($\uparrow$ $\downarrow$) and $\downarrow$ $\uparrow$) and equivalent symmetry ($\rightarrow$ $\rightarrow$) are, on the surface at least, relatively stable. They appear to be those which can characterize a relationship over a longer period of time. Although such a conclusion seems consistent with common sense, it is probably not the case, however.

A "healthy" relationship contains some symptoms of several kinds of relationships—competitive symmetry, submissive symmetry, complementarity, etc.— at various times during the course of the interaction. As we shall see later, the healthiest and most cohesive social relationship is often characterized by periods of conflict. A decision-making group without conflict is not very productive. Equivalent symmetry is by no means the most desirable social relationship in every circumstance if "most desirable" implies the exclusion of other kinds of symmetry or complementarity.

A Note on Terminology

One of the problems in explaining relatively new and complex material in a text-book is that many new terms are required. You have undoubtedly been aware of the use of unfamiliar language in the preceding paragraphs. We do not apologize for it. Jargon is necessary and eminently worthwhile, and learning the language of a discipline is essential for students new to that discipline—it is probably tanta-mount to learning a foreign language.

We are digressing here in order to show you that we are aware of having used jargon. Further, we are aware that you may be experiencing difficulty in learning this new vocabulary, and even of the possibility that you may resent it. We can assure you that we are not coining new words for the purpose of making simple material more difficult. Rather, the discussion includes concepts that cannot be expressed, or can be expressed only with difficulty and with undue ambiguity, in everyday or familiar terms. New terminology (such as "symmetry," "complemen-tarity," and "schismogenesis") will occur again in later chapters without the ex-planations that have been presented in the preceding pages. We have included Ap-pendix 1 as a reference to jargon; it gives explicit definitions of terms as they are used in this book. Develop the habit of referring to Appendix 1 (the glossary) as you continue to use this book.

GROUP INFORMATION PROCESSING AND STRUCTURATION

We know a fair amount about how humans develop individually. We know, for example, that each individual selects and interprets information from the vast quan-tity of data available in the environment. But some aspects of information process-ing are unique to the group—that is, to the social process (or social system) of group decision making. Group members control their own behavior, within the constraints of other forces. Groups must work within an environment, deal with internal group rules and structures, and accommodate their members' behavior.

While there are many theories of individual cognitive processing, there are relatively few theories of group social processing. Poole, Siebold, and McPhee (1986) have been working out a theory called group *structuration*. This theory is concerned with how groups develop by making use of certain rules and resources. It recognizes that groups are always in the process of changing and processing information and that every act of communication influences the group in some way and thus affects its decision-making process. These influences might be trivial at times, but they are significant at other times. For example, a significant problem frequently encoun-tered by groups is how to deal with inconsistent information. A jury, for instance, must decide which witness to believe when the plaintiff's and defendant's witnesses contradict one another's testimony; even while individual jurors might have a way to resolve the apparent contradictions, the group as a whole must process all the input.

The structurational theory of how groups process and structure information begins by assuming that the decision-making processes in groups are primarily patterns of interaction and relationships (an assumption that we make throughout this book). The theory then examines how group members use rules and resources. *Rules* are statements about how things ought to be done, such as about how to behave in the group, what the group expects, and what certain terminology means; the rules guide and explain the communicative behaviors of the group members (e.g., if one of the group's rules is to behave politely, the members will communicate accordingly). *Resources* are materials and attributes that the group can use, such as special knowledge, money, status, equipment, and relationships. The group members use the rules and resources as their "tools" of interaction, and each group is unique in that it develops its own rules and resources.

In addition to being guided by its rules and resources, each group is also influenced by its external environment. For example, if a group is assigned a task but is not given enough time or information, it will not be able to structure and process information. Earlier in this chapter we examined some principles of group systems, such as structure, function, and evolution; we also described groups as open systems characterized by feedback processes. As a group evolves over time, it structures itself. In other words, the group employs the rules and resources of interaction that account for its behavior. Each group has its own ways of handling information and using rules and resources, but all groups are also influenced by things they cannot control. Group *structure* is the result of the tension between internal decisions and external constraints.

Let's consider briefly how groups might structure themselves in such a way as to make nonrational decisions. Groups must interpret and utilize a lot of information, and in doing so they make many judgments. Often these judgments are made on nonrational bases; that is, in the language of structuration, groups apply *rules* that lead to nonrational behavior. One rule for group information processing compares a piece of new information with the previously established position of the group. The group's previously established position is a resource; it is something the group uses. One counterproductive rule that groups often employ is that if a new item of information contradicts the group's previously established position, then the new information is rejected out of hand. At such times the members consider the information irrelevant or of inferior quality, whether it is or not. Thus, group members treat the information nonrationally. They reject the information first; then they search for a basis for rejecting it (their previously held position) and use that to rationalize a judgment they have already made.

The importance of timing as a resource is also apparent in the above example. The point at which information is introduced is sometimes more important than the quality of the information itself. If the information is introduced after the group has already established an ideational position, the quality of this information might have little impact on the process of group decision making. The structural process is important, and we will encounter it again in Chapter 8.

NONVERBAL FUNCTIONS AND GROUP INTERACTION

In Chapter 3 we discussed some structural elements of nonverbal communication, showing how spatial arrangements and territoriality influence communication and group behavior. In this section we focus on the functional elements of nonverbal communication. Nonverbal communication is part of a pragmatic approach to communication that emphasizes meaning that is communicated in a context. It is usually very difficult to separate nonverbal communication from verbal behavior; in most communicative situations, body motions and vocal qualities are used in conjunction with language (i.e., nonverbal behavior usually "accompanies" words). If, for example, someone makes a fist, it would be very difficult to attach meaning (at least very specific meaning) to such behavior. But if he makes a fist while saying, "You've just got to listen to me!" then the fist is a body movement that functions to intensify his verbal message. It makes sense only in the context of his language. Nonverbal communication signals listeners about how to interpret a message. We will now discuss the functional nature of nonverbal communication by examining how nonverbal displays signal (1) clarification, (2) control, (3) emotional states, and (4) interpersonal relationships.

Clarification

As you know, *how* something is said can be more important than what is said. This is an overstatement (since you must say something in order to say it in a certain way), but it is true that tone of voice helps us clarify and interpret messages. There are many ways to say a word or utter a sentence. If someone says, "Do we want to meet tomorrow?" and you say, "Yes," the "yes" can be said in many ways. It can signal excitement and enthusiasm about meeting again so soon, or you can say it in such a way as to communicate that you are not happy about meeting.

People tend to believe vocal cues and body movement whenever these contradict verbal messages, because they think that nonverbal qualities are more difficult to hide. A group member can look you right in the eye and say whatever she wants. But if her body or voice contradicts what she says you will tend not to believe her words.

Most message clarification is accomplished by vocal qualities, and while it is impossible to be precise about how a group member is using his or her voice, there are some typical patterns of nonverbal communication. Generally, increased loudness is a signal of anger, hostility, or alarm; when accompanied by waving arms or violent body movements, loudness is a pretty good sign that someone is angry. Softening the voice conveys feelings of sympathy, powerlessness, and grief. Pitch is another important vocal feature. A high-pitched voice usually indicates alarm, anxiety, and fear; a low-pitched voice typically indicates emphasis on a certain point the speaker is making. Gestures are also used to clarify and add meaning to messages. Comedians raise their eyebrows or move their bodies in certain ways to emphasize suggestive or humorous remarks. Members of a group who are trying to emphasize what they say will use their arms, head, shoulders, and torso to add meaning to their words.

Control

Some people can exert considerable control without being obvious about it. And others are simply very effective and persuasive people either individually or in a group. Both types of people are very good at using nonverbal control signals. Certain nonverbal cues are positively reinforcing for other group members. In other words, when a member of the group is talking and accompanying his communication with smiles, nods, eye contact, gestures, facial expressions, body leans, etc., these not only help clarify his meaning but are also reinforcing to the listeners. And positive reinforcement is a fundamental way to control others. The converse is also true. Negative reinforcement will diminish the likelihood of certain behaviors. So if someone yells, threatens, reduces eye contact, and uses cold vocal cues, these are not reinforcing and can also signal attempts to control the communicative behavior of other group members.

Consider the example of someone in the group who talks too much. What are some ways you can use to control the person's voluminous verbal output? Sure, you can tell the person to "shut up" (i.e., resort to direct verbal confrontation), but most of us are uncomfortable with such techniques and prefer to communicate in a more polite manner. There are ways to accomplish this. You can deny the person the customary eye contact by shifting your gaze in another direction and by establishing eye contact for a prolonged period with another group member. This can be accompanied by turning your body away from the person and focusing your attention elsewhere. Neutral facial gestures and cold vocal cues will also negatively reinforce the talkative group member. In this way you can withhold the signals of approval that a communicator generally needs. On the other hand, you may want to encourage a group member who is presenting valuable information. Encouraging the person with head nods, eye contact, and approving vocal cues will reinforce a speaker and prompt him or her to continue talking.

Many group members also signal dominance and status in the group as a way to exert control. Dress is an important signal of power. People in organizations wear suits and ties or expensive women's clothing to communicate that they are to be taken seriously.

Body and vocal cues are the most typical signals of control when a group member must state his or her ideas in a credible manner. The following summarizes some of the techniques for exerting control in this manner:

1. Present yourself physically with a solid presence of steady eyes, calm hands, and a comfortable body position. Try to look like you belong where you are.
2. Be animated when necessary, but do not overdo it. If you feel passionately about a point you are making, communicate your ideas with force and confidence; however, you will lose your impact if you communicate this way too often.
3. Speak in a low or hushed voice to make a sensitive or emotional point.

4. Learn to speak fluently. This increases your credibility with listeners.
5. Use an authoritative tone. Speak slightly more loudly and rapidly than you might normally. Vary your intonation so that you emphasize points you want to make and provide some tonal variability; this helps you maintain your listeners' attention.
6. Use your voice and body to signal confidence and authority. Cues that communicate liking and approval are also effective control devices, for listeners are influenced by people they like.

Emotional States

Nonverbal behaviors are key indicators of emotional states and feelings. Again, the most significant cues are vocal cues and body movements, but the area of the face is the most important sector of the body for communicating emotion. We use the face to signal anger, disgust, fear, pleasantness, happiness, surprise, anger, and boredom. Different parts of the face display different emotions, and group members can learn to control these expressions. Cultures vary with respect to emotional expressions, but of all the areas of nonverbal communication the face is probably the most conventional in any given culture. There are relatively standard ways of signaling fear, interest, pain, surprise, and disgust. We express interest with eyebrows that move downward and eyes that have an intentional focus. Enjoyment is manifested by wide eyes and broad smiles. Surprise or startlement sends the eyebrows upward, and our eyes blink as if they are trying to focus. Anguish and distress make our mouths turn down and eyebrows arch. Fear causes our eyes to fix in a frozen position, the body trembles, the face turns pale, we sweat, and our hair bristles. The face is a source of emotional leakage. That is, even when we are trying not to express emotions, certain feelings leak out of the face. The eyes, mouth, and forehead portray people's responses and inner feelings. Even when people are trying to control their emotions, their faces often give them away.

The second most predominant emotional channel is the voice. Anger is most easily identified by the tone of voice alone, but people have a little more trouble identifying other emotions from the voice. They often confuse such emotions as fear, sadness, and nervousness. That is why it is important to become sensitive to a variety of nonverbal channels; group members will use their voice in conjunction with facial expressions, body movements, and other microcues. Individuals vary in their ability to interpret vocal cues, and this ability is directly related to one's amount of experience. Individuals with more group experience simply do better at interpreting nonverbal cues in the group.

Interpersonal Relationships

Group members use many channels of nonverbal communication to signal their attitudes about interpersonal relationships. In a broad sense, relational messages involve anything that has to do with how two or more people regard each other, themselves, and their relationship. Interpersonal attraction and liking are a part of any group process. People decide that they like or dislike other members of the group, and the relationships they form are crucial to the group's performance.

There are basically four types of information about relationships carried by nonverbal communication. The first is inclusion or exclusion: that is, whether a person is considered to be a part of an interaction or not. The second is confirmation or disconfirmation: whether messages are supportive of others or negative. The third and fourth are control messages and emotional messages, respectively, both of which have been discussed above.

Certainly eye contact functions to orient two people toward one another. Sustained eye contact has always been associated with people who like one another. Eye contact is confirming and inclusive. Group members who make direct and serious eye contact with the rest of the group will communicate to others that they respect them and want to include them in their relationship. And, as we said above, eye contact is a way of communicating emotions and control.

The face and the body are also carriers of relational messages. Smiling while leaning toward other group members is a pretty clear sign of empathy and concern. People who like each other usually nod their heads as the others speak, lean toward them, maintain similar postures, and generally orient their bodies toward the others. People who like each other mirror each other's nonverbal behavior. Some studies have shown that doctors and nurses achieve the most rapport with their patients when their bodies mirror their patients' expressions and gestures (Mansfield, 1973). Next time you are in a group, see if those group members who have good interpersonal relationships fall into the same postures.

SUMMARY

Communication, in terms of pragmatic functioning, is viewed as a pattern of behaviors in which the acts of each communicator constrain and are constrained by the pattern created by his or her own and others' behaviors. All people who engage in communication develop to some degree an interdependent relationship with one another, a relationship that embodies both the structural and actional (functional) attributes of a process. This interdependent relationship is the process of communication.

Viewed as sequences of actions, communication is unavoidable in the same sense that one cannot *not* behave. In this way, all communication is behavior, and the understanding of communication focuses on the social system—the connectedness of actions performed by individual group members in an ongoing, turn-taking sequence. Furthermore, every communicative action contains both a content dimension (information) and a relationship dimension (how the information is to be interpreted), analogous to the interdependence of the task and social dimensions of a group process. Thus, communication and the group process are defined similarly and may be said to constitute a single process.

The ongoing stream of communicative behaviors can be understood by analyzing each action as being of a certain type of function performed. Every communicative act can then be analyzed within a category of communicative functions. All the categories for analysis thus constitute a list of functions that can be performed by communication. To understand the ongoing process of communication, one must focus on the connectedness of those categorized actions. Acts are thus punctuated (organized, or grouped) into recognizable sequences of interacts or double interacts on the basis of their familiarity, or recognizability. And certain sequences become recognizable as interacts or double interacts on the basis of their frequency of occurrence during the history of past interaction.

The perspective on groups derives from systems theory, in which groups are characterized as whole entities that have structural, functional, and evolutionary processes. These systems are open in that they have a free exchange of information with the environment and can regulate themselves in fundamental ways. Group systems employ feedback sequences to regulate and control the group process. And members of a social system process information and structure themselves in ways that are different from those used in the information processing performed by an isolated individual.

Nonverbal communication is also a part of pragmatic group functioning. Group members use the various channels of nonverbal communication (e.g., face, voice, and body movements) to signal communicative functions. The nonverbal channels function predominantly to indicate message clarification, control, emotional states, and interpersonal relationships.

CHAPTER 5

Observing and Analyzing Small Group Communication

It should be clear by now that human communication is a very complex phenomenon. Perhaps because of this complexity, scholars from Aristotle's time to the present have been interested in studying human communication, but its subtleties and difficulties continue to thwart every attempt to understand it completely. It is extraordinarily difficult to analyze and describe.

A major obstacle to understanding human communication is the tendency to think of it as someone doing something to someone else. This is a conveyor-belt concept of communication. It assumes that messages travel along channels from senders to receivers and that communication thus exists in physical space and has material components (see Fisher, 1978, pp. 98–134). Accordingly, people apply the language of spatial properties to communication. They speak, for example, of "upward" and "downward" communication, of relationships that are "close" or "far apart," and of communication "barriers" and "breakdowns" (as discussed in Chapter 3). A "breakdown" in communication implies that something is wrong with the sender or receiver, and a "barrier" to communication implies that something has deflected a message from its path—which assumes that a message has material components and is supposed to travel unimpeded in a straight line from one person to another. This concept of directional linearity leads to the assumption that the most important goal of any message or speaker is to *affect* a listener.

The structure of our English language (subject-verb-object) encourages this view of human communication. Our most basic sentences, such as "The child hit the ball," suggest that someone (the child) is performing some action (hitting) on some object (the ball), or in general that the action is moving from one object to another. Thus, we often describe communication as one person "persuading" another, or we say that a speaker "informs," "entertains," "dominates," or "leads" the listener. We talk about communication as a transitive action in which A leads to B, which in turn leads to C. This view of communication is at odds with our view of communication as a process—an interdependent relationship developed between communicating people who willingly engage in a system of interstructured behaviors.

Linear ex.

Much communication research (and social science research in general) is conducted from a linear perspective. That is, the logic of communication experiments is formulated to establish causal relationships, such as how message A, traveling through channel B, has effect X on condition C. The experimental methods used are attempts to control environmental factors in order to note the influence of one variable on another (Bowers and Courtright, 1984, pp. 29–32). For example, researchers such as Hirokawa (1982, 1983a, 1983b) and Gouran (1983), who have been studying the influence of communication on decision quality in groups, pose their research questions in experimental language. They identify a communication variable A (which might represent the degree of high-quality communication, the amount of communication, or the inferences from communication), establish a research condition in which this variable is activated, and then note its effect X on some issue C in the group, where C might represent the quality of the group's decision. Although these procedures have led to many valuable and insightful conclusions about communication (see, for example, Hirokawa and Poole, 1986); they, are not consistent with the communication process as we have defined it.

However, the following section overviews some observational methods which are more consistent with our assumptions about communication and group interaction and which are better-suited to observing communicative behavior in small groups. This overview serves as a preliminary step toward understanding why the method of interaction analysis, discussed later in this chapter, is probably a superior method for observing communication in small groups as an interactive process. The procedures discussed in this chapter form the foundation for the model of decision emergence presented in Chapters 6 and 7. A specific interaction-analysis system is included in this chapter as an example of how the system may be applied to the observation and analysis of communication in ongoing decision-making groups. A second interaction analysis system is also presented.

COMMON OBSERVATIONAL METHODS

There are many different methods used to observe small group communication. Nearly every method employed in the broad spectrum of social and behavioral sciences has, at one time or another, been applied to group communication. This section reviews only a few of these methods and does not describe any single method comprehensively. (See Bowers and Courtright, 1984, pp. 91–104.) It should soon be obvious that these methods, widely used and certainly valuable for certain purposes, provide only a limited insight into communication and the group process, which naturally is our primary interest.

Self-Reports

To discover what people think or feel, undoubtedly the most simple method (and one that is thus often overlooked, is to ask them. The Gallup polls of public opinion, along with the Nielsen ratings of television programs, reflect specifically this method of social observation. Members of small groups often complete self-reports in the form of oral interviews or written questionnaires. The diary is another self-report measure. Members of classroom groups are often asked to record in such diaries their impressions and reactions immediately following each group meeting. Usually the diary does not require specific answers to specific questions, but asks only what the member thinks has happened to the group and to his or her own role in that group during that specific meeting.

Members' diaries are valuable as an observational method in that people frequently record in their diaries those feelings and thoughts which they might not wish to express during interaction with fellow group members. People are generally more willing to confide in the impersonal diary those thoughts which might otherwise escape observation. They tend to be much more frank in their diaries than in actual communication with other people, particularly in a newly formed group. Self-reports thus provide important additional information to the observer of group interaction. This information is particularly valuable in order to gain insight into the group's social dimension.

Self-report measures are typically paper-and-pencil tests in which an individual is asked to respond to a series of questions or statements. These questions or statements have been designed to identify attitudes or traits, the relatively enduring characteristics that describe a person or a situation. You might believe, for example, that a friend of yours is shy. But if you or a communication researcher designs a series of questions that ask people about how they feel in certain social situations, and these questions are an attempt to measure shyness, then you have used a self-report measure to establish that someone is shy. The measures can take on numerical values that make it possible to identify people as "very shy," "very outgoing," or somewhere in the middle. McCroskey's (1977) measure of "communication apprehension," is related to shyness and has received a great deal of attention. It measures an individual's fear or anxiety about communication by asking the person the extent to which he or she agrees with such statements as "I get nervous when speaking in front of groups." In this way McCroskey has been able to establish an individual's self-report of communication apprehension. And researchers have demonstrated that shyness, or fear of communicating, has negative effects on a group (McKinney, 1982). There are many self-report measures that attempt to measure individual traits such as self-esteem, introversion, dogmatism, authoritarianism, and recently recognized traits such as interaction involvement (Cegala et al., 1982).

Despite the obvious value of the self-reporting method of observing small groups, there are problems inherent in the method itself. In many respects, the least knowledgeable source of information about any specific person is that very person. We are often unaware of how we behave, what we do, and particularly what we are thinking or feeling. Many behaviors are performed from habit, or at least without willful concentration. If it is true that people act in accordance with behavioral "rules" even though they need not be aware of those rules, then people are not necessarily aware of what they do or why they do it.

It is also extremely difficult to put thoughts and feelings into words. We just don't have the appropriate language or ability to express a feeling. Most of us find it difficult even to put our sensations into words. Try, for example, to describe the taste of an avocado or an artichoke to someone who has never tasted one. Describe the smell of some exotic cologne or perfume to someone who has never experienced that aroma.

Furthermore, self-reports often distort things. All of us have naturally developed defense mechanisms that serve to protect our ego, our personality. When the truth is harmful to our self-image or when reporting reality would embarrass us, we typically distort our perception of our true feelings, behaviors, or motives. Perceptual distortion is not necessarily conscious prevarication. In fact, we often believe the distortion to be the truth and are not even aware of having distorted anything. Under any circumstances, self-reports from group members are to be suspect. Relying on such an unreliable method as the principal means for observing group communication can easily lead to inaccurate, as well as incomplete, information. The members' degree of involvement in their group and their group task may also stimulate distorted self-reports. The overly involved member tends to idealize the group and to evaluate his or her behavior differently than it probably merits. Conversely, the member with an extremely low level of commitment to the group tends to judge it as less effective than it is.

Finally, self-reports should be suspect because they inherently rely on the individual's memory. The human memory is quite fallible, with incomplete and distorted information typically present. You may be familiar with the classroom exercise in which one person tells a story to a second person, who in turns relays that message to a third person, who tells it to a fourth person, and so forth. After the second or third transmission, the story bears little resemblance to its original form.

Rating Scales

Rating scales are one solution to the problems inherent in self-reports, for rating scales ask an objective observer to evaluate the behavior of someone else. The rater is supposed to be more objective and less ego-involved in the evaluation. Teachers are using a form of rating scale when they test students; a student answers questions on a test, and the teacher assigns an evaluation.

In addition to their objectivity, another advantage of rating scales is that they are less disruptive of the actual communication process. If a researcher wanted to keep a running record of a group's progress toward a decision, it would be very obtrusive to stop the group every few minutes or so, ask the members to fill out self-report forms, and then tell them to continue. Rather, a rater could sit off to the side and make observations without bothering the natural development of the group.

A third advantage of rating scales is that they let the researcher control the definition of the construct. A construct is a concept that has been created specifically for a scientific purpose. It is part of a theory and usually measurable. If a researcher asks an individual to report on his or her "friendliness" or "fear of communicating," the result will be a subjective definition of the construct, which in some cases is desirable (but subject to the biases discussed above). But a rater who is evaluating the communication of others can be trained to observe things in a particular way, ignoring certain behaviors and paying particular attention to others. A researcher will provide a rater with a very specific and theoretically rigorous definition of a construct such as "fear of communicating." In this way the researcher knows that all behaviors are being evaluated the same way, according to a consistent set of principles.

A good example of a rating scale is The SYMLOG Adjective Rating Form (Figure 5-1) developed by Bales and Cohen (1979) for their work in evaluating and observing group behavior. Bales and his associates explain interpersonal behavior in groups by referring to three basic dimensions:

1. *Dominant versus submissive,* or what is called upward (U) versus downward (D).
2. *Friendly versus unfriendly,* or whether a person is positive (P) or negative (N).
3. *Instrumentally controlled versus emotionally controlled,* or what is called forward (F) versus backward (B).

An observer uses the rating scale in Figure 5-1 to rate individuals on the dimensions of interpersonal behavior.

As a result of using these rating scales, Bales can create what are called *directional profiles.* These are descriptions of how the group members are communicating (verbally and nonverbally) according to Bales's principles of interpersonal behavior and the three dimensions. For example, a group member named Tom might have a profile that characterizes him as upward (U). This means that his communicative behavior in the group has been described as dominant (upward); for instance, he takes the initiative in speaking, speaks loudly and firmly, and addresses the group rather than individuals. Nonverbal behaviors are also rated; if Tom were dominant, he would sit straight, keep alert and active, and move confidently. As Figure 5.1 shows, Bales's directional profiles account for multiple traits; for example, Tom might be both upward and friendly (UP), which means that in addition to his dominant behaviors he would be positive, such as talking in a friendly way and initiating relationships.

Group Outcomes

Perhaps the method most commonly used for observing group decision making is measuring the outcome of group discussion—the quantity or quality of decisions reached by the group members. This procedure typically involves determining the attributes of the group as it begins its task efforts and observing the results that accrue from the members' efforts, allegedly as a result of the particular combination of attributes. For example, a five-man group and a five-woman group may be given the same decision-making task. The decisions reached by these two groups are then observed and compared. Any difference between the decisions reached by the two groups is then attributed to their predominant structural characteristic of difference—in this case, sex.

Concentrating on the outcome from group discussion has serious shortcomings. For example, the quantity of decisions that a group makes is often irrelevant.

Your Name_____Group_____

Name of person described_____Circle the best choice for each item:

		(0)	(1)	(2)	(3)	(4)
U	active, dominant, talks a lot	never	rarely	sometimes	often	always
UP	extroverted, outgoing, positive	never	rarely	sometimes	often	always
UPF	a purposeful democratic task leader	never	rarely	sometimes	often	always
UF	an assertive business-like manager	never	rarely	sometimes	often	always
UNF	authoritarian, controlling, disapproving	never	rarely	sometimes	often	always
UN	domineering, tough-minded, powerful	never	rarely	sometimes	often	always
UNB	provocative, egocentric, shows off	never	rarely	sometimes	often	always
UB	jokes around, expressive, dramatic	never	rarely	sometimes	often	always
UPB	entertaining, sociable, smiling, warm	never	rarely	sometimes	often	always
P	friendly, equalitarian	never	rarely	sometimes	often	always
PF	works cooperatively with others	never	rarely	sometimes	often	always
F	analytical, task-oriented, problem solving	never	rarely	sometimes	often	always
NF	legalistic, has to be right	never	rarely	sometimes	often	always
N	unfriendly, negativistic	never	rarely	sometimes	often	always
NB	irritable, cynical, won't cooperate	never	rarely	sometimes	often	always
B	shows feelings and emotions	never	rarely	sometimes	often	always
PB	affectionate, likeable, fun to be with	never	rarely	sometimes	often	always
DP	looks up to others, appreciative, trustful	never	rarely	sometimes	often	always
DPF	gentle, willing to accept responsibility	never	rarely	sometimes	often	always
DF	obedient, works submissively	never	rarely	sometimes	often	always
DNF	self-punishing, works too hard	never	rarely	sometimes	often	always
DN	depressed, sad, resentful, rejecting	never	rarely	sometimes	often	always
DNB	alienated, quits, withdraws	never	rarely	sometimes	often	always
DB	afraid to try, doubts own ability	never	rarely	sometimes	often	always
DPB	quietly happy just to be with others	never	rarely	sometimes	often	always
D	passive, introverted, says little	never	rarely	sometimes	often	always

Figure 5-1 The SYMLOG Adjective Rating Form. (Bales and Cohen 1979).

123

Often a group has only one decision to make, such as "guilty" or "not guilty." But the quality of decisions is also difficult to measure when no objective method outside the group interaction is available to validate the group decision. When a group decision-making task is involved, there is no externally valid decision; the sole criterion of quality is the extent to which the decision achieves group consensus. How, then, can the quality of the outcome of a group decision-making task be reliably measured? No adequate answer to this question is currently available.

Because of the difficulty involved in measuring the quality of group decisions, observers of group decision making often observe groups performing tasks more suited to individual decision making (Hirokawa, 1983a). Such tasks have a single "best" or "correct" answer, and their quality is objectively evident. But groups performing tasks intended for expert individuals are doing little more than playing games. Such tasks severely restrict the group process and encourage expert individual members to dominate other group members. At the very least, no advantage is gained from observing groups that perform tasks unsuitable to the social context. But such observations unfortunately occur routinely.

Observing the group from the perspective of its outputs also assumes that structural conditions at the time of group formation determine what outcomes the group will eventually achieve. That is, a structural characteristic (for example, all males) or combination of structural characteristics causes the group to arrive at its decisions. Such an assumption denies the inherent interdependence of the members, their behaviors, the group dimensions, and so forth—interdependent relationships inherent in the nature of a process. In fact, the assumption that group structure determines group action is patently impossible in an open system, which is the perspective of small groups employed throughout this book.

Finally, observing only the group's outcomes is highly incomplete. At best, such an observational method answers only questions of *why* and *whether* group members achieve their outcomes. But it ignores the more important question of *how* groups achieve consensus. And only answers to the latter question can provide any insight into how we might increase the potential effectiveness of group decision making.

In summary, the three general types of observational methods used to analyze and describe small groups are generally unsatisfactory for our purposes. Certainly each of these methods provides highly valuable information about small groups, but that information is of a highly specialized and restricted scope. As far as communication and the group process are concerned, these observational modes are only indirectly useful and only partially relevant.

First and foremost, all three methods—self-reports, rating scales, and group outcomes—ignore the interdependent structural and actional aspects of any process. Each method is capable of observing the group at only a single instant in time and can therefore discover something about the group's structure at that time only. If the group is observed several times by using one of these methods, the observer can discover aspects of group structure as they exist at several different points in time. Comparing each observation with the others allows the observer to determine whether the group experienced any changes in its structure from one point in time to another. But how those changes occurred—the process of structural change—escapes observation. If we are committed to the perspective of communication and the group process, as we are, these methods cannot be considered satisfactory for our purposes.

All three types of observational methods discussed above also ignore the actual communicative behaviors of group members in preference to observing indirectly the internalized feelings of the members. The methods seek to discover what the members or raters feel about something rather than to observe how group members communicate. That is, the methods ask the group member to become introspective about his or her experiences, but not one of the methods strives to discover what those experiences have actually been. The members' communicative behaviors escape the observer's eye as the observations emphasize the effects of those behaviors. The viewpoint of this book stipulates that the interstructured behaviors of members precipitate the effects, or outcomes, and are therefore the most important element of all small groups to be observed.

Finally, the principle of interdependence employed by these methods is radically different from the principle as it has been discussed in preceding chapters of this book. Earlier chapters have consistently viewed interdependence as a relationship greater than the sum of its components, in which every component affects and is mutually affected by all other components. The observational methods discussed above, however, seek to discover interpersonal relationships solely from the viewpoint of an individual member. Thus, the observer discovers what one group member feels or perhaps does vis-à-vis another member but forsakes the interdependent relationship that structures the behaviors of the two members and transcends the individual viewpoint of either. Because these methods focus on a single component (or characteristic) of a group, they deny the principle of interdependence and wholeness—which requires that the observational viewpoint be the gestalt of the entire group taken as a whole, single entity. Self-reports, rating scales, and group outcomes are indeed valuable methods for observing selected structural aspects of decision-making groups. But when we look at these fundamental observational methods from the viewpoint of communication and the group process, we find that each of the three methods is too restricted in its scope and has too many inherent limitations to be consistent with our perspective on groups.

OBSERVING COMMUNICATIVE BEHAVIOR

Obviously, any method of group observation satisfactory for our purposes must directly observe the communicative behaviors of all group members. Equally obvious is the fact that observing communicative behavior is extraordinarily difficult. There are no yardsticks or microscopes with which to observe a communicative act. Communicative acts, first of all, are not physical objects that exist principally in space, such as a molecule of water. Rather, a communicative act exists only in the dimension of time. It is fleeting and transient. It ceases to exist immediately and is not permanently available for observation. And any relatively permanent record of communicative behavior, such as film or videotape, is useful but still incomplete.

Of course, not all human behavior is necessarily communicative. Although any behavior may be communicative in a given situation, some behaviors performed during group interaction are not relevant in that they do not significantly affect the group process of interaction. Thus, any observation of communicative acts must judge which behaviors are significant or relevant and which are not. No concrete guidelines are available to enable an observer to make such judgments with unquestioned validity and reliability. And authorities in communication even disagree on what communication is.

Observing all the communicative behaviors, or even just the verbal behaviors, of group members during group interaction requires that an observer be present in one form or another throughout the entire period of group interaction. The observation, of course, may not require the physical presence of an observing person. But some observational device, such as a camera or a tape recorder, must be present in order to provide a semipermanent record of the group's interaction. The question inevitably arises as to whether the presence of an observer or observational device significantly affects the behavior of group members during their interaction. That is, do members of a group behave differently because they are aware that they are being watched?

If you are a member of a group and someone is watching you with clipboard in hand, you will certainly feel some effects of that observer. And the more obtrusive the observations, the more your behavior will be affected. If, for example, an observer wanted to monitor your behavior during group interaction by wiring you to elaborate machinery and putting you in a room with all sorts of equipment and devices, you can be pretty sure that your behavior would not be very natural. On the other hand, a hidden and unobtrusive piece of equipment or an observer quietly taking notes would not dramatically disrupt group interaction. Indeed, we have witnessed classroom groups whose members concluded a meeting and left the room without turning off the tape recorder. They had simply forgotten it was there. And we also have numerous examples of classroom groups whose use of language certainly indicates that the members were not inhibited. Some authors (such as Barker and Wright, 1955) have argued that the effects of observers on group behavior are most pronounced during a brief period at the beginning of the group's development and then diminish over time.

Karl Weick, a noted psychologist and expert on observational methods, writes that the goal of an observer is "to be objective in close" (Weick, 1985, p. 567). No observer is purely objective and distanced from a group, but there are strategies and procedures for acquiring data in a useful and appropriate manner. The trained observer knows how to standardize the act of observing so that not only his procedures are understandable to others but also their impact on the subject(s) of the observation. The goal of an observer and the act of systematic observation is to organize, amplify, and impose meaning on social phenomenon so that all observers gloss or reinterpret what they observe (Weick, 1981). Suppose that, as an observer, you encounter the following example of interaction:

Tom: Our marketing trend data indicate that the future looks good for VCR sales. We anticipate another 15 percent penetration due mainly to improvements in the lower income markets.

Sue: Actually, I think the market is saturated and sales will be sluggish.

Tom: Where is the evidence of that?

Sue: Well, I don't have hard evidence, but it just seems like VCRs are so affordable now that everyone who is going to buy one has already done so.

Your goal in analyzing this communication would be to translate the natural "talk" into categories or concepts that specify the functions (or purpose) of the communicative behaviors. You might "reinterpret" the above interaction as follows:

Tom provides information in support of a desired action (selling VCRs).
Sue disagrees with Tom.
Tom questions Sue, seeking a justification for her statement.
Sue provides a subjective rationale justifying her previous statement.

The actual participants in communication do not use the above behavior-descriptive language to describe their talk. It is the observer who approaches the group armed with particular ways to interpret and understand the functioning of the group. The above interaction between Tom and Sue might be used to identify disagreement or conflict in the group, or it could mean that Tom is emerging as a dominant member of the group. In either case we can probably safely assume that the observer will not seriously distract group members and should be in a position to draw useful conclusions about the group. Below we will examine the nature and performance of interaction analysis in more detail.

INTERACTION ANALYSIS

The method of observation most pertinent to communication and the group process is interaction analysis. *Analysis* typically implies breaking down some whole into its component parts. For example, an analysis of the content of pure water reveals the presence of two units of hydrogen and one unit of oxygen. In this example of analysis, the content of water is analyzed into its compositional elements. The principle is the same for the first step in an analysis of interaction—reducing the whole of interaction into its compositional factors and the relative quantity of each.

"Now is the time for all good men to come to the aid of their party" is a familiar sentence used for a variety of purposes. The sentence may also be submitted to various systems of content analysis. One system might analyze the sentence into categories of "parts of speech" and use "words" as the units to be measured or counted. Such an analysis would reveal sixteen words analyzed as four nouns, two verbs, four adjectives, one pronoun, one adverb, and four prepositions.

Often this sentence is used to test the functional operation of a typewriter in much the same way that the prospective automobile buyer kicks the tires of an automobile. But a second content analysis of that same sentence using letters of the alphabet as units of measurement as well as analytical categories reveals that eight letters are not included in that sentence. Thus, the typewriter inspector would fail to observe the function of eight different keys. A better sentence used for the purpose of testing typewriters would be, "The quick brown fox jumps over the lazy dog's back." A similar content analysis of this latter sentence reveals at least one instance of every letter of the alphabet. (Go ahead and check it.)

Interaction analysis, then, is a general method for analyzing the content of communicative behaviors by breaking down the whole of interaction into its component acts. Experts in many fields of study have employed numerous varieties and methods of interaction analysis, but the remainder of this section offers only a few of those varieties. This section will further emphasize one particular method of interaction analysis exemplified by two specific systems. For a more complete description of the various methods of content analysis, many books are available that describe such procedures in much greater detail. One source that focuses on various methods of content analysis and systematic observation is Weick (1985).

Characteristics of Interaction Analysis

Interaction analysis is *long-term systematic observation*. This means that a trained observer uses a measuring instrument to select and record the communicative behaviors that are occurring within a situation. *Long term* implies prolonged and continuous observation; the emphasis is on observing a phenomenon over time in order to observe patterns and instances of connectedness. *Systematic* inquiry means that an observer works out a method of operation and adheres to it; the method of operation is theoretically and empirically sound. And *observation* is "standardized looking." When social scientists observe, they are looking for particular things in particular ways. If a communication researcher is interested in "verbal aggressiveness," for example, she will begin with a definition of the phenomenon or with some way to recognize verbal aggressiveness when she sees it. She will be armed with definitions and cues as to when verbal aggressiveness is occurring, and her observations will be controlled by these standards.

Categories   The categories (or pigeonholes) that things are classified into are perhaps the most important characteristic of interaction analysis. If the researcher's definition of a category of content (such as verbal aggressiveness) is weak or inaccurate, then the results of the research will be useless. The categories used for interaction analysis should possess three essential characteristics: When you create categories, they should be exhaustive, mutually exclusive, and sensitive to contexts.

To require that the category system be *exhaustive* means that each and every unit of behavior to be assigned can fit into some category. Some very simple category systems may have only two units: the unit of interest (e.g., "verbal aggressiveness") and a category for all other units (e.g., "not verbally aggressive"). But most category systems have more substantive categories of interest to the researcher. The system of categories is supposed to exhaust the communicative possibilities, at least in the theoretical sense. If a researcher is working with a ten-category system, then all communicative behaviors of interest must be assignable to one of the ten categories. If there are communicative behaviors that cannot be assigned, then either the category system is flawed and missing important data or there are behaviors that are not of interest to the researcher.

The categories in a system must also be *mutually exclusive*. This stipulates that a communicative behavior can fit in one and only one category. In other words, no two categories can overlap. For example, if two of a system's categories were "verbal aggressiveness" and "acts unfriendly," some behavior could be assigned to both categories. If one member of a group turned to another and said, "You never contribute much to the group," this might be both an aggressive statement and an unfriendly act, and this confusion about the function of the act would indicate a problem with the category system. The problem could be solved either by eliminating one of the categories, by refining the category definitions, or by making one category (such as "acts unfriendly") a subdimension of the other category. However, recognizing that interaction is often multifunctional, Hewes (1979) has made a case for violating the rule of mutual exclusivity. (Although Hewes's arguments are too technical for our introductory concerns, he does offer a theoretical and statistical solution to the problem of assigning a behavior to multiple categories.)

Finally, category systems should be *sensitive to contexts*. Contexts are situations; more specifically, contexts are configurations of people and things that give messages important meaning. The meanings of verbal and nonverbal utterances are not fixed; even an innocuous query such as "What is your name?" can be understood as a simple request for information (e.g., a clerk is taking information) or as a solicitous comment (e.g., asking the name of a member of the opposite sex at a party). An interaction analyst should understand the contextual constraints on a group. For instance, a corporate decision-making group is probably different than a group in the public sector, and it is often important that category systems reflect this difference. On the other hand, there may be times when a category system is relatively context-free; that is, acts representing a category are the same in one group as another. Disagreement, for example, might "look" the same in the corporate group as in the public group.

Devising a set of workable categories is not especially difficult, but it does require attention to the principles of reliability and validity. Herbert and Attridge (1975) specify thirty-three criteria for creating category systems that are reliable and valid. A *reliable* system is one that can be applied consistently across observers; that is, it ensures that there will be few judgmental errors and much agreement among observers. A *valid* system is one that is credible and yields true and useful results. Interaction researchers are always concerned with validity, for they must be able to demonstrate that their measurements are accurate. They demonstrate this by providing evidence and support for their reasoning processes (Agar, 1980) and by showing that their conclusions are plausible and can withstand the test of criticism.

Unitizing A second important characteristic of interaction analysis is the unit of measurement—determining what should be counted and placed into a category. There is no standard unit of measurement. A unit should be inclusive enough that the object of interest is available to the researcher, but it should also be of a manageable size. Some researchers have used time intervals as the unit of analysis (Hawes, 1972); they will code every 10 seconds, or 30 seconds, or however long a time metric they choose. Others have identified the "thought unit" as the unit of analysis; every time a speaker finishes a complete thought, it is coded into one of the categories. This may sound like a difficult and potentially confusing unit of analysis, but Crowell and Scheidel (1961) and Bales and Cohen (1979) developed coding systems that were specific and rigorous enough to code thought units successfully. Some researchers interested in decision making (e.g., Fisher, 1970b) have used the "decision proposal" as the unit of analysis; they are interested in tracking the various changes and modifications of decisions, so they code each time a group member modifies a decision category.

But perhaps the most common unit of analysis in communication research has been the act. An *act* is an uninterrupted verbal utterance; it is one stand on the floor; the act begins when a speaker starts talking and ends when he or she finishes. Most communication researchers are interested in functional category systems—systems that capture what people *do* in a communication context. People do such things as "ask questions," "act unfriendly," and "give information." An act can usually be categorized as a single function. The following example is composed of three acts (three stands on the floor) that are categorized into three functions:

ROGER: What is this little venture going to cost? (*Request for information.*)
BILL: Oh, we should be able to pull it off for under a hundred thousand. I mean it depends on loan interest rates and what sort of production schedule we work on. (*Answer.*)
PETE: I don't know, I think this is bad time to be incurring that much debt. (*Statement of opinion.*)

It is true that each of these three acts could be performing more functions than the ones indicated, but if our category system is reliable and valid, and if our theory about what we are observing is sensible, then it does not matter if these acts are multifunctional, because they are suitable for our purposes.

Contingency After developing categories and establishing units of analysis, it is important to turn your attention to *contingent* relations. These are relations concerned with the order of events, or what follows what. The units now become *sequences of units*. The contingency level of interaction analysis is very important because it is here that elements are grouped into recognizable patterns. Without these groupings, it would be impossible to recognize interaction patterns; there would be only a series of acts, one following another with no pattern or meaning. Try to figure out the unpunctuated sentence "ilikebillbutidontcaremuchforron." Our use of spacing, punctuation, and capitalization helps us "pattern" letters in the English language and make interpretation easier. You have no trouble understanding the sentence written this way: "I like Bill, but I don't care much for Ron."

The notion of punctuation applies to communicative acts (see Chapter 4). The goal is to identify the groupings of utterances—the patterns—that recur (or repeat) over time. In the above three-act exchange between Roger, Bill, and Pete, we saw the following pattern of functional communication:

Roger: Request for information
Bill: Answer
Pete: Statement of opinion

Each contingent pair of acts forms an interact. In other words, Roger performs a single act (requesting information), and Bill answers. Their two acts together are connected, or contingent, and form an interaction. Bill's answer then becomes the preceding utterance for Pete, and Bill and Pete also form an interaction. There are two interacts in the example above (Roger-Bill, Bill-Pete). Sequences such as these can go on for hundreds or thousands of utterances.

You might be wondering what use can be made of this type of interaction analysis. The following sections offer numerous examples, and many of the issues discussed in Chapter 6 and others were discovered through interaction analysis. But you can see even with the simple example above what interesting patterns might emerge. If you continued to find the above pattern, it would tell you what roles the various group members were playing. Perhaps Bill is a group expert and information source; Roger might emerge as a clarification and information seeker and be responsible for moving the group in new directions; and if Roger and Bill continued to form the same contingent pattern, it would be apparent that their relationship was responsible for stimulating this type of interaction. Moreover, it is possible to note change over time. Roger and Bill may form this relationship in the early stages of group development but change later in the group's history. Or there may be many "requests for information" during the beginning of the group's deliberations as they work to acquire information and get organized; we might see communication rich in information in the beginning and watch it dissipate later in the process. A consultant working with a group would find any of these findings valuable and would use them to improve the group's effectiveness at decision making.

In short, interaction analysis favors an evolutionary view of process. It is a technique for tracking the functional nature of communication over a group's history and identifying the patterns of interaction that characterize the group. No system of interaction analysis attempts to observe all aspects of human communicative behaviors. Rather, any analysis inherently focuses on those communicative aspects which relate to the categories. Hence, the categories are vitally important to the outcome of the analysis; they have the effect of imposing "reality" on whatever it is you are analyzing. The category system contains the meaning that you are trying to discover. Interaction analysis, unlike many other methods of observing groups, emphasizes what happens during group interaction, how it happens, and how changes occur over a period of time.

The following subsections describe two interaction-analysis systems. The detailed explanations of how these systems were developed and applied will help you understand the methods of interaction analysis and how communication researchers have discovered a number of interesting findings about the process of group decision making.

One System of Interaction Analysis: Decision Making

Since the model of decision emergence discussed in Chapter 6 results from applied interaction analysis, the system that led to discovering that model of group decision making seems appropriate to illustrate how interaction analysis might function. This system is admittedly imperfect, as are all others. It includes only verbal communication and probably places undue emphasis on the task dimension of the group process (see Chapter 4). Despite its imperfections, however, the system provides a general example of how interaction analysis might be utilized to observe group communication.

Central to this system of interaction analysis is the concept of a decision proposal. As a member presents an issue for consideration by other group members, this issue is potentially an item that will achieve group consensus—that is, the issue is a proposed decision being considered by the group members. As each member comments on this proposal, he or she implicitly attempts to influence the group's perception of it. (Naturally, a member need not be aware of attempting to influence the other members.) Thus, each comment "functions" on the proposal in some specific manner. The different functions that a member can perform on a decision proposal through an act of communication constitute the list of categories used in the analysis.

Each member's uninterrupted comment, or act, is considered a unit of communication. If an uninterrupted comment contains an instance of two functions (that is, if a single comment crosses functional categories before it is interrupted by a comment from another member), it is considered two units. During actual observation of groups, nearly all uninterrupted comments are found to contain but a single unit of communication.

These functionally defined units are quite obviously not of uniform length in either number of words or number of seconds. A single person performing a single function on the decision proposal in a single uninterrupted comment is considered to be a single unit of communication regardless of its relative length.

The categories for this system of interaction analysis are as follows (the same as presented in Chapter 4):

1. Interpretation
   - **f**   Favorable toward the decision proposal
   - **u**   Unfavorable toward the decision proposal
   - **ab** Ambiguous toward the decision proposal, containing a bivalued (both favorable and unfavorable) evaluation
   - **an** Ambiguous toward the decision proposal, containing a neutral evaluation
2. Substantiation
   - **f**   Favorable toward the decision proposal
   - **u**   Unfavorable toward the decision proposal
   - **ab** Ambiguous toward the decision proposal, containing a bivalued (both favorable and unfavorable) evaluation
   - **an** Ambiguous toward the decision proposal, containing a neutral evaluation

3. Clarification
4. Modification
5. Agreement
6. Disagreement

Several additional symbols are employed to simplify the analysis of interaction in practice. For example, the symbol O_n is used in addition to one of the categories above; it designates that an act is the one that originates a new decision proposal (identified by a subscript number) by introducing this proposal into the group discussion for the first time. Likewise, the symbol D_n represents an act that reintroduces into group discussion a decision proposal (identified by its original subscript number) that the group members had discussed previously. These two symbols do not represent categories of acts. Rather, they are used in addition to the actual analysis of interaction so that the observer may at all times keep track of which decision proposal is under consideration.

A category designated "procedural," not included in the above list, specifies acts which do not actually discuss a decision proposal and which are not substantive to the process of group decision making. Such acts coded into the "procedural" category rarely occurred during group interaction and were excluded from the final results of interaction analysis.

Although the categories are not difficult to understand, a brief explanation of each is probably necessary. The category of "interpretation" (1) reflects a simple value judgment without evidence, reasons, or explanation offered to support the credibility of that judgment. "Substantiation" (2), on the other hand, refers to an act that does include supporting evidence or reasons to enhance the believeability of the expressed value judgment. Thus, an act of "substantiation" may be considered more argumentative than one of "interpretation."

Both "interpretation" and "substantiation" are subject to further classification in one of four subcategories, or dimensions of the larger category. The "favorable" (f) and "unfavorable" (u) categories should be self-explanatory. The two varieties of "ambiguous" categories may be less clear. The comment "That seems like a good idea, but it has some flaws" is ambiguous because it includes both a favorable and an unfavorable evaluation of the proposal—hence, a bivalued evaluation and an instance of the "ab" category. The comment "That is a very interesting suggestion" is unclear because it evaluates the idea without expressing clear approval or disapproval of the suggestion—hence, a neutral evaluation and an instance of the "an" category. Both comments, of course, reflect interpretation rather than substantiation and also both the general and the specific dimensions of the category—that is, "1 ab" and "1 an," respectively.

The category of "clarification" (3) indicates those acts which function to render an idea pertaining to the decision proposal more readily understandable. No evaluation is evident in such a comment. Rather, the act restates some previous act in more concrete language.

"Modification" (4) signifies an act functioning to amend the decision proposal under consideration by direct means. The section in Chapter 6 that discusses the group process of modifying decisions notes that instances of this category rarely occur during group interaction.

"Agreement" (5) and "disagreement" (6) express support or nonsupport of the immediately preceding act. A typical "5" comment, such as "Yes," "You're right," or "Okay," does not function directly on the decision proposal. But such a comment indirectly affects the members' perception of this proposal by adding weight to the act that precedes the agreement. Whatever the preceding function unit, the "5" unit assumes the functional meaning of that antecedent category and underscores it. If "5" follows a "2f" unit, for example, it reinforces by agreement the substantiation favoring the decision proposal.

If "6," or "disagreement," follows a "2f" act, it expresses disfavor through negatively reinforcing the favorable substantiation. The "6" unit, then, indirectly functions as a negative evaluation of the decision proposal by disfavoring the specific preceding act that favored it. An excerpt from an actual group discussion may serve to clarify how one may apply this system of interaction analysis. The following excerpt is from a management training group (all-male) discussing budget allocations for its hypothetical corporation. Decision proposal 1 might be phrased, "The corporation should seek to discover what its fixed costs will be after the proposed plant expansion has been completed." The first comment in the excerpt below initiates this proposal, and all other comments are directed toward this single proposal. The symbols that appear to the left of each communicative act indicate the classification of each unit according to the categories of the system. When in doubt, refer to the previous listing of the categories and their identifying symbols.

$1an0_1$	*A:* Would we want to spend \$2,000 this first quarter to find out what the cost of our plant expansion is going to be?
3 (asks for)	*D:* The cost of what?
3	*A:* Our fixed expenses. Would we like to know how much they are going to be?
1 u	*B:* No. I'm not really worried about that.
1 u	*D:* No. I'm not concerned about that.
2 f	*A:* But if we are concerned about production and profit, that's a factor. That is a fixed operating cost we are going to have to live with. We should know in advance what it is going to cost us.
6	*B:* No.
2 u	*C:* But knowing it won't influence our decision to expand or not.
2 u	*D:* Why pay \$2,000 to get it if we are going to have to pay it anyway?
2 f	*A:* Until we do it the first time, we've got no idea if this is going to be another \$6,000 or whether it's going to be as high as \$30,000. That might influence us considerably on our long-range goals.
2 u	*B:* We are going to have to expand in spite of that, though.

2 u	*D:* I don't think we are ever going to refuse to expand. So the first time that we do expand, we are going to find out the fixed operating cost.
5	*G:* Yes.
2 u	*D:* By rights, it shouldn't be more. By normal operating procedures, it shouldn't be more than we pay right now. It should be less because our main plant has already been built.
3 (asks for)	*A:* Do you mean less than $6,000?
3 (restates)	*D:* Yes, I do.
2 u	*A:* Well, if it is anything less than $6,000, it would really be silly to spend $2,000 to find it out.
2 u	*D:* By just using common business sense, you have to say it is $6,000 or less. It can't be more unless they have to blast a hillside out of the way to get the addition to the main plant in.
5	*C:* Yes, I think you're right.

The above excerpt should explain by example how this system of interaction analysis may be utilized in actual practice. Note the several comments that ask for clarification. In both cases, the comment immediately following the request provides the clarification. Member *D*'s "Yes, I do" might appear, outside the context of the interaction, to be agreement. But it is really a clarification of his preceding comment in direct response to *A*'s request for clarification of his intended meaning. The other coded acts appear to need no further explanation.

After the group interaction has been analyzed into acts, the interaction is then divided into interacts. Figure 5-2 illustrates the interacts included in the excerpt coded above. The rows of the matrix in this figure are the categories of the interaction analysis system, which include the first (or "antecedent") comment of each interact. The columns across the top of the matrix are the categories of the second (or "subsequent") act of each interact. Thus, each cell in the matrix represents an interact. The first act is the row across, and the second act is the column down.

The nineteen acts appearing in the excerpt above translate into eighteen interacts. The first act, "1 an," is the antecedent of the second act, "3." Together the two acts compose the first interact in the excerpt. The second act, "3" is also the antecedent of the third act in the excerpt, also "3"; together they form the second interact in the excerpt. Thus, a sequence of three acts includes two interacts, and the entire excerpt of nineteen single acts contains a total of eighteen interacts.

Figure 5-2 shows that during even this brief excerpt, a trend develops regarding the group's treatment of decision proposal 1 in its interactive patterns. Note that the only acts expressing favor of the proposal, two "2f" units, are immediately followed by acts that conflict with the favoring function. One of the subsequent acts is outright disagreement, "6", and the other argues the opposing side, "2u." Once the argument started, the other members "piled it on" by positively reinforcing the seven "2u" units with additional "2u" units a total of three times, and twice with agreement, "5."

Subsequent acts

	1f	1u	1ab	1an	2f	2u	2ab	2an	3	4	5	6
1f												
1u		1		1								
1ab												
1an									1			
2f					1							1
2u					1	3			1		2	
2ab												
2an												
3		1			1				2			
4												
5					1							
6					1							

Antecedent acts

Figure 5-2 Interacts contained in interaction analysis of decision proposals.

A table such as that in Figure 5-2 is called a contingency table. Such an analysis provides the basis for analyzing possible phases of group decision making. A single matrix can be used to summarize all the interacts during a specified time period; for example, if the period is 5 minutes, a 60-minute group discussion will require twelve matrices (as illustrated in the figure). Each matrix can then be compared with the next, and any changes in interact patterns can be easily discerned. In this way, phase progressions during group decision making were discovered. In the next chapter we will study in much more detail how phase progressions can be discovered.

Another System of Interaction Analysis: Relational Communication

The concept of "relational" communication was discussed in Chapter 4 and will be encountered again in Chapter 9. The relationship dimension of communication is concerned with the ways in which verbal messages indicate how participants in an interaction "see" one another in relation to themselves. The most common relationship dimension is control, or the manner in which group members use communication to direct and dominate relationships. Chapter 4 also examined the various control modes and definitions of complementarity and symmetry (see pages 108–110). The conclusions about leadership in Chapter 9, and other issues regarding relational communication (e.g., Ellis, 1979), were arrived at using interaction-analysis techniques. The control dimension of relational communication has been operationalized by a category system called REL/COM (Ellis, 1979). The system includes the following five categories:

Dominance (↑ +): An attempt to restrict severely the behavioral options of the
    other
Structuring (↑ −): an attempt to restrict the behavioral options of the other, but
    leaving a variety of options open; an attempt to control the flow of interaction
Equivalence (→): An attempt at mutual identification; an interactional mode in
    which one does not seek to control or submit to control
Deference (↓ −): An expressed willingness to relinquish some behavioral options
    to the other while retaining some choice of options; a "following" behavior in
    which one relinquishes control of the flow of interaction
Submissiveness (↓ +): An expressed willingness to relinquish behavioral options
    to the other while retaining little choice

Each communicative act—one speaker's turn—is assigned to one of the above five categories. And to remain theoretically consistent, each act receives its assignment on the basis of how it relates to the previous act. No utterance is coded in isolation from the sequence of acts, and each speaker's act acquires relational meaning by how it relates to the previous act.

Assume that member *A* makes an assertion. Member *B* challenges that assertion by demanding proof of documentation for that belief. Because *B*'s response is a challenge (an "I dare you" assertion), that demand would be coded as an attempt to control the other's behavioral options—a dominant (↑ +) act. Member *A* may respond to that challenge by providing the information or documentation that was demanded. Relationally, *A*'s response is a confrontation of the challenge and would thus be coded as another dominant (↑ +) act. If *A* fails to respond to the challenge, the action relationally submits to *B*'s control and exhibits relational submissiveness. Failing to respond to a challenge is tantamount to a retreat in the face of the enemy's attack.

The interaction coded earlier into the decision-proposal system can also be coded into the five categories of REL/COM:

A: (not codable; no preceding act)
D: →   (equivalence)
A: →   (equivalence)
B: ↑ −   (structuring)
D: →   (equivalence)
A: ↑ +   (dominance)
B: ↑ −   (structuring)
C: ↑ −   (structuring)
D: ↑ +   (dominance)
A: ↑ +   (dominance)

B: ↑ + (dominance)
D: ↑ − (structuring)
G: ↓ − (deference)
D: ↑ − (structuring)
A: → (equivalence)
D: → (equivalence)
A: ↑ − (structuring)
D: ↑ + (dominance)
C: ↓ + (deference)

   Again, we can create a contingency table (Fgirue 5-3) for the relational communication codes. Figure 5-3 is an example of an interact matrix with each code as an antecedent and each as a subsequent act. If the patterns in Figure 5-3 were to remain consistent over the life of the group, we could assume that competitive symmetry (↑ ↑) was a prevalent pattern and that submissive symmetry (↓ ↓) was not characteristic of the group. An even more interesting analysis would be to create an interact matrix for every relationship in the group. We could then see who was dominant, who was submissive, and what relationships each individual had with the other people in the group. This type of analysis was used to discover the leadership behaviors that are discussed in Chapter 9. For our purposes here, it is sufficient that we understand how interaction analysis works and how it is possible to observe decision making and relationship development in groups. There are, of course, much more sophisticated treatments of this subject matter (e.g., Hawes and Foley, 1976; Fisher, Glover, and Ellis, 1977; Fisher, 1977).

Figure 5-3 Interacts contained in REL/COM analysis.

SUMMARY

It is important that you understand how to observe and analyze groups systematically. We have argued that groups are a system of interdependent communication behaviors, and it is possible to analyze groups in a manner consistent with this perspective, a perspective that preserves the importance of communication as a process. Several methods of observational research have been employed in the past. They include: (1) Self-reports, in which individuals complete paper-and-pencil questionnaires querying them about attitudes and beliefs. (2) Rating scales, which have observers rate or evaluate the behavior of others; these have the advantage of avoiding the biases of self-reports. (3) The measurement of group outcomes, which utilizes a method of manipulating some structural variable in the group and noting its effect on an outcome measure, such as decision quality or member satisfaction. Each of these perspectives is useful, but none emphasizes the observation of communicative behaviors over time.

Interaction analysis was posed as a most effective technique for measuring the group process. This is a method for analyzing group communication by breaking it down into its component parts and classifying these parts. This type of inquiry is systematic and depends on careful preparation of methods. The analyst begins by developing categories (or pigeonholes) to classify messages. Units of analysis are also established. The categories are then placed in contingency tables, where recognizable patterns of communication emerge.

Two examples of interaction analysis were presented. The first was an example of an interaction-analysis system designed to track the various modifications on group decisions; Chapters 6 and 7 continue to elucidate the various ways this system can be used. And the second example demonstrated how relational communication can be operationalized and studied as an interaction process.

CHAPTER 6

The Process of Group Decision Making

The past several decades have witnessed a growing concern over the allegedly clandestine nature of some decision-making groups in our society. The specter of a decision-making group in the proverbial smoke-filled back room is familiar to all of us. More often, the group making vital decisions is quite visible, but entrance into the group is highly restricted. Thus, concern has been concentrated on gaining a voice in the group decisions. For example, the "student power" movement of the 1960s resulted in student representation on most university committees, faculty senates, and even boards of regents. Now that a voice in the decision-making process has been, or is being, secured by previously powerless minorities, the problem might appear to be solved. Unfortunately, nothing could be further from reality.

The sentiment of one newly named student member of a university's governing board aptly described the persistent problem. He stated that he had worked long and hard for student representation on that board, but now that the students' voice could be heard he didn't know what to do about it. The fact is that membership in the decision-making group is necessary but not sufficient for effective decision making. A knowledge and an understanding of the process of group decision making are absolutely essential for effective membership. Hundreds of business organizations seek assistance from professional consultants so that their management personnel can function effectively in decision-making groups. Being a member of a group is simply not enough. An understanding of how groups actually make decisions—the process of group decision making—is necessary for effective participation in group decision making.

The purpose of this chapter is to describe the process that characterizes group decision making. But there is one thing that must be emphasized. There is no simple formula that will ensure good decisions. Groups are complex entities and they belie simple and sure answers. We have two general goals for this chapter. First, we want you to understand the natural and emergent process of group decision making, that is, what groups do when they are left on their own to establish their own patterns and to produce decisions based on true consensus. But secondly we are going to present some standard, or commonly accepted, group procedures. These are designed to help beginning students of group interaction get started. It is important to emphasize that forcing a group to go through a set of standard steps and procedures can often lead to problems. The group can become more concerned with the procedures than with the quality of the decision. Nevertheless, our perspective throughout this book has been one where we try to equip the student with intelligent choices about performing in groups. We present standard prescriptions for group success in that light. We want you to become sensitive to, and aware of, all aspects of what is occurring during group interaction. And while awareness of the group process is no guarantee of group success, it will certainly increase the chances for success.

AN OVERVIEW OF KEY TERMS

Preliminary to reading the ensuing discussion of the group decision-making process, one should have a full understanding of several key terms that will be used extensively in this chapter. All these terms are familiar and prompt immediate definitions. But, in a sense, these terms are jargon. That is, each of them specifies a rather precise meaning, probably narrower than the meaning used in everyday conversation. It is for the sake of precision, then, that the following definitions are included.

The relationship between *decision making* and *problem solving* is not a source of universal agreement. Some view the two terms as virtually synonymous; others draw rather clear distinctions between them. Our concern is with all decision making, which, for our purposes, includes some types of problem solving while excluding others. Recall the earlier distinction between tasks more appropriately performed by individuals and those uniquely adapted to the group process. The basis for that distinction also differentiates between two types of problem solving. One kind of problem possesses a "best" or "correct" solution, which is determined by external and objective means. Such problems may be typified by a mathematical problem for which only one solution is acceptable, by a logic puzzle governed by the invariable rules of induction and deduction, or by a crossword puzzle. Certainly these problem-solving tasks are not within the province of group decision making. They are best handled by a trained individual.

On the other hand, some problems have no solution that is subject to external validation. The solutions to these problems can be discovered only through group acceptance—the willingness of the members to commit themselves to implementing the solution. Thus, the only possible check of the validity of the solution is whether it achieves group consensus. Such problems would include determining how to combat pollution or crime most effectively, questions of penal reform, the rising costs from inflation, and so forth. The value of such solutions may ultimately be determined by how well they work after they have been put into practice. But at the time of their achieving consensus in the group, only validation through group consensus determines their worth.

Some decision-making tasks, of course, are not strictly within the scope of problems to be solved. Juries make decisions on questions of value and unverifiable facts. Voters make decisions on candidates for political office. Such decisional situations do not stem directly from problems that require solving, and they include even such prosaic decisions as what clothing to wear tomorrow, what the theme for homecoming should be, what color to paint the house, and what brand of toothpaste to buy. Certainly decision making includes some types of problem solving and much more.

A *decision*, ultimately the outcome of group interaction, is inevitably a choice made by group members from among alternative proposals available to them. Rarely, if ever, does a group make a single decision in isolation. Although only one decision is sometimes apparent, such as a jury's decision of guilty or not guilty, many preliminary decisions are essential to that final decision and are made by the group on its way to achieving consensus on the final decision. The jury, for example, must decide which witness to believe, which piece of evidence is stronger, whether there is a reasonable doubt, and so forth. Group members, then, focus their attention on various proposals during their interaction and choose, from among those alternative proposals, which ones they will accept or reject. The sum of the accepted proposals constitutes the productivity of the group.

Although the quantity of proposals initiated during group interaction is not a reliable measure of productivity, the fact remains that only those proposals which are initiated during interaction are available for final decision making. It is not yet clear whether more decision proposals yield higher-quality decisions. Results of research efforts aimed at answering this question, particularly those efforts studying brainstorming techniques, are varied and conflicting. Common sense indicates that the quantity of ideas proposed is somehow related to the quality of the decisions achieving consensus, but one must not neglect the factors of social conflict and intermember influence during interaction. As members discuss alternative proposals, they attempt to influence one another, directly and indirectly, to accept or reject a given proposal. The process of reciprocal influence during group interaction is one focus of this chapter.

A group reaches a decision as its members achieve consensus on a proposal. The term *consensus* implies a variety of differing meanings. Some think of consensus as the will of the majority that results from democratic voting procedures. Some believe that unanimous agreement is necessary for consensus. Often consensus implies the absence of a formal vote but implicit agreement not necessarily verbalized by the group members. Obviously a consensus decision is one on which members typically agree, but agreement, while often necessary, is not a sufficient condition for consensus. That is, members may agree with a decision, even unanimously, but may not achieve consensus.

For our purposes, consensus implies not just agreement with the decision reached, but commitment to it. In fact, members may be committed to a decision to the extent that they work to put it into effect without ever fully agreeing with it. Zaleznik and Moment (1964, p. 142) clarify the nature of consensus as commitment:

> Our meaning of consensus lies in the degree of personal commitment the
> members feel toward the group decision after it is reached. This means, for
> example, that even though some members might disagree with the decision

Q: relation of consensus, commi...
consensus
&
agreement

on principle, they will accept it and personally carry out their part. Their emotional commitment to the group is measured by willingness to put the plan decided on into effect, in their own personal behavior.

Simple agreement on a decision proposal, then, does not necessarily guarantee that the decision has achieved group consensus. In fact, group members who submit to pressures or external authority might express agreement without really accepting the proposal itself. In such instances the decision achieves false or superficial consensus: that is, agreement masquerading as consensus. The phenomenon of consensus without real agreement is not extraordinarily rare. For example, unsuccessful candidates for their party's nomination for political office often campaign strongly for the winning candidate. People may disagree on a new law or new tax passed by their elected representatives, but they generally obey those laws and pay those taxes.

The prime requisite for consensus, then, is not agreement with the decision, although agreement is highly common and even typical. The essential ingredient of consensus is the extent of group loyalty shared by members. To the extent that the members are cohesive or have developed groupness, the decisions reached by that group are most likely to achieve consensus as well as agreement. Thus, the rather cohesive group is more likely to be effective as a decision-making body.

The interdependence of the task and socioemotional dimensions of a group is again evident. As Zaleznik and Moment (1964, p. 155) point out, "Although this [consensus] may seem to be a purely task requisite, it is clearly a connecting link between task and social-emotional problems."

Consistent with the emphasis on communication and group process, the concern of this chapter is the *process* of group decision making. That is, this chapter is most concerned with questions of *how*—how groups achieve consensus on decisions over time; how members try to exert influence on one another during various periods of group interaction; how members' communicative behaviors occur in interstructured patterns during interaction. In short, the process perspective emphasizes how members actually interact during discussion of decision proposals and how certain proposals achieve consensus during group interaction; it is a descriptive approach to decision making. But first we will examine a prescriptive approach to decision making.

PRESCRIPTIVE APPROACHES TO DECISION MAKING

A prescriptive approach to decision making is one in which the group adopts a standard set of steps based on theories about how groups *should* make decisions. These are prescriptions for good decision making in the same way that a doctor's prescription is a prescription for good health. Prescriptive decision making is based on an "ideal" process; it implies a "best" way to make a decision. Below we will describe a prescriptive model for good decision making based on a rational approach to problem solving. The steps in this model are useful and can be applied in many situations; they offer a reasonable and intelligent way to approach group decision-making problems.

Nevertheless, we must once again offer a caveat. It is unwise to force groups to go through a process that they are unwilling or unprepared to experience. All groups should examine their composition, resources, time, energy, commitment, goals, and problems before deciding on a particular approach.

There are essentially three criticisms of prescriptive approaches to decision making. First, while following a standard approach can be practical, it can also stifle creativity; groups usually get through the task, but they accomplish it with little imagination or true excellence. Second, prescriptions typically assume that group members will act rationally and unemotionally, but we all know that not all members will. In fact, some nonrational (not irrational!) behavior is often good for the group. And third, there is simply conflicting evidence about whether prescriptive procedures improve the quality of groups' outcomes.

On the other hand, prescriptive procedures do help avoid inefficiency, redundancy, and delay. They often succeed in coordinating group members and focusing their attention on common issues. Moreover, prescriptive procedures gather the attention of the group around a jointly agreed-upon activity; for example, if the group declares itself in the "problem analysis" stage, then each group member is focused on the same activity.

Of the many useful standard group procedures (see Siebold, 1988), the procedure described below is a typical systematic and rational approach to decision making. It is based, in part, on Dewey's (1910) reflecting-thinking model and contains major additions from current research. One research project concluded that a procedure similar to the one below actually improved group decision making; Hirokawa (1983a) compared successful and unsuccessful groups and found that successful groups were ones that adhered to a problem-solving technique that seemed to reflect a more rational and systematic approach to problem solving.

Define and Limit the Problem

The group begins by defining and limiting the problem. The group discusses only the definition of terms and how the problem relates to other issues. Limiting the problem is important. It is important not to define a problem so broadly that it generates never-ending discussion and does not lend itself to concrete solutions. Ideally, everyone in the group should agree about what the problem includes and what it excludes. The following are some tips for how to proceed and what to talk about during this step:

1. Define the problem specifically. Try to phrase the problem as a question.
2. Discuss the group's goals.
3. Identify the resources available to the group.
4. Determine the relevance and importance of the problem to the group.
5. Clarify all procedural constraints, such as meeting times and places and when the final report is due.

Analyze the Problem and Gather Information

This is the essence of the decision-making process. It is important to spend time on this step before suggesting solutions. Hirokawa (1983b) found that successful groups do not jump quickly into the solution phase; they spend much time analyzing the problem and gathering information. The purpose of this step is to collect evidence and information that will help you explore and clarify the problem. Think about your audience; who will be reading the final report? For example, if you are discussing the rising cost of tuition on your campus, your group report must reflect your primary audience; the university administration will be interested in one sort of evidence and information, and students will perhaps be interested in another. In either case you must always know who you are working for. The following are important issues for the problem analysis stage:

1. Determine your audience.
2. Research and establish the history and causes of the problem.
3. Discuss how the problem relates to other issues.
4. Collect relevant information.
5. Discuss this information in your group.
6. Critically examine the facts and information. This means to challenge the facts and assumptions to make sure that they stand the test of scrutiny.
7. Make sure you have enough information.

Establish Decision Criteria

The group now decides what criteria (standards, or requirements) an acceptable decision must meet. The group should agree on specific criteria, and these criteria should provide methods of evaluation. If the decision criteria are properly developed, they will help the group recognize acceptable decision proposals and reject inappropriate ones. During this stage the group's discussion should focus on the following:

1. What an ideal decision would look like, and what it would include and exclude.
2. What a reasonable, but less-than-ideal, solution would be. This is important because it is not always possible to reach an ideal decision.
3. What standards the group should use to judge the decision.
4. What the group would consider valid and feasible about the decision.

The group should try to develop criteria as specific as possible. The following are some examples of decision criteria. They are responsive to the problem that one group was discussing concerning "What the role of the state should be in integrating public schools."

1. Maintain the quality of education.
2. Ensure a balanced racial environment.
3. Guarantee no increase in taxes or costs to families.
4. Do not displace only minority groups.
5. Generate simple and workable transportation facilities, including options for extracurricular activities.
6. Design a phase-in program for a smooth transition.

Discuss Possible Solutions

Now it is time to discuss and explore the most useful solutions. It is important to wait until now, because premature discussion of solutions is associated with poor decision making. Now that you have defined the problem, gathered information so that you can discuss it intelligently, and established some ground rules for what is acceptable, you are in a much better position to examine solutions. The goal is to come up with as many ideas as possible. You should seek quantity before quality. During this stage you should not be afraid to propose as many alternatives as possible; record every suggestion, regardless of how absurd it might seem. Some questions to be considered are:

1. Have all possible solutions been considered?
2. What is the evidence in support of each alternative?
3. Has the group used brainstorming techniques to produce ideas?

Determine the Best Solution

This is the point where the group agrees on a final solution. The group does this by testing the possible solutions against the decision criteria it established. The goal is to find the best solution relative to the original issue and the decision criteria; the method is to discuss each decision possibility in light of the decision criteria, including feasibility and desirability. The group should discard the unsatisfactory solutions, concentrate its discussion on the the remaining alternatives and make sure that the discussion includes the following:

1. Does the solution minimize the problem?
2. Is it workable?
3. What are its limitations?
4. Are there more advantages to the solution than disadvantages?
5. How does the solution compare to the decision criteria?
6. Are the facts and the information gathered consistent with the proposed solution?

Determine How the Final Decision Should Be Implemented

It must be possible to implement a solution. The group should begin to discuss plans for implementing a decision. Implementation is often not possible in classroom groups, but in other groups it is a very important component of the group's decision making. Sometimes only a final report is due; when this is the case, the group should assign individuals to the various tasks of report preparation.

DESCRIPTIVE APPROACHES TO DECISION MAKING

The section above presented a prescription for rational decision making. It is based on the assumption that groups can benefit by going through the steps that we outlined. But the approach that we will concentrate on for the remainder of this chapter is a descriptive approach. A *descriptive* approach does not say how groups *should* make decisions, but how they *do* make decisions. These are "descriptions," based on observations of groups, of what interactive processes are common to groups. Whereas a prescriptive approach is based on an "ideal" process, the crux of the descriptive approach is the "reality" of observation.

There are several assumptions of the descriptive approach to decision-making groups. The most basic is that a "natural" process of group decision making does indeed exist. That is, groups develop their own interdependent task and socio-emotional dimensions in a normal and fairly consistent interactive pattern that leads to validation of decisions by consensus. The process is assumed to be natural because it occurs in most effective and successful decision-making groups. This natural process can be disrupted to the extent that the group is influenced by outside forces. For example, a group that adheres strictly to a prescriptive method will not experience this natural process. External authorities, resource constraints, special instructions, and many other factors will also interfere with the process to various degrees.

The perspective of communication and the group process is best served by emphasizing descriptive approaches to group decision making. We will focus on the pragmatic interaction patterns of group members—their interlocked communicative behaviors—as they occur and change over time. We will trace these patterns throughout the group's history. Poole and Doelger (1986, p. 35) state that "The essence of group decision-making is interaction." Our concern, therefore, will be on the patterns of interaction that characterize decision development in groups.

Early Models of Group Development

Although formal instruction in group decision making is a twentieth-century phenomenon, the historical roots of group communication date back to the classical age of Greece and the philosophical origins of dialectic. The ancient Greek philosophers viewed the practice of dialectic as the search for truth through the exchange of opinions or arguments in free discussion. While the classical philosophers regarded dialectic as a branch of philosophy (specifically, logic), the contemporary view of group decision making is more closely aligned with the social sciences.

Sociologists, psychologists, and psychotherapists, as well as communication scholars, have long been concerned with studying how groups develop over time from a mere aggregate (or collection) of individuals into full-fledged groups. A few of those early models of group development are described in the following paragraphs in order to provide some background and perspective for the models that constitute the major thrust of this chapter.

Equilibrium Models One conceptual approach to the study of groups is to explain the group process in terms of a balance, or equilibrium, between two opposing forces. An equilibrium model is popular in many social-psychological explanations in the sense of an approach-avoidance conflict (opposing forces favoring and disfavoring some course of action), cognitive dissonance (simultaneous knowledge of positive and negative information concerning a course of action), along with numerous other explanatory models.

Such equilibrium models are popular, perhaps because they are easily conceptualized and easily adapted to the structural elements of social behavior. They are conceptually consistent with physical phenomena. That is, the equilibrium principle is evident in the axiom that actions have equal and opposite reactions, the balance scale, in the positive and negative forces of magnetic energy, etc. Furthermore, such models of group decision making implicitly assume the rationality of human beings, an assumption difficult to sustain in explanations of human behavior.

Although Robert F. Bales is known for his development of the categories for interaction process analysis, or IPA (Bales, 1950), he also developed an equilibrium model to explain group behavior. His IPA categories were probably developed as a way of observing actual interactional behavior in terms of an equilibrium between task and social forces. Bales (1953) hypothesized that every group has a problem of adapting to its environment. During this adaptation, it develops social mechanisms that serve to differentiate members from one another—for example, differences of roles, differences of status, and the development of a leadership structure. As a result of this emphasis on differences between group members, the social dimension of the group (in terms of its cohesiveness and interpersonal solidarity) suffers.

According to Bales's equilibrium hypothesis, then, the work that the group performs in accomplishing its task leads to a deterioration of the group's social structure. Conversely, as the group attempts to increase the interpersonal ties between its members and to perform work in the social dimension (that is, to raise the level of cohesiveness), its work on the task suffers. Groups tend to fluctuate back and forth between task and socioemotional activities: that is, between attempting to solve their task problems and maintaining group solidarity.

Bales's IPA categories (see Figure 6-1) are consistent with the equilibrium hypothesis. You will note that the twelve categories are divided equally between the task dimension and the socioemotional dimension—six categories each. Note further that the twelve categories are also divided equally between polarized (or mutually opposed) categories oriented to specific problems in either the task or the social dimension. Bales thus conceptualizes each and every act as directed toward solving some task or social problem confronting the group. Furthermore, every action that a member contributes to the group discussion is oriented to either a task problem or a social problem, but not both. Bales's categories are still very popular.

The best way to use the equilibrium models is to understand the group process in terms of the continuing presence of its two dimensions—task and social. While progress is being made in the socioemotional dimension of the group process, it is also being made in the task dimension. Thus, even as we focus our attention on one of these dimensions in order to understand it more specifically, we should keep in mind that our view is restricted by the one-dimensional spectacles we are using to understand the group process. We should realize that although we may not be *seeing* both dimensions functioning at the same time, the group process is continuously functioning in both—for the two dimensions remain interdependent and inseparable.

Phase Models The most popular approach to understanding the developmental process of groups over time is to describe group activity moving through a sequence of different kinds of interaction. This sequence develops into stages, or phases, of group interaction from the beginning of a group's activity as an aggregate to its eventual maturation as a group and the establishment of full-fledged groupness. From a task-oriented perspective, the phases of group development chronicle the group's interaction from the beginning of a group's task performance to the achievement of consensus on decisions. Although numerous models of group development have appeared throughout the past several decades and reflect differences in their authors' interests, the following brief survey of some of these models should also reveal similarities in their description of the phases of group development.

The most familiar of all descriptive models of the group process is the three-phase model advanced by Bales (1950) and Bales and Strodtbeck (1951). These authors discovered that decision-making groups, most of which were problem-solving groups, tend to discuss different kinds of task-related problems at different periods of time in their group interaction. Their three phases may be briefly described as follows:

Stage 1: Emphasis on problems of *orientation* (deciding what the situation is like)
Stage 2: Emphasis on problems of *evaluation* (deciding what attitudes should be taken toward the situation)
Stage 3: Emphasis on problems of *control* (deciding what to do about it)

Bales and Strodtbeck base their three phases of the group decision-making process on data compiled from using Bales's (1950) system of interaction process analysis. Figure 6-1 illustrates this system. The IPA classifies each communicative behavior performed by members during group interaction. The classes of behavior include twelve categories—in reality, six bipolar pairs of categories. Each category in the pair is the antithesis of the other: for example, "agrees—disagrees," "shows solidarity—shows antagonism." The IPA also separates the group's task and socioemotional dimensions by labeling three pairs of categories in each area. And each bipolar pair of categories is assumed to deal with a particular kind of problem confronting the group. Each of the first three types of problems—orientation, evaluation, and control—is emphasized in order by each decision-making group in three successive phases during group interaction.

Bales and Strodtbeck also emphasize the cyclic nature of the three phases of group decision making. As a group completes one decision-making task by progressing through the phases of orientation, evaluation, and control, it tends to recycle back to the initial orientation phase as it performs each subsequent task. Thus, according to Bales and Strodtbeck, the three phases characterize each performance of a single group decision-making task. We will see this activity again in Poole's (1983b) work.

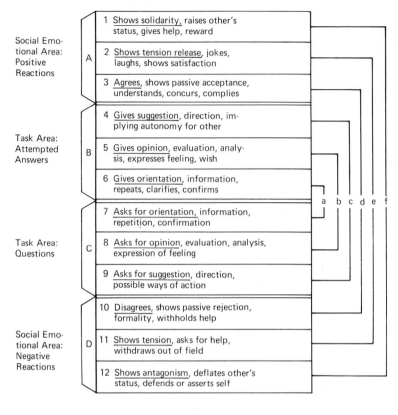

Social Emotional Area: Positive Reactions — A

1 <u>Shows solidarity,</u> raises other's status, gives help, reward

2 <u>Shows tension release,</u> jokes, laughs, shows satisfaction

3 <u>Agrees,</u> shows passive acceptance, understands, concurs, complies

Task Area: Attempted Answers — B

4 <u>Gives suggestion,</u> direction, implying autonomy for other

5 <u>Gives opinion,</u> evaluation, analysis, expresses feeling, wish

6 <u>Gives orientation,</u> information, repeats, clarifies, confirms

Task Area: Questions — C

7 <u>Asks for orientation,</u> information, repetition, confirmation

8 <u>Asks for opinion,</u> evaluation, analysis, expression of feeling

9 <u>Asks for suggestion,</u> direction, possible ways of action

Social Emotional Area: Negative Reactions — D

10 <u>Disagrees,</u> shows passive rejection, formality, withholds help

11 <u>Shows tension,</u> asks for help, withdraws out of field

12 <u>Shows antagonism,</u> deflates other's status, defends or asserts self

a   b   c   d   e   f

Key:

a Problems of orientation   d Problems of decision
b Problems of evaluation   e Problems of tension-management
c Problems of control   f Problems of integration

Figure 6-1 Bales's categories for "interaction process analysis."

Dunphy (1964) also depicted a sequential analysis of group development. He advanced a four-phase model of group development in terms of emotionality cultures:

Stage 1: Dependency (group members look to the leader for direction of their activity)

Stage 2: Fight-flight (group members resist the leader's direction and develop their ability to work independently of a leader's guidance)

Stage 3: Pairing (group members demonstrate a marked increase in group cohesiveness)

Stage 4: Work (little emotionality of any type appears during the final stage of group activity)

You will note that Dunphy's developmental model is highly similar to Bennis and Shepard's (1956) model of levels of work, which will be discussed in the following paragraphs. Dunphy also emphasizes the socioemotional dimension of the group process. This emphasis clearly reflects his interest in training groups (or T groups) rather than in groups specifically oriented to decision-making tasks.

Bennis and Shepard developed a four-phase model to describe group development. Their observations were much more subjective and interpretive than the direct observational method of interaction analysis (see Chapter 5). They derived their description from the reactions of nonparticipant observers. Their findings, according to the authors, also reflect their interpretations over a five-year period of teaching classes in group dynamics. The following four phases of group development are labeled according to the level of work the group is able to accomplish:

Phase 1: One-level work. Personally need-oriented—not group-oriented (Dependence and Authority Relations).

Phase 2: Two-level work. Maintaining the group task. Group-oriented and necessary—but routine (Resolution-Catharsis and beginnings of feeling of interdependence).

Phase 3: Three-level work. Group-focused work with new methods of attack, goal establishment, idea-testing (Interdependence with group focus and sense of direction).

Phase 4: Four-level work. Creative and integrative interpretation with immediate relevance to present problems of group task (Consensual Validation and maximum Productivity). (1956, pp. 753–755)

Several interesting observations emerge from Bennis and Shepard's model. For example, it illustrates a group's progressive ability to do more sophisticated work. This ability is apparently gained in successively progressive stages as the group develops interdependence among its members. As the group begins its process of development, it is dependent on some external authority responsible for the group task. In a T group, that authority is the trainer; in an organization, it is the boss; in a classroom, it is the instructor. The group can do two-level work only as the members begin to reject the external source of authority. By the time the members are able to do three-level work, they have completely rejected their dependence on the external authority.

Bennis and Shepard's model also maintains a clear separation between work and emotionality—the task and socioemotional dimensions. Although recognizing their close relationship, the authors emphasize the importance of achieving social interdependence as a prerequisite to task accomplishment. They feel that a group accomplishes the major part of its task during the period of four-level work.

Tuckman (1965) employed still another method for observing groups as he devised his four-phase model for group decision making. In fact, he himself did not observe any groups but synthesized the results of other published observations. He notes that groups simultaneously confront two kinds of problems in each phase of decision making. He labels these two problem types (a) group structure (how to get along) and (b) task activity (how to proceed). Essentially, these two types of problems are "social problems" and "task problems," thereby denying the inseparable interdependence of the two dimensions of the group process. Tuckman characterizes his four phases and their corresponding social and task problems with a catchy rhythm of four rhyming words:

Phase 1: "Forming." (a) Testing and independence; (b) attempting to identify the task.

Phase 2: "Storming." (a) Development of intragroup conflicts; (b) emotional response to task demands.

Phase 3: "Norming." (a) Development of group cohesion; (b) expression of opinions.

Phase 4: "Performing." (a) Functional role-relatedness; (b) emergence of solutions.

Tuckman's point of departure, like Bales and Strodtbeck's, is the type of problem under discussion at various stages in group interaction. He also clearly separates the members' communicative behavior into task and socioemotional areas. And, like Bennis and Shepard, Tuckman assumes that the group accomplishes most of its productive output in the latter stages of the decision-making process.

Despite the different methods used to observe group behavior, these three descriptive models share common characteristics. Although the perspective of each observer is quite different, they agree on many elements of the decision-making small group. Quite naturally, all three descriptions reflect a greater emphasis on the socioemotional dimension than on the task dimension. But this emphasis should be expected, since all the authors are psychologists or social psychologists whose primary interest is personality and social structure—not communication.

Although the three descriptive models do not reflect identical characteristics of each phase, several phases include characteristics common to all three models. That is, the first stage of group decision making in all three models is a period of orientation—a period in which members adjust their individualities to group membership and accustom themselves to the task at hand. This orienting period generally involves a search process in which members search for ways to view their task with no particular focus or established opinion toward the task.

One of the middle phases in each of the models includes a period of social conflict among members, differences of opinion on task ideas and social norms. This similarity seems to confirm that social conflict and deviance are indeed a normal part of the group process. Moreover, social conflict and deviance are normal during only one period of group interaction. And this period of normal conflict is near the middle of the process and not near the beginning or the end of group task performance. Thus, the norm of social conflict and deviance characterizes a specific intermediate phase in the process of group interaction that ultimately leads to validation of decisions through consensus.

A final stage of interaction in which members apparently accomplish most of their work on their task is common to all three models, although the exact nature of this stage is not abundantly clear. Bales and Strodtbeck indicate that the final stage is characterized by a maximum number of positive reactions. The other two models indicate that the group becomes capable of creative and effective task performance. But all three models agree that the group members achieve consensus and thereby validate their decisions during this last phase.

THE PROCESS OF DECISION EMERGENCE

Chapter 9 will discuss the phenomenon of leader emergence—the fact that groups do not "select" leaders so much as the leader and other roles "emerge" during group interaction. If the task and socioemotional dimensions of group process are truly interdependent, it seems logical that the decision-making process should be similar to the leadership process. Moreover, group decision making, like leadership, possesses no single "best" or "correct" answer to be discovered in a "Eureka!" or "Aha!" manner. It is reasonable to conclude that groups do not *make* decisions. Decisions *emerge* from group interaction.

If you were to observe a decision-making group as a participant or as a nonparticipant attempting to determine the point at which the group makes its decision, you would find such a task extraordinarily difficult, if not impossible. During some period of the group's interaction, the decision is probably apparent to you even though the group members continue their discussion. Even groups following prescriptions don't know exactly when they have made a decision.

The process of emergence is gradual and cumulative. A specific point in time at which decisions are made is not apt to be found. In fact, the emergence process presupposes that groups achieve consensus on their decisions *after* those decisions appear to have been made. The very final stage of interaction, then, fulfills the purpose of procuring members' public commitment, the essence of consensus, to decisions already reached.

Phases of Decision Emergence

Using interaction analysis (see Chapters 5 and 7) as the method for observing group decision making, Fisher (1970a) discovered four phases in the process of group decision making. Unlike other observational schema, Fisher's method identified each alternative decision proposal suggested during group interaction and attempted to observe the process whereby preliminary ideas are transformed into consensus decisions. Thus, each member's communicative act functions on the decision proposal under discussion by expressing some opinion (favorable, unfavorable, or ambiguous) toward that proposal, providing evidence to support that opinion, modifying the proposal, clarifying it, and agreeing or disagreeing with another member's opinion. The group interaction is thus anchored to the subject matter of the group interaction—the decision proposals—and to members' attempts to influence the perceptions of other members toward these proposals.

The observed pattern of communicative behaviors—acts and interacts—indicates four rather distinct phases of group decision making, each characterized by a different pattern of interaction. These phases are orientation, conflict, emergence, and reinforcement.

Orientation Phase A group's early problems of socializing and excessive primary tension affect the interaction patterns in this early phase. Members clarify and agree most often in this phase. Because the members are unaware of their social position initially and not sure of how to handle the task, they do not quickly or strongly assert themselves or their opinions. Consequently, they make assertions tentatively in order to test the group, and they agree with virtually everything. For example, a member states an ambiguous opinion toward the decision proposal, a second member agrees with that ambiguous opinion, and this is followed in turn by another ambiguous opinion. Since members agree even with comments serving only to clarify points of information, agreeing with another member's comment seems to function in the orientation phase not so much to reinforce other members' beliefs and opinions as to avoid disrupting the developing social climate.

Group members in the orientation phase search tentatively for ideas and directions to aid their decision-making efforts. They are unaware of the direction the group will eventually take, so they don't commit themselves, favorably or unfavorably, to the newly introduced decision proposals. Rather, they express attitudes that are ambiguous toward proposals—attitudes that don't really take a stand one way or the other.

Many of the ambiguous opinions expressed in the first phase probably reflect favorable attitudes in the making. That is, since members assert opinions and arguments favoring the proposals with increasing intensity as the discussion progresses, these opinions must be in the preliminary stages of formation during this orientation phase. As the issues become clarified and as the social climate becomes more conducive to the honest statement of one's true position, many members apparently change their ambiguous opinions to opinions favoring the decision proposals.

Characteristic of the orientation phase, then, is getting acquainted, clarifying, and tentatively expressing attitudes. This stage is a period of forming opinions, not rocking the boat, and getting rid of social inhibitions—in short, the orientation phase.

Conflict Phase The second phase of group decision making is characterized by dispute—ideational conflict over decision proposals. In the orientation phase, members only tentatively express their opinions, which are typically ambiguous. In the conflict phase they appear to have made up their minds. Members are now aware of the direction the group is taking toward the decision-making task and of the relevant decision proposals emerging from the group deliberations. Thus, members typically express either a favorable or an unfavorable attitude toward these proposals. Gone is the tentativeness of ambiguity. Gone, too, is tentativeness due to social inhibitions.

Polarization of attitudes means disagreement and conflict. In the conflict phase, expressing a favorable attitude is generally followed by another member's expressing an unfavorable attitude (and vice versa). Members have different opinions and express them in argument with one another. Not only do members express less ambiguous attitudes, but they also express them more tenaciously. They now provide data and evidence to substantiate their beliefs and engage in full-fledged debate with other members.

The interaction patterns of the conflict phase reflect the formation of two coalitions resulting from polarization of beliefs. That is, two coalitions are present in this phase—one favoring and one opposing those decision proposals that ultimately achieve group consensus. To illustrate, members *A* and *B* favor the proposals and reinforce each other's favorable opinions; *C* and *D* oppose the proposals and reinforce each other's unfavorable opinions. Expression of ambiguous attitudes or the presence of a "mugwump" (independent) member is not normal in the conflict phase. The norm is dissent, controversy, social conflict, and innovative deviance. In fact, mugwumps are deviates in the conflict phase in that they do not participate in the debate over ideas and opinions.

It is quite probable that the coalitions centered around leader contenders are the same coalitions formed by polarization of ideas during the conflict phase. The interdependence of the task and socioemotional dimensions seem to confirm this explanation.

Emergence Phase Social conflict and dissent dissipate during the third phase. Members express fewer unfavorable opinions toward decision proposals. The coalition of individuals who have opposed those proposals which eventually achieve consensus also weakens in this phase. The interaction patterns in the emergence phase reflect significantly less positive reinforcement of one another's unfavorable attitudes. A few residues of overt social conflict remain, but they are not significant. Comments expressing unfavorable attitudes are not only not reinforced by subsequent agreement or more unfavorable attitudes from other members in the coalition; they are not expressed so tenaciously either. That is, opposing members typically assert unfavorable opinions without including supporting evidence or reason to substantiate them.

The hallmark of the emergence phase is the recurrence of ambiguity. As in the orientation phase, some members express opinions ambiguous toward the decision proposals and tend to reinforce them by responding with further expressions of attitudes ambiguous toward the proposals. Thus, ambiguity toward decision proposals is prominent in the orientation phase, declines significantly in the conflict phase, and rises again during the emergence phase.

But although the proportionate number of comments expressing ambiguous opinions and interacts reflecting reinforcement of ambiguous comments does not differ substantially from the orientation phase, the function performed by ambiguity in the interact patterns of the emergence phase is significantly different. During orientation, members express opinions tentatively in the form of ambiguous attitudes toward the decision proposals. Some of these ambiguous comments are undoubtedly the initial expression of favorable or unfavorable opinions in rudimentary form of development. But group members have no reason to be tentative in the emergence phase. They are certainly no longer searching for attitude direction. They have plotted that direction in the orientation phase and debated it during the conflict phase. In the emergence phase, task direction is obviously no longer at issue. It is quite unreasonable to conclude that expressing an ambiguous opinion at this late point in the discussion reflects a tentative expression of a developing opinion.

The key to the function of ambiguity in the patterns of group interaction lies in associating the emergence phase with the conflict phase. Ambiguous communicative behavior functions in the third phase as a form of modified dissent. In the conflict phase, members either favor or disfavor the decision proposals. In the emergence phase, the bimodal distribution has shifted to favorable or ambiguous attitudes toward these same proposals. That is, the group member who expresses opposition to decision proposals in the conflict phase is in the process of changing from disfavor to favor through the mediating step of expressing ambiguous opinions.

Members expressing ambiguous opinions in the emergence phase have already committed themselves to a stand of opposition in the conflict phase and cannot be expected to change their opinions so abruptly. Thus, their dissent changes to assent by way of ambiguity. A dissenting member in the conflict phase responds to another member's comment favoring a proposal with an opinion disfavoring it. In the emergence phase, in the same situation the response will be an opinion ambiguous toward the proposal. Opposition to the proposal is still being expressed, but opposition is dissipating as attitudes are modified.

The two coalitions present in the conflict phase also dissipate during the emergence phase. The coalition of dissenting members opposing the decision proposals does not immediately disintegrate but turns to ambiguous comments as a final form of dissent. Just as the exact point in time at which a leader or a decision emerges cannot be pinpointed, neither can one determine the exact moment of the death of the dissenting coalition. The dissipation of dissent and the dissipation of the coalition are gradual and mediated by ambiguity. In the absence of outright social conflict, decisions may appear to have been reached. But the expression of ambiguous opinions, while not totally unfavorable, is not yet favorable. As disfavor dissipates to ambiguity, however, favorable opinions toward the decision proposals increase concomitantly.

The third phase is probably the crucial stage in the group process of decision making. During this third phase the eventual outcome of group interaction becomes increasingly more apparent. Therefore, this third phase is called the emergence phase.

Reinforcement Phase While group members tend to reach decisions during the emergence phase, they achieve consensus on these decisions during the reinforcement phase. Substantiating one's opinion toward the decision proposal is no longer necessary. After all, the ideas were thoroughly tested during the conflict phase, but members continue to provide evidence and reasons to support their opinions favoring the decision proposals, thus adding additional fuel to the fire of emerging consensus. Members constantly and consistently express opinions favorable to the proposals and positively reinforce one another's favorable opinions with expressions of agreement and additional social support. This overwhelming preponderance of interaction patterns that favor the decision proposals and positively reinforce the favorable opinions clearly identifies the final phase of group deliberations.

Dissent has all but vanished in the reinforcement phase. This phase includes the lowest number of comments opposed to the decision proposals and virtually no interacts of social conflict—that is, a favorable comment followed or preceded by an unfavorable comment. Of course the orientation phase contains few interacts of social conflict too. But whereas the low level of conflict during orientation reflects the members' conscious avoidance of conflict due to social inhibitions, the reinforcement phase reflects unity of opinion among group members. The dissipation of dissent, both direct (unfavorable opinions) and modified (ambiguous opinions), is virtually complete in this phase of group interaction.

Pervading this final phase in group decision making is a spirit of unity. All members seem to agree and strive to show this agreement by positively reinforcing one another. Their interaction patterns reflect virtually no tension; rather, the members are jovial, loud, boisterous, laughing, and verbally backslapping each other. This is the phase of developing members' commitment to those decisions which were the object of conflict in the second phase and which emerged during the third phase. This is the reinforcement phase.

Orientation, conflict, emergence, and reinforcement, then, are the four phases of decision emergence. They have been described here in terms of characteristic patterns of interaction. Where possible, they have been associated with elements of the socioemotional dimension. The original purpose of the investigation that revealed these four phases was to observe verbal task behavior free from the confounding variables of the socioemotional dimension. That purpose, of course, was doomed to failure. The two dimensions are interdependent. Attempting to view only one dimension can only provide a perspective from which to recognize the interdependence of both.

The descriptions of the four phases are admittedly rather general and provide no examples of group interaction. In order to illustrate the phases more clearly and reveal the "flavor" of group decision making from the viewpoint of members' communicative behaviors, Chapter 7 provides detailed examples of interaction patterns from an actual decision-making group. Chapter 7 should clarify most questions raised in the preceding general description.

NONLINEAR MODELS OF DECISION MAKING

Although the prescriptive and descriptive models described earlier are different in many significant respects, they are all *linear* models. Each model is based on a step-by-step progression toward the completion of task objectives. The steps in the linear model assume a given order; a group completes discussion of one set of problems before moving to the next. Each model assumes that solving one set of problems is prerequisite to solving the next set of problems; that is, the group is incapable of solving the second set of problems until it solves the first, and so on. Groups cannot or should not deal with problems out of sequence. Any step out of sequence would be considered a lack of group progress and an error of that group. The linear model outlines progress toward task accomplishment as a methodical progression along a straight line.

The Spiral Model

Thomas M. Scheidel and Laura Crowell (1964) discovered that group interaction aimed at developing ideas does not correspond to a linear model. Using a system of interaction analysis as their observational scheme (Crowell and Scheidel, 1961), these authors describe the group process of idea development as a spiral model (Figure 6-2). One member introduces an idea, and other members respond with agreement or disagreement, extension or revision. The idea is the object of discussion, and it develops over time to reflect the group's viewpoint. When an idea is developed to the point that it is an object of agreement by all group members, the group anchors its position on that idea and introduces new preliminary ideas progressing from that anchor point of agreement. The spiral process, then, involves "reach-testing" forward from an anchored position of agreement. If the reach-tested idea is affirmed by the group, a new anchored position is established, and reach-testing proceeds from there. If the new idea is rejected, the group returns to its anchored position and reach-tests another new idea from that same anchor point.

The spiral process of anchoring and reach-testing is not linear in that the group constantly retraces its path of idea development. Groups develop new ideas not in linear sequence, but cumulatively. One idea leads to another. One idea is progressively modified and remodified during the course of group interaction until the group achieves validation of its final decisions by consensus. The spiral process is cumulative and progressive, reflecting continuous modification of ideas and back-tracking to agreed-upon ideas as members reconfirm positions.

As noted earlier, several descriptive models indicate that the bulk of the group's task activity occurs in the final stages of interaction. The spiral model denies this allegation, but it explains the appearance that groups accomplish more work during the final stages. The spiral process is cumulative, and all ideas developed in the latter stages of interaction are the direct result of earlier agreements and anchored

Figure 6-2 The spiral model of decision making.

positions. But in the final stages, the group has acquired a vast background of many agreed-upon positions. Reach-testing in the final phase therefore proceeds from a broader base of agreement with increasingly diminishing need to backtrack to earlier anchor positions.

The spiral model also accounts for the apparent inefficiency of group decision making regarding the use of time. Every beginning geometry student knows that the shortest distance between two points on the same plane is a straight line. But group decision making apparently does not conform to the straight line of a linear model. Rather, the group process is more like a spiral of anchoring and reach-testing. But the spiral process is certainly not a disadvantage of group decision making. Anchoring and reach-testing ideas illustrate the group's superiority when performing decision-making tasks requiring high acceptance. Actually, the Fisher (1970a) four-phase model assumes a spiraling process and is less linear than earlier models.

Using Communication to Modify Decisions

The spiral model of idea development, described by Scheidel and Crowell (1964) and affirmed in the phases of decision emergence, reveals that group decision making is a process of cumulative development of consensus decisions. Groups achieve consensus on decisions through interaction patterns that modify, reject, accept, or combine previously introduced decision proposals. Below, we present the specific nature of the interaction patterns that cumulatively modify decision proposals until they appear in consensus form.

Studying the interaction patterns of decision-making groups, Fisher (1970b) discerned a pattern of cumulative, step-by-step modification of decision proposals. That is, groups do not typically modify preliminary decision proposals by clear and direct amendments, but in sudden jumps to different formulations of the same root proposals. Consistent with Berg's (1967) discovery of a group's rather brief attention span, Fisher found that groups apparently do not discuss each proposal for an extended period. Rather, a group member introduces a specific decision proposal, and then members discuss it for some length of time, drop it in favor of discussing another decision proposal, and reintroduce the first proposal later during the group deliberations.

An example may illustrate this pattern of modification more clearly. A corporate management training group (four men, here called A, B, C, and D) was engaged in making decisions regarding the management of a hypothetical corporation. One of their consensus decisions was to concentrate their sales and advertising campaigns for their business in two market areas—one urban and one rural. Member B initially introduced this decision proposal in its rudimentary form—to withhold all attempts to sell their products until after the results of a market analysis had become available. The following excerpt is from the group's interaction at that point:

B: This is going to be our plan initially, to get this market analysis. I feel we should consider holding our market in inventory and not sell the first quarter until you find out where the market is.

A: What would you do with the sales representatives, then? Just let them sit around?

B: Pay their salary—$8,000.

A: But you're not getting any return on your money.

D: You've got to put them out in the field.

C: Put them out. It wouldn't cost us anything.

A: All right. What should we do about advertising?

The group members did not respond favorably to *B*'s proposal, and they quickly moved to another, as yet unrelated, proposal concerning advertising. Later, *C* reintroduced a substitute decision proposal regarding how to allocate the company's sales representatives:

C: As a matter of fact, if we were to take one area and blanket it with our sales reps and take another area for our market analysis, we might be able to calculate a second area based on the results of our sales.

A: We might be able to. At least it's a better possibility than...

D: It's an indicator.

C: An indicator. You've got more information.

B: We need to get a job description of the chairperson.

The group members responded favorably to the substitute proposal. Yet they dropped the second proposal, too, before coming to a final decision and before exhausting their discussion of it.

The decision proposal to concentrate their sales representatives in two market areas came closest to the form of a direct amendment to the decision proposal while it was being discussed:

C: Our first shot at sales is really to obtain a market coverage.

B: What do you mean by "market coverage"?

C: I'm sorry. A market forecast.

B: That's what we were saying. Get a forecast on each region and try to cover sales in each.

C: But I don't think we can do that. I think we can blanket only one area.

B: If you put two sales reps in each area, you use six sales reps. But I don't think you want to do that.

D: No. We can't reallocate. If we put two in each one of those areas and reallocate one of them to the other area, then we cover it.

B: You're covered if the first guy gets a sale.

A: You've got to gamble a little bit, but I don't think you want to throw your whole sales staff into one area. I think we ought to distribute three and three. [By allocating the six sales representatives "three and three," *A* proposes to distribute them equally in two market areas. He appears to amend the earlier proposal to concentrate them in a single area.]

C: Three and three?

A: Three and three. And then see what the results of our market analysis are. On the basis of this knowledge, we can better reallocate.

D: Where are we going to do our market analysis anyway?

Member *A* initiated a new decision proposal largely by amending the proposal under discussion—to concentrate all six sales representatives in one area—and introducing it in amended form—to distribute them equally in two areas. But, without exhaustively deliberating this proposal, the members quickly shifted to another decision proposal regarding the area of market analysis.

Earlier the group had discussed the decision proposal of whether the company should advertise:

B: How much for advertising?

C: Mr. Marketing, would you recommend two pages of advertising for each of the areas we are going to cover?

D: Yes. I think that's the least we can do. If we are going to put sales reps in an area, we ought to support them.

B: Remember, we haven't got much cost there.

C: You can't make money unless you spend it.

B: No. But we are just finding out where the market is right now. Why spend it for advertising?

C: But what if the other people spend? We'll find out, of course, if we lose a sale to the competitors.

B: Let's not advertise.

C: We ought to advertise something.

D: I think we should have one page.

C: One page, at least.

B: But we don't have the money.

A: How are we doing in formulating our long-range objectives?

Unlike the previous examples of decision proposals dropped after initiation and brief discussion, members responded to this proposal with a direct conflict of opinions. But without resolving the conflict, the group again shifted to a totally different proposal—formulating the company's long-range objectives.

The two decision proposals to concentrate their sales force in two areas and advertise in both areas were combined later in a further reformulation of the decision proposals:

A: With the marketing advantage you have getting this information, you'd better spend as much as you can on advertising and sales in that place and ignore the rest.

B: I don't know if we want to go into two areas or not. We aren't going to have enough to cover.

C: I would suggest that we take a shot at two areas. If we hit area 4, which is urban, and pick area 2 right above it, which is...

A: Strictly rural.

C: If we hit area 4 and area 2, we can draw conclusions and see if there really is a difference between the urban and rural markets.

Members *C*'s addition of "urban" and "rural" to differentiate the two market areas is not so much a modification of the proposal as it is an observation on the advantage of concentrating advertising and sales representatives in two areas. This point seemed to win over the obviously reluctant member *B*. And this configuration was the decision proposal that eventually achieved group consensus.

Each of the reformulations of the initial decision proposal is introduced, discussed, and dropped several times. The excerpts included above illustrate only those moments in the group's interaction in which members initiated the proposal in a modified form and does not include other reintroductions of the same proposal. Thus, members modify decision proposals by leaps, or jumps, rather than continuously by direct amendment and prolonged discussion.

In short, reformulations or modifications of the initial decision proposal do not typically emerge from direct criticisms of the proposal while it is being discussed. Rather, group members appear to wrestle with the proposal, sometimes with conflict and sometimes without, and then to put it aside temporarily until one of the members experiences an insight and suggests a reformulation that seems closer to what the group really wants. This can be frustrating for the group. One group's self-analysis reveals just such frustration:

> We would be talking about one subject and then all of a sudden in
> midstream change and start talking about something else. Our group has the
> trait of going around in circles.

This perceptive comment reflects the concern of a group member who considered this "going around in circles" as indicating some failure in group interaction. Unfortunately, the members of this group never realized during their interaction that they were behaving quite normally. The only disruptive factor was their frustration.

Some level of tension is normal throughout group interaction. The spurts of task activity probably indicate the natural tendency of a group to manage its social tension by frequently conserving energy through abrupt transitions to different decision proposals. Thus, the spiral model of the group decision-making process, though generally intended to describe the process of task performance, is closely interrelated with the group's social dimension as well.

Conflict and Decision Modification Although the evidence is not conclusive, there is a justifiable basis for believing that the patterns of decision modification do reflect the influence of conflict over decision proposals. That is, when members consistently respond to initiated proposals with a conflict of opinions, the successive reintroduction of those decision proposals follows a distinctive pattern. And when members experience little conflict of opinions toward initiated proposals, the successive reintroduction of those proposals corresponds to a different pattern.

The pattern of decision modification characterized by little conflict is generally a process of lowering the level of abstraction of the language phrasing the decision proposal. That is, each successive reintroduction of a substitute proposal is slightly more concrete than the previous one. The example of the corporate management training group corresponds to this essential pattern. Another example of this pattern of lowered abstraction appears in the interaction of a group of nursing experts planning a workshop-conference for educators in public health nursing.

Early in the nursing group's weeklong deliberations, the members discussed the present status of public health nurses and observed that public health nurses felt they were downgraded by the rest of the nursing profession. The group then felt that the public health nurses attending the conference would be defensive and would resist new proposals. Later, a member initiated a substitute proposal to begin the conference with "a nonthreatening something." After being discussed and dropped, the substitute proposal was reintroduced, proposing to "get the conference feeling good and then change them." A later substitute proposal suggested that they begin the conference "on common ground." Eventually the proposal was reintroduced in the form that achieved consensus—"Begin the conference with a history of the contributions that public health has made to the the field of nursing."

Each reformulated decision proposal follows from the previous one, and none elicited much dissent from the members. Furthermore, each succeeding decision proposal was more concrete or specific than the previous one. Thus, without conflict, group members modify decision proposals in an evolutionary and methodical process of lowering the level of abstraction of each successive proposal. This pattern might be illustrated in the following methodical sequence:

Statement of the problem: "Public health nurses feel their lack of status and will therefore be defensive and resistant to change."
Criteria for the solution: "Begin the conference with a nonthreatening something."
"Get the conference feeling good and then change them."
Abstract statement of solution: "Start the conference on common ground."
Concrete statement of solution: "Begin the conference with a history of the contributions that public health has made to the field of nursing."

In the absence of conflict or significant dissent, the lowering-of-abstraction pattern of decision modification seems to be painless, systematic, and eminently reasonable. But not all emergent decisions follow such a methodical route to consensus.

The presence of conflict and dissent stimulates a different pattern of decision modification in which members introduce successive decision proposals at essentially the same level of abstraction. The same nursing group proceeded through the following reformulations of another initial proposal. The final reformulation achieved group consensus and was prerequisite to several other decisions to include specific programs in the conference:

1. "The public health nurse is engaged in treatment of pathology."
2. "Public health nurses should have more clinical work with patients."
3. "Public health nurses do perform tasks that require clinical nursing skills."
4. "Clinical skills are required for working with patients in the home as well as in the hospital."
5. "Public health nursing is a clinical nursing specialty."

This second pattern also reflects the characteristic start-and-stop cumulative development of a consensus decision. But unlike the lowering-of-abstraction pattern associated with minimal conflict and dissent, this pattern reflects substitute decision proposals that are virtually restatements of each other. Each proposal is essentially the equivalent level of abstraction of every other.

The lowering-of-abstraction pattern is methodical in that members express little disagreement about the credibility of each decision proposal. In the absence of conflict, group members apparently perceive their task as one of seeking, or "discovery"—in this case, discovering what to include in the conference that would solve their problem and meet their established criteria.

The second pattern including conflict seems to reflect a different task for the members. To some members of the nursing group, public health nursing is a form of community social work or civil service in a government-sponsored clinic. To others, public health nursing is a clinical nursing specialty equivalent to, for example, psychiatric nursing. The issue produced disagreement and significant social tension between group members. Rather than being perceived as a task of discovery, the task in the presence of significant conflict was perceived to be "persuasion," or attitude change, in order to secure intragroup agreement. Whereas creativity is required to perform a task of discovery, persuasion is required to secure agreement.

Conflict, then, does not affect the basic start-and-stop process of decision modification, but it apparently does result in a distinctive pattern of that decision modification. When there is little substantive conflict, members methodically reintroduce substitute proposals in a pattern that consistently lowers the level of abstraction of that proposal. When a decision proposal precipitates conflict between members, the proposal is typically introduced at essentially the same level of abstraction in successive restatements of the root proposal.

Multiple-Sequence Models of Decision Making

All of the phase and development models of group process discussed above are useful for understanding how groups actually make decisions. You might have noticed that as these ideas developed there was increasing attention to the various cycles that groups experience. But all the phase models discussed above are single-sequence phase models; they generally posit a rather unitary and direct sequence of phases and these phases are assumed to describe most groups. More recently Poole (1981, 1983a, 1983b) has questioned these single-sequence phase models and presented data in support of what he calls multiple-sequence models.

Multiple-sequence models suggest that groups can take different developmental paths depending on such factors as the nature of the tasks, group procedures, and relationships between members. Poole argues that groups do not evolve from single phasic units, but interweave different patterns over time. This perspective on groups builds on the spiral model and the process of decision modification discussed above. Poole (see also Poole and Doelger, 1986) proposes three fundamental group threads:

1. *Task process activities* These are about how the group structures its procedures. Introducing subject matter, analyzing problems, and comparing solutions are all examples of task process activities.
2. *Relational character* This is concerned with the working relationships between group members at a particular point in time. Are they currently in harmony and integrated? Are they in conflict? Are they focusing on work, or are they socializing?
3. *Topical focus* This is the substantive issue being dealt with in the group. What is the group talking about at a point in time?

These three threads can be coherent or incoherent. Consider the following coherent thread: Task activity = problem analysis; relational character = focused work; topical focus = subject matter X. Assume that a student group, talking about how to stop theft from the library, is discussing the extent of the problem. The topical focus (or subject matter) is: the extent of theft in the library. Their relational character is focused attention, energy, and work on the topic. The group's members are not currently in conflict. The task activity is: problem analysis. This configuration corresponds to the problem analysis stage of the prescriptive model presented early in this chapter. Poole shows how these three threads vary and how the group goes through many sequences. At any time, for example, the members might shift their relational character to conflict, such as continuing to talk about the same problem but experiencing conflict over their analysis.

The three threads can change at different rates and at different times. Poole (1983a, 1983b) and Fisher and Stutman (1987) show how the group develops along different trajectories that can be identified by breakpoints. A *breakpoint* is the point in the flow of communication where one group sequence ends and another one begins. Some typical breakpoints are delays, disruptions, adjournments, topic shifts, and planning periods. One way for a group member to "manipulate" the work of the group is to inject breakpoints artificially. Fisher and Stutman describe *routing statements,* or statements that signal the group to follow a new or potentially different path. These can be procedural statements, such as "I think someone should take notes," or they can suggest a future direction such as "Why don't we talk about the fund-raising issues?" Statements that summarize the group's position also function as routing statements: for example, "I think most of us agree that we will take the following three steps."

Poole's multiple-sequence model allows for finer descriptions of the group process. It combines the unitary phase models of group development with the individual and structural characteristics of the group. The concept of breakpoint is important because it allows us to comprehend cycles and their disruptions in order to pinpoint critical moments in the group's history. It is difficult for the beginning student to understand and recognize all cycles, but it should be possible to describe the task, relational, and topical issues of the group and work toward sequences that are beneficial to the group.

What good is this?

FACTORS OF GROUP MEMBERSHIP

There has always been some disagreement about whether the results of a group decision are directly associated with the individual members of the group—their attitudes and abilities—or whether the communicative process in the group alters and counteracts the individuals' abilities. Most current thinking (Allison and Messick, 1987; Jarboe, 1988) holds that individuals' abilities and attitudes are significantly influenced by the communicative process in the group.

Many early studies tried to associate demographic qualities (age, sex, education, race, etc.) with group performance (see Shaw, 1981, for a review), but these approaches usually do not explain very much. Jarboe (1988) found that you cannot understand very much about a group's decision by considering only "input" variables related to group members; it is imperative to examine the communicative process during the group's deliberations. This process apparently mediates the effects of individual members' personalities and abilities.

But group members can improve their thinking ability. Certain ways of thinking that individuals bring with them to the group can be an important input factor.

Thinking Abilities of Members

It would be foolish to say that the members' abilities have no impact on group decision making. Certainly, groups composed of intelligent members will make more intelligent decisions than will groups of less intelligent persons. Similarly, groups of more capable or more expert members will make more capable or more expert decisions than will less qualified groups. It would also be foolish to attempt to discuss in any definitive sense the possible combinations of different abilities among members of decision-making groups. Shaw's (1981) discussion is the place to look for a more comprehensive discussion. Our present purpose includes discussing only a very few abilities which members may possess and which are relatively important to the process of group decision making. These abilities are not necessarily more important than others, but they are influential in terms of their potential impact on the outcome of group decision making.

Some research has supported Dewey's (1910) model of reflective thinking as it is typically used—as an agenda to guide group deliberations. Indeed, this is the typical and traditional use of reflective thinking in group decision making. The ability to think rationally can help the group. Group members who rank high in reflective-thinking ability are perceived by their fellow members as more capable and as contributing more to the group's decisions than members who are low on this ability. Moreover, groups of members with high reflective-thinking ability make higher-quality decisions.

Scheidel (1986) has discussed another personal ability that may be directly related to improving the quality of group decisions. Scheidel differentiates between two different types of thinking, which he calls convergent thinking and divergent thinking. He describes convergent thinking as comparing and evaluating ideas; it is consistent with logic, rationality, and reason. Mr. Spock of *Star Trek* is probably the fictional archetype of the ideal convergent thinker. Divergent thinking, on the other hand, deals with new and quite arbitrary ways of looking at problems; it is highly creative in the sense that it explores new and unorthodox views of familiar situations, and it is less rational and logical than covergent thinking. Whereas convergent thinking deals with a step-by-step approach to problem solving, with emphasis on the greatest probability of success, divergent thinking involves leaps of the imagination and a lack of concern with probabilities of success.

To illustrate the difference between convergent and divergent thinking, here is an example. You may be familiar with the puzzle concerning the cannibals and the missionaries crossing the river in a single boat. It goes something like this: Three missionaries and three cannibals must cross a river. They have but one boat, which will carry only two people. Since the river is filled with crocodiles and piranhas, no one can swim the river. The problem, however, concerns the cannibals' latent tendency to eat people. The missionaries are safe as long as their number is equal to or greater than that of the cannibals. But if the cannibals outnumber the missionaries on either side of the river, it's good-bye missionaries. How can all six people safely cross the river in the single two-person boat?

The exclusively convergent thinker may find this puzzle somewhat difficult to solve without numerous trials. The more divergent thinker, however, experiences little difficulty and typically uncovers the solution immediately. In case you have not discovered the answer, the step-by-step solution follows:

1. One cannibal and one missionary cross the river. The missionary returns with the boat.
2. Two cannibals cross the river. One of them returns with the boat.
3. Two missionaries cross the river. *Both a missionary and a cannibal return with the boat.*
4. Both remaining missionaries cross the river. One of the cannibals returns with the boat.
5. Two cannibals cross the river. One of them returns for the remaining cannibal.

The key to solving this little problem lies in step 3. The convergent thinker, concerned with efficiency and achieving the goal in the most direct manner, is apt to overlook the possibility of having *two* people return with the boat. But such a step is necessary if you are to keep the cannibals from outnumbering the missionaries on one or the other side of the river. The divergent thinker, on the other hand, is not blinded by the constraints of efficiency and "rationality at all costs." Such a thinker quickly sees the key to the solution and solves the puzzle with little difficulty.

You may be tempted to believe that divergent thinking is superior to convergent thinking, or vice versa. Such a conclusion, however, would be quite mistaken. Both types are complementary modes of thought. In some situations one will be superior, but at other times the other will prove to be more useful in solving problems. It would be wise, then, for everyone to develop abilities of both divergent and convergent thinking. Unfortunately, while convergent thinking can be (and is) taught and learned in contemporary classrooms, divergent thinking can be learned only through experience and revelation. It defies any formalized description or instruction and can be acquired only through experiences with the novel, the creative, and the unexpected.

SUMMARY

Decision making includes problem solving, which requires the group's high acceptance of the solution. Decision making also includes other types of activities that are not clearly classified as problem solving: A decision is a choice made from among alternative proposals, and the consideration of these proposals constitutes all or part of the group's task performance. Consensus signifies the members' commitment to a decision reached by the group, and this commitment is measured by the members' degree of willingness to implement the decision.

Prescriptive views of the group decision-making process attempt to illustrate how groups *should* make decisions. They assume rationality on the part of the group members, assume that there is an ideal process of decision making, and are assumed to improve the quality of group decisions. We presented an example of a rational problem-solving technique.

Descriptive models of the group decision-making process attempt to illustrate how groups *do* solve problems and assume the presence of a natural (or normal) development of consensus decisions. Such models differ in terms of of the observer's perspective and of the tools used to observe the group process. The most commonly used descriptive model is the three-phase model from Bales's IPA. Other descriptive models using different observational techniques reveal significant similarities with the three-phase model, but few models employ the perspective of group interaction patterns.

Unlike linear models of group decision making, the spiral model and the multiple-sequence model assume a pattern of anchored group positions of agreement and of reach-testing forward to develop new ideas. In this way group members refine, accept, reject, modify, and combine ideas progressively and cumulatively until the idea reflects the group's consensus. The spiral process, normal to the group process, accounts for the apparent inefficiency of group decision making as well as for the influence of the social dimension in achieving higher-quality decisions.

Decisions are not so much *made* by a group as they *emerge* from the members' interaction. This emergence of decisions is illustrated in the four-phase model of orientation, conflict, emergence, and reinforcement, each phase characterized by a distinctively different communication pattern.

Group decisions achieve consensus in a spasmodic and cumulative modification of decision proposals in which proposals are introduced, discussed, dropped, and reintroduced in slightly modified versions until the proposal appears in a form that achieves group consensus. Although this start-and-stop process of decision modification is typical of all introduced decision proposals, the presence of social conflict affects the pattern of reintroduced decision proposals and the members' perception of their group task. In every case, the spasmodic process of decision modification reflects the normal interaction patterns of group members and influences both the task and socioemotional dimensions of the group.

The individual characteristics of the members of the decision-making group may also affect the group's task performance. For example, a higher ability level of the group members will probably lead to a higher-quality group decision.

Anatomy of Communication in Decision-Making Groups: Improving Effectiveness

COMMUNICATION DURING DECISION MAKING

The purpose of this chapter is to take a closer look at how communication works during the process of decision development. In the previous chapter we described four phases involved in the process of decision making. These phases—orientation, conflict, emergence, and reinforcement—are characteristic of the normal processes of many groups. Groups certainly experience these phases in many ways: Some go through the phases quickly, and others more slowly; some groups spend a different amount of time in each phase; and, as Poole's (1983b) work indicates, some groups are very idiosyncratic and undergo different sequences of interaction. But the four phases, in addition to other research on group cycles and the group process, capture the essence of group development regardless of their variations. Almost all groups get organized (orientation), experience some sort of conflict (conflict), develop decisions (emergence), and justify what they have done (reinforcement).

This first part of this chapter focuses on the specific communicative utterances made by specific members during actual group interaction, reflecting the "flavor" of the group discussion. It describes the communicative exchanges of specific group members as the group progresses through the four phases of decision making. The second part of the chapter identifies the principles that contribute most to effective group decision making.

The interaction described below was taken from audiotaped transcripts of group meetings and illustrates the four phases of group decision making. It might be useful to review the model discussed in Chapter 6 during and after your reading of this interaction.

The Situation A six-member jury (all men) is deliberating over a verdict after observing a mock trial. The dramatized trial involved a civil suit seeking damages for alleged injuries suffered in an automobile-pedestrian accident. The plaintiff, Alfred Derby, was the pedestrian who brought the suit. The defendant, Roger Adams, was the driver of the automobile that struck Derby. The jury group ultimately decided in favor of the defendant, Adams, and did not award damages in any amount to the plaintiff, Derby. Instrumental to this final verdict, the jury achieved consensus on a key decision that the plaintiff was negligent and therefore contributed to the accident.

Orientation The opening excerpt of group interaction occurs during the first 5 minutes of the jury's deliberations. The six group participants are designated by the letters A through F. The ellipsis (...) signifies a pause in the interaction, not omitted materials.

A: First of all, we decide whether it's a case of liability or negligence.
D: Yeah...negligence.
A: It's the same thing. In other words, you all feel that Roger Adams alone was negligent without the contributory negligence of Derby—or was it Derby's fault as much as Adams's fault—or was it either's fault—or was it just plain accident?
C: Guilty or not guilty.
A: It's not just those two choices, though. We've got three choices.
D: What else can there be, though? I mean...
A: It's not a criminal action like whether he robbed a store. It's just whether he is negligent, both of them are negligent, or whether...
D: Yeah, I see. But there are still only two verdicts. Do we give the plaintiff any money or not?
A: First of all, how many people here feel that just Roger Adams alone was negligent and that Alfred Derby, the person who was hit, in no way contributed to this negligence and therefore should receive compensation?

Typical of a group's orientation phase are the members' attempts to accustom themselves to the topic and to the procedure. In this case they must accustom themselves to the procedure of the law and the legal directions they received from the judge.

In the excerpt above, the members proceed to discover what choices of final decisions are available to them. Essentially they are asking themselves, "What precisely is the task we are expected to accomplish?" With this fundamental step out of the way, the members proceed to probe one another's attitudes. Member A's final comment requests a preliminary survey of the first impressions of group members. How difficult will it be to achieve agreement? This first excerpt, then, typifies the early efforts of members to acclimatize themselves—first to the procedures, and then to one another.

Member B responds to member A's request for his initial opinion and stimulates responses that are typical of the orientation phase. As member B provides argument for his opinions, A and C seem to experience discomfort. They respond by invoking procedural rules formulated on the spur of the moment in order to keep

B in check. In essence, they are telling B to withhold his evidence and reasons until later, at which time the group will thrash things out. For the present, A and C don't want to "rock the boat." A more typical manner of expressing a member's initial attitude during the orientation phase is the following comment of A:

A: I feel that...I don't know about you guys, but it could have been me. I'm a reckless driver, and I can picture myself in a hurry to school. And there were a lot of mistakes brought out in the testimony...on both sides. First of all, I have always thought that the Banker's [parking] lot is the one next to Administration.

A is attempting to advance his opinion and includes supporting reasons. But his specific opinion is not totally clear from this comment. His manner of presenting his attitude is tentative and ambiguous. He even seems to apologize for attempting to express an opinion. He includes self-deprecation lest his attitude appear too forceful to the other members. He tempers his attitude by condemning "both sides" for having made mistakes in their testimony. He concludes by citing an innocuous error of fact—the location of a parking lot; he calculates that his remark will offend no one and even attributes it to his own misunderstanding. He delivers this comment with considerable hesitancy, with numerous pauses, and with trepidation. Such ambiguity is characteristic of nearly all substantive comments during orientation.

Another excerpt of the group's interaction demonstrates a series of ambiguous responses following the initiation of a decision proposal of questionable relevance to the forthcoming decision:

A: I'm a little bit confused about this whole thing. I don't know if we can assume that what the attorneys said is true or not.
C: Not in summation you can't—unless it was brought out in testimony.
D: That one in the gray suit based his mostly on emotion, and if we were to go by that alone without regarding anything...I mean emotion is fine, but...
A: You're right. A lot of it was based on emotion. I realize that, but still I don't know whether we should accept it or...
C: That was his job. We can't blame him for...
A: I guess not, but...

A originates this decision proposal by claiming that he is confused and is seeking clarification. He does not appear to be looking for any argument. Only C expresses a definite attitude or opinion toward this proposal concerning the credibility of the attorneys. A and D respond to the proposal with ambiguous reluctance. The members continue to participate hesitantly. Note the number of unfinished sentences and phrases left dangling. Two members, A and D, appear to favor the decision proposal, but they are carefully tolerant of other members' opinions. A twice agrees with the attitude that he apparently disfavors, but he qualifies his agreement with a hint of disagreement—for example, "you're right...I realize that, but"...and "I guess not, but...." Including the qualifier "but" and implying both a favorable and an unfavorable opinion toward the proposal typify ambiguous attitudes toward nearly all decision proposals during the orientation phase.

Conflict Following the transition to the conflict phase, the members have completed developing their opinions. The period of testing the group atmosphere is over, and the general trend of idea development seems to be clear. Opinions and ideas in the orientation phase existed in their formative states. During the conflict phase, the process of formulation is complete. At this point, the group members proceed to choose up sides and engage in verbal battle over substantive issues. The following excerpt is typical of the interaction during the second phase of group decision making—the conflict phase:

A: The thing to decide is, was Roger Adams in a hurry? And did he act in such a manner that a reasonable, adult, mature person would?

C: You have to consider him a reasonable, prudent person. He was waved on by another person who was going to make the turn, irregardless [sic] of whether he was in a hurry or not.

A: I would say that if he is reasonable, he wouldn't take another person's word for it.

C: Oh, come on now! There is only one car on the street.

A: I certainly wouldn't do it.

C: Do you consider yourself reasonable?

A: I'm not reasonable. I'll admit it, too. But what does that have to do with it? I wouldn't want to use myself as an example. That doesn't say that he wasn't reasonable.

B: Then we're not going to get anyplace. You have to give some criteria. You can't just say he wasn't reasonable and let it go at that.

The tentativeness of expressed opinions, characteristic of interaction during the orientation phase, is certainly absent during interaction of the conflict phase. Member *A*'s comment, which initiates the decision proposal concerning the possible negligence of the defendant, does not indicate his opinion toward the decision proposal. It is clearly a comment expressing an ambiguous opinion toward the proposal. But the tone of this ambiguous comment is clearly different from the tone of the typical ambiguous comment of the orientation phase. At this point, *A* does not hesitate, verbally or ideationally. He self-assuredly asserts, "The thing to decide is,...."

Tolerance for any dissenting opinion is not apparent in the language choices of any of these commitments. The comment implying "This is my opinion but I could be wrong," which was characteristic of the orientation phase, becomes, in the conflict phase, the comment indicating "This is my opinion and it is correct." *C* also asserts, "You have to consider him...," and *B* asserts, "You *have* to give some criteria. You *can't* just say..." These stylistic characteristics of the communicative acts implicitly *compel* the responding group members into a for-or-against choice. Neutral opinions are no longer acceptable. The language used during the interaction of the conflict phase virtually forces the members to express definite opinions. Essentially stylistic features of the interaction itself force members into conflict or ideas.

Member *A* is now clearly identified as a spokesman for the plaintiff, and *B* and *C* appear to be spokesmen for the defendant. The next excerpt from group interaction involves a discussion of the same decision proposal and illustrates more vividly the ideational division of the group members:

C: Most people, I think, would make sure that the other side was clear for him to go. I think it would be reasonably prudent to take a glance over there to make sure that the guy was still signaling you on.

A: I don't think you can trust another person. It's a fact that...I don't know if you've ever traveled on the highway behind a semitrailer...You're following, and semitrailers don't usually go as fast as you would like or necessarily the speed limit. You're back of the semitrailer. You keep swinging out to see if you can pass. You see the driver wave his arm out like this. That's illegal. You can't use this as evidence in court that it was safe to pass the truck.

C: We can't consider that. We judge on the testimony we heard in court today and yesterday.

D: That's kind of irrelevant.

A: But the truck driver said it was safe to pass just like this guy in court said.

D: It is the custom on the highway, illegal or not, for big trucks to be courteous enough to flick on and off their lights when it's safe for the guy behind him to pass.

A: How long has it been since you have traveled on the highway?

D: Last fall.

A: Well, most of them don't do it anymore. Besides, if this guy was a reasonable man, he would have wanted to find out for himself. Not just take another guy's word for it.

C: We shouldn't take in anything that we didn't hear in court.

A: But this pertains to what we heard in the courtroom. If he was a reasonable man, he wouldn't have taken this driver's word for it that he should go.

C: How many people agree with you on that statement? I don't, for one.

D: I don't.

B: I would take the driver's word for it.

A: No, you wouldn't.

C: A reasonable person would.

The dissident A is fighting a losing battle to have the group consider his analogy regarding highway driving. His antagonists continue to be B and C. These three members engage in a heated verbal exchange over this issue.

During the conflict phase, group members know which members are on which side in the conflict over ideas and feel fewer inhibitions regarding the necessity for social facilitation. Disagreement is not only definite; it is vehement. Comments such as "Oh, come on now!" and "No, you wouldn't!" are quite common during the conflict phase. In fact, some comments are virtual insults and certainly not intended to win close friends. The question, "Do you consider yourself reasonable?" may be insulting; but C's final comment in the excerpt above, "A reasonable person would," is more than insulting. In the context of this interaction, that comment is tantamount to character assassination.

At this point, A appears to be the sole member of the group who favors the plaintiff's side in the civil case. Member D, not very active in earlier interaction during orientation, sides against A on this issue. But D's comments don't appear to be as vehement as B's and C's opposition. Note that D tones down his charge of irrelevance by saying, "That's kind of irrelevant," while C flatly asserts, "We can't consider that." Later D dispassionately appeals to A's reason about "custom" and disregards the issue of its legality. In fact, D continues to discuss the issue as though it were relevant.

Eventually D disagrees with A on this issue, but his disagreement is clearly not equivalent in tone, language, or manner to the disagreement of B and C. The next excerpt from the conflict phase casts more light on the role D plays in this second phase of decision emergence.

A: Do you think our Roger Adams testified truthfully on the stand?

D: I think he fudged a bit.

A: I do, too. That was my opinion. I realize that these are fixed situations, but let's pretend that it isn't. I mean, I think that he was trying to get himself out of a bad situation...as any normal person would, I suppose.

C: But the three witnesses for the defense—they all collaborated [sic] his testimony perfectly.

A: Which ones?

C: All three for the defense.

B: The guy that waved him on, the girl...

D: That is not strictly true, because the girl was a little off.

A: One person said that he stopped for one or two seconds and then shot out. Another one said he was there for half a minute. They didn't collaborate [sic] on that.

E: But one of them was watching him, and the other one was driving his own car and getting ready to go. They collaborate [sic] on the things that were important, though.

A: I can't see how you can say that. They didn't collaborate [sic] at all. Time was just one of the factors they didn't agree on.

Member A seems to have procured a lieutenant in D. Both are now identified with the plaintiff, while B and C continue to favor the defendant. One of the two most infrequent contributors to the group interaction, member E, identifies himself with the defendant in the excerpt above. Hence, two coalitions appear to be developing in this second phase of the group decision-making process. A and D form one coalition, which favors the plaintiff. B, C, and probably E are members of the other coalition, which favors the defendant. Only member F remains clearly outside either coalition.

This jury is composed of six members. The sixth member, F, is still to be heard from in the excerpts taken from the group interaction. He has contributed to the group interaction sparingly, and his participation during the conflict phase is virtually nonexistent.

One can probably speculate that F's withdrawal from group participation results from a feeling of discomfort brought on by the vehement substantive conflict over ideas during this phase. He is undoubtedly aware of his low status in the group, which may or may not be of his own volition. Whether from apathy toward the group's purpose or from an abiding fear of social conflict, F has chosen to

withdraw from group interaction rather than take a stand and join one of the coalitions involved in social conflict over ideas.

In terms of the developing status hierarchy in the emergent group setting,
leader-contenders are clearly emerging during this conflict phase (see Chapter 9).
Member *A* is the most vehement spokesman for the "plaintiff's coalition." Member
C, or possibly member *B*, seems to represent the strongest leader-contender for the
"defendant's coalition." The conflict over substantive issues is undoubtedly relevant to the contention over the leadership roles too. But member *A*, the leader-
contender for the coalition opposed to the decision that will ultimately achieve group
consensus, will not remain in active contention for leadership much longer. As a
member who has committed himself to a position opposing the consensus decision,
his bid for leadership is doomed.

Emergence Following the transition to the emergence phase, the substantive conflict between the members begins to dissipate, as illustrated in a later excerpt taken
from the group's interaction:

A: Let me ask one more question. Do you think Derby the plaintiff was in the
crosswalk?

D: I don't think so.

C: No, I don't. I don't think that has too much to do with it, though.

D: I agree.

C: I know there are some statues about the crosswalk, but I mean the fact that he
was in...I don't know. That might be kind of important.

D: He was on the roadway is really the issue.

C: I don't think it really happened exactly the way the defendant described it. I
think he embellished it a little toward his side. I think it happened close enough
to it, though.

F: As far as that goes, Derby may have his own story too. I mean each would be
looking out for himself. That's only natural.

D: Of course you are going to get this in any situation.

F: That's just it. Both of them. You can't use the two prime subjects. You have
to try and go on the witnesses. Of course they are witnesses, too, and you have
to consider them. And they are important, too, but...

Member *A* has initiated another proposal for consideration, but his initiating
statement expresses an ambiguous opinion toward it. He uses simple and straightforward language without argument. The communicative acts in response to his
proposal emphasize the irrelevance of his proposal rather than attempt to deny its
factual nature. During the conflict phase, the responses to such a proposal would
probably have been an intense denial and consequently an additional substantive
conflict. In the emergence phase, though, the conflict over issues is muted.

In the second phase, the members hammered out the issues and proposals
they felt were important to getting their task accomplished. But their response to
a new issue in the emergence phase is to dismiss it as irrelevant rather than to engage
in additional conflict.

The level of social tension (see Chapter 2) seems to be appreciably lower during the emergence phase. Member *C* is now much more tolerant of *A*'s opinions and feelings, as illustrated in the last excerpt. He admits to the possibility that the issue raised by member *A* "might be kind of important." He even goes so far as to concede that the defendant "embellished" his testimony, an admission he would never have made in the conflict phase.

The emerging decision becomes progressively clearer during the emergence phase, and all members seem to sense the direction the group has taken. Even *F* joins the interaction, "jumping on the bandwagon" to offer his opinion in support of the defendant. When the other members don't wholeheartedly welcome his offer to join their side, *F* begins to flounder in his comments and becomes extremely ambiguous and vague in his comments. His final remark is a classic example of ambiguity. At any rate, the decision becomes increasingly evident, and even *F* knows it.

The overt conflict over substantive issues characterizing the conflict phase moderates during the emergence phase. Both *A* and *D* ameliorate their dissent from the decision proposals favoring the defendant. For example, while *A* vehemently and tenaciously expressed his dissenting view during the conflict phase, he expresses only ambiguous opinions without much tenacity during the emergence phase. The following excerpt clearly illustrates this change in *A*'s verbal behavior:

A: I just wondered. Maybe this isn't really relevant, but I never really understood exactly where the point of impact was. Not in relation to the car, but in relation to the street. How far out from the curb he was. It appeared from the drawing and three or four witnesses that it was in the lane closest to the curb that Derby stepped off of. If this is the case, Adams made an illegal left turn. Of course, I might be mistaken.

C: Yeah, Right.

B: I think it was right in the middle.

C: Was it in the middle?

D: It was probably about 20 feet off. That might be closest to this curb.

E: He said he was about 11 feet off the curb, but he also put him closer to the middle.

A: If it was closer to the curb than it was to the intersection, it wasn't an illegal left turn. But it might have been 11 feet this way, and that would have been an illegal turn.

D: Eleven feet puts it right about the middle. No illegal left turn.

C: Remember he's turning, so he's got to come a little bit into the other lane on the turn.

D: Well, not necessarily.

C: It's pretty hard not to, with at least his front bumper.

B: It's pretty close, but he was probably all right on his turn. If he was out 11 feet, he was right there in the middle.

D: In that case he was only...He's not negligent.

A: This is irrelevant, then.

C: I don't think it's possible to hit him in the middle. I don't think that it is physically possible.

A: No. He did make a wrong turn, but he wasn't completely out of his lane from where he should have been.

C: He was probably wrong in not watching exactly as he was turning. But I don't think it was too far away to be reasonable.

Another last-ditch effort by *A* to advocate the plaintiff's side in the discussion: Did the defendant make an illegal left turn? But *A* fails to raise many doubts concerning what is becoming increasingly apparent as the consensus decision. But the strength and tenacity of *A*'s argumentativeness have dissipated. He initiates his proposal with reluctant ambiguity. Note his apologetic phrases, which appear throughout his contributions—"I just wondered. Maybe this isn't really relevant," "It appeared...," "If this is the case...," and the final "Of course, I might be mistaken."

During the ensuing discussion, *A* contributes another ambiguous argument indicating only the possibility—not even the probability—that the defendant was negligent in making an illegal left turn. Compared with his self-assured stance in the conflict phase, *A* has moderated his attitude considerably. He does not express certainty about any opinion he expresses in the emergence phase. He qualifies nearly everything with ambiguous language, such as "if" and "might." He resigns himself to losing the fight over this issue. In fact, he doesn't even try very hard to win it. He offers his resigned statement of capitulation, "This is irrelevant, then,"even before the other members have completely rejected it. In fact, *C* again expresses amazing tolerance for *A*'s proposal and once more appears to give it serious consideration before he rejects it. *A* has evidently succumbed to the apparent consensus decision. *C* apparently knows it and is softening the blow somewhat. *C* is definitely the leading contender for group leader, and he is willing to accept *A* as a high-status member whose opinions are worthy of consideration.

The two coalitions of the conflict phase also appear to dissipate during the emergence phase. Members of opposing coalitions responded to their "opponents" with open hostility and even contempt in the conflict phase, but they now respond with active rational consideration. The prime example of this change is illustrated by *C*'s comments. He preferred to insult *A* during the conflict phase as a response to *A*'s position favoring the plaintiff. But, during the emergence phase, *C* considers *A*'s proposal, admits to its potential significance and credibility, and then rejects it.

Again, the basis for rejecting proposals favoring the plaintiff's case is irrelevance. Members argued against proposals during the conflict phase on the basis of their truth or falsity, but the basic issue on which members typically evaluate proposals in the emergence phase seems to be relevance.

Reinforcement In the reinforcement phase, decisions have completed the process of emergence. Interaction during this final phase of the group process confirms decisions already made and develops the members' commitment, or consensus, toward those decisions. The following excerpt appears very early in the reinforcement phase:

E: Everybody saw the car coming.

B: Besides that, he said his lights were on.

C: His turn signal was on. It was obvious that he was coming. That would make it all the more easier [sic] to see the car coming.

D: Practically everybody saw that car coming. His lights turning.

E: That guy that was on the sidewalk…He saw all this traffic, and he also saw Adams coming. That's why he didn't go. Why did Derby go? He has to be at some fault.

C: I feel sorry for him, and I'd like to help him out, but I just don't think I can.

D: I agree.

B: You can't base it on an emotion…

D: Of course not.

C: I don't think we should take into any account what they told us at the beginning, either—about Adams being a drunkard and that.

B: No. Don't even mention that.

F: No. Don't worry about it.

C: No.

Members *B*, *C*, *D*, and *E* all express agreement with the decision proposal that Derby, the defendant, was guilty of contributory negligence. They not only agree with one another, but they provide superfluous evidence to support their agreement. Interaction consistently includes statement after statement expressing agreement with the one before it. Member *C* initiates a "straw man" proposal contrary to the decision already made, but he immediately expresses an unfavorable opinion toward it. Members *B* and *F* promptly concur, and they drop the proposal at once.

The major dissenter, *A*, is conspicuously absent from the previous interaction. But his former lieutenant, *D*, has certainly joined the other coalition. Even *F* is growing bolder and bolder with his comments, now that absolutely no doubt remains regarding the decision made by the group. As the group's interaction draws to a close, *A* leaves no doubt as to his completely modified position:

A: I guess I'd have to say that it was both their faults.

C: I say it is both their faults.

A: Evidently it probably is.

B: Derby really never should have stepped off the curb.

D: Right.

E: And there he was out 11 feet already, and he was trying to avoid another oncoming car. That's just plain stupid.

F: When you step off the curb, you know you are taking chances. You have to stay on your toes.

A: Well, he obviously didn't see him turn. But he should have.

F: He was right in front of him. He should have seen him turn.

D: Right. He must have been looking someplace else.

A: I think Derby stepped off the curb, started walking, and was halfway through the first lane when this guy started to make his turn. It doesn't take long for all this to happen. Only a few seconds.

C: The plaintiff was making some kind of inference that Adams was going excessively fast across the turn. I don't think that's really possible.

D: No.

B: How fast can you take a turn without crashing into the corner or something?

D: Yeah. When you're accelerating, you still aren't going more than 9 or 10 miles per hour.

C: The average turn is about 6 miles per hour, maybe a little faster, but that isn't excessively fast.

B: It varies if he was trying to beat this other car.

C: But he couldn't have been going even 15 miles around a turn.

D: If you do, you're pulling out like a sports car.

C: If you have good cornering, you'll probably make it. If you don't, you might not.

A: We agree unanimously right now that it is both their faults.
(A chorus of "Yeah!")

A: It was both their faults. There is nothing more to do, then.

E: I would say that it was mutual negligence—more Derby's fault.

F: I say it is all Derby's fault.

A: You say all Derby's fault?

F: Yes.

A: I think it is more Adams's fault. But both are still negligent.

C: Okay. Then it's unanimous.

F: I say that Derby was completely at fault. He shouldn't even be suing.

C: You mean that Adams should be suing?

F: Right.

A: There are two possibilities on this sheet. Let me read them both. "Number 1: We, the jury, find in favor of the plaintiff and against the defendant and assess damages to the sum of..." In other words, we think it was Adams's fault, and Derby should pay.

C: Throw that one out.

A: Okay. We'll throw that one out. "Number 2: We, the jury, find in favor of the defendant and against..." In other words, if they think it is more Derby's fault.

D: No. Just the plaintiff.

C: In favor of the defendant legally means it isn't the plaintiff. It doesn't mean that the defendant can claim damages. It just means that the suit has been dropped.

B: We find in favor of the defendant.

C: Yes.

A: That's how we do it, then.

B: Write "Contributory negligence."

D: We are all decided.

C: Unanimous decision. No dissenters.

Throughout these final moments of group interaction, there is a pervading spirit of harmony and unity. All members agree, and everyone knows that all members agree. But they continue to discuss the decision while verbally slapping each other on the back, even to the point of initiating another straw-man decision proposal. Three of the members join in verbally demolishing the plaintiff's argument concerning Adams's excessive speed.

Meanwhile, A firmly commits himself to the position that Derby is also at fault. His language still includes traces of reluctance. But his expression of agreement is completely understandable, given his earlier attitude of vehement opposition during the conflict phase. He closes his comments in the language of willing reluctance with such statements as "I guess I'd have to say..." and "Evidently it probably is." Nevertheless, he is firmly committed to the consensus decision.

The nonparticipant in the conflict phase, F, is caught up in the spirit of consensus, and he overreacts to the obvious consensus decision. He goes so far as to assess 100 percent negligence to the plaintiff. Not even members B and C want to go this far. They don't pay too much attention to F's Johnny-come-lately enthusiasm. They have made their decision, and they have reinforced it.

To avoid any doubts, and probably in deference to A's rationale for making the decision unanimous, B suggests that the group explain to the court that the basis for its decision was "contributory negligence." The addition of the members' rationale is superfluous, but they do it anyway. The final comments allude to the written record, which they return to officials of the mock court, confirming their consensus decision.

Summary The process of group decision making thus progresses through four phases of interaction—orientation, conflict, emergence, and reinforcement. The decisional process, closely allied with characteristics of the social dimension reflecting the interdependent relationship of the two dimensions, is a cumulative and cyclic process. Group members anchor their interaction to tentative decision proposals that lead to and culminate in consensus, or final group decisions.

Excerpts from an actual group's interaction reflect the "flavor" of the discussion and the importance of stylistic features of the language and changes in individual members' attitudes as their group progresses toward consensus. Although the four phases seem to be clearly separate in the excerpted interaction from each of the four phases, the transitions between phases are in reality quite gradual and not nearly as dramatic as they appear in selected excerpts. This, then, is the process of group decision making in action.

IMPROVING EFFECTIVENESS IN GROUPS

Perhaps our most important goal in this book is to help you improve your performance in groups. By now you have read Chapter 6 and the first part of this chapter and should have a good understanding of communication and the group process. At least you should understand that groups and communication are complex processes. This is a first step toward improving effectiveness. But becoming really effective in groups takes time, and there are no easy answers. We will present many issues and recommendations below for improving communication in groups, but there is still no simple formula for success. You might think that because you communicate every day, all this practice would make you an effective communicator. Such an expectation is quite false. On the contrary, most people are not very effective communicators and do little more than practice bad habits.

But you can improve your communication with understanding, knowledge, and practice. Compare your communicative health to your personal health. You certainly do not think of health as taking medicines when you get sick. Health is living normally from day to day. And if you know and understand your biological processes, you will know what to eat, what to wear, what activities to perform, what to avoid, and so forth. So it is with communication. The healthy communicator does not rush around seeking miracle cures. Rather, he learns about communication and what behaviors are most appropriate.

Some Warnings

Beware of books and people who sell "cures" for ailing groups and "vitamin supplements" for successful communication. Our position here is very clear: It is possible to improve your communication and group behavior, but not by slavishly and uncritically applying all sorts of tricks and techniques.

Rationality Rationality is probably the biggest trap set for group participants. As we discussed in Chapter 6, rationality can be good for a group, but the problem is that group members think they must adhere to a *single* mode of rational thinking. They believe, perhaps, that it is better to be a convergent thinker than a divergent thinker (see Chapter 6). Certainly convergent thinking is useful to the group, but it is not the only way a group should proceed. There is much about the communicative process that is not very "logical."

Decision making does not always proceed best on rational grounds. If that were the case, there would be no juries. A defendant would be tried only before a judge trained in law and rationality. But there are many complex extenuating circumstances surrounding a criminal charge, and these often call for nonrational decision making. It is like respecting the spirit of the law rather than the letter of the law. Religion, codes of ethics, and moral positions are important guides for behavior, and they are typically based more on faith than on reason.

It is also true that humans simply do not always behave rationally. There is much about our culture that is nonrational. On warm days, men wear suits and neckties, and women wear nylon hosiery; they may be conforming to the norms of personal appearance, but it is not necessarily rational. Actually, groups are breeding grounds for nonrational behavior. We have touched on the concepts of groupthink and group polarization in Chapter 2 and we will encounter these concepts again in the next chapter. Decisions that led to the Cuban missile crisis in the early 1960s and the Watergate trials in the 1970s were thought to be rational but turned out to be disastrous.

Standard Agendas and Formats Agendas and formats are road maps for the group to follow in order to improve the efficiency and quality of its decision making.

Students in courses designed to learn about communication and groups will probably encounter these agendas and formats. They are useful tools for beginners. But they, too, can be overused and produce more problems than they solve.

It is true that groups can be inefficient, but the reasons for the inefficiency are also the reasons why groups sometimes produce high-quality decisions. Groups are slow and often tedious because good decision making is hard work; a thorough testing and analysis of ideas, such that group members feel truly comfortable with the decisions, is a time-consuming process. Also, ensuring that people feel as though they have been heard and included is an often-overlooked function of groups. Many organizations promote frustrating group experiences simply so that they can guarantee that everyone has had a chance to participate.

PRINCIPLES OF EFFECTIVENESS

Effectiveness comes with knowledge and practice. It is true that "practice makes perfect," but only when the practice is based on understanding. More experiences and a greater variety of group experiences will lead to more effective group participation. You must have knowledge and experience. Reading a book about how to shoot a basketball will not do much for your shooting. You must practice. A book will provide you with indispensable knowledge about chess, but it will not make you an expert. The same is true of communication. Reading a book and never participating in groups will not do much for your skill in groups; and, conversely, participating in groups without the requisite knowledge and understanding will also place you at a disadvantage.

The principles of effectiveness that follow are designed to capitalize on the interdependence between knowledge and experience. We present these principles in three areas—individual attitudinal factors, interpersonal factors, and group factors.

IMPROVING EFFECTIVENESS: ATTITUDINAL FACTORS

Probably the first place to begin the search for improvement of effectiveness is with oneself—the individual group member. Because every person is, in some respects, a unique human being, it is difficult to discuss the idiosyncracies of the members of any decision-making group. On the other hand, some general principles related to the attitudes and values that are typical of members of effective groups can be isolated.

Attitudes toward the Group

The psychological "set," or orientation, to the group and to other group members is vitally important to the success and effectiveness of group decision making. Rarely do such attitudes exist before the formation of the group, however. Rather, members develop a certain orientation to the group and to other members during the process of group development. If a member does possess an attitude before the group is formed, an attitude conducive to effective group process, this orientation is probably one of open-mindedness. That is, the member enters the initial group meetings without prematurely having decided whether the group experience will be undesirable. This state of open-mindedness will also involve a considerable amount of interpersonal sensitivity in which the member is sensitive and open to the beliefs and feelings of others. Such an interpersonal sensitivity persists even though the beliefs and ideas of the others are quite dissimilar from those of the interpersonally sensitive member.

We have consistently stressed the principle of commitment in the sense of group consensus and cohesiveness. Individual members who are committed to the group experience a strong feeling of loyalty to it. That is, members believe in the potential effectiveness of the group process to the extent that they will sublimate their own goals in favor of those of the group. Commitment requires a belief that the group process will fulfill the goals of the individual and that group membership will provide benefits important to the individual.

With the attitude of commitment toward the group comes a feeling of responsibility. The committed group member is willing to expend time and energy for the benefit of the group. Often members of classroom groups will excuse themselves from contributing very much to the group effort by citing other considerations (for example, the student has a part-time job, time is required for other classes, the class is not the student's major, or only three credits will be earned in the class). But the group member, if committed, feels a sense of responsibility and will find the time and expend the effort for the group.

Without that feeling of responsibility, most group members will be content to avoid becoming heavily involved in the group effort. They will be very willing to let some other member of the group assume most of the responsibility and do most of the work. The committed member, on the other hand, goes out of his or her way to volunteer for additional responsibility and does not wait to be asked. The committed member is a responsible member. Effective decision-making groups enjoy a virtual competition among members who are actively participating in the group efforts.

Attitudes toward Interaction

A member who is committed to the group is never a silent member. Regardless of any personality traits (such as shyness or apprehension), the committed group member simply cannot remain a low participant. Indeed, such members find that they cannot remain silent on issues that confront the group, even though outside the group the person may remain silent even when being negatively evaluated as an individual. Group loyalty is typically stronger in affecting the amount of interaction of individual members than other aspects of the individual's own self.

A classroom group of a few years ago exemplifies the problem of the uncommitted member whose attitude toward the group carries over into his or her participation in the group interaction. This particular group was engaged in discussing the current practice of evaluating the courses and instructors in the university. The group suffered from a woefully inadequate amount of information concerning the topic, and this inadequacy was reflected in its report of its task accomplishments. Knowing that the student association of the university was performing a lengthy and comprehensive analysis of the evaluation forms and recognizing that one of the group members was involved in the department's student advisory committee, we asked him whether he was aware of the universitywide study of course-evaluation techniques. His reply went something like this: "Of course I know about it. But this bunch of turkeys in this group wouldn't know what to do with the information, anyway. They already had their minds made up. I thought I would just let them hang themselves." Only a member with a very low level of commitment to the group would have expressed an attitude of so little responsibility and remained so inactive in the group's interaction.

Chapter 6 discussed the tendency of successful groups to engage in considerable disagreement and social conflict over task-oriented issues. Although conflict can be considered an effective format for the critical testing of ideas, the willingness of the individual members to engage in conflict may be more important to the effectiveness of group decision making. Why would anyone engage in conflict interaction and run the risk of being wrong unless one is concerned about the group and its successful outcome? For most people, argument with friends or peers is relatively painful and socially uncomfortable. But for conflict to exist and to result in successful task performance, group members must be willing to participate in conflict. For this reason we normally think of the cohesive group as a group that is not afraid to experience conflict, to overcome conflict, and to remain cohesive despite the potentially disruptive influence of conflict.

With a social climate that is less conducive to expressing conflict, members feel inhibited. Consequently, the level of cohesiveness in that group and its ultimate effectiveness in performing its decision-making task suffer. The committed member is thus willing not only to express his or her own point of view but also to encourage the expression of other viewpoints. The result is a free and open attitude toward group interaction. Unruly? Yes. Disruptive? Potentially. But more important, such attitudes toward interaction lead to more effective communication and group decision making.

Creativity

Although there is obviously a point of diminishing returns, the greater the volume of ideas and decision proposals that members contribute during group interaction, the higher the quality of consensus decisions. Also, leaders initiate a large number of themes during group interaction, as we will discuss in Chapter 9. Each of these two findings implies that one ingredient of communicative effectiveness is creativity. As a participant in group decision making, then, you would be well advised to increase your creative capacity. Let your mind go. Give your imagination a free rein. No relevant idea should be considered too irrational or too farfetched. The best advice for developing creativity is not to stifle the formation of ideas. Be a divergent thinker (see Chapter 6).

Certainly groups do not accept all ideas that members contribute during group interaction. In fact, the more ideas the members contribute, the more ideas the group will reject. Indeed, the period of idea testing during group interaction, particularly during the conflict phase, involves the rejection of many decision proposals. But this is the period during which members should be encouraged to contribute new ideas too.

Members who do not fully comprehend the nature of the group process will probably consider the group's rejection of their ideas a rejection of their selves, a rejection of their value as group members. Consequently, such members tend to inhibit their creative impulses, and this restraint leads to their contributing fewer ideas. Brainstorming techniques, which have been devised to account for this human tendency, do not allow brainstorming members to respond critically to any contributed idea despite its apparent irrelevance. Effective group members, on the other hand, know in advance that the other group members will reject many of their ideas, but this knowledge does not inhibit their creativity. They continue to introduce new and different proposals for group consideration. These members probably suffer psychologically from the group's rejection of their ideas, too, but their creativity does not suffer as a result.

Actually, the slowness of the group process and the inherent start-and-stop process of modifying decisions encourage creativity from group members. Each member has the time and the opportunity to mull over his or her own ideas and the ideas of others and to develop new insights. Experts in creativity consider the incubation period essential to the creative process.

The process of group decision making again suggests the importance of timing. New and different proposals benefit the group efforts most during the orientation and conflict phases. During these early stages of group interaction, the creativity of members in devising new and different ideas should be at a maximum. During the emergence phase, members should confine their creativity to reformulating and combining previously discussed proposals. During the reinforcement phase, creativity in any form is definitely not an asset to the group process, but a liability.

Criticism

A very normal and understandable human tendency of inexperienced group members is to avoid criticism of, and conflict with, other members. Normally, no one wants to run the risk of hurting another person's feelings. Inexperienced group members tend to avoid criticism for fear of harming the developing feeling of groupness. All of us have been taught from childhood that courtesy and tact are infinitely superior to rudeness and boorishness. So we examine an atrocious painting on our neighbor's wall and call it "interesting." We may suffer through a boring party, but we will invariably tell the host and hostess as we leave that we had a great time.

Certainly, effective group decision making does not require that we rid ourselves of good manners and respect for others during group decision making.

Group decision making is in some respects a unique social situation. What we would consider courtesy and tact in one situation is tantamount to ineffectiveness and avoidance of social problems during group decision making. The fear of hurting the feelings of others and suppressing realistic opinions characterize members of a group with rather low cohesiveness. Criticism and conflict are typical norms of a highly cohesive group. In fact, group decision making may not be so unique after all. For instance, we rarely if ever have arguments with acquaintances, but we argue vehemently and say whatever we feel with our very close friends. Knowing that you can be honest with one another is knowing you are in the company of good friends.

The amount of criticism is irrelevant to the group process, but the timing of criticism is again all-important. Criticism in the wrong place at the wrong time is as harmful to the group process as no criticism at all. Let yourself go in exercising all your critical faculties during the conflict phase. At other times, you should probably control your critical impulses and use them sparingly.

Basic to the principle of criticism during group decision making is the avoidance of neutrality. It is absolutely impossible to remain neutral and be an effective participant during group interaction. High-status members are invariably dynamic contributors who take stands and defend them. Other members consider these stands to be helpful to the group's performance of its task. A "mugwump" is destined to be a low contributor and an ineffective group member. Group interaction virtually compels members to speak out on issues and to assume an argumentative stance. (The opening section of this chapter illustrated how the very language used in a comment by one or another member often forces the other members into taking a stand during the conflict phase of group decision making.) A neutral member is usually perceived to be wishy-washy and is generally peripheral to the action of group decision making.

One vital ingredient of group decision making and one of its principal advantages over individual decision making is the process of testing ideas. Such idea testing among multiple sources of criticism results in higher-quality decisions when high social acceptance is a key criterion of decisional quality. This process of socially testing ideas is the principle behind the "free and open marketplace of ideas," in which criticism is absolutely essential. During idea testing, the group norm should encourage as much criticism as possible, both in the amount and the diversity of that criticism. Effective group members are not necessarily tactless but are highly critical of others' ideas as well as of their own.

The following are some tips for improving your critical effectiveness in groups; these are questions you can ask yourself or the group to ensure that the group exercises the best judgment possible:

1. How well are the members using communication skills to discuss issues? Do they focus on information? What is their vocabulary, word selection, and phrasing like?
2. What is the quality of the information? Are there ample data, evidence, and facts? Has this information been tested and discussed?

3. What is the social climate like? Is the group cohesive, and why or why not? Can the group disagree without serious tension? Do the members reward one another? Are the interpersonal relations good? Do the members share an identity?
4. How good are the group's work norms? Are the members committed to the task? Do they complete assignments? Do they work to think creatively about problems? Do they follow procedures outlined by the group?
5. How effective is the leadership? Is the leader skillful in procedural matters, such as agendas, meeting schedules, and resources? Does the leader keep things on track? Does he or she manage conflict skillfully? Does the leader summarize, provide useful information, and generally structure the group?

IMPROVING EFFECTIVENESS: INTERPERSONAL FACTORS

By first discussing attitudinal factors and now interpersonal factors of communicative effectiveness, we do not imply that these factors are clearly separable. Just as a person's attitudes or psychological orientations will affect that person's participation in decision-making interaction, so also will one's interaction with others affect one's orientations and attitudes. Improving one's effectiveness in communication is plainly an attitudinal, as well as an interpersonal, phenomenon.

Active Verbal Participation

It should be intuitively obvious that effective group decision making is highly correlated with the active verbal participation of the members. In other words, the effective participant actively participates verbally during group interaction.

The silent member does little to benefit the process of group decision making. Moreover, contributing only infrequently to the group's interaction does not significantly benefit the individual member. Bench warmers on a football team do not contribute much to the team's success or to the development of their own abilities. Spectating is not playing. One learns to play the game by playing it. The bench warmer may have little choice about getting to play, but the group member is silent solely of his or her own volition.

Active verbal participation does not imply equal participation of all members. Obviously, equal participation is not only abnormal and impossible, it is also not even desirable. The contributions of some members are more valuable than those of others. The more capable members should participate more. Abilities and expertise vary among the members. Each member should seek during group interaction to participate actively, but not necessarily equally, with every other member.

Also, active verbal participation does not imply that any member should attempt to monopolize the discussion or control the group interaction. Active participation implies frequent contributions, but not necessarily lengthy ones. The knowledgeable and verbally active member contributes brief comments but does so without inhibition. The first general principle for increasing one's communicative effectiveness in group decision making may seem overly obvious but is nevertheless essential: The effective communicator has something to say and says it.

Communication Skills

There exists an old and hackneyed controversy among authorities in communication. The controversy dates back to ancient Greece, centuries before Christ, and is heard even today. It concerns the relative importance of *content* and *delivery* in the effectiveness of communication. Which is more important for effective communication—what is said or how it is said? Most authorities today consider the controversy naive and largely incomplete. Not only is the content of a message inseparable from its delivery, but the communicative process includes additional and highly significant elements that the controversy ignores.

First of all, the value of an expressed idea is determined in part by the manner in which it is presented. A skillful presentation affects the perceived importance of the message. Only the most naive student of human communication would argue that an idea has intrinsic worth apart from its use in the communicative situation and its expression within the sequence of communicative acts. The evidence that communication skills do affect the message content is virtually indisputable.

Specific characteristics of communication skills are rather unclear. Certainly the skillful communicator is fluent, articulate, and above all dynamic in the conversational situation. Communication skills also involves a knowledge and an understanding of the communicative process and the ability to be flexible, adapting to the demands of the social system and the situation. Without such knowledge and adaptive ability, the communicator is perceived to be not so much fluent and articulate as merely glib. The stereotyped used-car salesperson, for example, is considered glib and smooth, but these are negative characteristics, while skill is generally considered a positive attribute.

Learning communication skills is not at all similar to learning the skill of hitting a baseball or playing a trumpet. These kinds of motor skills are based on mastering techniques and performing those techniques as an individual. Communication, however, never occurs in isolation, but always in a social system with the interconnected communicative behaviors of other persons. The ability to analyze the other person and the situation and to be perceived as articulate and dynamic requires a thorough knowledge of the communicative process and a great deal of hard work. Certainly, experience and practice in many and varied communicative situations are essential for developing communication skills. And that experience always occurs in the presence of other people—the complex social system.

It would be pretty silly, and impossible, to attempt a very complete list or survey of all the communication skills useful to group members. In fact, this entire book is devoted to communication skills in groups. But in the spirit of working with a small and manageable set of principles that can help you most efficiently, we present the following as fundamental communication skills you can develop.

Language Strengthening Most of the meaning in messages is carried by language—

words and their use. People use language to communicate clearly, but they also use it to hide, deceive, and manipulate others. Some in the group will use technical or formal language to impress others by sounding as if they are knowledgeable. In the opening section of this chapter we saw how language varied with the stages of group development; some language was nice and polite, and at other times the language became intense and strident. Group members who do not have sufficiently developed language skills usually have trouble expressing ideas. For instance, listen to the following group member try to explain the distinction between two ideas:

SCOTT: Ah, you know, they just aren't the same thing. I mean one is not the same as the other. They don't really go together because they do different things.

Scott "feels" that two ideas are different, but he cannot find the words to express the differences.

The best way to improve is to pay attention to language. Read widely and listen to how people use words. Develop good habits, such as always using a dictionary, thinking about words, and taking the time to learn the meaning and use for new words. This all sounds simple, but it is fundamental to good communication. Your experiences in groups and with other people rely on meaning. And the only way to express specific and finer shades of meaning is to have the proper vocabulary. You must also think about the relationship between words and context. It might be appropriate to use slang or a vulgar word with your best friends, but not at work or in your group meetings. Try to use language that "fits" with the people around you.

Special Language As a communicator you are most concerned with conveying an idea. To do this well, you need many types of words at your disposal. Most words have a straightforward dictionary meaning, the meaning that any native language user would associate with the word, but these words can also have special meanings that are highly personal or individualistic. Say that you were irritated at a group member who was having problems and called the person "handicapped." There is a simple dictionary definition of this word, but it also carries extra meaning. It might be highly offensive to someone. How would you like to find out that the person had a handicapped family member!

In addition to the special meanings carried by words, there is an entire class of words called jargon. *Jargon* is the specialized language of a particular group of people who have training or experience in common. A group of doctors would use jargon to discuss a medical problem among themselves. But it would not be very good communication to use jargon with a patient who did not understand the language. There is nothing wrong with jargon if the others involved in the communication understand the terms; indeed, learning the language, or the jargon, is part of becoming a specialist or an expert in some area. Jargon can be quite useful when everyone understands it because jargon has specific meaning that helps avoid confusion.

The Ladder of Abstraction All language moves from concrete to abstract. Jane might refer to her "1984 Honda Accord" and we would know that she was talking about a very specific car. If she talked about "Honda Accords," that would be a little more abstract, because it could refer to any Honda Accord. The word "car" would be even more abstract. Group members should try to communicate as concretely as possible, for abstraction usually leads to confusion. If the group wanted to talk about "fuel economy," there would be a considerable difference between talking about fuel economy in all cars and talking about fuel economy in the 1984 Honda Accord. The latter is much more concrete and manageable.

Again, there is nothing "wrong" with abstract language. Sometimes it is perfectly communicative. In Chapter 3 we referred to Eisenberg's (1984) claim that some ambiguity and abstraction can be good for the group. Abstract language does not always lead to confusion. But generally it is best to start with concrete language. As the group develops and people adjust to one another and their language, it becomes easier to use abstract language effectively.

Message Functions The messages uttered by individuals perform various functions. A *message function* is the action that the message performs. In earlier chapters (5, 6) we have presented various interaction-analysis schemes, such as Ellis's relational coding schemes and Fisher's system for tracking decision development. These are attempts to capture the functions of messages. For example, a group member might say, "Sixty-five percent of property taxes are used to fund public schools." This utterance would function as a statement that *gives information*. Other statements might be composed of completely different content and subject matter but still function to give information.

You must learn to recognize what people are *doing* with their language. Are they giving information, stating opinions, disagreeing, acting friendly, or what? The function of a message is not always apparent. If a father sees a son's shirt on the floor and asks, "Is that your shirt on the floor?" he may not be asking a genuine question. The utterance may function to mean "Pick up that shirt and put it on a hanger!" Group members often say things indirectly. The ability to recognize message functions improves as groups and relationships develop.

Supportive Communication

Jack Gibb (1961) has discussed two different "climates" of communication that develop because of communicative actions performed by interactants. These communication climates include *defensive* communication and *supportive* communication. While a defensive climate results from defensive communicative behaviors, a characteristic of such a climate is a reduction of effectiveness due to an erosion of interpersonal trust and groupness. Gibb strongly suggests that the most effective-communication is that occurring in a supportive climate and resulting from supportive communicative actions.

Characteristic of defensive communication are behaviors that both threaten the other person and originate from a perceived threat from the other person. Such defensive behaviors include personal evaluation, attempts to control, and behaviors that appear to convey an attitude of superiority or extreme certainty of belief. Generally speaking, defensive communication tends to be perceived as judgmental, manipulative, insincere, or deceptive. Being defensive oneself tends to arouse defensiveness in the other person (reciprocity at work) and results in lowered effectiveness of group interaction.

Supportive communication generally proceeds from one person's feeling of empathy with another. Supportive communication is other-directed or problem-oriented to the extent that someone who communicates supportively is genuine, sincere, honest, and spontaneous. Supportive communication is characterized by actions that do not seek to evaluate others, although supportive communication could evaluate a problem or issue. Defensive communication results when evaluative comments appear to be directed toward the person rather than the issue.

Defensive communication typically involves little social risk, but supportive communication involves high risk. Individuals create a climate of mutual trust and respect. Although status differences will occur in the group (based on power, ability, etc.), individual members supportively communicating with one another appear to attach little importance to these differences. Group members thus generate considerable cohesiveness and consider themselves unified as a group even with the presence of a status hierarchy. To recognize leadership and status in an informal group with a supportive climate is not to disrupt the sense of groupness that members feel.

Attempting to maintain a clear distinction between attitudinal and interpersonal factors of communicative effectiveness becomes virtually impossible when discussing defensive and supportive communicative actions. Supportive acts create a climate of mutual trust and are tantamount to each person's trusting the other and perceiving that this trust is reciprocated by the other. Supportive communication is consistent with a feeling or attitude of mutual support on the part of each member. Conversely, this feeling of mutual trust develops as a result of the supportive communicative behaviors performed by the members. We are again faced with the dilemma of the chicken or the egg. Which came first—the *feeling* of trust or the trusting *behavior?* The supportive communicative *climate* or the supportive communicative *behaviors?* The answer, of course, is that they develop together. One is as much a result of the other as it is the cause.

Responding to Others

The tendency to emphasize the pragmatic perspective of human communication in previous chapters may have led to an implication that the actions performed by individual members are the key elements in the group decision-making process. Actually, the actions of each individual person are less significant than the *inter*actions among individuals. That is, one person's action may always be characterized as a response to the action of another person. Treating each action as a response to a previous action allows for the development of some general principles on how to respond to others. These principles may be used as guidelines in determining how one should respond to others in the interactive setting of group decision making. In any case, this view of communication involves thinking of communicative acts as always directed toward another person in response to the actions of that other person.

Failure to understand another person can result from a number of factors. The other person may misspeak or convey an unintended impression. You may mishear an utterance or receive some information that was not intended by the other. Or the language used by the other person may need clarification; it may be too abstract. Your response in all cases is quite similar. You should always ask for clarification. The lack of a clear understanding is frustrating. Often that frustration becomes a hidden agenda when we do not ask for clarification because we do not wish to appear foolish or stupid.

One group exhibited such a misunderstanding in its interaction because of one member's use of the jargonistic term "placebo effect." No other member responded to the term, but each continued to interact with no indication that anyone had any problem of understanding. After several moments, during which time little progress was made, one member finally asked what the speaker meant by a "placebo effect." The response was to express surprise that the other members were unfamiliar with the term. The subsequent interaction, which dealt not only with the issues at hand but also with the member's tendency to verbalize in a manner that was difficult to understand, undoubtedly led to increased effectiveness of that group process.

Because clarification is so significant when you are on the receiving end of the misunderstanding, you should always be prepared for the probability that other people will also misunderstand you. Consequently, you should develop the habit of checking to see whether your own expressed ideas were understood. Watch for the other person's reactions. Be prepared to restate your ideas in different ways in order to maximize mutual understanding. Realizing the fact that misunderstanding is a very common element in normal communication, you should also realize that any failure of others to understand your own communicative acts is quite normal. Their misunderstanding is not a reflection on your communication skills. In other words, be supportive rather than defensive when someone indicates a failure to understand you.

Another general rule of thumb in guiding your responses to others is, be as specific as you can. Avoid generalizing too much, particularly in responding to the other person's comments. If you are disagreeing, you should be careful to specify clearly the point of your disagreement and the reason for your disagreement. You should make your response as concrete and precise as you can. The fact that your disagreement is with a specific issue, not with the person who raised the issue, is significant to effective group decision making. It is also highly susceptible to misunderstanding.

Recalling that evaluative judgments tend to lead to defensive reactions, you might respond to others supportively by attempting to be as descriptive as possible. Some people have suggested that communicative responses should not attempt to describe the other person or the other person's ideas. Rather, the response should try to describe your own reaction. Rather than saying, "That's the most ridiculous thing I ever heard," you might say, "My first reaction to your statement is one of bewilderment. I'm not sure I agree with you." To be descriptive rather than judgmental is not to avoid disagreement on the issues. Rather, description refers to the manner in which disagreeing responses are phrased. They are directed at the idea, not the person. They describe yourself, not the other person.

Giving feedback and responding to others is important, because group members need to understand the positions of other members in order to perform their tasks adequately. Haslett and Ogilvie (1988, pp. 395–400) provide a valuable summary of suggestions for giving effective feedback:

1. *Be specific* If you just say, "I don't agree," you are not telling the other person very much. You are being vague. But if you say, "I disagree with your point about the product liabilities because...," you are being more direct.
2. *Give evidence and data* People want to hear a rationale for your opinions or beliefs. Provide evidence for statements of facts, and give justifications for opinions.
3. *Separate the issues from the people* Focus your response on the task and the subject matter, not on the person. Do not tell people that they are wrong; tell them that their ideas can be improved or that there is additional evidence.
4. *Use good timing* Respond to people about immediate issues. Instead of waiting and bringing the matter up later, give feedback soon after an issue is raised.
5. *Soften negative messages* This can be most easily accomplished with language that is neither intense nor offensive. Soften the force of negative messages with such phrases as "I'm not sure about this" or "Perhaps we can improve this by..."

IMPROVING EFFECTIVENESS: GROUP-IDENTITY FACTORS

Up to this point we have been concerned with the individual members as related to his or her own self (attitudinal factors) and as related to other individual members (interpersonal factors). The present discussion focuses on improving effectiveness in terms of an individual's sense of relationship with the group as a single identity. We continue to assume, however, that the attitudinal, the interpersonal, and the group factors are not three different elements of communication and the group process. Rather, these three sets of factors are so interrelated that it is virtually impossible to determine where one stops and the other begins. The member who feels commitment to the group begins to refer to the group in the first person (that is, "my" or "our" group). The identity of the group stems directly from the attitudinal and interpersonal factors of the group process.

Sensitivity to the Group Process

Because of the nature of a process, the importance of timing cannot be emphasized too much. Increasing one's communicative effectiveness is more than knowing what behaviors to perform or even how to perform them well. The most important principle of effective communication in group decision making is knowing when to communicate what.

Being sensitive to the group process enables the group member to judge fairly accurately in which phase the group is interacting. Sensitivity to the process allows the member to perceive roles and decisions as they emerge—probably before other, less sensitive members of the group are aware, and undoubtedly before the emergence process is completed. A group member who also possesses a modicum of communication skills is capable of adjusting his or her communicative behavior so as to behave appropriately in each specific phase in the process of group decision making.

Sensitivity to the group process also allows the member to pinpoint the causes of social problems and devise strategies to solve those problems. When a group is in trouble and is not functioning effectively as a group, the members generally recognize the existence of some problem. But knowing that the group is in difficulty and knowing what to do about it are two separate elements. The knowledgeable and sensitive group member becomes something of a consultant—an expert in the group process. He or she is able to discern the cause of the group's difficulties, which might, for example, be a problem member. Sensitivity to the group process does not lead the sensitive person to reject the member; rather, it establishes a desire to discover the cause of the problem member's dissatisfaction with the group and to do something to alleviate that dissatisfaction.

Commitment to the Group

Quite clearly the effective communicator in a decision-making group is a member who is deeply committed to the group and its task. In fact, active verbal participation is highly correlated with commitment. That is, committed members tend to assume a very active verbal role in the group interaction. And in true interdependent fashion, very active participants generally have a deep level of group commitment. If you feel strongly about something, you want to talk about it. Conversely, if you talk about something actively, you come to feel strongly about it.

One point must be emphasized. Effective communication in the group and low commitment of members are totally incompatible. If you feel that you are not committed to your group, you are a liability in the process of group decision making. You have but one recourse in such an untenable situation. If you are unable to perceive value in your group membership or in the group task, quit! You will undoubtedly think you are better off without the group, but don't be deceived. The group is infinitely better off without you! Without experiencing commitment to the group and the task, you cannot be an effective group member. Without your commitment as a member, the effectiveness of the group is severely curtailed.

Attitude toward Group Slowness

The member who understands the group process does not despair over the apparent inefficiency of the group's efforts. Particularly in the early stages of group interaction, the group mechanism seems excruciatingly slow. It is only normal to be somewhat frustrated and anxious. The inexperienced member will be distressed and eager to "get the show on the road." The effective member may be frustrated but will not be overly anxious. He or she will exercise patience and observe the process getting under way.

There is a sound rationale for not being overly eager for the group to increase its efficiency. What appears to be inefficiency at a snail's pace actually reflects one of the advantages of the group process of decision making. While the group sputters and spurts in pursuit of consensus, members are allowed time to develop new ideas and reformulate earlier proposals. Too often, time is at a premium, particularly if a group operates under pressure of a deadline. Nevertheless, the importance of "mulling time" must not be underestimated. It is a crucial step in creative and high-quality decision making. And it is an integral part of the group decision-making process.

The apparent inefficiency of the group process is also advantageous for the management of social tension in the group. Demanding greater efficiency of the group by placing tight controls on departures from the topic and by requiring prolonged discussion of specific proposals probably creates more severe social problems, which naturally affect the group's task efforts. The interaction process allows members some opportunities for venting their tensions and reducing the rate of their tension buildup through features inherent in the process—abrupt changes of topics and brief spurts of intensive interaction, particularly during the conflict phase.

Formula Answers

The talented Steve Allen once remarked that you can use just one simple sentence in virtually any conversation and gain typically excellent results. That sentence is, "Well, you know the old saying." This comment is universal and explains everything while contributing nothing. Allen emphasizes the point that a cliché or an adage of conventional wisdom is available for any and every issue. Strangely enough, the cliché often commands immediate and universal acceptance, even though for every cliché there is usually another that contradicts it. If you believe that "Two heads are better than one," do you also believe that "Too many cooks spoil the broth"? "Absence makes the heart grow fonder," but "Out of sight, out of mind." It is certainly true that "Haste makes waste," but everyone knows that "A stitch in time saves nine." Tidbits of conventional wisdom are often perceived to be truer reflections than they actually are of reality.

Some group decisions are similar to clichés in that they oversimplify at the expense of realism. Groups discussing such social problems as poverty, crime, or discrimination often agree that these problems are caused by the ingrained attitudes of the society's members. The group members then decide that changing the attitudes of society with a program of education will eradicate the cause and solve the problem. The solution is true, of course, but it is unmistakably naive, simplistic, and unrealistic. How will education change society's attitudes? Who will administer this educational program? How will they do it? Are they able to do it? Is such a program possible? How long will it take? What about the influence of peer groups and opinion leaders in the society?

Groups formed in a classroom situation and discussing a policy problem have a penchant for devising formula answers. But classroom groups engaging in policy discussions are not typical of most decision-making groups in this respect. Classroom groups discussing such remote problems do little more than participate in intellectual exercises. After all, no classroom group has the power to legalize abortion or marijuana or abolish censorship laws or affect the national economy. The members engage in interaction as a classroom exercise and often discuss problems remote from their own capabilities as a realistic group. The real-life group, however, cannot afford shortcuts to realistic wisdom. Groups in the "real world" generally have the responsibility for implementing the decisions they make. They can then observe the success or failure of their consensus decisions in actual practice. Nor does their job end with the conclusion of an academic term. The formula answer is potentially a much more prevalent problem for the classroom group than for most decision-making groups in the society.

Analyzing Group Episodes

Several previous chapters have included discussions recommending that groups engage in self-analysis as a means of promoting more effective decision making. Group members who engage in analyzing themselves and the group process typically do so for several reasons. One reason is to attempt to discover and confront social problems that may be inhibiting the progress of the group's task performance. A second reason is more pedagogical. Classroom groups involved in learning about group decision-making phenomena perform self-analysis for the purpose of furthering their understanding of communication and the group process. For whatever purpose, we cannot suggest too strongly the importance of self-analysis as a means for improving the group's communication and group process.

One focus of self-analysis is the pinpointing and analysis of "critical episodes." Typically, during the process of group development, certain events occur in the group's history that later come to exert a profound impact on the development of the group's social and task dimensions. Such events typically indicate a transition, or turning point, in the group's development; that is, the event serves to precipitate some subsequent interaction that either facilitates or disrupts the group's performance as a group. A group's analysis of itself may focus on these specific episodes rather than haphazardly attempt to consider the entire process of group development. Such a focus is beneficial in allowing the members to understand their own maturation as a group.

One of the most obvious questions in analyzing critical group episodes is probably "What was going through your mind at that time?" In this case, the group member is asked to engage in some self-disclosing communication concerning the episodes. Making the self-disclosures after the fact is undoubtedly more easily accomplished by the members than discussing frankly their own feelings at the time. Therefore, a successful analysis of a critical episode requires some elapsed time between the occurrence of that historical event and the time of the analysis. Typically, critical episodes bring on periods of increased social tension that further inhibit candid discussion of the episodes. An appropriate amount of time is necessary in order to allow this tension to dissipate.

A second question that may stimulate group discussion of critical episodes is to identify the critical figure or critical role in that episode. Which member of the group played the central role in either bringing about the episode or resolving the critical episode? That is, the critical episode may have involved confronting a problem member. In this case, the problem member played a central role, but an equally significant figure may be the member who initially confronted the problem member or encouraged other group members to confront him or her. After identifying these central or catalytic roles, the group may then concentrate on the reactions of those members as potentially more important than those of the other group members whose roles may have been observers more than anything else.

Another question of a more speculative nature may involve asking what the results of the critical episode were. What happened after the event? Why did those results occur? What might have occurred differently during the episode that would have led to a different outcome, either more beneficial or more disruptive? Should any action be taken at the time of analysis as a result of the retrospective analysis of the historical event? In other words, assess the significance of the effects (or results) of the critical episode.

Brown and Rothenberg (1976, p. 303) urge the use of critical episodes for group self-analysis and provide an example of their potential significance: "Although related to other components of group action—leadership, situation, the personalities of members, and social controls—the significant group episode in many ways predates all of these. The kind of person capable of coming to leadership in a group, for example, may be a function, to a greater or lesser extent, of some prior event in which another leadership style proved disastrous."

Group episodes are thus transitional events in the history of the group. They include events that led to either an acceleration or a disruption in the process of group development. Looking back on such events from the perspective of history allows the group members not only to understand "where they came from" and how they came to be what they are at that point but also to determine where the group is going. Analyses of group episodes provide valuable insights, leading to a more comprehensive understanding of communication and the group process. They may also lead to significant insights into improving communicative effectiveness during later group decision making.

Communication-Based Qualities of Effective Groups

In a series of studies, Hirokawa and his associates (Hirokawa and Pace, 1983; Hirokawa and Scheerhorn, 1986) set out to identify those qualities of groups which are most associated with effective decision making. They found a number of communication characteristics that separate effective from ineffective groups. The following are the most important characteristics of effective groups:

1. *Groups perform better when their members vigorously evaluate the validity of each other's opinions and assumptions.* Effective groups clarify, modify, and test the opinions of their members; ineffective groups gloss over the opinions of their members. Hirokawa found that whenever a member made a point in an effective group, some other group member would question the point and seek additional specificity and justification. Such communication patterns are quite prevalent in effective groups. Here is an example:

BILL: The city council will not support the building application because they are concerned about traffic congestion.
SUE: Really? Why do you say that?
BILL: Well, they haven't voted on it, but that's what I think.
JIM: Why do you think that? Did you read it somewhere or hear something about it?
BILL: No, not really.

In this example we can see that Sue and Jim challenged the quality of Bill's assertion. They did not let his statement that the city council "will not support the application" enter the group as a fact. Groups that make faulty decisions would not have challenged the statement, but would have proceeded as if Bill's assumptions about the city council were true.

2. *Effective groups provide a thorough and rigorous evaluation of decision alternatives.* Members of effective groups carefully test their decision alternatives. They match the alternatives against the group's preestablished decision criteria and critically evaluate each alternative in the same manner that they evaluate the opinions and assumptions of their fellow members. Forcing themselves to consider all aspects of an alternative, they ask whether or not it is fair, warranted, appropriate, reasonable, etc., to ensure that they have examined it adequately, and they analyze its potential consequences by asking such questions as "What is likely to happen if we implement this decision?" Ineffective groups do not discuss consequences; they go through a superficial discussion of alternatives and tend to settle on one alternative quickly. Here is an example of a superficial evaluation of a decision alternative:

JOHN: Shall we propose the parking lot to the city council?
ANN: Can we justify it?
JOHN: Yeah, we have all the data we have been collecting and it is possible to make the case.
PETE: How about the fairness issue? Do we think that is the best way to use the space?
AL: Yeah, sure.
JOHN: Sounds good to me.
AL: Let's go for it.

This group never really discussed the implications of its decision and therefore never uncovered any problems. The decision was ineffective and unrealistic because the members did not know enough about the problem they were trying to solve.

3. ***Decision quality depends on the accuracy of the premises the group uses.*** Hirokawa and Pace stated that this is a very important insight that resulted from their work. They found that high-quality groups use facts and inferences that are accurate and reasonable. This is easier to say than it is to do; many people get confused over what constitutes an accurate fact and an intelligent inference. Nevertheless, these skills can be learned. And the facts and inferences improve when the group is critical and evaluative, practicing the first two characteristics of effective groups discussed above.

4. ***The nature of the influential members' influence affects the quality of a group's decision.*** All groups have some members who exert considerable influence over the thinking of others by moving the group in certain directions. A group becomes effective when this influence is positive and facilitative, but a negative and inhibitory influence makes a group ineffective.

Positive contributions by influential members include such communicative behaviors as asking appropriate questions, introducing important information, challenging and persuading the group to dismiss unwarranted and questionable information, and keeping the group from digressing. In the group discussing the parking lot proposal, an influential member later asked pertinent questions about the proposal, such as "Where will it be located, what is there now, are there any other planned uses for the space, what will the community think, and are there important aesthetic issues?" These and other such questions forced the group to address many important issues, and this helped it reach a high-quality decision.

Negative contributions by influential members include introducing and supporting erroneous facts and assumptions, getting the group to accept poor information, making ridiculous suggestions, and distracting the group by leading it off in irrelevant directions. An influential member who makes negative contributions is a special problem when he or she is socially attractive. Although the members may like a person who is funny, pleasant, or otherwise appealing, these qualities alone do not make a person an effective task specialist. A group experiences the problems of ineffective groups when a socially attractive member who makes negative contributions exerts too much influence over the group's decision-making process.

SUMMARY

Developing effective communication within a group is not easy. There are no sure-fire principles for improving communication and group effectiveness. Such improvement ultimately requires a thorough understanding of communication and the group process. Misconceptions to be avoided include the naive assumption of human rationality and an overreliance on agendas.

Improving effectiveness depends on a number of interrelated attitudinal, interpersonal, and group-identity factors. Attitudinal factors involve each member's attitudes toward the group and toward group interaction, along with each individual member's creativity, critical ability, and honesty. Interpersonal factors include active verbal participation, communication skills, the use of supportive communication, and sensitivity when responding to others. When identifying with the group as a whole, effective members develop a sensitivity to the group process, a commitment to the group, and a reasonable attitude toward group slowness. Most important, perhaps, effective group communication often benefits from group members' engaging in interaction that is directed specifically at self-analysis, concentrating specifically on critical episodes from the group's history of past interactions.

CHAPTER 8

Behavioral Standards: Roles and Norms

Developing the socioemotional climate of the group is essentially a process of acculturation. Typically, the process of acculturation implies a new member's joining an already established culture, in the sense of a Vietnamese immigrant's coming to the United States to live, a midwesterner's moving to New York, or a southerner's relocating in the north. Certain modes of behavior are acceptable within a given culture, and others are unacceptable. Previous members of a culture have established certain expected patterns of doing and thinking. These patterns must be learned by the newcomer.

One familiar example of the impact of cultural differences on behavioral expectations is that of the North American in a Latin American country who arrives at 2:30 for a 2:30 appointment. The North American, considering the arrival to be "on time," is unable to comprehend why the Latin American should consider it rude to arrive so "early." Each culture develops its own rules for guiding behavior, and these rules may be quite different from those in another culture. The alien newcomer, then, must adapt to the new behavioral patterns or face the consequences of culture shock.

Every group develops its own standards to guide the behavior of its members. Even those groups which have formal requirements to direct members' behavior also develop informal rules during the process of group interaction. Every group thus establishes its own rules for guiding the behavioral patterns of its members. Of course, the development of those standards is typically cumulative and implicit, but it is nevertheless evident.

Members of every group soon realize that their membership in the group constrains, to some extent, their freedom to choose their own behaviors. That is, each member has a range of behavioral choices available to him or her. But the process of group development narrows this range of acceptable behaviors, so that some behaviors are appropriate and others are inappropriate within the group context. Each member soon learns what is expected of him or her and what is expected of others. In regard to the informal rules, at least, every member has had a voice in formulating those expectations.

You will recall that the discussion of groupness in Chapter 1 states that one of the characteristics of groupness is the development of behavioral standards. That is, one of the characteristics of groupness is "behavior based on norms and procedures accepted by all group members" (Brilhart, 1978, pp. 20–21). Although the rules that guide the behaviors of group members are seldom formalized in the sense of a written code, the members of groups soon develop expectations of how each member is to behave during group interaction. The normal process of group development leads to these expectations and the developing groupness.

This chapter will discuss the two most common standards for group members' behavior—roles and norms. Some roles and norms may be beyond the control of the group members themselves. That is, external standards may, in some respects, be stronger than the group's ability to devise informal norms and roles. Nevertheless, the development of informal roles and norms creates an extremely potent force that guides group interaction. The primary emphasis of this chapter, then, is on the development of these informal roles and norms.

ROLES

Comparing the concept of a social role to the dramatic role portrayed by an actor on stage is all too familiar. Even Shakespeare believed that all the world is a stage and life is just acting out one part after another. But we must not conform too closely to this analogy if we are to capture the richer meaning of the social role. The stage actor does create a role but is limited by the playwright's lines and the foreknowledge of the play's conclusion. The actor must also divorce the self, to a large extent, from the character portrayed. One's social role, on the other hand, is a direct reflection of one's self, and the specific behaviors that constitute the social role are much more spontaneous. And, of course, one cannot rehearse most of these behaviors beforehand.

Role Defined

The famed sociologist Erving Goffman (1961, p. 87) refers to a role as "the basic unit of socialization." As each individual member of any social system (a group, a culture, a society, etc.) identifies with and becomes identified with that system, the member assumes a role in that system. Goffman suggests, "It is through roles that tasks in society are allocated and arrangements made to enforce their performance."

A *role*, for our purposes, may be defined as a position in an interlocking network of roles that make up the group. But to define a role solely in terms of its "position" relative to the "positions" of other members of a group is to fail to comprehend fully how members function in their performance of roles and, ultimately, how the group functions as a decision-making system. A fuller definition, then, is that a role is a set of communicative behaviors performed by an individual and that it involves the behaviors performed by one member in light of the expectations that other members hold toward those behaviors. This definition also includes the behavioral tendencies which emanate from the person's own personality but which may or may not be expressed in actual role behaviors.

Considering a group member's role in terms of the expectations of other members, we can understand that the behavior of each individual member can be either consistent or inconsistent with what the other members expect that individual member's role to be. In other words, if the behavior of the member is similar to what other members expect, that behavior can be considered to be role behavior. Surely you know certain persons who create within you certain expectations that they will behave in a specific way. But if one of those persons were to do something that you didn't expect, you would probably describe such behavior as being "out of character." In other words, the behavior was not consistent with your expectations of that person's role.

To think of one's role solely in terms of one's "position" in a group network of roles is to provide only a partial picture of a group's social structure. Often a group that is subject to external pressures (e.g., a group within a larger organization) is also subject to a network of roles (within the larger organization) that is imposed on the group. A leader may be designated because of the status, seniority, or position which that member holds within the larger organization (for example, the company president and a group of advisors, or a supervisor and a group of subordinate workers). In this formal structure, each role position exists somewhat independently from the person who occupies that role. That is, when the person leaves the group, the position (or role) remains unfilled.

Furthermore, the person's behavior in such a formal role may not be consistent with the other members' expectations of the behaviors that should be performed by a person occupying such a role. Then, we say that the person occupying the position is not fulfilling the role obligations; for example, the leader is not doing the leading. Defined in terms of behaviors and position, a role becomes an inherently behavioral concept. Furthermore, a behavioral role exists only when a person is performing behaviors within a role. And those behaviors, in combination with the expectations of other group members, constitute our working definition of the role in a decision-making group.

Each role must be defined, to some extent, in terms of the communicative behaviors performed by the member occupying that role. The definition of a role solely as some preordained position that exists apart from the identity of the person occupying the position is incomplete. If we were to view a role in its broader sense, we might consider "president" of a government or a large organization to be a role. This type of role, defined solely as a position with attendant duties and privileges, exists independently of the person who actually serves as the president. Such a role definition governs many of the behavioral choices of the person filling that position. In addition, the position exists within the organization's structure despite the identity of the person who occupies it and continues to exist whether or not any person occupies it.

The role of "father" in a family group is also determined by factors other than behavior. The role of father is determined biologically (or legally, in the case of adoption) rather than simply by the actual behaviors performed. On the other hand, we also refer to the behavioral functions of the role "parent," regardless of who performs them. Therefore, an older child, for example, may perform "parenting" functions (that is, behaviors identifiable with the parent's role) even though that child does not occupy the formal position of parent, determined legally or biologically. The role, determined by behavior, is the informal role of parent.

To the extent that each group is capable of developing its own roles, norms, and social system, the members develop a system of informal roles. Such a system is created in addition to any preestablished network of roles that is "passed out" to the members by some external authority. Thus, each member (together with the other group members) works out his or her role through performing communicative behaviors. Each member's role, along with that role's relationships with the roles of other members, must be defined principally in terms of the behaviors performed by that member in combination with fellow group members. No role appears to be universally present in all (or even most) groups, with the probable exception of the role of leader. But because the leadership role is unique and so significant to the group process, Chapter 9 is devoted entirely to it.

Bormann and Bormann (1988, pp. 101–104) provide one possible explanation for the idiosyncracy of informal roles in decision-making groups. Their discussion of role emergence suggests that roles develop over time, owing to a pattern of response reinforcement during group interaction. As a member performs a given behavior, other members either encourage or discourage its continued performance through their reactions. They postulate that if the other members encourage this role function, the member will be likely to repeat that behavior until it becomes a full-fledged role function. If the other members discourage the behavior, however, the person will probably cease performing such a behavior during subsequent interaction. Thus, each individual member develops a role by consistently performing those behaviors which receive positive reinforcement from other group members. Furthermore, the other group members develop a set of expectations concerning a given member's role behavior on the basis of that person's repeated performance of similar behaviors.

Typically, group members acknowledge the roles of individual members and develop a set of expectations about each member's role retrospectively. That is, *after* the behaviors have been performed and the expectations have been developed, the role of each member becomes more easily identified. The identity of each member's role becomes more apparent to the group, and each member is increasingly seen as different from the other group members. Often the group's expectations and the role networks develop without the individual members being aware of the role that each is performing in the group. Nor are they necessarily aware of the expectations that other members have of them while the process of role emergence is taking place.

One member of a classroom decision-making group was informed by her fellow group members that they believed her role to be that of "blocker." She responded in her report of the group meeting, "I was considered a blocker. I can't figure out why." Her role behaviors during past group meetings, even though she was apparently unaware of them, were consistently critical of the group's directions and its potential decisions. She consistently characterized the progress made during previous meetings as "Not much." Hence, a role consists not only of the behaviors performed by each individual, but of those behaviors in conjunction with other group members' behaviors and expectations. After the fact, then, the members are able to discern the behaviors that are "typical" (that is, consistent with the role) and come to expect them.

Another member of a classroom group, in her diary of group meetings, wrote the following about her own role: "It is really nice to know that I have a role now, so that I can play it. Everyone says that I am a supporter and harmonizer....I really enjoy my group, and this has really helped me to understand people in groups. Before, I have been so scared of interacting. This class [group] has helped me come out of my shell more than usual." While one's private tendencies will affect one's behavior to some extent, every person's behavior in a group is more the product of the group interaction, taken as a whole, than it is product of the person's own tendency to behave in a certain way.

Each individual member develops that pattern of behaviors which constitutes his or her role in conjuction with fellow group members. Thus, the role—the behavior pattern—that a person develops in one group may be quite different from that same person's role in another group. A role, then, is not wholly determined by someone's innate personality traits. The human being does not carry a role from one group to another. A role is more like a suit of clothes that is put on or taken off to suit the occasion. The group's demands on the individual member's behaviors change because the group itself changes.

Role Performance

Role performance is the actual behavior of an individual while in the group. If we think of a role as a formal position in a network, the performance of that role by the person who occupies it is determined largely by the informal development of role behaviors in conjunction with the other members of the social system. Moreover, each person has an implicit notion of being "on duty" when performing that role. When on duty, the person is likely to perform role behaviors. But when a person is "off duty," his or her behaviors are less likely to conform to the expectations of other members of the social system.

We recall one classroom group in which the members recognized one of their group as their leader. At the same time, they resented somewhat his overbearing and arrogant approach to performing that leadership role. He talked constantly and tended to override any objections by other members to his directions. That same person rarely spoke during the meetings of the entire class. He never volunteered a contribution to classroom discussions. When called upon, he was very soft-spoken and acquiescent. Apparently he considered himself to be "on duty" as a "leader" only in his smaller group. In the larger classroom, he was "off duty" and felt no need to conform to the group's expectations of what a leader should do.

Goffman (1959, pp. 106–140) distinguishes role performance in terms of "regions" of behavior. In other words, a person performs a role when he or she is before the audience appropriate to that role (the "front region"). On the other hand, when the person is "backstage" (in the "back region"), there is apparently no perceived need to perform the role. Consequently, role performance is quite inconsistent with other people's expectations when the performer is in the back region; it is consistent with the expectations of others only when the performer is in the front region.

The noted psychologist Karl Weick adds an important insight to the notion of role performance when he talks about partial inclusion (Weick, 1979, pp. 95–97). *Partial inclusion* simply means that a person does not invest (or include) all of his or her behaviors in a single role. The various behaviors that you are capable of are dispersed among the several groups of which you are a member. You might be a leader in one group, a follower in another, aggressive at one time, and passive later. You can behave as a friend, a colleague, a son, a daughter, a husband, a father, and so on. All of us are capable of performing many roles, and it is important to remember that your role in a group is consistent with your own willingness to behave in a certain way in light of the expectations of the other group members. It is a mistake to equate personality with role behavior. The group needs only certain types of communicative behavior from you; you may have skills and ways of behaving that are simply not wanted or needed from the group. You do not invest your entire personality in the group. Group members perform certain roles because they are using particular patterns of talents or behaviors that the group and the individual desire or need. Their entire personhood is only partially included in the group.

Role Conflict

Occasionally role strain or role conflict occurs in a group in which a member finds that the demands of the group on his or her behavior are more than can be performed (*role strain*) or that the role behavior in that group is contradictory to her or his role performances in other groups (*role conflict*). Typically, the informal role structure is free from patterns of role strain, since every member works out a certain role performance in combination with other group members. Rarely does a person become committed to an emerging pattern of role behaviors which that person is unable to perform adequately.

Not typically, but occasionally, an individual member will perceive a conflict between role performance in the group and role performance consistent with the member's own personality or self-concept. One such member expressed just such a conflict in her reactions to a classroom group meeting. She wrote, "I started out with the feeling that I was going to remain passive and not contribute to the group— just to see if anyone would try to get things going. I was tired of trying to spark everyone and get them moving. I couldn't do it. I guess my personality is not suited for that role." Another individual expressed a similar role conflict when she confided, "I became very embarrassed when the group described my role (as they saw it) in the group. . . . I guess I'm not too 'big' on confrontations as well as tension. I can't confront others unless it's positively."

One student in a classroom group apparently experienced a similar feeling. She was the member delegated by her group to confront another frequently absent member with the group's ultimatum: "Put up or shut up." She wrote in her diary of her reaction to the group's decision to appoint her as the confronter. She considered herself a friendly and amiable person—one who was unable to perform such an aggressive task. Nevertheless, she did just that during the next group meeting. Her diary, written at the conclusion of that meeting, included the following comment: "I felt that my role [as confronter] in the group meeting had a stifling effect on me, but I felt that we accomplished a lot." Her successful performance, then, evidently compensated for her internal struggle with the role.

A more likely and perhaps more typical strategy of a person who is placed in an incongruent role is to modify perceptions of that role. Such a strategy may result in perceiving the role as something it is not or in perceiving the self in a different role. Another classroom group may provide a classic example of role-self perceptions that were quite unrealistic and quite inaccurate in terms of the individual member's perception of his role in the group. Bob, as we shall call him, perceived himself to be a natural leader and certainly the leader of his classroom group. After one meeting he wrote his personal reactions to that meeting in his diary (a class requirement): "I sort of felt insecure in my role as leader. I let John take it mostly, and he finally came to terms with the task and analyzed it well. However, everyone was unanimous in their support of me, so I guess they feel good about me as leader."

John's reactions to that same meeting appeared in his diary: "I do not object to Bob's trying to control every meeting. But if he slips or does something I do not agree with, I jump in and take control." Another member, after that same group meeting, wrote, "Bob tried to dictate to us again today, but I thought John handled him very well, under the circumstances." A meeting two weeks later brought the following comments from two other group members. One member wrote, "The meeting was short, but we accomplished everything we needed. I guess I'm feeling a little less annoyed with Bob." The other member wrote, "I was especially pleased with this meeting because Bob and I did not conflict as we did in the past. Perhaps this is due to two factors. First, he realized my right to have an opinion and respected my opinions more. Second, though, I might have been too tired to assert myself." Bob's reaction to that same meeting reflected quite a different perception of the situation: "My position as leader was more firmly established." Incidentally, at the end of the class when the group members voted on who they thought had led the group, John received every vote—except one (probably Bob's).

A more typical variety of role conflict is the inconsistency between a person's behaviors in the role of group member and a role in another group. One member of a classroom group, an older woman who described herself as "old enough to be the mother of any of my fellow members," found herself in role conflict in her group. The particular role conflict she perceived might have been something of a "generation gap." During one meeting especially, she found this role conflict to be virtually unbearable and described her reactions in her diary: "Because of the subject of the discussion [premarital sex], I am still reacting as a parent rather than a 'free-thinking' individual. I shall try to 'cure' this habit. Carefully taught and long-ingrained standards make it hard to compromise. They never change completely."

This particular member was quite committed to both groups (her family and her classroom decision-making group) and to the ideals of the two groups. She earnestly wanted to engage in appropriate role performances in both groups but found the carryover from one to be in conflict with the other. Consequently, she wanted to believe in opposite sides of the same issue. She never did completely resolve this role conflict.

One reason for the different roles developed by the same person in different groups is the interdependence of the social dimensions. The nature of the task stimulates certain expectations or requirements so that the network of roles is affected along with all elements of the social dimension. An example from a classroom group may illustrate this phenomenon. One woman, whom we shall identify as Margie, felt that her contribution to a group was limited to follower and information giver. Although bright, Margie was extremely shy and found it difficult to assert herself in any social setting. In a classroom group discussing problems of educationally disadvantaged children in urban ghettos, she found her behavior pattern quite different from what her personality traits might have predicted. Her fellow members discovered that she had had summer experience in social work and consistently turned to her for critical advice. They recognized her expertise based on personal experiences. Margie became a critic-evaluator and by far the most frequent contributor to her group. Rather than being a follower, Margie found herself in a role of dominance because of the nature of the task and her relationship with it. Of course, her personality was unchanged. She remained shy and nonassertive. But in the role network of this particular group working on this particular task, Margie's behavior pattern was assertive and her role was quite dominant.

In contrast to Margie, Steve was a BMOC ("big man on campus")—a starting member of the football team, an officer in his fraternity, handsome, and loaded with personal charm. It was impossible to dislike Steve. Everyone liked him from the first meeting, including his fellow classroom-group members. Steve was used to being a leader and seemed to have the knack of exerting the forcefulness of his personality on whomever he came in contact with. But as the pressure of time to complete their task impinged upon the group members, they became increasingly disenchanted with Steve's role behaviors. He discovered that his personality and charm were insufficient to meet the demands of task accomplishment. Bewildered by the social ostracism from his fellow group members and frustrated because his contributions were consistently rejected or ignored, he uncharacteristically remained silent and became a habitual absentee. For Steve, the experience of being in that group was obviously socially painful.

Role conflict can certainly occur, as it apparently did in Steve's case. Generally, however, a person is able to keep the role in one group fairly distinct from that in another group. At a common sense level, your behavior at home with your family group is different from your behavior with a group of your close friends. And both behavior patterns are different from your behavior in a classroom. You behave differently at a football game and a fancy restaurant. Implicitly, and often without consciously doing so, we make changes in our role patterns and performances as we move from group to group. And we do so as easily as we change shirts. This is the nature of social roles.

Baird and Weinberg (1977, pp. 164–168) summarize three different types of role conflict: "intrarole conflict, where someone experiences conflict while playing a single role; interrole conflict, where one person is simultaneously required to play two different roles; and interpersonal role conflict, where two or more individuals compete for the same role." The problems of role conflict, particularly those of intrarole and interrole conflict, are most pronounced in the network of formal role positions imposed by external sources on a group. The informal network of roles, developed by a group in its capacity as an LGD, typically avoids the intense role conflicts. The individual person and the group are able to devise their own role network and expectations in a form that is comfortable for most group members. In other words, role conflict is rarely a problem, except in the structure of formal roles. Any problems of role conflict that are evident in the formal structure are often ameliorated in the informal role structure worked out by the group members during the process of group development.

The problem of interpersonal role conflict, in which two or more persons attempt to perform the same role, is more evident in the leadership role. The problems associated with developing the leadership network of a group will be the subject for discussion in Chapter 9. Interpersonal role conflicts regarding nonleadership roles are rare in either the formal or the informal role networks. Every human being is to some extent a social chameleon, responding to the expectations of individual people in social systems. Maintaining a clear separation of those social systems and the respective roles within them is a typical method of coping with potential role conflicts.

Role Differences

As individual group members work out their own roles in cooperation with other group members, each member takes on a role that differentiates him or her from the other group members. That is, even though each member's role behaviors depend on the behaviors of other members, the resulting pattern of interactive behaviors distinguishes each member's role from those of other members. The group is thus composed of a network of roles, but each group member individually possesses an identity that distinguishes that member from other members. Group members therefore come to expect an identifiable set of certain behaviors from one person and a different set of behaviors from another person. In this way, each member maintains an identity as an individual, and the network composed of all individual identities becomes identifiable as the group.

It is impossible to identify a complete list of all the roles in a group, but some early group researchers (Benne and Sheats, 1948) classified roles that are commonly observed in groups. Their classification scheme is still one of the best descriptions of the various types of roles performed in groups. The scheme includes three types of roles: group task roles, group building and maintenance roles, and individual roles. Although it is difficult to make a clear distinction between all roles, it is surely the case that the three role types indicate that some roles are not oriented toward group goals, but apparently fulfill some purely individual needs. Below, each role is described and then defined with a sample communication representative of the role. All the communication examples come from transcripts and recordings of actual group interactions.

Task Roles   These roles are task-oriented and move the group toward its goal.

Initiator-Contributor   Presents lots of new ideas; initiates new ideas and directions. "Let's examine the social consequences of these taxes."

Information Seeker   Seeks information, clarification, and evidence. "Has anyone found research supporting this program?"

Opinion Seeker   Checks the opinion and agreement or disagreement of other group members. "How do the rest of you feel about this way of doing things?"

Information Giver   Provides and contributes important and relevant information. "The program was funded by property taxes in New York. There was a tax increase of 3 percent."

Elaborator   Explains, extends, and clarifies the ideas of other. "John was probably thinking about the magnet school programs in Boston. That was state-supported rather than locally supported."

Coordinator   Shows relationships between ideas and facts. "The Boston program can't be compared to the New York program because of the different ways in which the programs were funded."

Orienter   Keeps the group on track and moving toward the goal. "We are straying from the point. Let's get back to the issue on the floor."

Evaluator-Critic   Comments on group information and applies critical standards. "That proposal might work if we had an income tax in Connecticut, but we generate revenue by sales tax only."

Energizer   Stimulates the group to action. "Okay, let's go. Who'd like to handle the research on magnet schools?"

Procedural Technician   Deals with procedural tasks, such as scheduling, copying, and handouts. "I have reserved Room 233 and a slide projector for next week."

Recorder   Takes the minutes and keeps the group's records and history. "Last week we decided to have a long meeting this time."

Group Building and Maintenance Roles   These roles are communicative behaviors that focus on interpersonal relations in the group and on the general quality of the socioemotional environment.

Encourager   Accepts and reinforces the ideas of other group members. "Good idea, Bill. That really helps."

Harmonizer   Keeps the peace and resolves tensions in the group; often uses humor or sarcasm. "Nothing like a little friendly communication" (immediately following an argument).

Compromiser   Tries to offer ideas and solutions that satisfy everyone. "Okay, if the tax information is too difficult to find, I'll get the information about the tax laws, and you find the community stuff."

Gatekeeper and Expediter   Tries to encourage even participation. "Let Sarah talk. She usually has good ideas."

Group Observer   Makes generalized comments about the behavior of the group as a whole. "It seems as though we're stuck."

Follower   Goes along easily with the trends in the group. "Sounds okay to me if it is okay with you guys."

Individual Roles   These roles are self-centered and satisfy personal needs rather than the goals of the group.

Aggressor   Criticizes and attacks other group members in order to enhance his or her own status. "I am not impressed with this solution. I think we should do it the way I suggested earlier."

Blocker   Does not cooperate, and opposes much of what the group tries to do. "I don't like any of these ideas."

Recognition Seeker   Seeks to enhance his or her own status by citing past accomplishments. "Last year the group I led was very successful because we were organized."

Self-Confessor   Talks about himself or herself and offers irrelevant information about his or her own feelings and attitudes. "You know I always do that. I really have to try to change my habits."

Playboy   Behaves in a nonserious manner, always fooling around and joking. "Hey, let's bag this and go have a beer. We can talk more there if you want."

Dominator   Tries to monopolize the group with long speeches and suggestions on how to do everything. "Well, I think we should [etc., etc., etc.]." "My opinion is...."

Help Seeker   Tries to elicit sympathy and help from everyone; expresses insecurity a lot. "I am not good at writing. I think someone else should do it, or at least we should do it together."

Special-Interest Pleader   Has a private agenda and ideas, and pleads for these. "I still think the magnet school idea is a good one. Let's read this report and then talk about it again."

This list of roles, formulated by Benne and Sheats, certainly does not exhaust the list of all possible roles that can occur in groups performing decision-making tasks. An additional role, common to many groups, is that of "joker." Depending on the specific interaction, a joker may be a harmonizer, a follower, a tension reliever, a playboy, or even an information giver (although the joker's information is typically phrased in a humorous way). In cloaking information in humor, the joker may allow the group to accept information that would otherwise be unacceptable.

People tend to associate the joker's role primarily with the socioemotional dimension, rather than with the task dimension, and this association may possibly be valid. When the joker's role as the group clown arouses a set of expectations that the joker is not serious about the task or is disinterested in helping the group achieve consensus, however, the role is probably more disruptive than beneficial to the group process. Every role is inevitably relevant to both the task and socioemotional dimensions of the group process. In a decision-making group, any role performance (such as that of the joker) that leads group members to believe that the member is not serious about completing the task is likely to be detrimental to the most efficient functioning of the group process.

The "silent member," or low participator, is another role that may have important functions in the group process. If a member is characterized by other group members as a silent member, these others often come to believe that the silent one is not fully committed to the group or the group task. On the other hand, a silent member may develop into an important contributor to the group process if the group members do not perceive low participation as a symptom of low commitment.

One classroom group contained a silent member who later played an important role in that group's development, even though the total amount of talk he generated remained well below the average of all group members. His later contributions, though infrequent, consisted of volunteering to do the group's outside activities, to research materials, and generally to perform the less desirable legwork of the group. Not only did the other group members come to view his role as quite valuable, but the member himself became much more satisfied with the group and his membership in it. One of his reactions to a group meeting late in the class expressed his increased satisfaction: "I felt I made some very important, objective contributions. I have moved from being a low participator to an important, candid one. Meetings are more fun now."

When a group is sincerely and seriously interested in self-improvement, one assigned role that may well enhance the group's progress is that of "group productivity observer." The member assigned this role, while still carrying out his or her informal role developed through normal group interaction, takes on the additional responsibility of reporting at the end of each meeting on the progress that the group appears to have made during the meeting.

To benefit from the possibility that a group productivity observer may be beneficial to the group process, the other group members must be open to the observer's criticisms and observations. Moreover, they must have faith in the objectivity of the member they choose to be the observer and must be willing to trust that member. Of course, the person who is assigned the role of group productivity observer must be frank, candid, and honest in observing the group interaction and must give the group an accurate assessment of its productivity. If your group wishes to assign this role to one of your group members, you may find such a role performance quite helpful. But the group productivity observer is beneficial only to the extent that you are all willing to accept the member's observations and strive actively for self-analysis. On the other hand, if your group appears to be functioning quite normally and acceptably, you will find little reason for assigning such a role to anyone.

Because of the changing roles of women in society, there has recently been a great deal of interest in the roles played by males and females in the group process. Much attention has been directed at the influence of sex-role stereotypes on group functions, but some investigations have attempted to discover potential role differences between males and females in terms of their role performance and their influence on the overall group process; for example, Coates (1986, pp. 151–155) reports differences between all-female and all-male groups in terms of their role differentiation and communication. The findings suggest that all-female groups exhibit less differentiation between their members' roles than do all-male groups; at the same time, since female groups often outperform male groups in performing their assigned tasks, it appears that role differentiation does not necessarily lead to greater productivity.

Under any circumstances, one should expect that nearly every group will develop a network of roles that differentiate members from one another. Such an observation should not appear too controversial. After all, individual human beings are typically quite different from one another. We typically tend to distinguish one person from another and say that each has a unique personality and is an individual in his or her own right. At the risk of appearing undemocratic, we might even affirm the truism that all people are not created equal. Although all people may have equality of rights and privileges, some persons are more capable than others and have different kinds of capabilities. As a result, the roles that individuals perform during group interaction will probably lead to observed and expected differences between group members. Such role differentiation should not be considered "good" or "evil," but quite normal in human interaction.

NORMS

Conformity by members to certain behavioral conventions, specified or unspecified, is a normal and consistent phenomenon of every social system. The punishment for nonconformity is often not clear, but the pressure to conform is strong nevertheless. We consistently follow the changing fashions of dress and music, for example. What was conformist yesterday may be nonconformist today, but we continue to heed the changing social whims in an overt drive to avoid being abnormal.

The human animal apparently has a strong desire to follow the herd. At one time or another, you have probably proved this point with some variation of the "emperor's new clothes" prank. In one variation, for example, a group of people stops at a busy street corner and stares upward at a purely arbitrary point in the sky. They engage in totally meaningless, animated conversation about this imaginary phenomenon they are allegedly observing. They point to it, "oohing" and "aahing" over the magnificence of the sight. Within minutes a crowd gathers, and everyone stares, pointing at the sky. When the people in the original group feel that the crowd is large enough, they quietly slip away and congratulate themselves on their remarkable ability to manipulate human behavior.

As standards for behavior, norms vary considerably in the extent to which they are known. Some norms, such as the laws or bylaws of a formal organization, are very explicit; the organization's members know what its laws are and what the punishments are for violating them. Laws are easily recognized and understood. Other norms, however, are less explicit. Members of the social system may not realize what norms exist until having violated them. Newcomers to a group often learn the group's norms by the mistakes they make.

Also, even while some social norms apply to all members of a group, other norms apply only to one or another role; that is, a specific behavior considered normal in one role is not necessarily considered normal in another. For example, a superior can walk directly into the office of a subordinate, but entering a superior's office without permission would violate a norm. This illustrates that not all of a social system's norms apply equally to all members of the system. Rather, each role has its own limits of acceptable (or normal) behavior. Thus, playing golf and joining a high-class country club would be considered normal behavior for a business executive, but drinking beer with the "hard hats" in a saloon after work would be considered abnormal behavior for this executive.

Norms Defined

The most obvious definition of *norm* includes some characteristic of necessity or obligation—"oughtness." Norms describe how common behavioral and intellectual standards have developed in the group (Moscovici, 1985, p. 373). The degree of oughtness may vary from situation to situation and from role to role, and it may also determine the extent of the punishment to be meted out for deviating from the norms. That is, when one belches at a party, one is behaving contrary to some norm, but the punishment for this deviation is not likely to be as severe as the punishment for violating some codified norm, such as robbing a bank. Under any circumstances, however, to behave contrary to a norm is to do something that the system decrees ought not to be done.

Andrews (1988) distinguishes between explicit norms and implicit norms, a differentiation that is particularly relevant to our study of group decision making. *Explicit norms* include those which are formal and which are intentionally adopted by the group, such as the procedures the group adopts or the rules it abides by in its meetings; Robert's *Rules of Order,* for example, is a set of explicit norms. *Implicit norms,* on the other hand, emerge during the interaction of the group members and become "knowable" as the interaction continues. Group members may be aware of both explicit and implicit norms, but the implicit norms are more changeable as the members continue to interact with one another.

Some norms, which may be either explicit or implicit, also originate from the values of members. Davis refers to a *value* as "a basic belief or assumption about what is good, right, or proper." Such values probably originate in a larger culture or society to which the specific group members belong. The values of a business organization, for example, would be imposed on the members of subgroups within that organization. After all, the group members are also members of the larger organization. Members may also have values that they bring to the group from the larger society to which they all belong—the university community, a church, a national culture, etc.

Norms may thus originate in a larger society, in the group's interaction, or in the procedural rules officially adopted by the group. In this way, they may be imposed on the group as well as created or formulated during the process of group interaction. Like other behavioral standards (such as roles), norms may be formal or informal. In summary, norms may be imposed on the group from an external authority or may be developed by the group members during the actual process of group interaction.

DEVELOPMENT OF GROUP NORMS

Norms develop slowly in groups and are always a reflection of the values and information shared by the group members. As the members repeat behaviors over time, the developing patterns become norms. Even something as simple as seating habits are subject to norms. After a few weeks in most classes, you will notice the students (including yourself) seated in approximately the same seat every day. If you come to class late and find someone else sitting in "your" seat, you probably feel slightly irritated.

But the development of norms in decision-making groups is more complex than the simple repetition of behaviors. Norms develop through feedback loops and interaction. When an individual is in a group, he or she has some ideas about the subject matter under discussion. In a sense, individuals have norms of their own. But group membership means that the individual must exchange ideas (communicate) with others. Eventually people notice that their views on things do not coincide; they meet with disagreement. People become a little uncertain of their own opinions and information and work to reduce the differences by finding a consensus satisfactory to all. Thus, groups establish norms in order to reduce tension. Even the choice of where to sit in the example above is based on simplicity and consistency, which reduce tension. It is simply easier to sit in the same seat and allow others to do so.

Moscovici (1985) explains that groups do not establish norms as much as they transform individual norms into a single one. People come to the group with attitudes and opinions, and these are transformed by the process of interacting with others. Individual attitudes and opinions converge toward agreement with others, and the group transforms individual attitudes into group-held norms. There is a classic research study by Sherif (1935) that demonstrates this point with great insight. Sherif had subjects look at a stationary light shown in total darkness. This stationary light produces the autokinetic phenomenon, which means that the light appears to move; the light is actually stationary but creates the impression of motion. In the first phase of the experiment, people estimated how much the light was moving and established a personal norm. In the second phase, two or three people who had different personal norms were brought together for discussion, and in the course of the group discussion their judgments developed toward a common norm. The study showed that individual norms were transformed into a single one.

Some members of a group in an organization, observed by one of the authors, had established the norm of verbally forceful argument. Early in the group's history some new members were presenting documented evidence in a calm and professional manner, but they were attacked quite harshly by the other members. Their evidence was questioned and their arguments criticized. The new members tried to remain composed and to respond in a dispassionate manner, but they were almost shouted down. Soon the new members, too, adopted the norm of assertiveness and forcefulness to support their views. The group had now established predictable communication sequences that established a norm of verbal forcefulness.

In Chapter 4 we discussed the structuration process. The details of that theory are beyond our concerns here (see Poole, Siebold, and McPhee, 1986), but structuration is a very specific account of how individuals develop patterns of communication that create group structures. In some significant ways, structuration and group norms are related, because group norms help produce group structure. For example, all groups must have ways of legitimizing what is acceptable or unacceptable behavior. The legitimate use of power in the group is one important group structure; the group must have collective agreement (sometimes unstated, however) on who has power and how they can use it. A leader might call a group to order. The group norm about how leaders communicate might be, "one way to wield power is to call the group to order." This norm helps establish a legitimate power structure in the group.

Norms "belong" to the group and not to the individual member. Everyone, moving from one group to another, is subject to different norms because of the differences between the groups, not because of a new internalization of a different set of norms. We shall consistently refer to group norms with the full implication that the norms do indeed "belong" to the group.

As classroom instructors, we strive to encourage a classroom norm of argument—a free exchange of conflicting opinions and ideas. Students engage in verbal conflict with other students and with the instructor. Many students and instructors are uncomfortable with this norm and consider it inappropriate, disrespectful, and disruptive. The point is that no norm is more "correct" than another. Rather, social norms vary from one social system to another and may even conflict with one another. Therefore, a norm developed in one social system is appropriate within that social system but may be quite inappropriate in another.

Pressures to Conform

Although deviance from norms is the subject of Chapter 10, it is important at this point to provide some discussion of conformity pressures exerted by a group on its own members. We shall take the position that not all conformity is alike. Nor is all deviation alike. The typical reaction to conformity (and, paradoxically enough, to deviance) is rather negative. That is, people often feel that conformists have no minds of their own. They merely succumb to the will of some unnamed majority. Also, deviance is typically regarded as distasteful, and a deviant is regarded as a criminal or an immoral person. We shall consistently argue that neither conformity nor deviance is harmful or beneficial in principle. Some element of conformity is socially healthy, as is some element of deviation from group norms. The important principle is not *whether* conformity or deviance is good or bad, but *what* conformity or deviance is good or bad.

Few will disagree with the fact that groups, societies, and cultures exert enormous pressures on their members to conform to the norms established by the social system. Conformity and its counterpart, deviation from norms, will be present in all groups and in all societies. Furthermore, group pressures to conform to social norms and to sanction negatively those members who deviate from them are also likely to exist in all groups, both explicitly and implicitly. Even the suggestion of social pressure causes people to conform. Hocking, Margreiter, and Hylton (1977), in a very interesting study, gave subjects in an experiment either positive or negative information about a band. They found that positive information increased the positive evaluation of the band. Subjects were more likely to enjoy the band when they had previous positive information.

On the other hand, all norms (particularly those which develop informally through group interaction) are not consistently enforced to the letter of the law. A certain range of behaviors is expected, and a certain range of deviation from norms is expected. In this sense, members will interact and behave within a certain range of allowable behaviors without being perceived as deviants. But behaviors beyond those limits will be labeled as deviant, and group pressures toward conformity will be brought to bear on those members performing such behaviors.

Typically, informal norms are accepted by group members, so that members will generally conform to those norms. When members accept a norm, they not only acknowledge that the norm exists and that they understand it, but also that the norm applies to the behaviors of members within that group. Because norms develop as a product of the group interaction, rather than through an internalizing process of each individual member, informal norms are enforced by the group. Without enforcement of norms and punishment of deviants, the norms will cease to exist.

Certainly some of us are more likely than others to accept norms. For example, a person with a poor self-concept, a need for social acceptance, or a submissive personality trait will be more likely to conform with minimal group pressure. When conformity results from the personality characteristics of individual group members, however, the significance of those social norms to the group process decreases accordingly. More important are those norms which members accept because of the nature of the group process. That is, members who are committed to the group are engaged in active participation in the group deliberations. They feel that the group is important and are loyal to it.

Groupthink Perhaps the most dramatic consequence of pressures to conform to group norms, especially in cohesive groups, is the groupthink phenomenon. *Groupthink* is what happens when a group avoids conflict and reaches consensus without criticizing and evaluating ideas. When the members of a group are very attracted to the group and reap many rewards from their membership in the group, they are especially vulnerable to the groupthink phenomenon. These groups have developed strong norms about not "rocking the boat," and they encourage almost blind loyalty to the group by discouraging conflict and independent opinions.

The following is an example of a groupthink situation: Robert Lynne, chairman of Regal Airlines, is meeting with his board of directors to decide whether or not to purchase a small ground transportation company. Lynne organized the meeting and opened with a few words in support of the purchase. As soon as he finished, the rest of the board members began nodding their heads in approval and supporting the idea. No one disagreed. The conversation that followed was light, supportive, and sprinkled with positive predictions about what this would mean for Regal Airlines. The group voted to approve the purchase and commented, "This was a great meeting and an important moment in the history of our company."

"Bob Lynne is taking us in new and productive directions," stated another board member. "He certainly has my support."

This may appear to be a smooth and effective meeting, but the group is not really functioning well. The decision was made quickly and on the basis of normative pressures to "go along." It was a groupthink decision. Irving Janis, the sociologist who first wrote about groupthink, has observed these types of decisions in government policies. Janis studied documents and transcripts of meetings in the Kennedy administration during the 1962 Bay of Pigs invasion and concluded that the administration's decision to attack Cuba was a groupthink decision. It was the result of a cohesive group's reluctance to express private doubts about the decision. Janis has discovered groupthink tendencies in a number of government fiascoes (Janis, 1983).

Groupthink occurs because of the presence of certain group norms. And there are always pressures to conform to norms. Here are four norms that establish conditions for groupthink to occur:

1. *Mindless cohesion* This is when a group feels that it can do no wrong because it is extremely optimistic and committed. While cohesion is, of course, important, it becomes counterproductive when the members dismiss anything that might threaten the group. The people in the Regal Airline example were more interested in conforming to the norm of cohesion than in critically examining their decisions.
2. *Pressuring nonconformists* Group members are pressured into going along with the group. The pressure can be subtle, such as rolling one's eyes or frowning, or more direct, such as expulsion from the group. In time this leads to what Janis called self-censorship, which is a tendency for group members to avoid expressing opinions.
3. *Failing to reward critical thinking* Sometimes people give in to the pressures of high-status individuals. Very often groups that do not encourage critical thinking are those with strong leaders who demand support, not conflict. The group and its leader feel invulnerable. This feeling of invulnerability is a classic symptom of groupthink. Groups are ideal places for discussion and disagreement, and the quality of decisions suffers when honest opposition is not encouraged.
4. *Tendency to justify what they have done* Groups make poor decisions when they discount information because it is inconsistent with an established position. Groupthink decisions emerge from rationalizations. The group blindly believes that what it has done in the past is best. They reject new information and reaffirm the inherent "correctness" of their own group. This leads to a false sense

of consensus. The group is unified and spirited, so it appears that everything is fine. The members of the Regal Airline board of directors were congratulating themselves and felt very good about the decision; nevertheless, they had not reached a true consensus, one that emerges from discussion and critical evaluation.

Members of a cohesive group are most likely to accept the norms of that group and to conform willingly to them precisely because they perceive the norms to benefit the successful performance of the group's decision-making efforts. In the presence of low levels of cohesiveness (or little groupness), the pressures on members to conform to group norms (particularly informal ones) are less likely to succeed.

Since the level of cohesiveness and the members' loyalty to the group may vary considerably among groups, the pressures on members to conform to group norms are also extremely variable. One reason is undoubtedly that the norms of cohesive groups are much more apparent to the group members. Members of a cohesive group know what is expected of them; they know what they ought to do and what they ought not to do in order to exhibit their commitment to the group. With little groupness, however, members are not only less willing to conform to the group norms, but are even less aware of what those norms really are.

Conformity, when healthy or beneficial, is thus linked closely with the level of cohesiveness (or groupness) developed by a group during its interaction. Lacking cohesiveness, the members are unlikely to produce strong pressures for conformity on deviant members; they probably don't care whether deviant members conform to the group norms, since they are also less committed to the group process. In order to avoid groupthink, it is necessary to find the right balance between cohesiveness and conformity.

The Norm of Reciprocity

Chapter 2 has discussed the phenomenon of reciprocity, specifically the reciprocity of self-disclosing communication. This human phenomenon is so pervasive in groups that reciprocity has even been labeled a social "norm" (Gouldner, 1960). Humans tend to react to other humans in a manner similar to the way in which those humans behave toward them. Furthermore, humans apparently reciprocate the behaviors of others in a sense that they feel they "ought" to do so. The human value leading to reciprocal behaviors is embodied in the golden rule and even in the golden rule in reverse. When attacked, we tend to fight back. A small boy will justify his aggressive behavior by saying, "He hit me first!" Apparently this norm of reciprocity justifies reciprocal fighting.

Probably no one social norm is present in all groups. But if any social norm is nearly universal among social systems, it may be the norm of reciprocity. In its state as a do-unto-others norm, reciprocity functions by a member's tendency to reciprocate similar behaviors in response to the behaviors of others. That is, if A helps B, B feels compelled to reciprocate that assistance. If A likes B (and B perceives that liking), B feels compelled to reciprocate. Consistent with previous discussions, if A confides some rather intimate self-disclosing information to B, B will tend to respond with intimate self-disclosing statements. The norm of reciprocity creates something of a snowball effect as each person's behavior reinforces the similar behaviors of the others. For this reason, perhaps, a norm embodying a pattern of communicative behaviors develops rather quickly in the continuing interaction of the group.

Perhaps the most important principle in understanding norms as they function in the group process is that group norms "belong to" the group and not to its individual members. Moreover, in the presence of high cohesiveness and high levels of member commitment to the group, those group norms become very powerful forces in shaping the behaviors of the individual members, even sometimes to the detriment of the group.

Group norms are significant and potent forces in groups. There are studies that have found that preventing people from fulfilling group expectations is one of the most fundamental sources of frustration for people. Often, and perhaps typically, persons will sacrifice their own individuality and individual needs (even physical ones) for the purpose of furthering and realizing group goals and conforming to social norms. And this is perfectly normal social behavior. The important principle remains: Social norms are group norms, rather than merely norms that are internalized by individual persons.

SUMMARY

The two most common standards for group members' behaviors are roles and norms. A role may be defined as the set of behaviors performed by a member in light of the expectations of other group members toward those behaviors. Each person's role often varies from group to group. Role performance, however, encapsulates each set of role behaviors within the region of performance—that specific group.

Some persons may experience role strain or conflict when a role performance places too great a demand on the group member or is incongruent with role performances in other groups. Occasionally, role conflict occurs when the expected role performance is incongruent with the person's personality traits. In that case, a person typically employs one of several strategies in order to reduce the role conflict, short of leaving the group. Every group member typically performs a role that differentiates him or her from other group members. The number of available roles is very large and is typically idiosyncratic to each group, probably because of the fact that each member develops the role performance in conjunction with other group members during the process of group interaction.

Group norms provide standards for how each member ought to behave in the group. LGD norms nearly always reflect the values shared by group members. The members typically apply pressures on deviant members to conform. Those pressures are strongest and healthiest in a successful and cohesive group and sometimes lead to a phenomenon called groupthink, where groups make poor decisions because they discourage critical thinking. The most common norm of group interaction is reciprocity, the tendency to behave toward other people as they behave toward you.

CHAPTER 9

Leadership and Power

Probably the most familiar of all social phenomena is the concept of leadership. Although not studied extensively until the last three or four decades, leadership has intrigued philosophers for centuries. How and why do people come to power? Why do people so zealously follow leaders like Adolph Hitler? What do leaders do that nonleaders don't? What constitutes good or effective leadership?

It is amazing that so many people could study one phenomenon and gain such little understanding of it. The number of unanswered questions concerning leadership is staggering. The purpose of this chapter is to shed some light on leadership in a small group. Consistent with the perspective of communication and the group process, this chapter deals with leadership as an emerging process precipitated by the interstructured communicative behaviors of all group members.

POWER AND INFLUENCE

Some form of power is universal in human groups. It exists in small groups, organizations, families, and nations. Power and leadership are not uniquely human phenomena. Indeed, a leadership structure and power relations are present in all forms of animal life. The female lion dominates the pride. Usually the largest male ape is dominant in the colony. And insects of all sorts display power and status relations.

When an individual has power, he or she is in a position to demand compliance. It is best to consider power as a continuum: on the high-power end, a person is able to coerce one or more other people into behaving as the powerful person wishes, or they suffer the consequences.

Power is the ability to exert control over others—and it is different from influence, because influence suggests persuasion rather than control. The two concepts—power and influence—are really quite distinct because it is possible to exercise one without the other. Power is not required for influence. A group member can be persuasive and influential without "possessing" power; some other group member can be powerful because he or she can control the behavior or resources of other people, but he or she might not be personally influential (Hollander, 1985). But even though power and influence are different processes, they are typically interrelated because group leaders are able to use both, depending on the situation and other group members. In many respects, influence is a more important concept because most leaders, even the very powerful, must use influence (or be persuasive) more often than they use raw power; because unrestrained and bold power can be so disruptive and counterproductive, most leaders rely on persuasion more than on the full power at their disposal.

Discussions of power and leadership begin with a very basic premise, which is that a leader usually has power over others. The most fundamental sources of power in groups are structural and personal (Pfeffer, 1981). *Structural power* simply means that a person is in a position or place that has power attached to it. If you are a member of a five-person group and one person is designated as the "leader," then the person in that position has power even if he or she is incapable or unwilling to use it. People hired into such positions as vice president, dean, director, or foreman all acquire a certain amount of power simply because the position is a validated power position. A leader in one of these positions has "legitimate" power because the position has been sanctioned by some appropriate group or agency.

Personal power, on the other hand, refers to individual qualities that make them powerful. Some people have personal characteristics that make a person powerful. But personal power also refers to *resource dependency*, which means that if person *A* controls something that person *B* needs or wants, then person *A* has power. For example, if a friend of yours had to sign for every one of your financial transactions, you would be dependent on that friend for a resource: signatory authority. Your friend would have personal power over you. Anyone who has special knowledge or competence, regardless of his or her position, has personal power.

STATUS

Status comes with leadership and power. Status is the "prestige of the position" that is afforded an individual (Shaw, 1981, p. 271). A person newly appointed to a vice presidential position of an organization will not only be in a position of leadership where she can exercise power but will also acquire status. All social organizations (such as small groups, corporations, and societies) have status hierarchies. People acquire status from social class, background, professional membership, or the possession of certain objects, such as money, cars, and clothes. But the status hierarchy of a small group (especially an LGD group) is more dependent on the ability to influence other group members. High-status members in most groups are perceived by other members as having provided the greatest assistance to the group's task accomplishment. If the raison d'être of the group is to accomplish some goal, whoever helps the group make progress toward that goal is rewarded with a high-status position. Social groups award status on the basis of the person's past behaviors in the group, and achieved status is the most important status concern when there is no external authority that awards status to group members.

All organizations have *formal* and *informal* structures. When two status hierarchies exist side by side—one based on ascribed status and one based on achieved status—you have formal and informal structures. A business organization, for example, has its own status hierarchy ascribed by the organization, but the workers in that organization may have developed their own status hierarchy, which may not conform to that sanctioned by the organization. When the authority of the two hierarchies is in conflict, the resultant tension can be very great. Many organizational problems arise over a conflict between structural power and personal power. This sort of conflict emerges in classroom groups when an instructor designates one group member as leader. This ascribed leader has status only because he or she has been appointed to the position, and this person's success or failure as a leader now depends wholly on the behavior of the group. Since group members award the highest status to the person who has helped them progress toward the goal, the appointed leader might be in for a surprise if he or she fails to meet the group's expectations.

Groups also develop levels of status hierarchy. The leader is at the top of the status level, with other roles ordered in relation to this one. All groups have a leadership (or top-status) level, and once a group leader has been identified, other group members compare their roles with the leader's and attach a corresponding status level to their own roles. You will recall that status consensus is a very important component of member satisfaction in groups; groups that agree on who will occupy what levels of status—especially the leadership level—are typically the more cohesive groups. In fact, groups that have reached full agreement on the status hierarchy perform better than groups that are democratic but unsure of the status hierarchy.

A status hierarchy exists in every group and organization. It is impossible to avoid. But it does not mean that members who have less status than others are of little value to the group. Productive groups value the contributions of everyone. Nevertheless, it is natural for people to attribute importance and value to the behavior of others; some members are therefore assigned a higher status. But the attribution of status to group members is a rank ordering of members' communicative behaviors relative to one another, not a judgment according to an absolute standard. Status, then, is something that is achieved in a particular group according to its goals and communication patterns. It is not a reward that a person can transfer easily from one group to another.

LEADERSHIP AND POWER

Several years ago one of us served on a committee charged with the task of selecting a chairperson for a university department. Several of the initial meetings were devoted to defining the role. We were unanimous in agreeing that we wanted a "chair" rather than a departmental "head." In other words, we agreed that we wanted leadership but that we did not want a dictator. The essential difference between "chair" and "head" was apparently the degree of power at the disposal of the leader.

The concept of extreme power in the hands of a leader is not novel. Indeed, nearly five centuries ago Machiavelli conceived of a political power so strong that rulers could use any means at their disposal to control the behavior of their followers. In fact, he believed that such power is essential for a centralized government. Machiavelli's name today refers to the unscrupulous exercise of political power. And the term *Machiavellianism* has been employed in reference to a person's ability or desire to dominate or control the behavior of another person during interaction.

It is important to distinguish between a *head* (for lack of a better term) and a *leader*. A head possesses the power to control the fate of others and thus has considerable power to coerce those under his or her leadership. A small group head would determine the goal of the group, give directions that must be obeyed willingly or unwillingly, and levy direct sanctions against nonfollowers. There would be considerable social distance between the head and the followers. In short, the relationship between head and followers is unidirectional: The head can influence followers but is less susceptible to any influence from them.

The LGD, of course, has a leader rather than a head in virtually every case. (It must be remembered that the term *leaderless* in "leaderless group discussion" indicates only that the leader, along with norms, roles, etc., is determined by the group members themselves and not imposed by an authority *outside* the group.) But a leader has power too. The difference between headship and leadership is not the amount of power, but the basis from which the power is derived. As we saw earlier, one common basis of power is the control of resources that are needed or desired by others. Saudi Arabia, for example, possesses much more power than its size warrants because the country controls a vast quantity of oil needed and desired by all industrialized countries of the world. And when we think of powerful countries, we immediately think of those countries with the capacity of nuclear weapons. In short, power resides in the possession of some relatively scarce resource needed or desired by others. Such a concept of power is expressed in conventional wisdom by the adage "In a country of the blind, the one-eyed man is king."

Most groups do not typically provide such a basis of power. While intelligence, for example, might be considered a personal resource, it is not something that can be transferred from one person to another or acquired by a person in the same sense that the resources in the examples above can be acquired. Nevertheless, the leader of the LGD does have a kind of power, even though its basis is not so easily defined. Unlike the unidirectional relationship between a head and the followers, the relationship between a leader and the followers is reciprocal. Consistent with the doctrine of interdependence, a leader leads at the discretion of the followers. That is, the basis for a leader's power is "consent of the governed." A leader may be deposed at any time. When a leader fails to satisfy the followers, his or her basis of power is undermined. Hence, the leader ceases to lead. A basis of power, such as the control of scarce resources, defines a leader in isolation, regardless of the will of other group members. Such a definition is contrary to the elements of process and interdependence inherent in groups. For our purposes, then, a leader is defined only in terms of followers. To discuss leadership is to discuss followership. One cannot exist without the other.

A leader is, of course, recognized by group members as the leader. Their recognition takes the form of deferential behavior. That is, members accede to the leadership moves made by the leader. They accord the leader respect and, generally, liking. (We shall return later in this chapter to the subject of the leader as an object of liking.) Members perceive the leader to be aiding the group in making progress toward their group goals. Normally, such progress implies the leader's activity in aiding the group in accomplishing its task. Perhaps more important than any other definitive characteristic, the leader is the person who consistently acts like a leader by performing leadership acts.

The definition of leadership at this point is admittedly quite general, but it does provide a basic understanding of what constitutes leadership in the small decision-making group. A more precise description of why certain persons achieve leadership status is provided later in this chapter.

PERSPECTIVES ON LEADERSHIP

The vast quantity of research and philosophical writing about leadership reveals considerable confusion. The reason for the confusion stems from the many perspectives used to view leadership. People commonly consider leadership to be embodied in a person occupying a given position in the group; therefore, a leader is a person first and a position in a role network second. While this viewpoint is a common one, it may have hindered progress in discovering the nature of leadership. In order to provide the basis for this book's perspective on leadership and to enrich our understanding of this elusive phenomenon, an evaluative survey of the most common perspectives on leadership follows. Hollander (1985) also provides a concise summary of some recognized perspectives on group leadership.

Traits

Letters of reference to employers, universities, and scholarship or loan agencies often ask for evaluations of the applicant on selected personality characteristics. A characteristic often included in such lists is "leadership ability." The assumption underlying this characteristic is the belief that a leader is a unique person possessing some innate ability that allows him or her to assume a leadership position in any social system. Further assumed is the belief that leaders are born, not made. Our conventional wisdom contains this same assumption in such well-worn phrases as "a natural leader" and "born to be a leader." It is not surprising, then, that the early approach to leadership searched for those individual characteristics or traits which leaders possess. The traits approach still influences contemporary views on leadership.

The traits approach attempted to distinguish leaders from nonleaders on the basis of how they differ in terms of personal characteristics. The very earliest research using the traits approach highlighted physical characteristics, consistent with the notion that the childhood leader is the biggest bully on the block. Because of consistently fruitless efforts to discover distinctive physical characteristics of leaders, this perspective soon focused on the distinctive traits of a leader's personality. The results from the traits approach have been contradictory and disappointing, however. Many personality traits have, at one time or another, been linked to leadership, including such traits as dependability, intelligence, self-confidence, enthusiasm or dynamism, originality, responsibility, verbal facility, critical thinking ability, and creativity.

A list of such traits appears consistent with common sense. One would normally think that a leader should have all these traits. But the traits approach to observing leadership has failed to achieve consistent results. Indeed, a leader of one group does not consistently achieve leadership in other groups. In fact, the leader of one group often cannot maintain leadership even in the same group. The traits approach plainly cannot account for the change of leadership in the same group.

It is probably impossible to assume that leadership can be explained simply by referring to the personality traits of individuals. Hollander (1985) explains that there have been two persistent questions about the qualities of leaders. The first asks what qualities *distinguish* leaders from followers. This is essentially the traits approach to leadership, where one assumes that leaders "possess" certain characteristics that cause them to be successful leaders. And, as Hollander argues, "this effort has not been very productive" (p. 492).

The second concern is what makes *effective* leaders. This is a very pragmatic question and can be studied by evaluating leaders in situations and noting effectiveness with respect to outcome criteria. This second approach is still concerned with leadership qualities, but only to the extent that situation-specific conditions are accounted for. Followers perceive leaders to have certain qualities, whether these qualities are apparent or not. There is currently considerable interest in leadership qualities with respect to how a leader's qualities are related to task demands (Boyatzis, 1982). This approach (discussed in more detail below) recognizes that the problem of assessing leaders in different situations is more complicated than simply identifying who is the leader.

In short, a strict traits approach to leadership is unsatisfactory. Personality traits are difficult to measure and people often disagree about personalities. Moreover, there are different traits required for different activities. The traits approach cannot differentiate between a good leader and a bad one, and it fails to explain the difference between achieving leadership and maintaining it. The variations in leadership qualities and requirements are so great that any list of traits would surely exclude some successful leaders and include some unsuccessful ones. The styles approach to leadership was an attempt to solve some of these problems.

Styles

The traits approach to leadership attempts to distinguish leaders from nonleaders and to identify those personality traits which characterize persons who rise to leadership status. The styles approach proceeds from a different perspective. Leadership styles assume an a priori identification of the leader through either ascription or achievement and a general description of how the leader leads. This approach seeks to determine which style of leadership is best, or most effective, in a group by comparing one predetermined style with another.

The early research utilizing the styles perspective differentiated between three general styles of leadership. These three styles were generalized descriptions of the relationship between leader and followers based on the leader's general pattern of behavior—democratic, autocratic, and laissez-faire. The laissez-faire style of leadership was soon discarded because it was so difficult to define. Essentially, the hands-off policy indicated by the laissez-faire style implies that the leader leads through not leading at all. Even on a commonsense level a laissez-faire style of leadership is an anomaly. Nonleadership is viewed as leadership?

Numerous studies have compared the democratic and autocratic styles of group leadership. Those in business management commonly refer to the two styles as "participatory" and "supervisory" management styles. Unfortunately, because the two styles are considered diametrically opposed to each other, the comparisons between them are not always realistic. Typically, an extremely democratic style is compared with an extremely autocratic style. That is, the democratic leader is totally unselfish, seeks group participation at all times, and consistently functions in the best interest of the group as a whole; the democratic leader, then, tends to overemphasize the socioemotional dimension of the group. On the other hand, most comparisons require the autocratic leader to behave with an absolute minimum of group participation, give blatant orders, and work for highly selfish goals; the autocratic leader, then, overemphasizes the task dimension of the group. Realistically, of course, there are many leadership styles that exist between these two extremes. And a single leader may even be democratic at times and autocratic at other times.

Past comparisons, however, have discovered some differences between groups functioning under these two styles. For example, the group with a democratic leader typically experiences more satisfaction, and the group with an autocratic leader is more efficient and more productive—particularly when productivity is measured on the basis of efficiency (for example, fewer errors). But the differences between the groups tend to diminish over time as the group members accustom themselves to the style of their leader. Since the task and social dimensions are interdependent, the success experienced in one dimension affects success in the other. That is, because members experience greater satisfaction with a democratic leader, they tend to work harder and increase their productivity, and because groups are highly efficient and productive under an autocratic leader, the members experience greater pride in their achievements—hence, an increase in satisfaction.

The styles approach is not a fully satisfactory perspective from which to view leadership in a small decision-making group. It is intuitively obvious that no one style is most desirable or most effective for all groups and all situations. For example, a military leader in battle and an airplane pilot in a storm are autocratic leaders and undoubtedly should be. When the going is rough, neither of these two leaders can stop to take a vote. Rather, they give orders that must be followed immediately and without hesitation. Naturally, in less trying situations the pilot or the military leader often adopts a more democratic style.

It is possible for leaders to use a characteristic style, but this style cannot be entirely divorced from the requirements of the situation that the leader and followers are involved in. Leaders must utilize a range of behaviors, depending on the demands of the task and the nature of the followers with whom the leader must interact. Even leaders who have a consistent style are controlled by external factors. So a style might be a *typical* tendency, but it is still *relational* because the leader responds to the qualities of followers and situations.

Situations

Because of the inability of the traits and styles approaches to provide robust explanations of group leadership, many investigators of group behavior have turned to other perspectives. A common perspective that is currently popular for studying group leadership is the situational approach. When people who rise to leadership positions are assessed from this perspective, the main consideration is given to what the leader does or needs to do for effective group functioning.

The situational approach to group leadership requires a thorough description of the group situation. Of the many situational variables that could be examined, perhaps the one most commonly studied is the group members' particular combination of personality traits—their level of interest in the task, their motivation, and so forth. A second variable often believed to have some bearing on the particular kind of leader required in a situation is the nature of the group's task. Other, less commonly studied situational variables include factors of the physical setting; for example, sitting at the head of a table has been associated with leadership in our culture (although seating arrangements have not proved to be highly successful indicators of leadership). The size of the group has also been thought to have some bearing on leadership. Obviously, as the group increases in size, the reduced availability of each member becomes more of a problem; on the other hand, charismatic leadership is closely associated with very large groups and with a corresponding increase in social distance between leaders and their followers.

At first glance, the situational approach to group leadership appears to solve most of the problems associated with the traits and styles approaches, but it has its problems too. First, it offers very few general principles to help prospective group leaders know what they should or can do in a given situation. Of course, there are many lists of do's and dont's to guide prospective leaders, but such lists have not proved very successful. Second, no comprehensive list of situational ingredients now exists; even compiling such a list may be quite impossible. Third, even for those variables which have been observed to exist within a situation, there is no way of determining which variables have the greatest impact on the situation. A fourth problem stems from the fact that what *functions* the leader should fulfill is the significant element in the situational approach. The head of a student group gathering information on campus activities needs to function differently and to draw on different skills than does the leader of a town council or a labor union; although each leader must direct followers and influence the group process, the situation and the content of the activity make for different behavioral needs. Overall, the fundamental problem with the situational approach is the generality of the term *situation*; thus, analyses of situations have failed to distinguish clearly between task demands, group size, resources, and so on (Hollander, 1985).

But the situational approach has drawn attention to how leaders are affected by the perceptions of their followers (as opposed to concentrating solely on the behaviors of individual leaders). Therefore, what began as a strong response to the traits and styles approaches has led to significant developments in understanding leader-follower relationships. One of the most important of these developments has been the contingency model of leadership.

The Contingency Model of Leader Effectiveness One specific situational approach to group leadership is the contingency model, developed by Fiedler (1964, 1967). Central to his contingency model is the assessment of a particular leadership "trait" measured by a paper-and-pencil test. Originally Fiedler developed two such tests—one to measure the "assumed similarity of opposites" (ASo) and the other to evaluate the "least preferred coworker" (LPC). A score on the ASo test would be high if the individual perceived himself or herself to be quite similar to the group member who was perceived to be the most different. In the LPC test, the higher the leader rated the group member whom he or she liked least, the higher would be the leader's LPC score. Fiedler discovered that the scores on these two tests were highly correlated. Therefore, the contingency model is typically based on only the LPC test.

In regard to the behavior of leaders, leaders with high LPC scores have been found to be more socially oriented. That is, they generally concern themselves with the group's social dimension. Conversely, leaders scoring low in the LPC test tend to be more task-oriented and concerned with order and structure. The contingency model, however, does not attempt to determine how leaders behave in certain situations. Rather, the model tries to place a particular leader (that is, a high-LPC or a low-LPC leader) in a group situation in which that leader will be most effective. Thus, the contingency model provides something of a combination of the traits and situational approaches. That is, a leader with a particular trait (high LPC or Low LPC) is thought to be most effective in a specific situation.

Fiedler determined that a leader's effectiveness would vary as a result of several characteristics of the situation. The most notable of these characteristics include the amount of structure or external demands that the task places on the group, how well the group members get along with one another (similar to cohesiveness), and the formal power given to the person occupying the leadership position (such as the power to reward and punish group members).

Numerous investigations of LPC leaders in different situations have resulted in conclusions concerning the favorability of various situations for the leader. For example, a situation is quite favorable for leadership when it contains a highly structured task with a low level of difficulty, high commitment of group members to the task, and high formal authority of the leadership position. The more "favorable" the situation, then, the more directive the leader (that is, the leader will have a low LPC score). The less favorable the situation, one might assume, the more likely it is that the socially oriented leader (one with a high LPC score) will be most effective.

Such conclusions, however, are tempered by investigations suggesting that in extreme situations (i.e., those situations extremely favorable or extremely unfavorable to the leader) low-LPC leaders tend to be most effective. Such leaders apparently function with high task motivation even under arduous conditions and are able to get the task accomplished. Conversely, high-LPC leaders are apparently most effective when the situation is moderately favorable or moderately unfavorable. Evidently, their social orientation to the group's performance allows the group to function most effectively when the situation is neither extremely favorable nor extremely unfavorable.

Fiedler's contingency model is a combination of traits and styles approaches to leadership, also. That is, the LPC trait, measured by the paper-and-pencil test, is associated with a particular leadership style (directive or nondirective) that is very similar to authoritative and democratic leadership styles. Consequently, the approach to determining the potential effectiveness of the leader, contingent upon situational characteristics, is an attempt to match leadership traits and styles to a particular group situation. We therefore interpret the contingency model of leader effectiveness as a specific situational approach to leadership.

Fiedler's contingency model has been very influential in explaining leadership effectiveness. Proponents of the model report strong confirming support in a number of experiments (Strube and Garcia, 1981). Still others claim that since a leadership "style" is matched with a situation, the subordinates in those situations are more satisfied with the group experience. Chemers (1983) believes that the Fiedler model can predict and explain group member satisfaction as well as performance.

There are other contingency models of leadership (e.g., Vroom and Yetton, 1973; House and Mitchell, 1974), but each is similar in that leadership tendencies are typically described along a continuum from highly directive, or autocratic, to participative and democratic and are then matched with situational contingencies, such as the nature of the task, member relationships, and environmental factors. These models then predict leader effectiveness and group member satisfaction. But the models are also incomplete in some significant ways. There is a tendency to assume that an LPC score, for example, is associated with particular behaviors. As we will see later in this chapter, leaders adapt their behaviors to a wide range of situations and are not often strictly "person-oriented" or "task-oriented." In fact, one study (Offermann, 1984) reported evidence that a leader's LPC score *changed after group interaction*. This study raises serious questions about the stability of the LPC score to measure leadership style. It is also true that many individuals can operate very effectively in both the task and social realms and cannot be easily categorized by the LPC measure. Nevertheless, contingency models, and Fiedler's LPC model in particular, have helped link individuals with situations and have provided the rudiments of an interactional approach to leadership.

Group Composition Gilstein, Wright, and Stone (1977) also provided insight into group leadership from a situational perspective in their investigation of leaders in groups with differing compositional "mixes" of members. They attempted to determine the specific types of groups in which directive or nondirective leaders would be most effective. Among their conclusions, they state that, in their investigation, groups whose members had conservative sociopolitical orientations developed higher member satisfaction (that is, cohesiveness) with a directive leader. Conversely, liberal members preferred a nondirective leader. According to this and other studies cited by the authors, groups with nondirective leaders tend to generate more member-centered and task-responsive interaction; the members apparently perceive a greater degree of freedom to participate and thus have a feeling of greater responsibility to participate in the group interaction. Members of groups with directive leaders, on the other hand, often turn to the leader for guidance and succeed in shifting the responsibility for interaction to the leader rather than assuming the responsibility themselves.

One should not be led to conclude that nondirective leaders will diffuse the responsibility for the group's interaction among the group members. Rather, members with particular personality traits and with specific sociopolitical orientations tend to respond differently to the perceived directiveness of their group leader. Thus, persons who are more assertive, more interpersonally sensitive, and more ideationally flexible tend to interact more and thus allow for greater group effectiveness when they are in groups led by a nondirective leader. But groups composed of less assertive, less sensitive members with more fixed ideas apparently prefer situations that are more structured. They therefore respond more favorably to a more authoritative, or directive, leader.

The situational approach to leadership, although highly popular and traditionally the most accepted approach to group leadership, underscores the complexity of the group situation. The number of factors that can differentiate one group situation from another is extraordinarily large. Among such factors are the personality attributes of individual members, the nature of the task, the amount and kind of external constraints on the group, the degree of cohesiveness in the group, ad infinitum. Moreover, each of these situational factors is subject to change as the group continues to interact. To account for all the factors, let alone the variation of each factor over time, is an extraordinarily challenging and probably impossible task. Even though the situational approach to leadership is conceptually attractive, it is extremely difficult to implement.

The Task and Social Dimensions of Leadership

With the exception of the functional approach that follows, all perspectives on leadership have considered leadership to be a role filled by one person. Bales and Slater (1955), however, began to consider the possibility that leadership duties might be divided among group members and that more than one person in the group could perform leadership duties. Moreover, there is general agreement that there are two dimensions to any leadership situation—the task and social dimensions. The *task* dimension pertaining to goals, production, structure, and the general accomplishment of tasks. The *social* dimension pertains to the quality of interpersonal relationships, consideration for others, socioemotional support, and individual feelings. Sometimes the task and social leadership functions in a group are handled by two different people. One person might be particularly adept at organizing the group and accomplishing goals, and another person might be skilled at forming and maintaining good personal relationships between group members. When both of these qualities are present in one highly capable individual, you might have the "great man" model of leadership.

Some people are quite uncomfortable with the notion that there is a task and social leader in a group. And, in fact, it is possible to argue that most members of groups perceive task competence to be the primary determinant of leadership and expect a competent person to be a directive and assertive leader. The leader-follower relationship becomes important here, because of the following: When group members are highly involved in a task, they value a directive leader and expect the competent leader to guide the group toward its goals. But when group members are uninvolved, they resent directive leaders and look more for social support, which is to say that group members who, not satisfied with the situation, look to other people for agreeable social experiences; hence, uninvolved and unhappy group members perceive some people to be task leaders, whom they do not appreciate, and others to be social leaders, whom they do appreciate. It is true that many studies of leadership take place in the laboratory, where student subjects are "captive" and relatively uninvolved. But most groups in organizations are composed of committed group members. We will assume, then, that the notion of more than one leader is unusual and not very representative of actual groups. However, the notion of dual leadership does call attention to the fact that leadership requires different functions and that followers in groups significantly influence leader behaviors. Later we will examine what Hersey and Blanchard (1982) call a "life-cycle theory of leadership," which accounts for the development of leader-follower relationships over time.

THE FUNCTIONAL PERSPECTIVE ON LEADERSHIP

All the perspectives on group leadership—traits, styles, situations—have one element in common. Each assumes that leadership is centered in the *person* who occupies the leadership position in the group's network of roles. The functional perspective shifts the point of emphasis from the person to the communicative *behaviors* performed. Although the functional approach is certainly not new, no consistent search for leadership functions has developed over the years. The function perspective has never achieved the significance or popularity enjoyed by each of the other perspectives at one time or another. One reason for this lack of popularity may be a confusion over what is meant by "functions." While some have considered group functions to be general principles essential to group operation, others discuss functions as specific behaviors capable of being performed by one person.

The view of functions as general principles necessary for maintaining the group fails to serve our purposes and is not congruent with the perspective of communication and the group process. The concept of group functions, which can be useful if made specific, becomes diluted through overgeneralizing. Most group functions are generalized "good advice"—principles with insufficient practicability. For example, some commonly listed group functions include: (1) to advance the purpose of the group, (2) to inspire greater activity among members, (3) to administer procedural matters, and (4) to build group cohesiveness. Essentially, these group functions imply some sort of influence that achieves desired results, such as greater cohesiveness, increased productivity, or greater group unity. Group functions, then, are little more than desired goals achieved rather than specific communicative behaviors that help achieve these goals.

Although there is no single acceptable list of individual functions—that is, communicative behaviors—several suggested lists indicate some individual behaviors that have been associated with leadership in the past. Cartwright and Zander (1968, p. 306), for example, distinguished between group functions and individual functions and provided such a list:

> It appears that most group objectives can be subsumed under one of two
> headings: (*a*) the achievement of some specific group goal and (*b*) the
> maintenance or strengthening of the group itself. Examples of member
> behaviors that serve functions of *goal achievement* are "initiates action," "keeps
> members' attention on the goal," "clarifies the issue," "develops a procedural
> plan," "evaluates the quality of work done," and "makes expert information
> available." Examples of behaviors that serve functions of *group maintenance* are
> "keeps interpersonal relations pleasant," "arbitrates disputes," "provides
> encouragement," "gives the minority a chance to be heard," "stimulates
> self-direction," and "increases the interdependence among members."

Mortensen (1966) devised five categories of individual behaviors that he labeled "attempted leadership." These five categories include "introducing and formulating goals, tasks, procedures," "eliciting communication from other group members," "delegating, directing action," "showing consideration for group activity," and "integrating and summarizing group activity." These five categories imply several characteristics of leadership behaviors. For example, Mortensen conceived of a leader as initiating proposals for action, asking focused questions, and summarizing group activity. These functions are also reflected in Cartwright and Zander's list.

Hugh C. Russell (1970) discovered four dimensions of a leader's communicative behaviors. These dimensions are "goal facilitation," "emotional control," "objectivity," and "communication skill." They indicate that a leader directs the group toward the group goal, attempts to reduce tension and resolve conflicts, contributes balanced information, and possesses the qualities of a skillful speaker. Unfortunately, Russell's list of dimensions did not attempt to specify those behaviors which exercise influence or which a leader specifically uses in order to exert leadership. He did not, for example, specify a behavior that could reduce tension or resolve conflict. These dimensions are only descriptive characteristics of the totality of a leader's behavior—not types of communicative behaviors themselves.

Functional Communicative Behaviors

It is, of course, impossible to identify all the behaviors that leaders perform, and labeling any single message as functional and serving the needs of the group is probably an oversimplification. Nevertheless, we want to give you as workable a list as possible for learning and identifying leadership behaviors. Although you cannot learn to be a leader simply by reading a list of typical leadership behaviors, you can improve your effectiveness in groups by becoming familiar with common leadership behaviors and practicing them, always keeping in mind that an appropriate behavior depends on the situation and on your relationships with your followers. Deciding how to communicate in a group is a matter of making informed strategic choices about what communicative behaviors will be most effective. The following discussions are designed to help you make intelligent choices. The leader must function in three areas—groups procedures, task requirements, and social needs.

Group Procedures All groups must be guided through their tasks in an orderly manner. Every type of group, including LGDs, establishes procedures for accomplishing goals. Putman (1979) explains how some groups prefer very rigid procedures while others are quite casual. The leader can perform the following functions to facilitate the procedural requirements of the group.

Plan an Agenda Most people appreciate a sense of order. An agenda is a list of topics to be discussed during the group's meeting. The leader should either prepare an agenda before the group meets or direct the group before the meeting actually begins to agree on what it will talk about. The leader should also be prepared to stimulate discussion on each of the agenda items; the leader should not control the discussion, but should simply generate discussion and make sure that relevant issues emerge.

Handle Routine "Housekeeping" Matters These are tasks that typically must be completed before the group begins considering the central issues of the meeting. The tasks could be such things as taking roll, calling the meeting to order, distributing handouts, or making any necessary announcements or modifications to the agenda. Handling all such tasks ensures that the group is prepared to complete its work.

Prepare for the Next Meeting Group members need to be informed about such things as the meeting's location, date, and time. The leader should make sure that the physical conditions are appropriate; that is, the room is of sufficient size, there are enough chairs, and any equipment (e.g., projectors and slides) is available and operating. These may sound like small tasks to perform, but they are very important to the work of the group. The truly efficient leader gains the respect of the group by attending to small details.

Task Requirements The leader plays an extremely important role in accomplishing the work of the group. Leadership behaviors that help the group achieve its goals are task-oriented behaviors. It is important to remember that leadership behaviors can be performed by any member of the group; as we will see later, research indicates that leadership communicative behavior is often shared by group members, or at least that no single person is the only one to communicate in a leaderlike manner. There are obviously many leadership functions that group members can perform, and it is sometimes difficult to separate task functions from procedural or social functions, but the following represent the most important task requirements.

Initiate a Structure Effective leaders organize and direct things so that the group makes progress toward its goals. The leader suggests ways of doing things and proposes tasks and goals for the group. The "initiate a structure" function is general enough to include procedural matters as well as others. When a leader proposes an agenda, directs the group to proceed in a certain way, or suggests solutions to a problem, he or she is initiating a structure for the group. When group members withhold suggestions or wait for others to initiate ideas, they are not contributing to the orderly progression of the group.

Seek Information We said earlier that groups can perform some tasks better than individuals because they have the advantage of collectivity. In order for groups to utilize all of their resources and perform at their best, they must seek out all the relevant and pertinent information. Functional behaviors in this area include requesting facts, asking questions, and getting clarification on unclear points of information; the dysfunctional group member is neither aware of necessary facts nor takes the time to seek out information. Some leaders will prepare for group meetings by writing down questions to be asked.

Give Information Every member should be contributing valuable information to the group, but individuals who are leaders contribute more than others. They spend more time reading and preparing for the group than other members do. Very simply, leaders offer facts and information relevant to the group's concerns. Members who carry out fact-gathering assignments and report the results of their work to others gain an influential position, because access to information is always associated with power. Of course group members who exert leadership by providing information should do so in a manner that benefits the group rather than the individual leader.

Offer Informed Opinions Perhaps you have heard the quip "Opinions are like rear ends; everyone has one." This may be true of general opinions, but it is not true of informed ones. Very few people have *informed* opinions. Whereas a general opinion is an unsupported belief about some issue or matter before the group, an informed opinion is a belief supported by data, evidence, and argument. Leaders seek information so that they can offer informed opinions; it is counterproductive to confuse the members with ambiguous or indefensible opinions. Leaders also offer their informed opinions at the right time, neither stating them too soon nor remaining silent too long. For instance, a member who knows that his or her opinion is likely to sway the group might let other members express themselves first so as not to influence them unduly.

Clarify and Elaborate Reducing ambiguity and clarifying ideas by asking questions and making statements are important leadership functions. A good leader can recognize when the members are confused or unclear about an idea because it has been expressed in abstract language. Technical or socially inappropriate language can sometimes be a problem too; if the group is preparing a public document, the leader should make sure that it is appropriate for the external audience, free from jargon or specialized language that might not be very communicative. The leader should also be capable of relating one idea to another and of seeing the big picture. Because group members are often preoccupied with their own ideas, it is up to the leader to clarify the connections between ideas so that the members understand the ideas' implications.

Summarize the Group's Main Points and State Its Consensus Group members usually express many opinions and ideas during the course of a discussion. Some of these are carefully thought out, but others are rather haphazard and superficial, and in either case it is important that they be summarized. A leadership function has been performed when someone restates the main points in clear language and summarizes the member's various arguments. A truly skillful and balanced summary will include all the main points and arguments, and it is dysfunctional for a leader to favor one position over another. At some point in the group's deliberations the leader will say, "I think we have agreed on the following points," then state what he or she believes to be the group's consensus, and engage the group in additional discussion about those points on which there is no consensus.

Social Needs Groups also have social needs. A leader who attends to social needs is concerned with promoting a harmonious and pleasant social environment in the group; this requires the leader to be sensitive to the group's individual members and their interpersonal relationships. But it is impossible to separate a group's task requirements from its social needs completely, because each influences the other, so the task and social dimensions should really be considered together. The group's success depends on both, and conflict between the two can be disruptive to the group. If a group's leader and members are concerned only with achieving their task goal, their interpersonal relationships and sense of personal well-being will suffer; on the other hand, if the leader and members spend all their time socializing and "liking" each other, the task will suffer.

It does not take much imagination to see how a member's performance on the group task can be hindered by a poor social environment. If the member feels unappreciated and has tense social relationships with other group members, he or she is not going to perform well. The following example shows how the task and social dimensions are related in a significant way. Jim states an opinion and Bill disagrees with it.

JIM: Since so many minority students are concentrated in a few schools, the only way to achieve racial balance is by busing.
BILL: Well that's a pretty dumb idea. It's been tried before and always causes all sorts of problems. Forget it.

Although Bill is responding to a particular idea that pertains to the task, he is doing it in such a way that Jim is likely to feel personally inadequate. Bill's comment is a clear enough statement of his opinion about a task-related matter, but it also says something about how he views Jim. Because Jim is surely going to interpret Bill's statement as an expression of a negative attitude toward himself, Bill's message about a task matter will have a deleterious effect on his social relationship with Jim.

A leader must analyze the group at any moment and decide which behaviors are best to meet the group's needs. Should a leader decide that the group members would benefit by some dialogue in an attempt to understand one another and get along better, the following types of communicative behaviors might prove useful.

Express Feelings   This is very difficult in most work groups. People simply feel vulnerable and weak if they express feelings that are highly personal. Nevertheless, there are times when it is important. A leader should not force group members into a soul-searching session but can call attention to feelings that are bothering people. A leader can provide support for a group member who has been personally attacked and can reinforce a less confident member. A leader who freely expresses feelings and shows concern for the feelings of others will establish a friendly and productive work environment. And the best way to stimulate others to talk about their feelings is to do it yourself. So if as a leader you say what is on your mind, others will likely follow.

Facilitate Involvement and Communication   Almost all groups have members who do not participate or are not very involved in group life. Some people are simply apathetic, and others are shy or feel overwhelmed by the group. Leaders must work to keep everyone participating; otherwise, the group loses valuable input. And if members are not stimulated enough to participate, they emotionally withdraw from the group and become part of the problem rather than part of the solution. There are a number of ways to stimulate communication and involvement, but the following three are the most common and effective:

1. *Make sure you reinforce any attempts to participate by shy or reluctant members*   Verbal reinforcements are simple and effective, such as saying, "Good idea, I hadn't thought of that." Everyone likes to think that his or her ideas are being treated seriously and appreciated. Studies show that verbal reinforcement is very likely to increase the frequency with which a group member participates. Even if you do not agree with what a member says, you can communicate disagreement in a socially acceptable manner. In the example above, Bill could have said something like "That's one solution that has worked, but there are a few others we haven't considered."

2. *Directly engage people in communication*   A leader might find it necessary simply to remind group members that they have an obligation to participate, telling them directly that the quality of the discussion depends on their participation. It is always easier to sit back and listen, so some members need a little prodding. Also, a leader can address questions directly to individuals; this will pull a person into the interaction, and then if the person's contributions can be reinforced,

there will be even stronger incentives to continue participation. It takes practice and skill, however, to do these things tactfully; if the leader is perceived as being condescending, then his or her efforts will not only fail but will do more harm than good. Giving assignments is another way to encourage involvement in the group. At the close of a meeting or work session, a leader should give directions for the next time, and group members who are responsible for some type of work and must come prepared to report will naturally be involved in the interaction. When such an assignment makes use of an individual's experience and expertise, the individual is even more likely to succeed.

3. *Increase the chances for participation* Sometimes groups are so large that people find it difficult to "jump in"; the leader might consider dividing the group into small clusters to give everyone an equal chance to participate. There is also the problem of the overpowering member or subset of members who dominate the discussion. Just as there are shy people who hesitate to be involved, there are extroverts who are ambitious and have an opinion about everything; a leader should not allow one member to dominate the discussion. Finally, the leader can use the structural arrangement of the group to advantage. Recall that Chapter 3 discussed the concept of structural centrality; that is, a person who is in a more central position sends and receives more messages. Place a group member in a central position (such as in the middle of a network or at the head of a table), and this will increase the frequency of the member's participation.

Harmonize A leader should attempt to reconcile disagreements and reduce tension. This can be achieved either through humor and relaxing comments or through more direct attempts at conflict resolution. (Conflict resolution will be discussed in the next chapter, but here it is important to identify it as a social skill that a leader should possess.) *Harmonizing* is getting the members to cooperate and creating a supportive climate in the group. The skilled harmonizer knows the difference between (1) a healthy and valuable exchange of ideas, which may include honest disagreement, and (2) nasty arguments that interfere with the group's productivity and are based on individual egos and ambitions. All of the theories and techniques of conflict resolution notwithstanding, a leader can always simply restate opposing positions, ask the members to clarify their views, and then try to find compromises.

Functionalism and Leadership: Conclusion

In sum, the list of leadership functions given above does note some specific behaviors associated with leadership. Moreover, the functions emphasize those behaviors which facilitate group task accomplishment. A more specific list of behaviors comprising all the functions performed by a leader is probably unrealistic, but the partial list given above may be used as a springboard for further consideration. Certainly the performance of appropriate leadership functions requires a social awareness of what function needs to be performed, when it needs performing, and the ability to perform it.

The functional perspective on leadership is not without its shortcomings, however. While the approach itself has potential, the state of knowledge about leadership functions is small. First, the leadership functions that researchers now recognize and use are still too global and not easily applied. Second, most past efforts to discover leadership functions attempted to describe communicative behaviors or their consequences in isolation, without viewing leadership acts within the interstructured sequence of group interaction. What type of act precedes and follows a leadership act? Perhaps the leadership act can be defined as a leadership function only in terms of the act that precedes and follows it. If leadership involves a reciprocal relationship of leader and follower, the behavior of the leader is probably meaningless when isolated from the behaviors of the followers. Thus, leadership functions should reflect the interdependence of communicative behaviors performed by both leader and followers during the process of group interaction.

Indeed, the overall perspective on communication and the group process underlying this book rests on the functional perspective of leadership. In other words, group leadership is a process in which communicative behaviors associated with leadership are performed by one or more group members. These behaviors, then, develop the pattern of leadership that characterizes the decision-making group. If leadership is a process, it is not best viewed as a personal quality that some people have and others do not. Nor can leadership be viewed simply as a structural position occupied by some person within a network of roles. Leadership develops over time as group members interact with one another. And their interaction patterns eventually reflect leader-follower relationships between their members.

The problem of identifying leadership acts is real. In fact, the cop-out of the situational perspective is not completely absent from the present treatment of leadership. Although the explanations should be more explicit in the description of leadership emergence given later in this chapter, the basic axiom identifying a leadership act is appropriateness within a given interaction sequence. That is, what may be a leadership act at one time during the group's interaction may be quite inappropriate at another time.

Shifting the focus of leadership from the person to his or her communicative behaviors, the functional approach no longer implies that leadership acts are necessarily performed by only one person. Typically, members of a decision-making group have a single member as their leader in that the bulk of the leadership acts is generally performed by just one person. But it would not be extraordinary if several persons performed the leadership functions and hence provided the group with shared leadership. But shared leadership in no way implies that one person is a task specialist while the other is a socioemotional specialist. Rather, inherently implying the interdependence of the two dimensions, group leadership functions are shared in that several members perform these functions without partitioning their leadership responsibilities into neat pigeonholes.

The functional approach also allows for, and serves to explain how, leadership changes from one person to another within the same group or in different situations. Mortensen (1966) discovered that some leaders consistently performed leadership behaviors throughout all periods of the group's interaction and hence maintained their leadership positions. Other leaders, however, noticeably declined in their attempted leadership acts, thereby indicating their fall from leadership status. As the deposed leader decreased his or her performance of attempted leadership acts, another member or members apparently performed those acts and took over as leader.

Finally, the functional approach makes it possible to define which functions characterize good, effective leadership and, conversely, which functions characterize poor, ineffective leadership. Other perspectives are less capable of defining the qualities of effective leadership, for to do so requires evaluating what the leader actually does. Hence, the functional perspective is necessary in order to be able to evaluate leadership behaviors.

LEADERSHIP EMERGENCE

In the event that a leader is appointed by some authority outside the group, the process of leadership emergence applies to the emergence of the informal leader. Most groups have a leader who emerges gradually over time, in which case the process is important. When people achieve leadership status gradually, the process is termed *leadership emergence*. This process is especially apparent in juries where no leader is appointed, in battlefield promotions, and in the development of political and organizational leadership.

Most religious and political emergent leaders, as well as small group leaders, inspire allegiances and positive associations in their followers. When leaders are popular and successful, it is usually because they are not autocratic. Most emergent leaders have a large and impressive following who identify with the leader, and sometimes the identification is so strong that the followers fail to examine their reasons for feeling so strongly about the leader. This is not a typical problem in small groups, but there are ample examples of political and religious leaders who fit this model. Leaders emerge with a dedicated following because they treat people well and tell them what they want to hear. Actually, the notion that leaders emerge from a consensual base is exaggerated, because most leaders spend considerable time encouraging and cultivating followers.

People want to lead for numerous reasons, but most of them fall into one of the following five categories:

1. *Information* The leader is often a person who has special information that cannot be communicated easily to others.
2. *Rewards* The individual seeks the rewards associated with leading.
3. *Expectations* The individual believes that the task can be accomplished and that he or she can do it.
4. *Acceptance by other group members* Individuals who are reinforced and affirmatively evaluated by group members are likely to attempt leadership.
5. *Status* People who bring status to the group often attempt to lead. This status can be in the form of a previous leadership role or of some other valued activity or resource.

Who emerges as a leader has been an important subject of study, and research shows that communication is the major determinant (Hollander, 1985). In fact, the amount of talking, as opposed to its quality, is the most important determinant. The person who makes many contributions to the group is perceived to be motivated and therefore to be an attractive leader for the group. The *quality* of what is said becomes more important later in the group process, when the members can be impressed with content. Who speaks first is another indicator of who will emerge as a leader, for people who speak up immediately are perceived to be motivated and self-assured, characteristics that group members find appealing in a leader. Moreover, group members who speak up first have the attention of the remainder of the group and can exercise influence.

Schneier and Bartol (1980) found that women are less likely than men to emerge as leaders, but one interesting difference is that women are often rated the same as men on certain leadership behaviors. In other words, women are perceived to be the same as men when it comes to communicating in a leaderlike manner; however, when leaders are actually identified, there are fewer women than men. We will take a closer look at sex differences and leadership later in this chapter.

Fisher's Model

Fisher (1980) created what he called a hypothetical model of leadership emergence. Based on his observations of classroom groups, he proposed a model in which members of groups contend for leadership and then go through a process of elimination. The model can be understood as an explanation of how the leadership *process* works after some members make leadership attempts (perhaps seeking leadership for some of the five reasons listed above). Figure 9-1 is a pictorial representation of this hypothetical model; it shows that there are three stages in the process.

At least theoretically, all members of the group are candidates for leadership. Some members, through the quantity and quality of their communication, will make their interests known immediately. During stage 1, some members (e.g., member *E* in Figure 9-1) will fall from contention immediately for any number of reasons. They simply feel uninterested or are incapable of emerging as a leader because of their personality (such as being overly shy), their lack of expertise, or their general failure to communicate as a leader. Stage 1 is usually pretty brief. Noncontenders are quickly recognized by other group members and just as quickly eliminated as leader contenders.

During stage 2, several members are strengthened in their bids for leadership by gaining the assistance of other members to support their candidacies. Thus, members *A* and *C* remain contenders for group leadership while members *B* and *D* drop out of personal contention and serve as lieutenants of *A* and *C*, respectively. As a lieutenant, each becomes less an initiator of action and more a supporter of proposals initiated by one of the contenders. In stage 2, two opposing factions (or coalitions) develop around each of the remaining contenders. Stage 2 is typically a lengthy phase and often involves some verbal sparring. But as this stage comes to an end, one of the contenders loses the bid for leadership and leaves the remaining

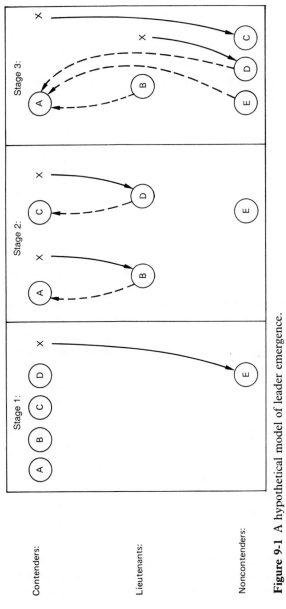

Figure 9-1 A hypothetical model of leader emergence.

contender alone at the top. The member who characteristically drops from contention during stage 2 tends to be overly directive and uses offensive verbalization,
such as stilted language or incessant talking.

Stage 3 concludes the process of leader emergence as member A remains the
sole contender after the demise of member C. Member E may reenter the emergence process by supporting member A, thereby swinging the balance of power to
the A-B coalition. Realistically, however, member E's support is probably not particularly significant, especially if E has continued to be a low-participating member
during stage 2. If, on the other hand, member E takes a more active role in group
interaction, E's support is sought by members A and C during stage 2. Then E's
decision to side with one or the other is a crucial factor in the final emergence of
member A. Of course, member C could also drop out of contention if the support
of member D as a lieutenant is lost, particularly if member C is overly directive and
verbally offensive as perceived by D. Member D could easily shift the balance of
power by transferring his allegiance and support to member A.

Figure 9-1 represents a basic model from which many variations might occur.
For example, successful leader emergence may involve only two stages, in which
just one contender picks up a lieutenant and all other members jump on the bandwagon. This variation is not at all uncommon and signifies a socially painless process of leader emergence. It evolves very quickly and allows time for the group
members to develop their status hierarchy and level of cohesiveness quickly and
generally satisfactorily.

Another variation involves the early emergence of a group leader who is then
deposed as group leader, leaving the group once again in a leaderless situation. The
process of leader emergence would then recycle back to the beginning of stage 2 and
begin all over again. Unless the nonparticipating member's level of participation
and involvement has abruptly increased, he or she remains out of leadership contention. The deposed group leader could even regain leadership status but would
undoubtedly have more difficulty the second time around.

A third variation of successful leader emergence involves the absence of stage
3. In this case, two or more members share the leadership functions and are recognized equally as leaders. While shared leadership is not extraordinary, neither is
it the typical case. One can generally expect a single person to emerge eventually
as the leader of a small decision-making group.

THE LEADER-FOLLOWER RELATIONSHIP

Earlier in this chapter, in the Functional Communicative Behaviors section, we
outlined some specific behaviors that leaders typically perform and said that you
can improve your effectiveness in groups by practicing these behaviors. While the
odds are that such behaviors will serve you well, you must not forget that leaders
exhibit communicative flexibility. They adjust their communicative behaviors and
interpersonal relationships according to the favorableness of the situation and the
nature of the people they must work with: that is, their followers. In some ways this

is counterintuitive, because we usually assume that leaders affect followers' behavior, but an important issue in the study of leadership and group processes is the reciprocal effects of leader-follower relationships.

In an early experiment, Farris and Lim (1969) tested whether or not leadership behaviors might be significantly influenced by the performance of subordinates. Leaders were assigned to work with groups. One group of leaders was told that the members of their group were highly competent and among the best-performing group in the company. In a second situation the leaders were told that their groups were poor performers and among the worst-performing in the company. Later the behaviors of the leaders were described, and it was found that there were important differences between the two situations. The leaders were seen as more considerate and respectful of the high-performance group and as less considerate of the low. When leaders are working with competent and motivated followers, they tend to be more considerate, create less structure, and include their followers more in decision making. A number of other early studies in communication and psychology confirmed these findings. Followers can significantly influence the communicative behaviors of leaders.

Some recent research has suggested that the communicative functions performed by a group leader during the group process may vary considerably. That is, the group leader varies in his or her interactive behaviors, depending on the specific member of the group with whom he or she is interacting. Rather than perform consistent "leadership functions" throughout the interaction, the leader will function differently with different group members.

Ellis (1979) performed an analysis of the relational interaction (e.g., the symmetry and complementarity of the one-up, one-across, and one-down control modes) in decision-making groups. He discovered that the perceived leader of the group performed communicative functions quite distinct from other group members, not in terms of different behaviors that function to set the leader apart, but in terms of adapting specific functions to nearly every member of the group individually. That is, the leader, when interacting with each member, differed from the interaction patterns characteristic of the group as a whole. No other members of the group consistently demonstrated variable interactive patterns with other group members. They all tended to interact with everyone else in much the same fashion.

Ellis's results suggest that the primary leadership function may not be in the form of specific communicative behaviors that differentiate a leader from nonleaders. Rather, the leadership function may be the adaptation of specific functions to specific group members. At the same time, nonleaders apparently interact with other members in the same way in which they interact throughout the entire group interaction. Ellis (p. 163) writes: "The leader does not 'do' one thing which sets him apart from other group members. Apparently, the leader takes stock of the individuals in the group and enacts behaviors which he considers appropriate for each individual."

We sometimes believe that the leader assumes the leadership role by structuring the interaction, by influencing the flow of the ideas and relationships in the interaction. Ellis's research implies that the leader may indeed attempt to structure the interaction with some members; but in interacting with other members, the leader may defer to their structuring and may not attempt to exert any relational authority over them.

One conclusion from Ellis's research may be that there is no such thing as leadership functions that a leader performs consistently throughout the group interaction. Rather, a leader functions as a leader in adapting different communicative functions to different group members. In one case, he or she may be an authority figure and initiate the direction of the interaction's flow. In another case, however, he or she may be a respondent to some other member's attempts to structure an interaction.

Thus, all group members perform important contributions to the group's interactions. Furthermore, these contributions may serve as "leadership functions" overall. But the leader, as an initiator, a respondent, and a reactor to these functions, is adept at knowing when to initiate and when to respond and with whom. The leader's interaction with each member is distinctive. The leader is able to adapt to every other member as a unique, contributing member of the group. Apparently nonleaders do not interact in such an adaptive manner.

The leadership function of adaptation is also the subject of an investigation performed by Wood (1977). She indicated in her report that leaders are able to adapt to situations and to past failures of the group. In terms of specific communicative behaviors, Wood indicated that leaders tend to promote what she called a collective identity—apparently similar to groupness. Perhaps the adaptation of specific functions to other members as unique individuals, such as Ellis depicted, is one way to weld individuals into a collective group identity.

One very interesting theory based on leader-follower relationships is proposed by Hersey and Blanchard (1982). They have been working with a *life-cycle theory of leadership*, which is a response to the difficulties of defining *situation* and to the importance of leader relationships with group members. The central tenet of Hersey and Blanchard's theory is that leaders should communicate and interact with followers based on the level of maturity of the followers. The emphasis is on followers. The followers determine the leadership style and the power of the leader. Hersey and Blanchard define effective leadership according to how well the leader operates within a particular situation. Rather than describing leadership as a single style or set of behaviors, they argue that a leader's style must be integrated with the behaviors of followers. A leader is *effective* when his or her style is appropriate to the environment and the other members of the group or organization. When leadership effectiveness is based on the interaction of leader behaviors and the environment (followers and other situational variables), it means that no single leadership style is always best. In a crisis-oriented organization, such as the military or the police, it is best for a leader to be highly directive and task-oriented because success depends on fast action and immediate responses; group members do not need as much socioemotional support.

The life-cycle theory of leadership is based on the life cycle of group development, and the fact that groups develop toward levels of maturity. The primary element of effective leadership is the *maturity* of followers, and maturity is based on a number of components. First, mature group members are able to set obtainable goals and to accept feedback about how well they are progressing toward their goals. They are more interested in how well they are doing than in how well they are liked. Second, mature group members take responsibility and are both motivated and competent to handle responsibility. Third, mature group members are psychologically confident and able to perform their various tasks. They feel secure as individuals and are not easily threatened or shaken. And finally, mature group members realize that flexibility is important to goal accomplishment. They realize that many situational variables can influence a task and that they must diagnose and respond to these variables.

The life-cycle theory of leadership is displayed in Figure 9-2. The graph shows how task- or relationship-oriented a leader should be, depending on the maturity of the followers.

Quadrant I begins with followers who are low in maturity; that is, they are insecure, not very motivated, lack competence, and seek feedback that is irrelevant to the task. The theory predicts that an effective leader would concentrate on task behaviors. He or she would get the group organized, direct its activities, and oversee specific tasks. Relationship behavior would be kept to a minimum because the group requires much help in order to make progress on its tasks.

The bell-shaped curve in Figure 9-2 shows how the maturity level of a group or organization develops along a continuum from immature to mature. Quadrants II and III are medium levels of maturity where the leader would concentrate more on relationship behavior and alternate between being more or less task-oriented.

Figure 9-2 Relationship of leadership style to group maturity.

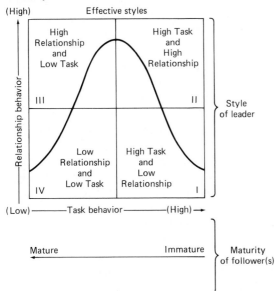

Quadrant IV is where groups and organizations have developed into more mature organizations. Followers are now capable of performing their tasks and are more self-confident. Individuals can provide their own rewards in quadrant IV and do not need the leader to provide their "strokes." The leader can reduce his or her close supervision and include the followers more in decision making. The leader trusts the other members of the group and feels comfortable delegating responsibility. The essential principles of the life-cycle theory are pretty sound and have applicability to groups, organizations, and even families.

Legitimacy and Leader Behavior

The principle of legitimacy is generally defined as prescribed or ascribed approval of norms, values, roles, or other behavioral standards. Typically, an organization endows certain roles with legitimate status by prescribing a formal status hierarchy independent of the persons occupying positions in that status hierarchy. For example, a colonel in the armed forces has legitimate authority of leadership over all those of lower rank by virtue of the rank given by the organization itself and not necessarily because of any achieved informal status. A familiar theme of war movies is a story of veteran soldiers who resent the leadership of a young "90-day-wonder" second lieutenant who does not have the experience or achievements of some of the soldiers of lesser rank. But nevertheless, the veterans formally recognize the authority due to the legitimate rank of commissioned officer. All leaders depend on followers for legitimacy.

Normally, legitimacy refers to formal recognition or approval by some external agency that has authority over the group. In some groups no such agency exists outside the group. In a university classroom, the instructor and the values of the student culture both exert an impact on the classroom group. Some members may have legitimate approval of their roles by virtue of the instructor's designation or campuswide status as a "big man on campus." Such quasi-legitimate recognition may endow a member with some vestige of formal leadership. But the member then must earn informal recognition of leadership status during the process of leader emergence.

Legitimacy exerts little direct influence on the LGD, but the group itself manufactures its own symbols of legitimate recognition. Certain symbols of authority are endorsed with a kind of legitimate approval, and the member who possesses one or more of these symbols takes on the aura of legitimate recognition of authority. Numerous examples of such symbols may be found in a classroom group. Some instructors ask classroom groups to record their interaction during each meeting on audiotape. The member who takes possession of the tape recorder, adjusts the microphone, and controls its operation possesses a symbol of authority. It is not uncommon for members who are contending for leadership to fight over the right to possess this authority symbol.

One classroom group using transistor cassette recorders encountered a problem in operating the machinery. For some reason it did not work properly, and the member who had habitually taken charge of it was unable to get the recorder working. Another member who conveniently owned a similar recorder easily spotted the trouble and fixed it. His leadership status received a big impetus with this seemingly unrelated act. His fellow members insisted that he take charge of the group's cassette recorder in subsequent meetings. He did—and later emerged as the group's recognized leader.

Often a group sits around a rectangular table and leader contenders race to the meeting room in order to be able to sit in the chair at the head of the table. One classroom group typically held meetings in an instructor's office with the alleged seat of authority the instructor's swivel chair behind the desk. Perhaps not coincidentally, the group's emergent leader turned out to be the member who consistently occupied the swivel chair during group meetings. He admitted afterward that he initially wanted to sit in that chair because it was the most comfortable one in the room. He also expressed his surprise on several occasions when he had arrived late for a group meeting to discover that the other members had left the swivel chair vacant for him. He believed that seat was a symbol of his leadership authority apparently recognized, perhaps at a low level of awareness, by his fellow group members.

Another classroom group's emergent leader was the sole member who took notes during group discussions. As a result of his trusty legal pad, he was always an expert on what the group had decided and accomplished during past meetings and was able to organize its future activity. He often referred to his legal pad, and he was consistently asked by other members what was written on it. For him and his group, that legal pad became a legitimate symbol of authority.

But a legitimate symbol of authority need not be a physical object. Often an activity by a group member receives formal recognition by the group and takes on a legitimacy by itself. One group frequently met outside class hours at the apartment of one of the members. She became the hostess of the group meetings, served coffee and pop, potato chips and snacks, and enveloped herself in the legitimacy of being the authority in her own apartment. She was recognized as the emergent leader—quickly and painlessly.

Although there are many more examples of manufactured legitimacy in groups, all cases have one ingredient in common. Whether a physical object or an activity, the legitimate symbol of authority is associated with (1) a single person who has assisted the group in making progress toward its goal and (2) this person's relationship with other group members. The symbol is not prescribed by some outside authority, but receives formal and relatively permanent recognition by the group members themselves. Instances and symbols of manufactured legitimacy do influence the process and highlight a person who is contending for leadership. The combination of leader-member relationships and symbols of manufactured legitimacy allows the group or an outside observer the opportunity to perceive the process of leader emergence in operation.

MALES AND FEMALES IN LEADERSHIP ROLES

What effect does sex of the leader have on the group? Do males and females differ in their contributions to group interaction when they are in the leadership roles?

Are leaders more likely to be male or female? Questions such as these are significant elements in group phenomena in light of the increased emphasis on the role of women in our society. Unfortunately, the answers to these questions are impossible to determine definitely. Sex-role stereotypes, although still prominent in our society, are currently in a state of flux with the increased appearance of women in nontraditional societal roles. Any attempt to answer such questions, then, is destined to be incomplete and outdated within a very few years. The following discussion, then, is not intended to be definitive, but to suggest the flavor of the transition of changing stereotypes and human perceptions in the American culture.

Researchers have consistently discovered that the attitudes of group members significantly affect the members' perceptions of males and females occupying leadership roles (see, for example, Yerby, 1975). Depending on the extent to which the members hold stereotypes of men and women and on whether these members are men or women, a group's level of cohesiveness and its attitudes toward leaders will vary considerably. On the other hand, because of the extent to which androgyny (self-concepts that include a combination of characteristics socially attributed to males or females) affects the perceptions, one is tempted to doubt whether any attempt to depict perceptions as either male or female can be successful. Furthermore, few researchers have attempted to determine whether the communicative behaviors of males and females actually differ from each other when they are performing leadership roles. Typically, the researchers have tried to learn whether group members *perceive* that male and female leaders differ in the leadership functions.

One of the rare studies, designed to observe directly the interactive behaviors of male and female leaders, suggests little discernible difference in their interactive contributions: DeStephen (1977) discovered that, overall, the male and female group members in her study did not differ significantly in terms of the communicative behaviors they contributed to the group's interaction process. On the other hand, leaders differed considerably from nonleaders in that they showed a greater tendency to clarify task issues and seek evaluations of task issues than nonleaders did. But in attempting to distinguish between the communicative functions of males and females in the leadership role, DeStephen found little difference. In fact, female leaders performed the same "leadership functions" as male leaders, only perhaps more so. For example, females tended to clarify even more than male leaders did. But leaders, regardless of their sex, appeared to perform more clarifying functions than nonleaders did. One may conclude, then, that the distinction is greater between leaders and nonleaders than between males and females in the leadership role.

Even though it is clearly difficult to draw any conclusions about males and females during this transitional period in our culture, one might speculate as to the reasons why people tend to perceive differences between male and female leaders, even though those differences may not be apparent in the actual behaviors performed. In other words, we might speculate that people tend to behave in a manner consistent with the way we think they should respond. That is, we have certain expectations about how males and females, leaders and nonleaders, are supposed to act. When our expectations are thwarted (for example, when males or females do not behave as we expect them to), we tend to perceive differences, but our perceptions may not be based on our actual observations.

On balance, there is considerable evidence that male and female leaders are likely to be perceived and treated differently. Studies continue to report that people prefer men to women as bosses and as professional colleagues. Many men mistrust the competence of women and assume that they are less capable of successful task completion than men are. One study (Rice, Bender, and Vitters, 1980) at the U.S. Military Academy compared male and female cadets as leaders. In this study, the gender of the leader did not appear to influence the cadets' performance and morale, but it did influence their perceptions of their leaders: The cadets attributed the success of female leaders to luck, but they attributed the success of male leaders to ability. Another study (Rice, Instone, and Adams, 1984) confirmed the finding that male leaders were more likely to be thought of as having succeeded through hard work and ability than female leaders were. This same study also reported that women were harsher judges of other women than men were.

The stereotype is that men are confident, dominant, skilled, achievement-oriented, and task-oriented. On the other hand, women are supposedly accommodating, democratic, and more concerned with relationships than with tasks. The problem here is that women and men are equally capable of leading, but they are evaluated differently. Many of the findings about differences between male and female leaders are based on outmoded ideas about dominance and competitiveness. Men are certainly encouraged to be aggressive and competitive, but women are just as active and competitive, except that they strive for achievement in different areas. Hollander (1983) writes that in time women will be judged more fairly. As more women move into leadership roles and perform capably, the disadvantages they encounter will dissipate.

HOW TO AVOID EMERGING AS LEADER

In many ways it is difficult to know how and why certain members emerge as group leaders. The process of eliminating leader contenders, however, suggests that it may be less difficult to determine how and why certain members do *not* become group leaders. If certain people truly wish not to become leaders (as some people are quick to assert), the following list of "rules" should allow them to fulfill their goal. These principles are guidelines for assuring yourself of a low-status position in your group. Follow them faithfully, and we guarantee that you will definitely not emerge as your group's leader.

Rule 1 Be absent from as many group meetings as possible. You will be even better at avoiding leadership responsibilities if you provide no reasons for your absences. But with or without reasons, absence from group interaction is an effective tactic.

Rule 2 Contribute to the interaction as little as possible. You might also consider contributing incompetently to the group's interaction; such a strategy, however, is more dangerous, for other members may perceive competence in what you consider to be incompetent. The safer practice is to avoid contributing and thus let other members think you are incompetent or disinterested rather than to interact too much and thus remove their doubts.

Rule 3 *Volunteer to be the secretary or the record keeper of your group's discussions.* The role of recorder or secretary in a group is rarely associated with the role of leader. You do risk the problem of demonstrating interest and commitment to the group by volunteering for what is indeed a valuable role. You will probably be assigned a rather high status. You should probably consider this strategy a compromise. By avoiding leadership, you may be substituting a high-status role. But if you truly wish to avoid becoming a leader, you should be willing to compromise.

Rule 4 *Indicate that you are willing to do what you are told.* This strategy is sometimes as risky as becoming a secretary. By showing your commitment to the group in your willingness to perform activities beneficial to the group's task efforts, you may be indicating too much commitment to the group. Lack of interest in the group is more effective in avoiding leadership responsibilities, but a subservient or acquiescent commitment is the next best thing.

Rule 5 *Come on strong early in the group discussions.* The timing of your verbally aggressive and directive behavior is extremely important when following this principle. If you advocate something strongly later in the group interaction, your activity may be misinterpreted as an attempt to assist the group in solving its decision-making task. It is vitally important that your advocacy be extreme and that it demonstrate an unwillingness to compromise your position, especially if another member should resist your ideas. Attempt to be unsuccessful in your early advocacy of your positions. Failure in these early stages of the group process is important. Too much success, particularly in the early stages of group decision making, is likely to lead to the undesirable effect of having other group members think you are contending for leadership. Later stages in group decision making, during which time members are advocating ideational positions, are the times to show your apathy regarding which decision proposals will achieve consensus.

Rule 6 *Try to assume the role of joker.* By telling lots of jokes early in the discussion, you will get people to like you while you are in the process of avoiding leadership. Sometimes, contenders for low-status roles tend to be uncomfortable when other members show dislike of them. If you become a joker, however, you will probably avoid such negative reactions. On the other hand, they will probably not take you very seriously. Make sure, however, that your jokes are consistently off the topic and are not combined with any opinion or information concerning it. Your funny-person role should also be consistent. Don't do anything that would indicate that you are anything but a joker.

Rule 7 *Demonstrate your knowledge of everything, including your extensive vo-*

cabulary of big words and technical jargon. This strategy is also a bit risky in that members may misinterpret your know-it-all attitude and command of esoteric words as signs of intelligence and breadth of background. You can't afford to be timid when using this tactic. Express a comprehensive knowledge of every topic and a continuous use of words that other people probably don't understand. Consistency is the key to successful employment of this strategy.

Rule 8 Demonstrate a contempt for leadership. This method is rarely used, but it is always successful in avoiding the leadership role. One classroom group member, whom we shall call Sean, was quite successful and adept in utilizing this strategy. He verbalized frequently and vehemently his distaste for all leaders and the concept of leadership itself. He was a veteran of the war in Vietnam and had recently returned from southeast Asia. He consistently expressed his strong belief that all leaders are corrupt. One of his reactions to an early group meeting was most explicit in revealing his attitude: "I do not want to hear any fascinating facts about leadership. Leadership is for whoever wants it. If you have an average IQ and a corrupt tendency to dominate people, you can become a leader. Those who manipulate leaders are those who dominate very furtively." Sean succeeded beyond the highest expectations of all leadership avoiders. In his six-member group, he was unanimously voted the least liked member in both social and task areas. But one must be aggressive in using this strategy and must consistently resist and label every attempt at leadership contention by other members.

Of course, these "principles" for avoiding the leadership role are presented in a tongue-in-cheek manner. They are characteristic of those behaviors of persons who are eliminated from leadership contention. Rarely, if ever, does any person intend to avoid becoming a leader. Although individual group members may not intentionally attempt to be the group leader, they also do not intend to avoid leadership, at least at a very high level of awareness. During the normal functioning of the group process and group interaction, the group works out the role of each member, including the role of leader. Such functioning of the group process is quite normal and typical. Moreover, the process is functioning even though the members may not be aware of it until after the process has been completed.

The best advice to any group that is attempting to assess and understand the social and task dimensions of the group process is to become aware (at least as fully as possible) of the probable stage of group development occurring at that time. Attempting to intervene in the normal group process is likely to be successful only with such an understanding. Under no circumstances should a member attempt to counteract the normal functioning of the group process except as a desperate act of last resort. A better action would be to encourage and take advantage of your comprehensive understanding in order to manage more effectively all facets of communication and the group process, including that of leader emergence.

If your group appoints a group-productivity observer, one task of this observer should be to look for the stage of development of decision making and for leader emergence (probably the same process) and for the interdependent social and task dimensions of the group process. Such an observer must be highly sensitive to the group process and have a comprehensive understanding of how communication and the group process function. It is to be hoped that members of your group will have such a comprehensive understanding.

SUMMARY

Perhaps the most pervasive element of social systems is the existence of leadership and a status hierarchy. In the LGD, roles fall into several hierarchical levels, typically two or three, proportional to the contribution of each member in helping the group achieve its goals. In some groups, each member achieves a status level through communicative behaviors rather than through being given status by some authority outside the group. The leader's status is based on the reciprocal influence of leader and followers—an interdependence among the communicating members in the group.

Several perspectives of viewing leadership have been popularly employed in the past. They include the traits, styles, situational, and functional approaches to group leadership. The functional perspective, unlike any of the others, focuses on the communicative behaviors of individual members and their relative contributions to the group's progress. This perspective deemphasizes leadership as defined by the person who occupies a given position in a network of roles. Because there have been so few studies of leadership utilizing the functional perspective, no comprehensive list of communicative behaviors associated with leadership yet exists. But a partial list of behaviors is available.

Employing the functional perspective, leadership is viewed as a process whereby a group leader achieves status gradually over time as a direct result of group interaction patterns. This process, termed *leader emergence*, may generally be described as a process of elimination in which each member is a contender for leadership, but each is eliminated, one by one, until a single person remains and is recognized as the group's leader.

A basic model of leader emergence hypothesizes three stages of elimination. In stage 1, uninformed, low-participating members are eliminated. In stage 2, two or more contenders emerge by gaining lieutenants who support their leadership contention. Those contenders eliminated in stage 2 are typically overly directive and use offensive verbalization. In stage 3 there is only one remaining contender, who achieves recognition as leader. Several variations of this basic model are possible in a particular small group.

The leader-follower relationship is very important. Behaviors associated with leaders include being verbally active, demonstrating communication skills, consistently initiating themes, seeking opinions and information in the early and intermediate stages of group development, stating opinions and attempting to persuade other members in the intermediate and later stages of group development, and adopting an informed and objective argumentative stance. The life-cycle theory of leadership relates leadership style to the group members' maturity.

Groups manufacture formal symbols of legitimacy in group interaction. Such symbols, which may be physical objects or member activity, are associated with a particular member and with the formal authority of leadership, although they may vary from group to group.

Although stereotyped attitudes of sex roles remain prominent, our society's attitudes are currently in a state of rapid change. Consequently, males and females who function as group leaders probably do not differ significantly from one another in terms of the communicative actions they use in leading. However, the group members or followers may perceive differences because of their previously held attitudes regarding sex-role stereotypes.

CHAPTER 10

Social Conflict and Deviance

The past four decades have witnessed numerous instances of social conflict and deviant behavior within our society. Many people believe that this upsurge of dissent is unparalleled in our history, but dissent has been present since our system was founded. Many eligible young men resisted the draft during the Vietnamese war, but draft resistance has been prevalent since the first Selective Service during the Spanish-American War. Hundreds of thousands of protesters marched on Washington, D.C., several times during the decade of the 1960s, but so did veterans of World War I some forty years before. The civil disobedience of Martin Luther King, Jr., led to his imprisonment, just as civil disobedience led to the same for Henry David Thoreau, Eugene Debs, and countless labor organizers during the early struggles of the labor movement in the United States.

Dissent is not unique to the present. Many people believe that such social conflict is detrimental and reflects some failure within our culture. Others believe that social conflict is symptomatic of a healthy society. The truth, as in most cases, undoubtedly lies somewhere between the two extreme positions. Obviously some conflict within a social system is detrimental, just as some conflict is beneficial. The point to be emphasized is that social conflict, both good and bad, is normal and a recurring phenomenon of our social system throughout its history. Moreover, social conflict has been normal in the functioning of every social system throughout the history of human civilizations.

MUCH CONFLICT ABOUT SOCIAL CONFLICT

Many sociologists view a social system as a delicate balance of opposing forces—forces which threaten to disrupt the system and forces which maintain the system. According to this view, a social system is perpetually in a state of conflict that may at any time tip toward the disruptive forces and destroy the system.

The perspective of this book—communication and the group process, with emphasis on their interdependence—is not consistent with viewing the system as a balance of opposing forces. The process viewpoint assumes that such forces, if they exist, are interdependent, so they cannot be separated or be in opposition to each other. For example, "temperature" is hardly an arithmetic difference between forces of heat and forces of cold. If it were, one would be comfortable if one held a block of ice in one hand and a burning coal in the other. Temperature is a single reading, not a balance of two readings, one high and one low.

It is important to know that not all experts agree on the nature of social conflict, its effects, or its solution. Understanding social conflict from the communicative process perspective requires an understanding of the varied and often conflicting views about social conflict.

Intergroup, Cognitive, and Interpersonal Conflict

To understand the nature of social conflict, one must first identify who or what is in conflict. Probably the most common view of social conflict is *intergroup conflict*— that is, conflict between opposing social systems. Intergroup conflict involves conflict between groups or societies rather than between single individuals. It embraces labor-management relations, particularly during periods of contract negotiations, as well as conflicts between nations. An individual human being, when involved in intergroup conflict, participates not as an individual entity, but as a representative of an entire social system.

Although intergroup conflict is a fascinating area of concern and some examples will be drawn from it, a study of this type of social conflict does not suit the purposes of this book. Since our purpose is to understand the communicative process that characterizes group decision making, intergroup conflict is not highly pertinent.

Cognitive conflict, as the term implies, involves the psychological conflict that rages within the individual (Roloff, 1987, pp. 486–489). The cognitive view alleges the existence of opposing forces within a person's mind that determine actions, beliefs, and values. Numerous balance theories attempt to explain individual behavior through cognitive conflict. They include cognitive dissonance theory, congruity theory, equity theory, exchange theory, and consistency theory, among others. Roloff (1987) has also explained conflict through the concept of ambivalence—a balance of internal forces that attract or repel.

But an investigation of cognitive conflict does not serve the purposes of this book either. In the first place, internalized conflict cannot be directly observed through communicative behaviors and may or may not be indirectly reflected in group interaction. Then, too, cognitive conflict utilizes the psychological makeup of the individual person as the basis for understanding the small group rather than the process of interaction based on the interstructured communicative behaviors of all members.

Interpersonal conflict is most pertinent to the perspective of communication and the group process. But interpersonal conflict, for our purposes, does not necessarily imply a personality conflict between individuals. Quite the contrary, it is defined solely in terms of interact patterns. Thus, interpersonal conflict is directly observable through sequences of communicative behaviors performed by members of the group. The personalities of individual members are not considered to be in conflict; rather, it is the behaviors performed by two or more members that conflict with one another.

Affective and Substantive Conflict

A second view of social conflict considers the basis of that conflict—whether conflicting issues are affective or substantive. Typically, in reference to interpersonal conflict, *affective conflict* implies emotional clashes between individuals within a social system, generally over procedural or how-to-do-it problems. Such conflict does not ordinarily stem from a disagreement on opinions or beliefs, but from a struggle based on selfish or personal issues. *Substantive conflict,* on the other hand, involves an intellectual opposition of group members to the content of ideas or issues pertinent to the group task.

Since social conflict and deviance are considered a single phenomenon in group interaction, the affective-substantive differentiation of conflict may also be called *role deviation* and *opinion deviation*. While an opinion deviate disagrees with other group members about the content of ideas, a role deviate is a type of person who is not desired by other group members. One member of a student group found herself to be a role deviate in her group. She received low sociometric rankings from nearly all her fellow group members. Concerned, she asked them why. Her diary immediately following that group meeting describes their reactions:

> They also said that they had projected me as being the type of person I
> played in class; they projected that role as being my true personality....Now
> that they know me a little better, they could see I wasn't "Susie," a
> dominating woman, but "Susan"—a different individual altogether.

Role deviation and opinion deviation differ significantly in their impact on group interaction (Putnam, 1986). Other group members increase their interaction with an opinion deviate and exert pressure on him or her to conform to their majority opinion. But the group virtually ignores the role deviate, apparently perceiving that this type of person is a hopeless case not worthy of pressure. A social system tends to view deviance either as a behavior apart from the individual personality of the deviate or as a personality trait of the individual. As behavior, deviance affects the group process of interaction and is therefore central to the perspective of this book; as a personality trait, however, deviance has less of an effect on the group's interaction patterns.

The opinion deviate is tolerated and perhaps even admired by fellow members. After all, we have been taught from childhood that rationality and independence are virtues in our society. We are urged to be masters of our own fate, to make up our own minds. "Know thyself" was the advice of Socrates. Advertising campaigns appeal to our rational independence by urging us to buy the product that gets us away from the crowd. The virtues of rationality and independence are often reflected in adolescents' rejection of their parents' ideas and beliefs. Their parents, often to their chagrin, had experienced the ultimate success in teaching two of our cardinal social virtues.

Lewis Coser (1956, pp. 48–55), the eminent sociologist, distinguishes between realistic and nonrealistic conflict, which appears to be another dimension of substantive and affective conflict. According to Coser, *realistic conflict* is a means to an end; it is a deviant behavior intended to further the group's progress toward its goal. But *nonrealistic conflict* is an end in itself not directly associated with any goal. For example, one worker may go out on strike to gain higher wages and better working conditions, but another worker may engage even in the same strike because of some oedipal hatred of the employer, and this displaced hatred could as easily be directed against any authority figure. The point is that the first worker, the person who performs deviant behavior as a means to achieve some goal, is said to be engaged in realistic conflict.

The view of conflict that best serves the purposes of this book is, of course, substantive conflict—that conflict expressed as a deviant behavior in intellectual opposition to ideas or issues associated with the group's task or goals. Substantive conflict is realistic to the extent that it serves as a means toward accomplishing some goal.

Destructive and Constructive Conflict

There is enormous disagreement over the effects of conflict on the social system (Folger and Poole, 1984, pp. 5–7). One school of thought seems to view conflict as inherently undesirable since it inevitably leads to disruption of the social system. An opposing view considers social conflict essential to the effective functioning of every social system. It is intuitively obvious that neither view is absolutely accurate. Some conflict and deviance disrupts the system, and other instances of conflict and deviance are beneficial to the system. Discriminating between the two kinds, however, is no simple task.

Many functions of the social system of the United States are predicated on the existence of conflict. Our economic subsystem of free enterprise assumes conflict and free competition among producers and retailers for the consumer dollar. The basis of our political system is the free and open marketplace of ideas in which societal values gain social consensus. Candidates for political office air conflicting views on the issues during the course of a political campaign. Our judicial system is based on the adversary system in which the accuser confronts the accused. Many of our recreational activities include games based on conflict—football, tennis, handball, chess, Monopoly, among others. Conflict is undoubtedly an integral part of our nation-society.

But despite the pervasive influence of social conflict in our society, most Americans are ambivalent about many of its forms. Probably the best example is the right of minority dissent, constitutionally assured in the Bill of Rights. Freedom of speech is one of our most cherished national values, epitomized in such statements as Voltaire's "I disapprove of what you say, but I will defend to the death your right to say it." National opinion polls have reaffirmed that nearly all Americans steadfastly uphold the freedom of speech of all Americans—majority and minority. But many of those same Americans, the polls tell us, would refuse to allow a professed Communist to give a public lecture. Battles over censorship laws are common in our social system. Apparently not all members of our society consider all realistic and substantive conflict (or opinion deviation) to be constructive. Indeed, many people consider much substantive conflict highly destructive.

A social system is too often viewed as an abstract ideal—a system of pure cooperation—so that any deviance must be unnatural. If a social system is idealized, members of the system are constrained to strive for the perfection of pure cooperation. Any deviant behavior, then, is construed as a failure of the social system and must therefore be eradicated. The typically shortsighted view of common sense would have us believe that a "perfect" social system is worth striving for. But as we hope to illustrate, the "perfect" social system free from conflict and deviance is doomed to failure because of its inherent inflexibility, its inability to cope with environmental stresses, its lack of capacity for growth and progress.

Assuming the idealized social system and its corollary that social conflict is inherently destructive leads to an incredibly naive outlook on social conflict among many members of our nation-system. Too often, realistic conflict is camouflaged and dissenting views are suppressed in order that our social system shall masquerade as an absolutely perfect and ideal system, without fault or information to the contrary. But perfection is hardly possible in human beings or in their creations. Our nation's heroes had faults, just as every other human being has had from the beginning of time. But most important, the consistent effort to "accentuate the positive and eliminate the negative" makes us naive about social conflict and more susceptible to dissenting views.

Most of our nation was shocked when some U.S. soldiers elected to remain with their Communist Chinese captors at the close of the Korean war rather than return to their homeland. Many people reacted by advocating stronger teaching of only the positive aspects of our society. Others advocated a greater emphasis on comparative politics—to show the realistic faults and virtues of all political systems—so that our citizens would be fully aware of all alternatives. Indeed, all of us probably believe that our system would fare well in such a comparison. At least we would no longer be naive and uninformed about social conflict and deviance.

The positive side of social conflict is represented by the functionalists—George Simmel (1955), Lewis Coser (1956), and Talcott Parsons (1951), among others. The functionalists do not deny that some social conflict disrupts the functioning of a social system and is therefore destructive. But the functionalists do emphasize the socially constructive functions of conflict and advocate an understanding of social conflict so that the social system shall be able to take advantage of its positive aspects (see also Putnam, 1986, pp. 177–178). Some of the positive functions performed by social conflict are included later in this chapter.

Reactions to Social Conflict

The typical reaction to social conflict is to search for ways to resolve it—that is, to get rid of it. At the very least, according to this view, conflict must be controlled so that it doesn't get out of hand. Naturally, some conflict must be resolved or controlled because it is potentially destructive. Destructive conflict, unchecked, would lead ultimately to dissolution of the system itself. Hence, methods of conflict resolution are essential for instances of destructive conflict. Modes of conflict resolution include such devices as compromise, bargaining, appeasement, negotiation, and mediation.

Occasionally, cure-all "formula" solutions are offered as substitutes for genuine methods of conflict resolution. Such formulas are usually not realistic and stem from a grossly oversimplified view of social conflict. One such formula answer is "more cooperation." If cooperation were so simple, the conflict would not have to be resolved in the first place. A more commonly suggested formula, offered to solve virtually any social conflict, is "more communication" or "opening channels of communication." If there is no communication at all between conflicting parties, which is rarely the case, some communication is obviously called for. But communication inherently assumes specific forms, such as negotiation. "More communication" is meaningless. If present communication is ineffective, increasing the amount of communication does not render it suddenly more effective. More often, "more communication" is suggested as a substitute for any real effort to resolve conflicts. Such a formula stems from an overly naive and grossly inadequate understanding of the nature of the communicative process.

When parties in conflict cannot satisfactorily resolve their disagreement, they search for modes of controlling that conflict. One common and often effective means of controlling conflict, particularly intergroup conflict, is *encapsulation.* Conflict that is encapsulated does not cease to exist, rather, it continues under the governance of an agreed-upon set of rules. In international conflict, for example, people have referred to the "cold war" between the United States, the Soviet Union, and the People's Republic of China. "Cold war" is a euphemism for international conflict that has been encapsulated within the rules of international diplomacy—embassies in each country, exchanges of diplomatic notes, treaties limiting nuclear testing, talks and treaties on arms limitations, trade agreements involving nonstrategic materials, reciprocal visits by high-ranking dignitaries, etc. All conflicting nations agree to the rules and thereby control the conflict between their countries without attempting to resolve it.

Even wars are encapsulated, in part, by certain international "rules" of warfare, such as those of the Geneva Convention and the Geneva Accords. Thus, even armed conflict with the avowed purpose of annihilating the enemy nation is governed by rules and therefore encapsulated. Encapsulation of conflict is a common ingredient of international relations.

The belief that conflict must be resolved or controlled is consistent with the view that conflict is inherently destructive. But resolution and control are inappropriate reactions for numerous instances of social conflict—particularly the kind that serves socially positive functions. In fact, such conflict should even be encouraged and utilized to further the system's progress toward its desired goals. Utilizing social conflict in the best interests of the system requires a thorough understanding of the phenomenon itself and the ability to manage conflict in order to benefit from its positive aspects.

For the purpose of understanding the process of small group decision making, our primary interest is social conflict that is interpersonal, substantive, and constructive. Our goal is to understand social conflict and deviance as a process and to manage it constructively to the benefit of the group. This view does not deny destructive forms of conflict, but it does emphasize a view of conflict too often overlooked. While instances of destructive conflict do not typically exert significant impact on the general process of group interaction, constructive conflict plays an instrumental role in shaping the process of group interaction. Such conflict is vitally important, then, to the purposes of this book.

FUNCTIONS OF SOCIAL CONFLICT AND DEVIANCE

According to one of the foremost functionalists, Georg Simmel (1955, p. 13), conflict is inevitably a "form of sociation." It is impossible to have social conflict without interaction among the parties in conflict, and interaction is certainly a form of sociation. Simmel says of social conflict, "it is a way of achieving some kind of unity, even if it be through the annihilation of one of the conflicting parties." Although the reference to annihilation may be tongue-in-cheek, it is indisputable that social conflict cannot exist with an individual person in social isolation. Certainly conflict is a distinct type of interaction between at least two persons. And interaction is one of the basic requisites of a social system (Folger and Poole, 1984, pp. 8–9). One can only conclude that anything that encourages interaction must be a potentially positive force in the development of a social system. It is on this deceptively simple assumption that the positive social functions of conflict are based.

While we might think of conflict as some disruption in the interaction process, quite the opposite is more accurate. In fact, social conflict inevitably requires social interaction. Likert and Bowers (1972, p. 117) are quite emphatic on this point: "Every conflict, other than those internal to a particular individual, involves an interaction among persons, groups, organizations, or larger entities and occurs through an interaction-influence network." When people engage in conflict, they inevitably engage in interaction, and we should not be overly concerned that conflict is present in the interaction. We should be more concerned if and when conflict functions to disrupt or discontinue the group's efforts. The important point to remember is that conflict requires interaction among parties to the conflict. Conflict is thus an active ingredient of the group process.

Furthermore, the distinction between conflict interaction and nonconflict interaction is the nature of how the actions relate to each other. According to Deutsch (1973, p. 10), "*Conflict* exists whenever *incompatible* activities occur." A conflict thus involves a sequence of activities that are incompatible with each other. For example, a statement favoring a decision proposal followed by a statement opposed to the decision proposal is an instance of a conflict interact. A one-up comment (see Chapters 4 and 5) followed by another one-up comment is a symmetrical and incompatible interact, thus reflecting a relational conflict. Conflict would also be present in a one-down comment followed by another one-down comment. A statement followed by disagreement is a very common form of conflict in group decision making. In any case, social conflict requires interaction for it to take place. Furthermore, conflict is characterized by a sequence of incompatible activities performed by the parties to the conflict. Being able to distinguish social conflict is one thing, but understanding the functions it performs in group decision making is another. And those functions performed by social conflict and deviance provide the subjects for the following discussions.

Influence on Cohesiveness

Social conflict breeds not only social interaction but also increased involvement (Tjosvold, 1982). The member who is apathetic toward the group and toward the worth of the group task has little reason to engage in the painful process of social conflict. Moreover, the virtual absence of social conflict in group interaction is a trustworthy indication of the low involvement or commitment of group members. If the group develops even a moderate level of cohesiveness, its members will engage in rather frequent, though not extended, periods of social conflict. Thus, the natural development of group cohesiveness presupposes social conflict. In this sense, social conflict is not only desirable for the development of groupness; it is quite inevitable and should be expected as part of the *normal* sequence of group interaction.

Of course, social conflict, if it is to be beneficial to group cohesiveness, must not be perceived as threatening the group's social fabric. Substantive conflict serves to precipitate secondary tension. Therefore, the successful group develops mechanisms for managing social conflict as it arises. And a history of successful conflict management builds group cohesiveness.

Lest the term *conflict management* be misinterpreted, it is important to note that the group does not necessarily resolve the conflict or even control it through limiting its boundaries. Conflict management refers to the interaction sequences developed by a group to deal with social conflict and consistently used by the group when social conflict occurs. Generally, conflict management implies that social conflict will definitely occur again, although probably in slightly different form. The normal process of conflict management is part of the process of decision modification.

Social conflict also aids group cohesiveness by providing an outlet for hostility. According to Napier and Gershenfeld (1985), a group must discover methods for venting hostility in order to gain and maintain even a moderate degree of cohesiveness. If the group develops norms that do not permit the expression of hostility, the group members either become apathetic or drop out as their deep-rooted negative feelings become ingrained. As group members shed their inhibitions about expressing negative feelings, they develop stronger ties to their group membership. One student group member, after a particularly fruitful meeting, experienced just such a reaction. Her diary contains her sentiments about what occurred during that meeting:

> We began to function as a group. Each of the individuals in the group expressed feelings. Before really talking about our topic, we only had some "small" talk. . . . There were real differences of opinion. . . . The group became more cohesive.

> I began to think of myself as a member of the group. I felt more at ease with the members in my group to the extent that I felt free to disagree.

The more inhibited the group members are in expressing their feelings, the greater the frustration they experience because of their suppressed conflict. And frustration leads directly to secondary tension. Thus, social conflict may in fact serve as a form of releasing social tension.

Conflict performs a catalytic function in developing the social organization of the group. Putnam (1986, p. 186) emphasizes the role of conflict in increasing a group's social organization, particularly the interdependence of group members. Roloff (1987) goes further to say that groups go so far as to induce, permit, and sustain deviant behaviors of members in order to develop a social organization. Deviant behaviors allow the group members to identify and strengthen their norms and other behavioral standards. As an analogy, a law on the books that is never violated and hence never enforced soon loses its strength and visibility as a law. It becomes a "blue law" without any impact on governing the behavior of the society's members.

The deviate also allows the group to focus on a concern common to all members—the deviate himself or herself—about whom something must be done. Since the deviate is of concern to the group as a whole and not to each member individually, the group's visibility becomes greater than any individual's self.

For these reasons, then, a group induces deviant behavior from one of its members when deviance does not occur through the initiative of one of the members. In order to maintain group solidarity and organization, the successful group not only permits deviant behavior, but ensures that it is evident in the group interaction. The group is in trouble when members avoid or ignore deviant behavior. Recall that the socially successful group learns to confront problems head on by recognizing deviant behavior and doing something about it. It may be said now with some confidence that the cohesive group thrives on social conflict—or, in more memorable words, "The group that fights together stays together!"

Influence on Productivity

Since this book deals with group decision making, its major concern is substantive conflict—intellectual opposition over ideas and issues. It seems paradoxical that a group whose members continually argue over ideas and issues can be very productive. But group productivity is measured in terms of the quality of its decisions and not by its efficient use of time. Obviously a group with substantive social conflict will utilize more time making decisions than a group without any conflict. But efficient utilization of time is not a characteristic of the group process anyway.

Substantive conflict leads directly to consensus owing to the increased involvement of group members with their task performance. As conflict over issues increases, group members tend to concentrate greater effort on those issues in order to bring about solutions. Donohue (1981) discovered that conflict over ideas causes groups to search for more alternatives and thereby to improve the quality of their group decisions. Conflict, then, serves as a stimulus to critical thinking and stimulates members to test their ideas. It logically follows that the issues that precipitate social conflict exert the greatest influence on those decisions which eventually achieve group consensus. And since those issues have survived the critical tests of ideational conflict, the decisions are probably of higher quality.

All members of the group benefit from the critical exchange of ideas. Committed members who engage in substantive conflict quite obviously receive the rewards of stimulated critical faculties. The undecided members, the low participants, also gain information necessary to commitment through observing the committed members "fighting it out." This principle is also present in a political campaign. Uncommitted voters apparently make their decisions after hearing the partisan voters air all sides of the issues.

One student member of a classroom group maintained that she played the role of a deviate in her group for just this reason—to stimulate the uninvolved members of her group. She analyzed her own role in the following excerpt from one of her diaries:

> I am the negative force in the group, i.e., I *can't* agree with everything that is being said. Other members in the group don't agree with decisions but are *too polite to say anything!* I voiced my opinion both for the silent majority and for myself. Also, it was a means of manipulation to get things rolling. It worked! Without this, nothing would have been accomplished. The group members agreed with me after some discussion.

One of the problems that haunts every decision-making group is the possibility of superficial or false consensus. That is, members agree on the final decisions but remain uncommitted to them. Hence, the decisions are never put into effect or are implemented only halfheartedly and consequently fail. An early study by Riecken (1952) found quite the opposite with decisions reached after uninhibited social conflict. Phillips and Erickson (1970, p. 77) also asserted, "Once the public conflict has been played out in a democratic group and a consensus of policy and action has been derived, there is a strong personal commitment on the part of the members that motivates them to act legitimately to implement group decisions rather than to subvert them." If members are committed enough to sustain social conflict over issues, they should remain committed once consensus is achieved. Superficial or false consensus is more likely to result from suppressed conflict than from expressed conflict.

Influence on Consensus

If consensus is the goal of group decision making, it is important to note the influence of social conflict on consensus if we are to understand fully the influence of conflict on productivity. The most commonsensical response to the relationship between conflict and consensus is probably to think of conflict as the opposite of consensus. After all, conflict indicates incompatibility of actions, and consensus should reflect compatibility. When we think of consensus as the result (or outcome) of group decision making, conflict is probably opposed to consensus. On the other hand, if consensus is a process, conflict interaction may perform a valuable function during that process and lead to the successful outcome of group decision making.

Torrance (1957), investigating the relationship between group decision making and disagreement, provides evidence to suggest that conflict (in the sense of interaction sequences involving disagreement) is highly valuable in achieving consensus. Among other characteristics he discovered, he found that effective decision-making groups tend to exhibit a wide divergence of judgments expressed by their members. Certain members of these groups are apparently quite willing to oppose the opinions of others and to disagree whenever they feel that the situation requires it. The conclusion of Torrance's investigations provides a strong link between consensus and conflict. In fact, greater consensus is obtained when a group experiences a greater amount of disagreement during decision-making interaction.

The four-phase model of decision emergence, discussed in Chapter 6, supports Torrance's conclusions. You will recall that the conflict phase (the second) is one element in the process of successful group decision making. This phase contains significant amounts of disagreement and the formation of coalitions of members opposed to one another on the substantive issues of the task. The evidence appears sufficient to warrant the belief that social conflict (at least substantive conflict) is an integral part of the process of achieving consensus in group decision making.

One problem in viewing the relationship between consensus and conflict may be a mistaken belief in the notion that consensus is somehow similar to cooperation. If that were true, conflict would be quite different from either consensus or cooperation. A greater similarity exists between conflict and cooperation than between cooperation and consensus. There are three basic differences between consensus and cooperation. Consensus indicates internal agreement, but cooperation does not include such an assumption. Consensus specifies agreement on the content of behavior (the substantive ideas), but cooperation means agreement only on the form of behavior. For example, we agree to disagree and thereby cooperate. Finally, cooperation requires that cooperating persons tolerate one another's differences, but consensus requires that any substantive differences should be abolished.

Whether this analysis of consensus, conflict, and cooperation is accurate is not really the important issue. More significant is the fact that conflict interaction requires considerable cooperation. Of course, conflict may exist as a struggle within one specific group member. That is, a member may have ambivalent feelings toward an object or idea and simply not have formed a firm opinion. Or conflict may be bound to the situation in the sense of a struggle over scarce resources. For example, whole nations engage in conflict in order to ensure a supply of strategic products, such as petroleum or uranium. But conflict, in terms of interaction sequences, requires a certain amount of cooperation in order for it even to occur. When people are engaged in substantive conflict over ideas, they are engaged in communication with one another. In the process of communication, they are essentially cooperating with one another.

In group decision making, the parties to the conflict are united in their quest for a common goal. Typically that goal is consensus. When the United Auto Workers and General Motors engage in collective bargaining, they are involved in conflict interaction. At the same time, they are cooperating in order to realize their common goal—agreement on a new contract. Without that common goal, the United Auto Workers and General Motors would find little reason for interacting with each other. Nor would there be any reason for their conflict. Social conflict provides a strong influence on group productivity. Not only does it influence consensus, but it also reflects cooperative interaction among persons or groups that are oriented toward a common interest.

One final note on the influence of social conflict and deviance on productivity concerns the *assembly effect*—the nonsummativity of group members that distinguishes group decision making from the decision making of its individual members working alone. Social conflict is one of those group elements which a decision-making individual is inherently incapable of replicating. Quite assuredly, social conflict—particularly realistic substantive conflict—contributes to the assembly effect. Without it, the group decision-making effort adds nothing to a lone individual performing the same decision-making task.

Influence on Social Growth and Change

Viewing a social system from a process focus highlights the perpetual change that every social system undergoes through time. Our nation, for example, has experienced phenomenal growth and change within the brief two centuries of its existence. As conditions within and without the system change over the years, the social system adapts to those changes if it is to continue to exist. If any system is to keep up with the times, it cannot stagnate. Progress is essential. And progress can occur only through innovation. And innovation is, by definition, deviant from the traditional norms of the past.

Social growth and change are usually explained through the principle of feedback—a concept borrowed from the field of cybernetics. Feedback, as it functions in the form of interaction sequences, has been explained and illustrated in previous chapters—especially in Chapter 4. Social growth and change in a social system occur through the amplification of deviant behavior: that is, through feedback cycles. Negative feedback loops serve to counteract deviant behavior. The conflict phase of group decision making (discussed in Chapter 6) exemplifies the existence of negative feedback cycles, and these cycles begin to show their strength and effects during the emergence phase. The reinforcement phase includes many positive feedback cycles as they occur to further the commitment of group members toward the decision already made.

The normal process of managing conflict and deviance in group decision making undoubtedly involves the functioning of positive and negative feedback cycles. Perhaps the most critical factor in conflict management is the element of time. Attempts by group members to resolve conflict too quickly or to control deviant behavior prematurely are unfortunately shortsighted. As Tolar (1970) states, "No matter how conducive to conflict resolution circumstances are, after a certain critical phase in the dispute has been attained [perhaps the conflict phase of group decision making], further progress must await the passage of a 'respectable' amount of time."

Patience is a virtue of members in effective decision-making groups. This book has continually emphasized the importance of allowing the natural process of group decision making to occur. Particularly in regard to managing social conflict and deviance, premature intervention in the natural process is more likely to be disruptive than beneficial. Decision-making groups that are burdened by undue time pressure or unrealistic deadlines are destined to make decisions that are below their capabilities.

THE "NORM" OF SOCIAL CONFLICT AND DEVIANCE

To call social conflict and deviance a "norm" appears to be a contradiction in terms. Deviant behavior is by definition contrary to group norms. But the perspective of communication and the group process must not be ignored. To view conflict and deviance as either constructive or destructive is to consider only their effects and to deny the *process* of conflict. When viewed from the perspective of communication and the group process, realistic substantive conflict and deviance can readily be seen to serve positive functions in the group, which leads to the startling observation that conflict and deviance are normal in group interaction patterns. That is, since realistic substantive conflict and deviance exist in nearly all groups, occur in many phases of group interaction, and constitute a significant part of this interaction, they must be considered normal.

Idea Testing in Decision Making

Some conventional wisdom maintains that since group decision making is a cooperative venture (which it certainly is), arguments, disagreements, and conflicts over ideas should be avoided. But even if it were possible to avoid interpersonal disagreements, a highly unlikely event, such conventional wisdom is simply bad advice. Interaction during group decision making is a curious blend of persuasion, compromise, negotiation, argumentation, flexibility, and firmness of opinions. Issues are thrown into the hopper of group interaction and provide the raw materials for the group's final consensus decisions.

During group interaction, every idea, opinion, proposal, or suggestion contributed to the group is tested under fire. Involved members focus their critical abilities on these ideas and submit them to rigorous examination. During this process of critical discussion, some ideas are accepted, others are rejected, many are modified and combined with others. The eventual outcome of idea testing includes those decisions which achieve consensus. Because the group task is to achieve consensus on decision, the critical exchange of opinions, ideas, and information is quite normal in the process of group interaction during decision making. A more detailed description of this process is included in Chapters 6 and 7.

Formation of Coalitions

Within every social system of any size, subgroups form around some issue or idea. Subgroups typically form and maintain themselves because of some social conflict within the larger system. These groups within groups often command greater loyalty from their members than does the larger social system of which the subgroup is a part. Criminals in our society, for example, have a legendary code of conduct that the larger society has apparently been unable to break. "Honor among thieves" and the "code of silence" are familiar terms to describe this particular subgroup's norms. A small work group in a large organization also has a greater influence on its members than the large organization does. In a university, for example, students and faculty alike often identify most closely with their affiliated departments. The students generally consider themselves communication majors, education majors, physics majors, or engineering majors first and members of the larger university community second.

The formation of subgroups is neither desirable nor undesirable to the larger social system. It is inevitable and should be fully expected as a normal occurrence. Too often subgroups, particularly those representing a minority, are ignored. The larger social system would do well to recognize their existence and take advantage of their apparent group strength.

Even a small group typically contains subgroups during the normal process of group decision making. Since the subgroup is usually temporary, a more appropriate term is *coalition*. This type of coalition is *a temporary alliance, among two or more members of the group, oriented toward a difference of opinion regarding the means to achieve the group's goal*. Specifically, a coalition unites certain group members who agree with noncoalition members on the nature and value of the group goal but who disagree on how that goal can best be achieved. Such a coalition, then, involves social conflict and deviance over means but, typically, agreement on the goal itself.

Coalition formation requires a minimum of three members in the group. With only two members, social conflict is either destructive or unmanageable. Social conflict in a dyad (a two-member group) exists without deviance. There is no minority, no prevailing opinion upon which to base a norm. Thus, dyadic conflict is resolved typically by one member dominating the other. And dominance-submission relationships thwart the group process of idea testing during decision making. Any consensus following conflict in a dyad is destined to be false or superficial consensus.

With at least three members, two-one coalitions are possible. In a four-member group, several three-one and two-two combinations are possible coalitions. The five-member group is often viewed as the optimum size for small group decision making because of the numerous possibilities for coalition formation and management. But there is no hard-and-fast rule governing the number of members required in a small group as long as the minimum membership is three. As long as groupness can be achieved, no maximum limit is placed on the size of a small group.

Small group coalitions based on realistic substantive conflict are generally temporary and revolve around a specific issue or group of issues. The normal process of achieving group consensus gradually merges the coalitions into the unitary whole of the group.

The Leadership Paradox

Leadership is a most fascinating role in a small decision-making group. As a high-status member who is committed to the group, the leader is a strong conformist. Numerous research studies have illustrated the tendency of a leader to conform closely to group norms. The conformity of a leader has even found its way into the conventional wisdom of corny jokes. You are probably familiar with the story of the rotund little gentleman during the French Revolution who was observed huffing and puffing in the wake of a riotous mob. When asked why he was chasing after the mob, he replied innocently, "I have to follow them. I am their leader."

The humor of this little story stems from the paradoxical nature of the leader's role as both conformist and deviate. A leader functions as an innovator who aids the group's progress toward goal achievement. In times of crisis, the leader must find new directions contrary to traditional norms in order to maintain the group and save it from impending disaster. A leader who doesn't innovate is soon deposed in favor of someone who can. Thus, the leader gains and maintains that role by functioning both as a conformist and as a deviate.

Several explanations account for this self-contradictory behavior of the group leader. Hollander (1985) has suggested perhaps the most plausible explanation. He describes gaining and maintaining leadership as an economic model whose central concept is "idiosyncrasy credits." In early stages of leader emergence, the leader conforms to the group norms and accumulates credits, much as one deposits money in a bank account. Later, the leader who successfully exerts influence through innovative behavior is not regarded as a deviate, having accumulated sufficient credits from a bank account and cashes them in in order to innovate. According to Hollander, strict adherence to traditional group norms during periods of crisis is fatal to the leader's position and damaging to the group. Members perceive a leader who continues to conform in a stress situation as not knowing what to do and not helping the group achieve its goals.

Hollander's economic model of idiosyncrasy credits is a credible explanation for how a leader is able to deviate as well as conform. But the model should not be construed to imply that a leader innovates only during group crises. Indeed, a leader innovates through initiating themes and performing other leadership functions throughout group interaction. In fact, the leader must be recognized as an innovator before the crisis period so that the members expect innovative behavior and look to the leader for assistance.

If there were any doubts that deviant behavior is beneficial to a group, those doubts should not be dispelled. Maintaining the social organization of a group virtually demands deviant behavior. And the group demands deviant behavior not just from low-status members, but from the highest-status member of all—the leader.

Moreover, the leader's deviant behavior is not only beneficial; it is normal and to be expected.

THE PROCESS OF SOCIAL CONFLICT AND DEVIANCE

It is important to keep in mind that the process perspective inherently defines the deviance and conflict instrumental to the group process as *behaviors* performed by members and not as roles occupied by one or more of the members. While role deviation may be present in a group, it has no significant impact on the pattern of group interaction. The process view, emphasizing the principle of interdependence, also stresses the interdependence both of conformity and deviance and of cooperation and conflict in forming and maintaining groupness. As interdependent elements, they are viewed not as different processes, but as different dimensions of a single process. And this process embodies all the communicative behaviors of all group members.

Flight Patterns

Several independent studies of small group interaction have discovered what appears to be a phenomenon common to many groups. When confronted with social conflict within group interaction, members typically run away from it, that is, take flight in their interaction patterns. Some observers, for example, find that a period of social conflict will typically be followed by a period of interaction in which members avoid discussing the task. Gouran and Baird (1972) found that group members tend to change the topic under discussion soon after a period of social disagreement.

Why a group's interaction pattern exhibits flight from social conflict can be explained in several ways. One explanation assumes that conflict and deviance are unpleasant stimuli that group members wish to avoid. But this explanation is not very plausible in that it smacks of ignoring a problem and hoping it will go away. Sooner or later the group members must face the problem and resolve, manage, or control the conflict. Such a view also alleges that members invariably view social conflict as destructive.

A second explanation is that flight patterns are not an avoidance of anything, but merely a reflection of the short attention span of groups. A third explanation is that flight patterns reflect the normal process by which groups progressively modify decisions on their way to achieving consensus. Neither of these views assumes that conflict is inherently destructive or constructive.

Whatever the explanation for the apparent flight patterns in group interaction, it is obvious that disagreement spawns more disagreement, at least temporarily, in brief flurries of social conflict. It is also apparent that groups do not overtly attempt compromise as their initial response to social conflict; groups often perceive compromise to be an unsatisfactory solution to group conflict. A group's first response to conflict between its members is apparently to fight it out in frequent, albeit brief, periods of interaction and then abruptly cease consideration of the issue.

Innovative Deviance

Robert K. Merton (1957, p. 140) a noted sociologist, has discussed several varieties of deviant behavior in social systems. His classic discussion of deviance suggests four different varieties, not all of which are beneficial to the successful functioning of the social system. In fact, three of his classifications of deviance are probably disruptive and harmful to effective functioning.

One form of deviance in Merton's classifications is *ritualism* (which we have tended to call blind conformity). A ritualist is a person who conforms blindly to social norms solely for the sake of conformity, merely going through the motions of conformity without any real understanding or realization of why the norms are being followed. Another form of deviance is *retreatism*, a withdrawal from society (as a hermit or dropout does). And a third is *rebellion*, a disruptive form of deviance that involves rejecting the social system's values. Rebels seek to overthrow the existing social system and replace it with a new and presumably better one.

The lone form of deviance that appears to be most conducive to providing benefits to the social system is what Merton calls *innovation*. Innovators in a social system are members who are quite committed to the goals of the system or group but who believe that the socially approved means to achieve these goals need to be revised. Innovative deviance is perhaps the most common type of deviant behavior in the interaction patterns of group decision making. The silent or uncommitted member might be a retreatist, the member of a classroom group who wants to get an A but is concerned only with satisfying the instructor might represent a ritualist, and the person who hates leaders would probably represent a rebel. But innovative deviance, according to Merton, involves behavior that reflects a rather strong commitment to the group in the form of an agreement with the goals of the group; the innovator simply disagrees with the prevailing (or majority) view of the acceptable means for achieving these goals.

Valentine and Fisher (1974) utilized Merton's concept of innovative deviance as the basis for a system of interaction analysis. They attempted to observe the sequence of group interaction more closely in order to determine how deviant behavior functions during the process of group decision making. The results from their interaction analysis, although not conclusive, provide some interesting speculation about how innovative deviance functions to benefit the natural process of group decision making.

Oddly enough, Valentine and Fisher discovered that innovative deviance is not associated with any particular member or members. That is, nearly all members of the group contribute some innovation to the interaction. Moreover, no one or two members appear to contribute significantly more innovatively deviant behaviors than other members. This phenomenon may not be true of all forms of deviance, but innovatively deviant behavior is apparently a phenomenon of group decision making that is not necessarily associated with one or two particular members who would then be labeled "deviants."

Valentine and Fisher also discovered that innovatively deviant behavior accounts for a rather significant proportion of the entire group interaction. An average of 27 percent of all the communicative actions performed by the group members they observed was characterized as deviant behavior. Furthermore, all but 1.75 percent of deviant behavior was innovative deviance. Innovative deviance during group interaction appears to be most acceptable during the conflict phase and, to a lesser extent, during the emergence phase of group decision making. On the other hand, such deviant behavior is probably detrimental to the group process during the formative phase of group development (the orientation phase) and during the final phase of reinforcement as the group nears consensus (see Chapter 6).

Valentine and Fisher also suggested that during the conflict and emergence phases, innovative deviance appears to stimulate further innovative deviance. That is, during the two middle phases of group decision making, the group members they observed appeared to interact in bursts of social conflict and deviance. Such patterns of deviant behavior precipitating further deviant behavior seems to indicate the presence of positive feedback cycles. These cycles appear to stimulate further deviance, at least innovative deviance.

What does innovative deviance look like during group decision making? According to the interaction categories utilized by Valentine and Fisher, innovative deviance occurs in the form of a contradiction or rejection of an assertion. Continuing a disagreement initiated by others is also classified as an innovatively deviant act, as is advocating a previously attacked assertion or negatively modifying another member's assertion. A statement that supports a previous innovatively deviant statement is also classified as innovative deviance.

While the greatest proportion of innovatively deviant behavior occurs in the intermediate phases of group interaction, innovative deviance is apparently also present throughout nearly all the group discussion. The only exception to this rule may be during the final phase of reinforcement. During the latter stages of group interaction, as the group is achieving final consensus, virtually no deviant behavior of any kind is evident in the interaction sequences. This conclusion from Valentine and Fisher's study appears to confirm the earlier hypotheses that any temporary coalitions that have formed around the substantive issues appear to dissipate in a spirit of unity as the group nears its final goal—consensus.

Another result consistent with the analysis reveals that most innovatively deviant behaviors appear in the interaction before the majority position of the group is clearly established. That is, most innovative behavior occurs before consensus and is apparently instrumental in formulating that consensus. This discovery seems to confirm the belief, stated earlier, that conflict leads to consensus.

While innovative deviance may generate further deviant behavior, these spurts of deviant interaction are not sustained indefinitely. That is, decision-making groups interact in bursts of deviant behavior followed by periods of interaction in which little deviant behavior is present. After a period of nondeviant interaction, the members then engage in another spurt of deviant interaction patterns. These peaks and valleys of deviant interaction suggest patterns of "flight" behavior in which members appear to avoid deviance and social conflict after brief periods of deviant interaction. But the suggestion of the fight-flight pattern in group interaction does not necessarily indicate that group members typically avoid conflict and deviance. Rather, group members may be able to withstand only so much social conflict and deviance before they abruptly change the topic under discussion. The fact that group members are apparently not avoiding conflict is even more evident when one realizes that the group members invariably return to those topics which had earlier precipitated deviant behavior and social conflict.

The conclusion from Valentine and Fisher's study regarding the identification of members as deviants is worthy of further discussion. You will recall that the results of their interaction analysis indicated that nearly all members of the decision-making groups they observed performed innovatively deviant behaviors. This conclusion emphasizes the fact that deviance, at least innovative deviance, is probably best defined in terms of behaviors. That is, innovative deviance constitutes a normal and rather substantial proportion of group interaction. Furthermore, it is apparently not a role position occupied by one or two members within a group's network of roles.

Innovative deviance, as it affects the group process, is a function of the communicative behaviors of many members, not of an individual member's personality or self-concept. Therefore, deviance should be considered normal to the process of group decision making, not the province of a few "oddball" members. Innovative deviance is part of the normal communication performed by all group members who are committed to the group's goals.

Phases of Conflict

In an additional study, Ellis and Fisher (1975) attempted to observe conflict interaction during group decision making. The purpose of this study was to provide some insight into the potential of conflict for social integration, that is, for developing groupness. This particular investigation, utilizing interaction analysis, suggests the possibility that group decision making can be classified into three phases of conflict integration. The first third of the group interaction involves *interpersonal* conflict, the middle third of the interaction can be characterized as *confrontation,* and the final phase involves *substantive* conflict.

Ellis and Fisher described the interpersonal-conflict phase as resulting from the individual differences between the personalities of the group members. During the early stages of group decision making, the members have not had sufficient time to generate group-centered issues; therefore, they involve themselves in conflict that is based on their identities more as unique human beings than as group members.

The second phase of conflict, confrontation, includes interaction that tests ideas. Present in such interaction patterns are agreement and disagreement with specific decision proposals. In the sense that confrontation involves choosing up sides and fighting out the issues, it appears to pit one coalition of members against another. The second phase of conflict interaction probably includes both the conflict and emergence phases of group decision making.

The final phase of conflict interaction is characterized by the positive functioning of information in group interaction. Nearly all contributions by the members involve statements directly addressing those issues and proposals which achieve group consensus. Substantive conflict clearly indicates effective management of social conflict or, at least, the outcome or result of effective conflict management during earlier phases of group interaction.

Ellis and Fisher pointed out that for effective decision making, groups need to devise conflict management techniques that are adapted to the specific type of conflict occurring in the interaction. For example, the techniques for managing interpersonal conflict differ significantly from those used for managing confrontation (or substantive conflict). Interpersonal conflict results from a lack of information about task issues; therefore, having all group members generate more information directed at the group's task is an effective way to help manage the interpersonal conflict that arises during the early phase of group decision making. On the other hand, confrontation results from the problem of integrating voluminous amounts of information; that is, the members have generated so much information that they are having difficulty determining which information is the most and the least valuable. Thus, whereas managing interpersonal conflict involves *generating* additional group-related information, managing confrontation involves *integrating* existing information. By being able to make such distinctions between specific types of social conflict, effective decision-making groups become able to develop techniques for managing each particular type.

Folger and Poole (1984, pp. 20–23) concluded from a comparison of phase theories that groups go through a *differentiation-integration* cycle. Every group experiences a differentiation phase—it experiences conflicts that draw out sharp differences between its members. At some peak point, when the group cannot tolerate the conflict any longer, integration begins—the group moves toward a solution that is at least acceptable to its members. If attempts at integration are not successful, then the group returns to differentiation and begins the cycle again.

Understanding the phases of conflict development in groups is important, because they put each type of conflict in a meaningful context and thereby teach group members what they must deal with in order to move through conflict. Phase theories suggest that there are patterns of conflict that help shape the expectations of group members. The study by Ellis and Fisher, for example, showed that ambiguous comments occur in both the early and late phases but are interpreted differently in each. Ambiguity in the early phase represents indecision; ambiguity in later phases represents movement from one idea to another to help the group reach a decision. Therefore, an understanding of the general phase the group is experiencing provides a way to interpret specific communicative utterances.

MANAGING CONFLICT

Up to now we have been talking mostly about conflict as a normal characteristic of group decision making, and we have noted that conflict needs to be controlled. We have also discussed the control of conflict as a problem of management, not as a problem of getting rid of conflict. Since conflict is inevitable and can be a positive characteristic of the group process, it is important to *manage* conflict rather than eliminate it. Group members should thus be careful to avoid the tendency to think of conflict and deviance as harmful, disruptive, or simply "bad"; they must think about conflict both as potentially disruptive *and* as beneficial. The problem of management thus becomes one of how to maximize the benefits of conflict and avoid the consequences of destructive conflict.

Standard Conflict-Avoidance Techniques

The following are some ways that groups can make decisions by avoiding substantive conflict. These techniques are sometimes counterproductive because they force decisions the group is not ready to make. None of the techniques is based on the group's working through conflict and arriving at a decision that reflects consensus, but each is used quite often to force decisions and bring conflict (and communication) to a close.

Majority Vote Our democratic traditions have conditioned us to take majority-rule votes. After a little discussion in a group, there is always someone who says, "Well, let's take a vote." Majority votes make for quick decisions and certainly save time. But have you ever heard the phrase "the tyranny of the majority"? Majority votes satisfy only one portion of the group. And if a coalition consistently votes together and constitutes a majority, it can certainly become tyrannical. Groups that solve all problems by taking majority-rule votes are thwarting the benefits of the group process and placing too much value on closure at the expense of consensus. Majority votes also divide the group; after the vote there are "winners" and "losers," with all the accompanying hurt feelings and animosity. Majority-rule votes are not very effective for small group decision making.

Compromise Compromise should be considered a last-resort measure. People think of compromise as reaching agreement by each party's giving in a little bit. More often, however, compromise results in a superficial consensus—that is, an agreement with little commitment. Group members often think of compromise as everybody winning something, when actually everybody loses something. Compromise sounds very democratic, but it rarely works in practice. The typical outcome of a compromise is some dissatisfaction felt by all group members.

One member of a group wrote in a journal, "We went back and forth . . . without reaching accord. A compromise was in need. I gave in as much as possible, and she just gave in. Not a harmonious compromise, but tolerable." The other party to the compromise reacted, "I tried to get a group discussion going . . . but they weren't really interested in what I had to say. Finally I gave up and decided to agree with them so that we could get our task accomplished. Maybe I should have persisted longer, but I don't think it would have done any good." This compromise consisted of one member giving in to the other. The result was a superficial consensus. There was agreement, to be sure, but there was no consensus on the decision.

Authoritative Rule A group member who has power, authority, and status can always force a decision. Say that an executive vice president who has been leading a problem-solving group for the past few months says: "We have been working on this for some time and are unable to come up with a decision. Rather than continuing this any further, I am going to make the decision for us." This will force closure and avoid additional conflict, but it can also lead to anger, anxiety, and other adverse effects on the group. If group members are not committed to the decision, they will not work to make it succeed.

Third-Party Arbitration This is when a disinterested third party is brought into the group to make the decision. Arbitrators are not common in small discussion groups. They are, however, used extensively to solve disputes among large competing groups, such as labor versus management, government versus citizens, and situations with many competing interests, such as environmental disputes (Goldmann, 1980). Arbitrators can have special respect and credibility in the eyes of the group because they are supposed to (1) be disinterested, (2) be requested by each side of the issue, (3) have special skills in conflict management techniques, and (4) bring fresh ideas to the process. In practice, third-party arbitrators are often imposed on groups and force decisions that have the same problems as compromises. Sometimes groups are neither committed to the process of arbitration nor respectful of the intervenors. This is very harmful because it encourages the parties to avoid responsibility for the decision.

Regulating Conflict

In this section we will give you some help putting conflict management into *practice*. We will suggest ways to improve a group's chances of working with conflict constructively. As usual, we provide no pat answers or tried-and-true rules. Rather, we offer intelligent strategies distilled from much of the best thinking about conflict management (see Folger and Poole, 1984, especially Chapter 6; Filley, 1975).

Clarify the Issues A group's first task is to clarify the conflicting issues about the problem it is addressing. This clarification is one of the group's most important tasks, and it is accomplished during the differentiation phase—in which the group identifies, defines, and sharpens the issues. Once the group has successfully differentiated the issues, it has a clear and accurate picture of the areas of conflict, understands the consequences of the conflict, and has some idea about what kinds of action are necessary. During this phase, the group must strive for communication which defines the problem's issues clearly and which encourages flexibility and creativity.

Folger and Poole (1984, pp. 192–194) suggest four ways to help clarify a problem's conflicting issues. These four strategies have been used effectively by group members as well as for third-party intervenors.

1. *Discuss the historical roots of the problem* The issues become more distinct when the group has a thorough understanding of the factors that created the problem. Sometimes the issues become clearer as the group argues about the problem's historical development. Groups often gain new insights as they discuss the problem's chronological development.

2. *Create a positive discussion atmosphere* One of the most basic reasons why a group does not define a problem's issues clearly is that its members feel insecure about stating their opinions. They often believe that being honest will result in argument and personal animosity; moreover, they sometimes feel vulnerable and subject to retribution if they express their opinions openly. The group should work to ensure that the general communication climate is sufficiently open and free that all members will express their opinions. The leader can play an important role here, because he or she is in a position to encourage good hard-hitting discussion and to discourage any of its negative consequences. The leader can control the agenda, govern who talks to whom, and direct the general flow of communication. Dealing with people individually, the leader can also work to redirect destructive emotions and bad feelings.

3. *Discuss needs rather than solutions* When a group finds itself in conflict over unsatisfactory solution proposals, the cause of this conflict is that the members have diverse and incompatible needs that the proposed solutions do not satisfy. When such conflict occurs, posing further solutions does not help. Rather, the causes of the conflict need to be addressed. The group should (a) stop discussing solutions until the members' needs have been clarified, (b) insist that the members discuss their needs, and (c) work to avoid interpersonal conflict. In managing this aspect of conflict, a group leader can ask the members to deal with the following questions: What are the members' needs? How does solution X meet these needs? How does the member view the needs of other members?

4. *Categorize the issues* When the conflicting issues are complex and multilayered, trying to clarify them can be very frustrating. As a result, certain members might launch into personal attacks against other members or express frustration about something outside the group's control, and such behavior can disrupt the group's work. Loud, belligerent discussions are usually a sign of aggression and displaced personal antagonisms, and a perceptive leader (especially if he or she knows the members individually) can often recognize such sources of conflict. When such behavior occurs, it is useful to divide the problem into small categories and deal with each one individually. Furthermore, the group will be able to manage each category's issues more carefully if it will separate out extraneous matters and concentrate on one issue at a time.

Promote a Positive Climate Folger and Poole (1984, p. 84) define *climate* as "the relatively enduring quality of the group situation that (a) is experienced in common by group members, and (b) arises from and influences their interaction and behavior." The climate is the general environment of the group; it is the mood, feeling, or "air" that pervades the group situation. Changing a poor climate is difficult, but necessary. Group climates arise from communication and the relationships between group members. The climate can be positive or negative, flexible or rigid, enabling or thwarting, friendly or hostile, supportive or threatening, authoritative or participatory, and so forth. It takes time to make the group climate conducive to good conflict management, and it is certainly not something that can be changed easily. The best ways to analyze a group climate are to (1) observe the group over a period of time, (2) interview people, and (3) listen to the language of the members and how they talk about themselves. Here are two suggestions for promoting a more positive group climate:

1. *Encourage open discussion* The group simply must feel free to communicate without negative consequences. This is easier said than done, but it is something the group must strive for. Discussion should be focused on issues and kept away from personalized argument; the members should be free to communicate their feelings, but these should always be related to the central issue. The most useful technique for promoting open discussion is to reinforce it. A group member, perhaps the leader, should begin by honestly expressing feelings and disagreements. This will stimulate others to communicate in the same manner. The leader or group member then reinforces these others either by giving them direct feedback ("I'm glad you said that. Now I understand.") or by extending the discussion with contributions of his or her own.
2. *Change the talk* One way to alter the group climate is to begin talking about it differently. For example, all group members like the feeling of cohesion and unity that comes with group membership, and sometimes what makes it difficult to work through conflict is that the climate is not one of cohesion—so a simple way to correct this is to change the language to "we" when talking about the group. This gives the members the feeling of belonging to a social unit; it creates a comfortable environment where members feel as though they have something in common. There is the story of the fraternity pledge class that was asked by members how many pledges were in the group; each pledge would answer, "One, sir; we are a unit." This sort of dramatized example shows how changing the language can alter the perception of the group climate. Groups that give themselves special names and codes show that they have a climate of strong solidarity.

Allow Group Members to Save Face When people engage in face-saving communication, they are attempting to protect their image and personal identity (Folger and Poole, 1984, pp. 149–167). Face-saving is a very emotional group activity, responsible for numerous difficulties in conflict interactions, for group members want to be perceived as capable and competent and thus do their best to make sure that others have this image of them. A strong concern for self-image can surface when members are involved in conflict interaction, because in conflict situations they are exposing their opinions and attitudes and thus feel vulnerable, not only open to personal criticism but also risking the loss of other members' esteem; that is, conflict is a situation in which one's identity is threatened. (Consider, for example, that corporations often save face by making out-of-court settlements with injured customers, thereby making reparations and satisfying the injured parties without admitting to wrongdoing or criminal negligence.) Thus, conflict has to be conducted in a manner that allows group members to preserve their personal and relational identities.

The following are some useful techniques for promoting face-saving communication:

1. *Establish a proper climate* The climate established in the group is perhaps the most important means of preventing face-saving problems. If members agree that it is acceptable to state opinions and feelings openly without being threatened, they will have little concern for face-threatening communication. Such a climate develops from the previous behavior of the group. Reinforcing individual acts with support and tactful behavior is the best way to ensure a climate conducive to face-saving.

2. *Reduce defensiveness* Folger and Poole (1984, p. 182) show that people who are threatened become defensive. They feel "backed against a wall" and must do whatever necessary to save face and regain their image. Defensiveness can be reduced by having each party to a conflict state that he or she understands the other side of the issue and recognize its validity; for example, group members can explain that they understand how another member can feel threatened. Tying the current instance of defensiveness to a previous one is another way to show support and sympathetic understanding of the problem. Recognizing the other party's feelings will not necessarily make these feelings go away, but it is a step toward establishing a climate receptive to open discussion.

3. *Avoid accusatory and intimidating messages* Messages that accuse, intimidate, or generally threaten challenge the self-image of the other party. Some particularly manipulative individuals feel that such a message can be a show of strength and that it helps their position because it weakens the other party. But this strategy rarely works, for such a message requires a reaction, which is usually defensive or counteraccusatory. The group has then created a new problem that necessitates another response and redirects the communication away from productive conflict management. If the group ignores these messages, it is allowing this behavior to influence future interaction. Members who feel intimated must be encouraged to make their feelings known. They must describe why they feel as they do, addressing *specific* behaviors, and must encourage the intimidating members to explain their behavior. Escalation and increasing tension are the consequences of a failure to address acts of intimidation.

Some groups set aside some time to evaluate the group's progress and discuss problems and directions. This is an excellent time to address issues related to face-saving and intimidation, for the time period legitimizes such discussions and, moreover, does not interfere with the group's normal work.

Develop Integration Skills People generally spend more time learning about competition (e.g., sports, games, grades, business) than about cooperation. Our market economy and our society's traditions of individuality and success foster competitive attitudes. These attitudes have served us well in many arenas, but there are more occasions when cooperation is called for than competition is.

Some people think about group communication and decision making as primarily competitive, or a zero-sum game. In a zero-sum game, one person's gain (plus) is another person's loss (minus) and the result is zero. Athletic competition, poker, and most board games are zero-sum games because there is one winner and one loser and nothing in between. But solving group conflict should *not* be a zero-sum game. The best decisions and approaches to conflict are *integrative*, which means that the members of the group integrate their resources toward a common goal, much as in working on a jigsaw puzzle.

Group members must learn how to communicate and behave in an integrative manner. After they have clarified a problem's issues and clearly stated their differences, they must move to an integrative approach. The emergence phase of the decision-making process utilizes integrative behavior. To help groups become more specific and directive in approaching a problem from an integrative perspective, here is a description of divisive versus integrative communicative behavior from Patton and Giffin (1988, pp. 432–433):

Divisive Behavior	**Integrative Behavior**
1. Use purposive behavior in pursuing your *individual* goals.	Use purposive behavior in pursuing *common* goals.
2. Be secretive.	Be open.
3. Publicly disguise your own needs, keeping private what you really want.	Accurately and openly express your own needs.
4. Use threats and bluffs.	Use no threats and bluffs.
5. Be unpredictable, and use an element of surprise.	Be predictable; your behavior is flexible, but it is not designed for surprise.
6. Use nonrational and irrational arguments.	Use rational and innovative arguments.
7. Attempt success by stereotyping the other side and increasing hostility; demand ingroup loyalty.	Instead of stereotyping the other side, consider its merits; work to reduce hostility and to promote positive feelings.
8. Use a zero-sum approach; assume that preventing the other side from reaching its goals will facilitate your own goals.	Use a non-zero-sum approach; assume that the goals and solutions will benefit both parties.

Groups must avoid an us-versus-them or a superiority-inferiority approach to conflict. Both are divisive and just splinter the conflicting parties. There is a tendency during conflict, especially when issues are difficult to resolve, to stereotype the other side; statements such as "typical management" reflect the fact that group members see the other side as inflexible and of one mind.

Folger and Poole (1984, pp. 194–197) describe two other ways to induce integration:

1. *Develop common goals* There is usually more room for agreement in a conflict situation than most people think. It is likely that the parties in conflict will begin by accentuating the differences between them rather than discussing their commonalities. Have someone try to keep track of the points of agreement. If both parties can agree on goals, then they can focus the discussion on the means of reaching the goals. This is usually an easier problem than working out differences in goals. Communication that emphasizes common goals is also encouraging for group members, prompting them to adopt a more integrative approach to the conflict.
2. *Clarify the integrative process* The conflicting parties should state emphatically that they want to move toward integrative solutions, and attempt to control the process. This helps establish the proper attitudes and emotional conditions for integration.

Filley (1975, pp. 92–106) describes some ways to promote an integrative solution:

1. *Adjust relational conditions* This is similar to establishing a cooperative climate.
2. *Adjust perceptions* The group uses the procedures outlined by Filley to clarify the nature of the conflict.
3. *Adjust attitudes* The parties clarify the emotional issues including how they feel about the conflict.
4. *Problem definition* Depersonalize the problem and define it in a manner separate from individuals.
5. *Search for solutions* Generate solutions in a nonjudgmental way.
6. *Consensus decision* Evaluate the alternative solutions and choose a single solution.

In Conclusion

Managing conflict is not easy and is always risky. Even though we have offered a number of steps and strategies, there is no guarantee that all conflict can be regulated in a cooperative and integrative manner. Moreover, it is foolish and naive to think that all groups are trustworthy and will work for cooperative solutions. But this is a goal worth striving for, because even with the strong pressures in our culture to succeed and gain, often at the expense of others, it remains true that decisions of real quality and permanence are based on integrative communication that leads to mutually beneficial decisions.

SUMMARY

The right of dissent in our society is one of our most cherished privileges, although conformity, inescapable and inevitable, is more often the rule. Conformity to the behavioral standards of a social system implies not only uniformity of behavior, but uniformity based on conflict between alternatives and on avoidance of unpleasant social pressures. Pressures toward conformity in the small group are extraordinarily severe, although a deviating member gains strength to resist such pressures by having publicly committed himself or herself to a deviant position or when another member agrees with that deviant position.

Many people in our society are ambivalent about social conflict and deviance and often view the social system as functioning in a delicate balance of supportive and disruptive forces. Thus, conflict may be seen as existing within one person, between two or more persons, within the same social system, or between social systems. Social conflict is also classified as affective or substantive—emotional or intellectual.

When a perfect (or ideal) social system is assumed, social conflict appears to be a failure of the social system and inherently destructive. However, those who adopt a functionalist approach perceive social conflict and deviance as often performing desirable, constructive, and even essential functions instrumental to the effective operation of the social system. If conflict is destructive, it must be resolved or controlled. On the other hand, constructive conflict must be understood and managed in order to achieve its social benefits. The multifaceted nature of social conflict and deviance dictates the emphasis on interpersonal substantive conflict serving constructive functions for the small group.

Social conflict and deviance perform many functions beneficial to the group process. Conflict furthers group cohesiveness and increases productivity. Innovative deviant behavior is essential for progress as the group grows and changes through time. Groups manage deviant behavior through feedback loops and cycles.

Realistically, social conflict and deviance are so common to the process of group development that they are considered normal within the group process. A decision-making group invokes social conflict as members test ideas in a critical exchange of information and opinions. Coalitions form temporarily around conflicting ideas before typically merging as the group achieves consensus. And the leader, paradoxically enough, normally conforms to and deviates from group norms in the process of gaining and maintaining leadership status.

Verbal innovative deviance, an agreement on group goals but a disagreement on the means to achieve them, is suggested as an insight into the ongoing process of social conflict in group interaction patterns. Verbal innovative deviance seems to account for a significant proportion of group interaction and appears in clusters or spurts of deviant behavior that alternate with normal periods of group flight behavior. Normally, only innovative deviant behaviors exert a significant impact on group interaction patterns, and these behaviors are generally distributed among all involved group members.

Different types of conflict occur during the process of group decision making. Social conflict may be interpersonal, confrontational, or substantive, depending on the phase of group decision making in which it appears. Consequently, strategies for managing conflict and deviance during the group process vary considerably. Nevertheless, some general tactics for conflict management are possible. These strategies include clarifying issues, saving face, promoting a positive climate, and developing integration skills.

REFERENCES

Abelson, Robert P., and Ariel Levi. (1985) "Decision Making and Decision Theory," in G. Lindzey and Elliot Aronson (eds.), *The Handbook of Social Psychology*, 3d ed., vol. 1. New York: Random House, pp. 231–309.

Adams, J. S. (1980) "Interorganization Processes and Organization Boundary Activities," in L. Cummings and B. Staw (eds.), *Research in Organizational Behavior*, vol. 2. Greenwich, CT: JAI Press, pp. 321–355.

Agar, M. (1980) "Getting Better Quality Stuff: Methodological Competition in an Interdisciplinary Niche," *Urban Life*, 9:34–50.

Alba, R. D. (1982) "Taking Stock of Network Analysis: A Decade's Results," in S. Bacharach (ed.), *Research in the Sociology of Organizations*, vol. 1. Greenwich, CT: JAI Press, pp. 39–74.

Allison, Scott T., and David M. Messick. (1987) "From Individual Inputs to Group Outputs, and Back Again: Group Processes and Inferences About Members," in Clyde Hendrick (ed.), *Group Processes*. Beverly Hills, CA: Sage, pp. 111–143.

Alpert, M., and H. Raiffa. (1982) "A Progress Report on the Training of Probability Assessors," in D. Kahneman, P. Slovic, and A. Tversky (eds.), *Judgement Under Uncertainty: Heuristics and Biases*. Cambridge: Cambridge University Press.

Altman, Irwin, and Dalmas Taylor. (1973) *Social Penetration: The Development of Interpersonal Relationships*. New York: Holt, Rinehart & Winston.

Andersen, J. (1988) "Communication Competency in the Small Group," in Robert Cathcart and Larry Samovar (eds.), *Small Group Communication*, 5th ed. Dubuque, IA: Brown, pp. 450–458.

Andrews, Patricia H. (1988) "Group Conformity," in Robert Cathcart and Larry Samovar (eds.), *Small Group Communication*, 5th ed. Dubuque, IA: Brown, pp. 225–235.

Baird, John E., Jr., and Sanford B. Weinberg. (1977) *Communication: The Essence of Group Synergy*. Dubuque, IA: Brown.

Bales, Robert F. (1950) *Interaction Process Analysis: A Method for the Study of Small Groups*. Cambridge, MA: Addison-Wesley.

Bales, Robert F. (1953) "The Equilibrium Problem in Small Groups," in Talcott Parsons, Robert F. Bales, and Edward A. Shils (eds.), *Working Papers in the Theory of Action*. New York: Free Press, pp. 111–161.

Bales, Robert F., and Philip E. Slater. (1955) "Role Differentiation in Small Decision-making Groups," in Talcott Parsons et al. (eds.), *The Family, Socialization, and Interaction Process*. Glencoe, IL: Free Press, pp. 259–306.

Bales, Robert F., and Stephen P. Cohen. (1979) *SYMLOG: A System For the Multiple Level Observation of Groups*. New York: Free Press.

Bales, Robert F., and Fred L. Strodtbeck. (1951) "Phases in Group Problem-Solving," *Journal of Abnormal and Social Psychology*, 46:485–495.

Barker, R. G., and H. F. Wright. (1955) *Midwest and Its Children*. Evanston, IL: Row Peterson.

Bateson, Gregory. (1935) "Culture Contact and Schismogenesis," *Man*, 35:178–183.

Bateson, Gregory. (1972) *Steps to an Ecology of Mind*. San Francisco: Chandler.

Benne, Kenneth D., and Paul Sheats. (1948) "Functional Roles of Group Members," *Journal of Social Issues*, 4:41–49.

Bennis, Warren G., and Herbert A. Shepard. (1956) "A Theory of Group Development," *Human Relations*, 9:415–437.

Berg, David M. (1967) "A Descriptive Analysis of the Distribution and Duration of Themes Discussed by Task-Oriented Small Groups," *Speech Monographs*, 34:172–175.

Berger, Charles R. (1973) "Task Performance and Attributional Communication as Determinants of Interpersonal Attraction," *Speech Monographs*, 40:280–286.

Berlo, David K. (1960) *The Process of Communication.* New York: Holt, Rinehart & Winston.

Birdwhistell, Ray L. (1970) *Kinesics and Context: Essays on Body Motion Communication.* Philadelphia: University of Pennsylvania Press.

Blau, Peter M. (1960) "A Theory of Social Integration," *American Journal of Sociology,* **65**:545–556.

Bochner, Arthur P. (1984) "The Functions of Human Communication in Interpersonal Bonding," in Carroll C. Arnold and John Waite Bowers (eds.), *Handbook of Rhetorical and Communication Theory.* Newton, MA: Allyn and Bacon, pp. 544–621.

Bormann, E. G. (1986) "Symbolic Convergence Theory and Communication in Group Decision-Making," in R. Y. Hirokawa and M. S. Poole (eds.), *Communication and Group Decision.* Beverly Hills, CA: Sage, pp. 219–236.

Bormann, Ernest G., and Nancy C. Bormann. (1988) *Effective Small Group Communication.* Edina, MN: Burgess.

Bowers, John W., and John A. Courtright. (1984) *Communication Research Methods.* Glenview, IL: Scott, Foresman.

Boyatzis, R. E. (1982) *The Competent Manager.* New York: Wiley.

Brilhart, John K. (1978) *Effective Group Discussion,* 3d ed. Dubuque, IA: Brown.

Brown, Steven R., and Albert Rothenberg. (1976) "The Analysis of Group Episodes," *Small Group Behavior,* **7**:287–306.

Burgoon, Judee K. (1988) "Spatial Relationships in Small Groups," in Robert Cathcart and Larry Samovar (eds.), *Small Group Communication,* 5th ed. Dubuque, IA: Brown, pp. 351–366.

Cartwright, Dorwin, and Alvin Zander. (1968) "Leadership and Performance of Group Functions: Introduction," in Dorwin Cartwright and Alvin Zander (eds.), *Group Dynamics: Research and Theory,* 3d ed. New York: Harper & Row, pp. 301–317.

Cegala, D. J., et al. (1982) "An Elaboration of the Meaning of Interaction Involvement: Toward the Development of a Theoretical Concept," *Communication Monographs,* **49**:229–248.

Chemers, Martin. (1983) "Leadership Theory and Research: A System-Process Integration," in P. B. Paulus (ed.), *Basic Group Processes.* New York: Springer-Verlag.

Coates, Jennifer. (1986) *Women, Men and Language.* England: Longman.

Collins, Barry E., and Harold Guetzkow. (1964) *A Social Psychology of Group Processes for Decision-Making.* New York: Wiley.

Coser, Lewis. (1956) *The Functions of Social Conflict.* New York: Free Press.

Crowell, Laura, and Thomas M. Scheidel. (1961) "Categories for Analysis of Idea Development in Discussion Groups," *Journal of Social Psychology,* **54**:155–168.

Davis, James H. (1969) *Group Performance.* Reading, MA: Addison-Wesley.

DeStephen, Rolayne S. (1977) "Leadership and Sex: Behavioral Differences in the Small Group Context." A paper presented to Western Speech Communication Association, Phoenix, AZ.

Deutsch, Morton. (1973) *The Resolution of Conflict: Constructive and Destructive Processes.* New Haven, CT: Yale University Press.

Dewey, John. (1910) *How We Think.* New York: Heath.

Donohue, William A. (1981) "Analyzing Negotiation Tactics: Development of Negotiation Interact System," *Human Communication Research,* **7**:273–287.

Drecksel, Gay L. (1984) "Interaction Characteristics of Emergent Leadership," Ph.D. dissertation, University of Utah.

Dunphy, Dexter C. (1964) "Social Change in Self-Analytic Groups," Ph.D. dissertation, Harvard University.

Eisenberg, Eric. (1984) "Ambiguity as Strategy in Organizational Communication," *Communication Monographs*, **51**:227–242.

Ellis, Donald G. (1979) "Relational Control in Two Group Systems," *Communication Monographs*, **46**:153–166.

Ellis, Donald G., and B. Aubrey Fisher. (1975) "Phases of Conflict in Small Group Development," *Human Communication Research*, **1**:195–212.

Farris, G. F., and F. G. Lim. (1969) "Effects of Performance on Leadership, Cohesiveness, Influence, Satisfaction, and Subsequent Performance," *Journal of Applied Psychology*, **53**:490–497.

Festinger, Leon. (1950) "Informal Social Communication," *Psychological Review*, **57**:271–282.

Festinger, Leon. (1954) "A Theory of Social Comparison Processes," *Human Relations*, **7**:117–140.

Fiedler, Fred E. (1964) "A Contingency Model of Leadership Effectiveness," in Leonard Berkowitz (ed.), *Advances in Experimental Social Psychology*, vol. I. New York: Academic Press, pp. 149–190.

Fiedler, Fred E. (1967) *A Theory of Leadership Effectiveness*. New York: McGraw-Hill.

Filley, A. (1975) *Interpersonal Conflict Resolution*. Glenview, IL: Scott, Foresman.

Fisher, B. Aubrey. (1970a) "Decision Emergence: Phases in Group Decision Making," *Speech Monographs*, **37**:53–66.

Fisher, B. Aubrey. (1970b) "The Process of Decision Modification in Small Discussion Groups," *Journal of Communication*, **20**:51–64.

Fisher, B. Aubrey. (1977) "Interaction Analysis: An Underutilized Methodology in Communication." A paper presented to Western Speech Communication Association, Phoenix, AZ.

Fisher, B. Aubrey. (1978) *Perspectives on Human Communication*. New York: Macmillan.

Fisher, B. Aubrey. (1980) *Small Group Decision Making*. New York: McGraw-Hill.

Fisher, B. Aubrey. (1986) "Leadership: When Does the Difference Make a Difference," in R. Hirokawa and M. S. Poole (eds.), *Communication and Group Decision-Making*. Beverly Hills, CA: Sage, pp. 197–215.

Fisher, B. Aubrey, Thomas W. Glover, and Donald G. Ellis. (1977) "The Nature of Complex Communication Systems," *Communication Monographs*, **44**:231–240.

Fisher, B. Aubrey, and Randall K. Stutman. (1987) "An Assessment of Group Trajectories: Analyzing Developmental Breakpoints," *Communication Quarterly*, **35**:105–124.

Folger, Joseph P., and Marshall S. Poole. (1982) "Relational Coding Schemes: The Question of Validity," in M. Burgoon (ed.), *Communication Yearbook 5*. New Brunswick, NJ: Transaction, pp. 240–266.

Folger, Joseph P., and Marshall S. Poole. (1984) *Working Through Conflict: A Communication Perspective*. Glenview, IL: Scott, Foresman.

Gibb, Jack. (1961) "Defensive Communication," *Journal of Communication*, **11**:141–148.

Gilstein, Kenneth W., E. Wayne Wright, and David R. Stone. (1977) "The Effects of Leadership Style on Group Interactions in Differing Socio-Political Subcultures," *Small Group Behavior*, **8**:313–332.

Goffman, Erving. (1959) *The Presentation of Self in Everyday Life*. Garden City, NY: Doubleday.

Goffman, Erving. (1961) *Encounters*. New York: Bobbs-Merrill.

Goldmann, R. B. (1980) *Round Table Justice: Case Studies in Conflict Resolution*. Boulder, CO: Westview Press.

Gouldner, Alvin W. (1960) "The Norm of Reciprocity: A Preliminary Statement," *American Sociological Review*, **25**:161–171.

Gouran, Dennis S. (1983) "Communicative Influences on Inferential Judgments in Decision-Making Groups: A Descriptive Analysis," in D. Zarefsky et al. (eds.), *Argument in Transition: Proceedings of the Third Summer Conference on Argumentation*. Annandale, VA: Speech Communication, pp. 667–684.

Gouran, Dennis S., and John E. Baird, Jr. (1972) "An Analysis of Distributional and Sequential Structure in Problem-Solving and Informal Group Discussions," *Speech Monographs*, **39**:16–22.

Gouran, Dennis S., and B. Aubrey Fisher. (1984) "The Functions of Human Communication in the Formation, Maintenance, and Performance of Small Groups," in Carroll C. Arnold and John Waite Bowers (eds.), *Handbook of Rhetorical and Communication Theory*. Newton, MA: Allyn and Bacon, pp. 622–658.

Hackman, Richard J. (1968) "Effects of Task Characteristics on Group Products," *Journal of Experimental Social Psychology*, **4**:162–187.

Hall, Edward T. (1959) *The Silent Language*. Garden City, NY: Doubleday.

Haslett, Beth, and John R. Ogilvie. (1988) "Feedback Processes in Task Groups," in Robert Cathcart and Larry Samovar (eds.), *Small Group Communication*, 5th ed. Dubuque, IA: Brown, pp. 385–401.

Hawes, Leonard C. (1972) "The Effects of Interviewer Style on Patterns of Dyadic Communication," *Speech Monographs*, **39**:114–123.

Hawes, Leonard C., and Joseph M. Foley. (1976) "Group Decisioning: Testing a Finite Stochastic Model," in Gerald R. Miller (ed.), *Explorations in Interpersonal Communication*. Beverly Hills, CA: Sage, pp. 237–254.

Hecht, Michael L., and Pat Riley. (1985) "A Three Factor Model of Group Satisfaction and Consensus," *Communication Research Reports*, **2**:179–187.

Herbert, J., and C. Attridge. (1975) "A Guide for Developers and Users of Observation Systems and Manuals," *American Educational Research Journal*, **12**:1–20.

Hersey, P., and K. H. Blanchard. (1982) *Management of Organizational Behavior*, Englewood Cliffs, NJ: Prentice-Hall.

Heslin, Richard, and Dexter Dunphy. (1964) "Three Dimensions of Member Satisfaction in Small Groups," *Human Relations*, **17**:99–112.

Hewes, D. E. (1979) "The Sequential Analysis of Social Interaction," *Quarterly Journal of Speech*, **65**:56–73.

Hirokawa, Randy Y. (1982) "Group Communication and Problem-Solving Effectiveness I: A Critical Review of Inconsistent Findings," *Communication Quarterly*, **30**:134–141.

Hirokawa, Randy Y. (1983a) "Group Communication and Problem-Solving Effectiveness: An Investigation of Group Phases," *Human Communication Research*, **9**:291–305.

Hirokawa, Randy Y. (1983b) "Group Communication and Problem-Solving Effectiveness II," *Western Journal of Speech Communication*, **47**:59–74.

Hirokawa, Randy Y., and R. Pace. (1983) "A Descriptive Investigation of the Possible Communication-Based Reasons for Effective and Ineffective Group Decision-Making," *Communication Monographs*, **50**:363–379.

Hirokawa, Randy Y., and Marshall Scott Poole (eds.). (1986) *Communication and Group Decision-Making*. Beverly Hills, CA: Sage.

Hirokawa, Randy Y., and Dirk R. Scheerhorn. (1986) "Communication in Faulty Group Decision-Making," in Randy Hirokawa and Marshall S. Poole (eds.), *Communication and Group Decision-Making*. Beverly Hills, CA: Sage, pp. 63–80.

Hocking, John E., Duane G. Margreiter, and Cal Hylton. (1977) "Intra-audience Effects: A Field Test," *Human Communication Research*, **3**:243–249.

Hollander, E. P. (1983) "Women and Leadership," in H. H. Blumberg et al. (eds.), *Small Groups and Social Interaction*, vol. 1. New York: Wiley.

Hollander, E. P. (1985) "Leadership and Power," in G. Lindzey and Elliot Aronson (eds.), *The Handbook of Social Psychology*, 3d ed., vol. 2. New York: Random House, pp. 485–537.

Homans, George C. (1950) *The Human Group*. New York: Harcourt, Brace.

Homans, George C. (1961) *Social Behavior: Its Elementary Forms*. New York: Harcourt, Brace.

Horenstein, David, and Shirley J. Gilbert. (1976) "Anxiety, Likeability, and Avoidance as Responses to Self-Disclosing Communication," *Small Group Behavior*, 7:423–432.

House, R. J., and T. R. Mitchell. (1974) "Path-Goal Theory of Leadership," *Journal of Contemporary Business*, 3:81–97.

Hunt, Gary T. (1980) *Communication Skills in the Organization*. Englewood Cliffs, NJ: Prentice-Hall.

Janis, I. L. (1983) *Groupthink: Psychological Studies of Foreign Policy Decisions and Fiascoes*, 2d ed. Boston: Houghton Mifflin.

Janis, I. L., and L. Mann. (1977) *Decision Making: A Psychological Analysis of Conflict, Choice, and Commitment*. New York: Free Press.

Jarboe, Susan. (1988) "A Comparison of Input-Output, Process-Output, and Input-Process-Output Models of Small Group Problem-Solving Effectiveness," *Communication Monographs*, 55:121–142.

Johnson, David W. (1986) *Reaching Out*, 3d ed. Englewood Cliffs, NJ: Prentice-Hall.

Johnson, David W., and Frank P. Johnson. (1987) *Joining Together*, 3d ed. Englewood Cliffs, NJ: Prentice-Hall.

Jourard, S. M. (1964) *The Transparent Self*. New York: D. Van Nostrand.

Knapp, Mark L. (1978) *Nonverbal Communication in Human Interaction*, New York: Holt, Rinehart & Winston.

Lewin, Kurt. (1951) *Field Theory in Social Science*. New York: Harper & Row.

Likert, Rensis, and David G. Bowers. (1972) "Conflict Strategies," in Elliott McGinnies (ed.), *Attitudes, Conflict and Social Change*. New York: Academic Press, pp. 101–122.

McCroskey, J. C. (1977) "Oral Communication Apprehension: A Summary of Recent Theory and Research," *Human Communication Research*, 4:78–96.

McKinney, B. C. (1982) "The Effects of Reticence on Group Interaction," *Communication Quarterly*, 30:124–128.

Mansfield, E. (1973) "Empathy: Concept and Identified Psychiatric Nursing Behavior," *Nursing Research*, 22:525–530.

Marston, Peter J., and Michael L. Hecht. (1988) "Group Satisfaction," in Robert Cathcart and Larry Samovar (eds.), *Small Group Communication*, 5th ed. Dubuque, IA: Brown, pp. 236–246.

Merton, Robert K. (1957) *Social Theory and Social Structure*. New York: Free Press.

Monge, Peter R. (1987) "The Network Level of Analysis," in Charles Berger and Steven H. Chaffee (eds.), *Handbook of Communication Science*. Beverly Hills, CA: Sage, pp. 239–270.

Monge, Peter R., and Eric M. Eisenberg. (1987) "Emergent Networks," in F. Jablin, L. Putnam, K. Roberts, and L. Porter (eds.), *Handbook of Organizational Communication*. Newbury Park, CA: Sage.

Mortensen, C. David. (1966) "Should the Discussion Group Have an Assigned Leader?" *Speech Teacher*, 15:34–41.

Mortensen, C. David. (1972) *Communication: The Study of Human Interaction*. New York: McGraw-Hill.

Moscovici, S. (1985) "Social Influence and Conformity," in G. Lindzey and Elliot Aronson (eds.), *The Handbook of Social Psychology*, 3d ed., vol. 2. New York: Random House, pp. 347–412.

Myers, D. G., and G. D. Bishop. (1971) "Enhancement of Dominant Attitudes in Group Discussion," *Journal of Personality and Social Psychology*, **20**:386–391.

Napier, Rodney W., and Matti K. Gershenfeld. (1985) *Groups: Theory and Experience.* Boston: Houghton Mifflin.

Nokes, Patrick. (1961) "Feedback as an Explanatory Device in the Study of Certain Interpersonal and Institutional Processes," *Human Relations*, **14**:381–387.

Offerman, L. R. (1984) "Short-Term Supervisory Experience and LPC Score: Effects of Leader Sex and Group Sex Composition," *Journal of Social Psychology*, **123**:115–121.

Pacanowsky, Michael E., and Nicholas O'Donnell-Trujillo. (1983) "Organizational Communication as Cultural Performance," *Communication Monographs*, **50**:126–147.

Parsons, Talcott. (1951) *The Social System.* New York: Free Press.

Patton, B. R., and K. Giffin. (1988) "Conflict and Its Resolution," in Robert Cathcart and Larry Samovar (eds.), *Small Group Communication*, 5th ed. Dubuque, IA: Brown, pp. 429–441.

Pearce, W. Barnett. (1974) "Trust in Interpersonal Communication," *Speech Monographs*, **41**:236–244.

Pearce, W. Barnett, and Stuart M. Sharp. (1973) "Self-Disclosing Communications," *Journal of Communication*, **23**:409–425.

Pfeffer, J. (1981) *Power in Organizations.* Marshfield, MA: Pitman.

Phillips, Gerald M., and Eugene C. Erickson. (1970) *Interpersonal Dynamics in the Small Group.* New York: Random House.

Poole, Marshall S. (1981) "Decision Development in Small Groups I: A Comparison of Two Models," *Communication Monographs*, **48**:1–24.

Poole, Marshall S. (1983a) "Decision Development in Small Groups II: A Study of Multiple Sequences in Decision Making," *Communication Monographs*, **50**:206–232.

Poole, Marshall S. (1983b) "Decision Development in Small Groups III: A Multiple Sequence Model of Group Decision-Making," *Communication Monographs*, **50**:321–341.

Poole, Marshall S., and Joel A. Doelger. (1986) "Developmental Processes in Group Decision-Making," in Randy Hirokawa and Marshall S. Poole (eds.), *Communication and Group Decision-Making.* Beverly Hills, CA: Sage, pp. 237–264.

Poole, Marshall S., David R. Siebold, and Robert D. McPhee. (1986) "A Structurational Approach to Theory-Building in Group Decision-Making Research," in Randy Hirokawa and Marshall S. Poole (eds.), *Communication and Group Decision-Making.* Beverly Hills, CA: Sage, pp. 237–264.

Putnam, L. L. (1979) "Preference For Procedural Order in Task-Oriented Small Groups," *Communication Monographs*, **46**:193–218.

Putnam, L. L. (1986) "Conflict in Group Decision-Making," in Randy Hirokawa and Marshall S. Poole (eds.), *Communication and Group Decision-Making.* Beverly Hills, CA: Sage, pp. 175–196.

Rice, R. W., L. R. Bender, and A. G. Vitters. (1980) "Leader Sex, Follower Attitudes Toward Women, and Leadership Effectiveness: A Laboratory Study," *Organizational Behavior and Human Performance*, **25**:46–78.

Rice, R. W., D. Instone, and J. Adams. (1984) "Leader Sex, Leader Success, and Leadership Process: Two Field Studies," *Journal of Applied Psychology*, **69**:12–31.

Rieken, Henry W. (1952) "Some Problems of Consensus Development," *Rural Sociology*, **17**:245–252.

Roloff, M. (1987) "Communication and Conflict," in Charles Berger and Steven Chaffee (eds.), *Handbook of Communication Science.* Beverly Hills, CA: Sage, pp. 484–534.

Rosenfeld, L. B. (1988) "Self-Disclosure and Small Group Interaction," in Robert Cathcart and Larry Samovar (eds.), *Small Group Communication*, 5th ed. Dubuque, IA: Brown, pp. 288–305.

Russell, Hugh C. (1970) "Dimensions of the Communication Behavior of Discussion Leaders." A paper presented to the Central States Speech Association, Chicago.

Scheidel, Thomas M. (1986) "Divergent and Convergent Thinking in Group Decision-Making," in Randy Hirokawa and Marshall S. Poole (eds.), *Communication and Group Decision-Making*. Beverly Hills, CA: Sage, pp. 113–130.

Scheidel, Thomas M., and Laura Crowell. (1964) "Idea Development in Small Discussion Groups," *Quarterly Journal of Speech*, **50**:140–145.

Schneier, C. E., and K. M. Bartol. (1980) "Sex Differences in Emergent Leadership," *Journal of Applied Psychology*, **65**:341–345.

Shaw, Marvin E. (1976) *Group Dynamics: The Psychology of Small Group Behavior*, 2d ed. New York: McGraw-Hill.

Shaw, Marvin E. (1981) *Group Dynamics: The Psychology of Small Group Behavior*, 3d ed. New York: McGraw-Hill.

Sherif, M. (1935) "A Study of Some Social Factors in Perception," *Archives of Psychology*, **27**:(187).

Siebold, David R. (1988) "Making Meetings More Successful: Plans, Formats, and Procedures for Group Problem-Solving," in Robert Cathcart and Larry Samovar (eds.), *Small Group Communication*, 5th ed. Dubuque, IA: Brown, pp. 209–224.

Simmel, Georg. (1955) *Conflict*. New York: Free Press.

Sorensen, S. (1981) "Grouphate." A paper presented to the International Communication Association, Minneapolis, MN.

Strube, M. J., and J. E. Garcia. (1981) "A Meta-analytic Investigation of Fiedler's Contingency Model of Leadership Effectiveness," *Psychological Bulletin*, **90**:307–321.

Taylor, R. B., and J. C. Lanni. (1981) "Territorial Dominance: The Influence of the Resident Advantage in Triadic Decision Making," *Journal of Personality and Social Psychology*, **41**:909–915.

Thibaut, John W., and Harold H. Kelley. (1959) *The Social Psychology of Groups*. New York: Wiley.

Tichy, N. M. (1981) "Networks in Organizations," in P. Nystrom and W. Starbuck (eds.), *Handbook of Organizational Design*, vol. 2. New York: Oxford University Press, pp. 225–249.

Tjosvold, D. (1982) "Effects of Approach to Controversy on Superiors' Incorporation of Subordinates' Information in Decision Making," *Journal of Applied Psychology*, **67**:189–193.

Tolar, Alexander. (1970) "The 'Natural Course' View of Conflict Resolution," *Psychological Reports*, **26**:734.

Torrance, E. Paul. (1957) "Group Decision Making and Disagreement," *Social Forces*, **35**:314–318.

Tuchman, M. L., and T. J. Scanlan. (1981) "Boundary Spanning Individuals: Their Role in Information Transfer and Their Antecedents," *Academy of Management Review*, **24**:289–305.

Tuckman, Bruce W. (1965) "Developmental Sequence in Small Groups," *Psychological Bulletin*, **63**:384–399.

Tversky, A., and D. Kahneman. (1983) "Extensional vs. Intuitive Reasoning: The Conjunction Fallacy in Probability Judgement," *Psychological Review*, **90**:293–315.

Valentine, Kristin B., and B. Aubrey Fisher. (1974) "An Interaction Analysis of Verbal Innovative Deviance in Small Groups," *Speech Monographs*, **41**:413–420.

Vroom, V. H., and P. W. Yetton. (1973) *Leadership and Decision Making*. Pittsburgh: University of Pittsburgh Press.

Watzlawick, Paul, Janet H. Beavin, and Don D. Jackson. (1967) *Pragmatics of Human Communication.* New York: Norton.

Weick, Karl E. (1978) "The Spines of Leaders," in M. McCall and M. Lombardo (eds.), *Leadership: Where Else Can We Go?* Durham, NC: Duke University Press, pp. 37–61.

Weick, Karl E. (1981) "Psychology as Gloss," in R. Kasschau and C. N. Cofer (eds.), *Psychology's Second Century.* New York: Praeger, pp. 110–132.

Weick, Karl E. (1985) "Systematic Observational Methods," in G. Lindzey and Elliot Aronson (eds.), *The Handbook of Social Psychology,* 3d ed., vol. 1. New York: Random House, pp. 567–634.

Weick, Karl E. (1979) *The Social Psychology of Organizing.* Reading, MA: Addison-Wesley.

Wood, Julia T. (1977) "Leading in Purposive Discussions: A Study of Adaptive Behavior," *Communication Monographs,* **44:**152–165.

Yerby, Janet. (1975) "Attitude, Task, and Sex Composition as Variables Affecting Female Leadership in Small Problem-Solving Groups," *Speech Monographs,* **42:**160–168.

Zaleznik, Abraham, and David Moment. (1964) *The Dynamics of Interpersonal Behavior.* New York: Wiley.

Zeev, M. (1981) "The Decision to Raid Entebbe: Decision Analysis Applied to Crisis Behavior," *Journal of Conflict Resolution,* **25:**677–708.

APPENDIX 1

Glossary

Students often complain about the use of *jargon,* or language peculiar to an area of study. Most people deplore unnecessary jargon because it is cumbersome and awkward to use. Nevertheless, it is impossible to separate knowledge from language. Language is the package that ideas come in. If you are going to be knowledgeable or expert in an area of study, you must master the specialized language within that field. You may often feel overwhelmed with new terminology because as a university student you live in a virtual sea of language. It is not inaccurate to say that studying physics is to study the "language" of physics, just as studying philosophy, history, or agriculture is a matter of mastering ideas in those fields by mastering their language.

This glossary is an added effort on our part to help the student master the language associated with communication and decision-making groups. Distinctions and specialized meanings are important in any field of endeavor. The word "glossary" is a plural noun that refers to a collection of "glosses." A gloss is a brief explanatory note. It comes from the ancient practice of scholars making notes in margins or between lines explaining how a text should be interpreted. So a glossary is a list of new or specialized terms. New words are coined in order to describe new events and phenomena. Scholars assisted others with the interpretation of ancient texts by providing a list of definitions and commentary. If I told you that the computer I was working on at this very moment had a "20 meg hard drive" you would probably understand what I meant. It was not long ago that the two-word term *hard drive* would either have been gibberish or perhaps have referred to a long trip in a car. But the specialized use of those two simple words has created new meanings in the world of computer technology. You can be perfectly communicative when talking to a friend about computers and using the term *hard drive* because the term has established meaning.

This glossary is intended as a handy reference. We have tried to provide you with a manageable list of important concepts. The field of communication, particularly group communication, has more than its share of superfluous terminology. This is probably because there is no unifying theory that guides all who work in the area. So as people make new "discoveries" and identify new characteristics of groups, they create new terminology and new linguistic distinctions that perpetuate jargon. There is plenty of terminology in communication and group communication that does not appear below. This does not mean that those terms are not important or that they do not symbolize something important about groups or communication. It just means that they were not useful for our purposes. The concepts defined below are considered central to the understanding of communication and the group process.

One important warning for the reader who uses this glossary: Do not be misled by simple and overly general definitions. Definitions are easy; understanding is difficult. A brief definition is no substitute for understanding a concept. Although a single word may have a useful definition, it also implies other words. To understand a concept fully, one must understand an entire array of words and how they relate to one another. This glossary lists important concepts, but this book uses many additional terms not listed in the glossary that are necessary for a thorough appreciation of these concepts. So memorize definitions if you must, but do not confuse definitions with genuine understanding and knowledge.

Affective conflict   Emotional clashes between members of a social system, typically on procedural issues.

Assembly effect   The ability of a group to achieve collectively a level of productivity greater than the sum of the productivity of individuals when working by themselves.

Barrier or Breakdown   A cessation or blockage of communication, a concept based on the fallacious assumption that communication embodies only the structural aspects of sending and receiving messages along a channel.

Boundary spanner   A person who communicates and processes information between two or more networks.

Centrality   A characteristic of a communication network indicating the position in the network in which a member requires the fewest linkages to transmit a message to every other member of the group.

Channel capacity   The number of items of information that a person can effectively process at one time.

Coalition   A temporary alliance between two or more members of a social system, typically oriented toward a difference of opinion about the means used to achieve the group's goal.

Cohesiveness   The output of a group's socioemotional dimension; essentially, the degree to which members are attracted to one another and are personally committed to the group.

Collective structure   The repetitive pattern of behaviors that characterizes a group; when communication among group members becomes interdependent, interstructured, and predictable, a collective structure emerges.

Communication   The process of people exchanging messages, which are formulated according to the principles of a code, in a context.

Complementarity   A form of relational interaction in which a relational behavior and its response are combined to form a complete and coherent relationship; for example, question-answer, $\uparrow \downarrow$, or $\downarrow \uparrow$.

Conflict management   An accomplishment of the group when its members maximize the benefits of conflict and avoid the consequences of destructive conflict.

Conformity   Uniform behaviors exhibited by members of a social system resulting from the members choosing, from among conflicting alternatives of behavior, that alternative least subject to negative social influences.

Consensus   The degree of personal commitment the members feel toward the group's decision after it has been reached.

Contingency model   A model of group leadership, developed by Fiedler, that incorporates general predictions of leader effectiveness in selected situations. Predictions are based on scores of group leaders on LPC (least preferred coworker) tests.

Coorientation   The "strain toward symmetry" in which two persons (*A* and *B*) are oriented, positively or negatively, to the same object (*X*).

Decision   In a group, a choice from among available alternatives that is validated by achieving consensus among members.

Decision making   As a group task, the process of choosing among alternatives for which no "best" or "correct" answer can be validated by any means other than group consensus.

Density   The number of linkages in a network that actually exist in proportion to the number that would exist if everyone were linked directly.

Deviance   That behavior of members which is not in conformity with group norms or expectations.

Distance, communication   A characteristic of a communication network indicating the number of links required for one position in the network to transmit a message to another position.

Double interact   A sequence of three contiguous acts performed by group members.

Emergence   A gradual process describing how a group develops its roles, including that of leader, and its decisions.

Encapsulation   A method used for controlling social conflict through regulating conflict by a set of rules agreed upon by all parties to the conflict.

Evolution   The characteristic of a system embodying its history; that is, the enduring changes in the system's structure and function over an extended period of time.

Feedback   A mutually causal sequence of events or acts which, self-reflexively, exerts influence on the original act or event in the sequence. Feedback, affecting a deviant act or event, serves to counteract that deviance (negative feedback) or amplify the deviance (positive feedback).

Flight   The behavioral tendency of a group to cease considering its task as a means of avoiding some unpleasant stimulus, commonly social conflict.

Formal   A term used to describe the norms, status hierarchy, communication networks, etc., of a social system sanctioned or prescribed by legitimate sources of power or authority.

Formula answer   An oversimplified and unrealistic solution to a complex problem; typically so general that it cannot be implemented.

Function   The characteristic of a system denoted by the relationships among components in time and serving to regulate the ongoing action of the system.

Gatekeeping   The structural function of serving as an intermediary between source and receiver in the flow of messages; receiving and selectively relaying messages from the original source to the ultimate receiver.

Group   A collection of three or more persons whose behaviors are interstructured so that these persons exert a mutual and reciprocal influence on one another.

Group mind   A belief, now outmoded, in the independence of a group's manner of thinking and feeling apart from its members.

Groupthink   The phenomenon that occurs when members of a highly cohesive group disregard alternative courses of action in favor of maintaining unanimity of opinion in the group; an absence of critical idea testing and conflict, which are typical of the natural group process.

Group fantasy   The sharing of an interpretation of events that helps satisfy the group's need for organizing events and for communal bonds.

Identification   The extent to which a group member feels part of the group and has internalized its goals.

Idiosyncrasy credits   An economic model which explains the leader as both a deviant and a conformist and which illustrates the ability of a group leader to innovate after having conformed to the group norms for a period of time.

Informal   A term describing the norms, status hierarchy, communication networks, etc., developed through the emergent natural group process and not necessarily sanctioned by legitimate sources of authority or power.

Information processing   The process of using perceptions to transform data into information and then acting upon those perceptions; it may be performed by either one person or a group.

Innovative deviance   See **Verbal innovative deviance.**

Interact   A sequence of two contiguous acts performed by group members.

Interaction analysis   A method for analyzing the sequential process of communication.

Interaction management   The skill involved in regulating the direction and flow of interaction in the group.

Interaction process analysis (IPA)   The system of interaction analysis developed by Robert F. Bales.

Interdependence   A relationship between two or more elements so that each influences, and is influenced by, the other.

Interpersonal attraction   A characteristic of a relationship such that the people are drawn toward one another. Attraction usually occurs when group members hold similar attitudes.

Leaderless group discussion (LGD)   A task-oriented group whose members have the capacity to determine for themselves the group's structure, function, and behavior.

Leadership   A high-status position achieved in a group by performing leadership acts recognized by other group members as helping the group to perform its task; defined interdependently with followership.

Legitimacy   The principle of prescription or prior approval of norms, values, roles, or other standards imposed on a group by some person or source outside the group whose authority over it is recognized by the group members.

LGD   See **Leaderless group discussion.**

Life-cycle theory of leadership   The assumption that leaders should communicate with the group based on the maturity of the followers; the theory assumes that groups develop toward maturity.

Message   A single communicative act.

Motivation   A characteristic of group members who are stimulated to devote time, resources, and energy to the group.

Multiple-sequence models   The theory of group development which argues that groups do not evolve from single phasic patterns, but interweave different patterns over time. This theory is a response to and criticism of unitary phase models.

Natural process   A process of group development, nearly universal, that is based on "rules" governing behavior. Group members need not be aware of these rules.

Network   The structure of channel linkages among group members that illustrates the pattern of transmitting and receiving messages.

Nonsummativity   A principle, inherent in any system, which stipulates that the whole is greater than, or different from, the sum of its parts because of interdependent relationships among the parts.

Norm   A standard that regulates the behavior of all members of a group through feedback directed at members whose behaviors are contrary to that standard.

Open system   A characteristic of a system that has a free exchange of information with its environment.

Orienting communication   Group communication that maintains the group's focus by directing the discussion through clarification, questions, answers, and relevant information.

Partial inclusion   The notion that a person does not include all of his or her behaviors in a single role; the behaviors you are capable of are dispersed among several roles.

Polarization   The tendency of groups to make decisions that are more extreme than the initial opinions of its members.

Pragmatic perspective   A perspective on communication that emphasizes the role of contexts and relationships in determining the meaning and effects of messages.

Primary tension   The inhibitions of group members during the early period of group development; similar to the phenomenon of stage fright in an individual.

Process   A sequence of events or actions continuously changing over time in progress toward some goal.

Productivity   The output of a group's task dimension; the quality or quantity of work performed by a group.

Proxemics   The principles behind the ways in which group members use, arrange, and perceive physical space.

Punctuation   In a system, the process of organizing the sequence of acts or events in order to discover meaning and significance in the sequence.

Rating scales   A method of observing and evaluating the behavior of group members.

Reachability   The number of links in a network that it takes to connect one individual to another.

Reach-testing   The process of introducing a new idea from an anchored position of group agreement in the spiral model. Other group members test that idea through discussion and may accept it, reject it, extend it, or revise it.

Reciprocity   A norm typical of most social systems that encourages members to respond to the behaviors of others with similar behaviors.

REL/COM   A system of analyzing interaction into categories of relational control ($\uparrow$ $\downarrow$, $\rightarrow$).

Risky shift   The tendency of a group to make decisions involving greater risk (that is, bringing a bigger payoff but a lower probability of attainment) than individuals make.

Role   A position occupied by a group member in an interlocking network including all group members; defined in terms of the behaviors performed by the member.

Satisfaction   The extent to which group members enjoy and are satisfied with the group experience.

Schismogenesis   The escalation of either symmetrical or complementary relationships to a point that the social relationship is threatened with disruption.

Secondary tension   Social discomfort typified by abrupt and abnormal departures from the routine functioning of a group; induced by interpersonal conflict, environmental pressures, feelings of frustration, etc.

Self-disclosure Communication that informs another person about one's private self and provides information that the other person does not know and is unlikely to acquire through other means.

Social comparison The process of evaluating characteristics of one's self-concept by comparing them with those of another person or a group, typically performed by comparison with persons having similar characteristics.

Sociofugal arrangements A physical environment arranged such that it keeps people away from one another and discourages communication.

Sociopetal arrangements A physical environment arranged in such a manner that it encourages contact and communication.

Spiral model The process of decision making involving constant backtracking and reach-testing of ideas until the idea develops during group interaction to represent the consensus of the group members.

Status A social class or division rank ordered in a hierarchy from high to low. Status may be ascribed, that is, given the position by some higher authority. It may also be achieved through behaviors recognized by other group members as beneficial to the group.

Structuration The theory of how groups develop by using their resources to establish rules for processing information.

Structure The characteristic of a system denoted by the physical or spatial arrangement of the components at any given point in time.

Substantive conflict Intellectual clashes between members of a social system on issues pertaining to the group task.

Supportive communication Communication which is genuine, sincere, and supportive and which is directed toward another person. This type of communication is typically non-evaluative and respectful of the other person's identity.

Symbolic convergence A theory of group communication that emphasizes the extent to which group members identify with common symbols and meanings.

Symmetry A form of relational interaction in which the response to a relational behavior is the same as the antecedent act: for example, $\uparrow \uparrow$, $\downarrow \downarrow$, or $\rightarrow \rightarrow$.

System An entity that behaves as an entity because of the interdependence of its component elements.

Theory The basis for explaining, describing, and understanding any set of complex phenomena: for example, communication and the group process.

Tolerance threshold The maximum degree of tension that will not prohibit a group from functioning normally. Social tension at a level above the threshold disrupts the ability of the group to function as a group.

Unitary phase models The theory of group development which suggests that all groups develop in a similar linear sequence of phases.

Verbal innovative deviance (VID) The behavior of a group member reflecting agreement with the group's goal but disagreement with the majority on the appropriate means for achieving that goal.

Wholeness A principle inherent in a system which stipulates that every component of the system affects, and is affected by, every other component and that a change in any one component inherently brings change in all other components.

NAME INDEX

SUBJECT INDEX

303

Power, 222–223, 225
Pragmatics of communication, 86–100
Problem solving (see Decision making)
Process, 11–12, 87, 143, 194–195
  defined, 11–12
  natural group, 146
Productivity, 34, 58, 213
  and cohesiveness, 33–38
  and conflict, 264–265
  defined, 34–35
  reserve, 36–37
Punctuation of communication sequences,
    97–100

Rationality, 144, 146, 182
Reach-testing, 158–159
Reciprocity, 25–26, 42, 220–221
Reflective thinking, 144–146
Reinforcement phase of decision emergence,
    156–157, 178–181, 267
Relationship dimension of communication,
    93–95, 105, 108–110, 136–138
  complementarity, 109–110, 136, 138
  and leadership, 245–246
  symmetrical, 109–110, 136, 138
Risk, interpersonal, 29–30
Risky shift, 55–56
Role(s), 203–214
Role conflict, 207–210
  defined, 203
Role deviation, 258
Role differences, 210–214
  emergence, 205
  gender, 213–214
  group productivity observer, 213
Role performance, 206–207
  in terms of "position," 204
Role strain, 207
  types of, 210–212

Satisfaction, member, 43–45
Self-disclosure (see Communication, self-
    disclosing)
Small group communication, observational
    methods of (see Observational meth-
    ods of small group communication)
Social comparison, 24–25
Social dimension, 33, 41–46, 148, 232
Social structure, 77–78

Socioemotional climate, 41–46
  and attraction, 41–43
  and cohesiveness, 41
  group identification, 45–56
  and satisfaction, 43–45
Spiral model of decision making, 158–159
Status, 44–45
  ascribed and achieved, 223–224
  formal and informal, 223–224
  hierarchy, 176, 224
  in LGD, 223
Structuration, 111–112, 217
Structure:
  barriers and breakdowns, 78–79
  nonverbal communication and, 79–84
  social, 77–78
Symbolic convergence, 46–48
SYMLOG, 122–123
Symmetry, 109–110, 136, 138
System, 3, 92, 100–103
  defined, 15
  evolution of a, 15, 101–102, 131
  function of a, 15, 100–101
  nonsummativity, principle of, 15, 100–101
  openness of a, 102–103
  structure of a, 15, 101–102, 112

Task, 57–59, 232
  group, 57–59, 124
  oriented group, 2–4
  types of, 57–58
Task dimension, 32–33, 53–54, 148, 232
  defined, 54
Tension, social, 48–53, 177
  management of, 49–53, 196
  primary, 49–50
  secondary, 49–50
  tolerance threshold, 49–50
Theory, importance of, 100
Thinking:
  convergent and divergent, 166–168
  reflective, 144–146, 166
Trust, interpersonal, 28–29

Understanding versus knowledge, 3, 292–293

Wholeness (see System, nonsummativity)

Zero-history group, 19